Lecture Notes of the Institute for Computer Sciences, Social Informatics and Telecommunications Engineering 449

More information about this series at https://link.springer.com/bookseries/8197

Abdulhameed Danjuma Mambo · Assane Gueye ·
Ghada Bassioni (Eds.)

Innovations and Interdisciplinary Solutions for Underserved Areas

5th EAI International Conference, InterSol 2022
Abuja, Nigeria, March 23–24, 2022
Proceedings

Springer

Editors
Abdulhameed Danjuma Mambo 🆔
Nile University of Nigeria
Abuja, Nigeria

Assane Gueye 🆔
Carnegie Mellon University Africa
Kigali, Rwanda

Ghada Bassioni 🆔
Ain Shams University
Cairo, Egypt

ISSN 1867-8211   ISSN 1867-822X (electronic)
Lecture Notes of the Institute for Computer Sciences, Social Informatics
and Telecommunications Engineering
ISBN 978-3-031-23115-5   ISBN 978-3-031-23116-2 (eBook)
https://doi.org/10.1007/978-3-031-23116-2

This Springer imprint is published by the registered company Springer Nature Switzerland AG
The registered company address is: Gewerbestrasse 11, 6330 Cham, Switzerland

Preface

Many challenges continue to unsettle Africa. These challenges range from issues affecting housing, energy, transportation, water and sanitation, ICT infrastructures, poverty reduction, peace and stability, food security, environmental sustainability, climate change, education, health and social wellbeing, equal opportunity for all irrespective of gender, racial, religious, and tribal background, natural resource management, good governance, and strong democratic institutions.

These problems are many, complex, and interconnected. Their solutions require thinkers who are qualified and capable of thinking across fields and disciplines from all over our vast continent. Interdisciplinary approaches engender a wholeness that helps to integrate information, experiential learning, research skills, and methods of inquiry. This quest for solutions gave birth to the International Conference on Innovations and Interdisciplinary Solutions for Underserved Areas (InterSol) series among other things. The main objectives of InterSol are as follows:

(1) to encourage innovative interdisciplinary research, development, and education that focus on solving problems in underserved areas in Africa and beyond, and
(2) to create an international research and development community around "interdisciplinary solutions," which meets annually, publishes in international fora, and incentivizes members of the community to initiate interdisciplinary research projects that address needs.

Previous editions of InterSol were held in Dakar, Senegal (2017), Kigali, Rwanda (2018), Cairo, Egypt (2019), and Nairobi, Kenya (virtual, 2020/21). The 5th EAI International Conference on Innovation and Interdisciplinary Solutions for Underserved Areas (InterSol 2022) was held at the serene city campus of the Nile University of Nigeria in Abuja during March 23–24, 2022. The university is a member of the Honoris United Universities, a pan-African network of 15 private higher institutions in 10 African countries.

This year's conference touched on several grey areas that are important to Africa's growth and development. It provided an avenue for face-to-face and virtual interaction with experts in these fields. Contributions came from within and outside Africa. Papers were received from Nigeria, South Africa, Egypt, Cameroon, Sudan, Kenya, Tanzania, Burkina Faso, Turkey, Cyprus, China, India, Senegal, Germany, the USA, and the UK. There are papers on pest control, housing materials and designs, sustainable waste management, renewable energy applications, food preservation techniques, and research collaboration. Overall, 25 papers were accepted for publication in this proceedings. The papers were double-blind reviewed, with at least three reviews per paper.

The keynote speeches delivered at the conference underlie InterSol's passion for strengthening collaboration across disciplines, universities, and regions. For example, Ghada Bassioni, Faculty of Engineering, Ain Shams University, Egypt, talked about

"Intra-African Cooperation - Challenges and Opportunities". The second keynote speech by Mohammed Jibrin, Director General/CEO of the National Board for Technology Incubation (NBTI), Nigeria, looked at how to bridge Africa's research-industry gap through technology incubation centres. The third speech by Okechukwu Ugweje, University of Mount Union, USA, talked about an experiential learning program at the University of Mount Union that sends engineering students to developing countries to plan, design, and execute interventionist projects.

Although retreating, COVID-19 is still a potent force around us. Travel restrictions, together with the economic straits that come with COVID-19, and a dearth of conference registration and travel grants have continued to hamper the capacity of African researchers to submit to quality conferences like this one. African researchers needed support in this area.

Generous support for the conference was provided by the Nile University of Nigeria, which allowed the use of its state-of-the-art auditorium for free and provided refreshments for over 200 participants at the opening ceremony. Also, the university's high-powered delegation was at the conference, led by the Director of Academic Planning, Abdullahi Saleh, and the Dean of Engineering, Steve Adeshina. Both delivered speeches expressing appreciation for the hosting of InterSol 2022.

This conference was managed by the European Alliance for Innovation (EAI), a non-profit organization and a professional community established in cooperation with the European Commission to empower global research and innovation, and to promote cooperation between European and International ICT communities

The 6th edition of the InterSol conference is planned for Mauritius in 2023.

Abdulhameed Danjuma Mambo
Assane Gueye

Organization

Steering Committee

Assane Gueye	Carnegie Mellon University Africa, Rwanda
Abdulhameed Danjuma Mambo	Nile University of Nigeria, Nigeria

Organizing Committee

General Chair

Abdulhameed Danjuma Mambo	Nile University of Nigeria, Nigeria

General Co-chairs

Okechukwu Ugweje	University of Mount Union, USA
Steve Adeshina	Nile University of Nigeria, Nigeria

Technical Program Committee Chair and Co-chair

Assane Gueye	Carnegie Mellon University Africa, Rwanda
Ghada Bassioni	Ain Shams University, Egypt

Sponsorship and Exhibit Chair

Abdullahi Gimba	Nile University of Nigeria, Nigeria

Local Chair

Steve Adeshina	Nile University of Nigeria, Nigeria

Workshops Chair

Abdullahi Ahmad	Canterbury Christ Church University, UK

Publicity and Social Media Chair

Sehouev Mawuton Davidi Agoungbome	University of Delft, The Netherlands

Publications Chair

Abdulhameed Danjuma Mambo	Nile University of Nigeria, Nigeria

Web Chair

Petrus Nzerem   Nile University of Nigeria, Nigeria

Posters and PhD Track Chair

Abubakar Dayyabu   Nile University of Nigeria, Nigeria

Panels Chair

Cheikh M. F. Kebe   Université Cheikh Anta Diop, Senegal

Demos Chair

Jafaru Mahmud   National Agency for Science and Engineering
                                       Infrastructure, Nigeria

Tutorials Chair

Abdulazeez Rotimi   Baze University, Nigeria

Technical Program Committee

Okechukwu Ugweje   University of Mount Union Alliance, USA
Abdullahi Gimba   Nile University of Nigeria, Nigeria
Sadiq Thomas   Nile University of Nigeria, Nigeria
Mahmud O. Jafaru   National Agency for Science and Engineering
                                       Infrastructure, Nigeria
Musa Muhammad   Nile University of Nigeria, Nigeria
Omotayo Oshiga   Nile University of Nigeria, Nigeria
Petrus Nzerem   Nile University of Nigeria, Nigeria
Abdulhameed Danjuma Mambo   Nile University of Nigeria, Nigeria
Ibrahim Anka   Nile University of Nigeria, Nigeria
Muhhammad Suleiman   Nile University of Nigeria, Nigeria
Mustapha Alhaji   Federal University of Technology, Minna, Nigeria
Musa Alhassan   Federal University of Technology, Minna, Nigeria
Sop Maturin Desire   University of Bamenda, Cameroon
Muhammad Bello Ladan   IBB University, Lapai, Nigeria
Tanko Musa Umar   IBB University, Lapai, Nigeria
Abdullahi Ahmed   Canterbury Christ Church University, UK
Damaris Mbui   University of Nairobi, Kenya
Solomon Derese   University of Nairobi, Kenya
Kennedy Nyongesa   Bureau for Climate Change Resilience and
                                       Adaptation, Kenya
Ayuba Salihu   Nile University of Nigeria, Nigeria

Malo Sadouanouan	Université polytechnique de Bobo-Dioulasso, Burkina Faso
Bamba Gueye	Université Cheikh Anta Diop, Senegal
Jessica Thorn	University of York, UK/ACDI, South Africa/AIMS, Rwanda
Narcisse Talla Tankam	University of Ngaoundere, Cameroon
Assane Gueye	Carnegie Mellon University Africa, Rwanda
Mouhamadou Lamine Ba	Université Alioune Diop de Bambey, Senegal
Gaoussou Camara	Université Alioune Diop de Bambey, Senegal
Cheikh Mouhamadou Fadel Kebe	Université Cheikh Anta Diop, Senegal
Melissa Densmore	University of Cape Town, South Africa
Ghada Bassioni	Ain Shams University, Egypt
Moustapha Diop	University of Maryland, Baltimore County, USA
Tembine Hamidou	New York University, USA
Ababacar Ndiaye	Université Assane Seck de Ziguinchor, Senegal
Charif Mahmoudi	Siemens, USA
Gertjan van Stam	SIRDC, Zimbabwe
Maimouna Diouf	Dakar American University of Science and Technology, Senegal
Maissa Mbaye	Université Gaston Berger, Senegal
Timothy Onosahwo Iyendo	Nile University of Nigeria
Abdulazeez Juwon Rotimi	Baze University, Nigeria

Contents

Sustainable Development for Underserved Areas

Effects of Noise Pollution on Learning in Schools of Bamenda II Municipality, Northwest Region of Cameroon

Sop Sop Maturin Désiré[1]([✉]), Tizi Mirabel Ngum[2], Abdulhameed Danjuma Mambo[3], Fombe Lawrence[2], Babila Nuvaga Fogam[4], and Nuebissi Simo Joseph Landry[5]

[1] Department of Geography, Higher Teacher Training College, The University of Bamenda, Bamenda, Cameroon
`maturinsop@yahoo.fr`
[2] Faculty of Arts, Department of Geography, The University of Bamenda, Bamenda, Cameroon
[3] Faculty of Engineering, Nile University of Abuja, Abuja, Nigeria
[4] Health Post, The University of Bamenda, Bamenda, Cameroon
[5] Faculty of Arts, Letters and Social Sciences, Department of Geography, The University of Yaoundé I, Yaoundé, Cameroon

Abstract. In the modern world, unwanted noise pollution from a variety of sources has significant effects on the learning environment and on the academic achievement of students. In the Bamenda II municipality, both primary and secondary schools are exposed to noise pollution levels ranging between 37.66 dB and 65.82 dB during 7–8 am, 37.06 dB–67.68 dB during 9–10 am, and 49.16 dB–71.44 dB during 1–2 pm. The goal of this study was to assess the effect of noise pollution on schools and students' performance in Bamenda II municipality. The study used a cross-sectional study design to determine the sample size. Sampled schools exposed to different noises, such as traffic and business-related noises, were purposively chosen. 200 questionnaires were administered, involving 127 students and 73 teachers. A medical doctor was interviewed to assess noise impact on teaching-learning outcomes. Noise levels (A-weighted decibels) were measured using Extech 407732 Sound Level Meter. Data were analyzed using descriptive and inferential statistical methods. The results showed that noise in educational institutions harms learning and academic achievement. Over 90% of the teachers complained that noise affected their teaching and 92.2% of the students acknowledged that noise affected their learning ability. They also reported communication interference, voice masking, tiredness/fatigue, and headache as some of the major problems of noise pollution. The study suggests that school buildings should have sound insulation systems with double-glazed doors/windows, and awareness about noise pollution-related dangers to teaching and learning should be emphasized.

Keywords: Noise pollution · Schools · Learning · Teachers · Pupils · Decibels · Cameroon · Northwest Region

A. D. Mambo et al. (Eds.): InterSol 2022, LNICST 449, pp. 3–15, 2022.
https://doi.org/10.1007/978-3-031-23116-2_1

1   Introduction

Man has since creation desired to live in a comfortable environment; one worthy of purposeful and sustainable amenities; and having all the instruments of comfortable living (Makinde 2015). The aspiration of man for a desirable living environment comes to focus as an illusion, due to environmental pollution of all sorts. Environmental pollution is defined as the addition of any substance or form of energy (for example, heat, sound) to the environment at a rate faster than what the environment can accommodate by absorbing, dispersing, or breaking it down, and that would harm humans, flora and fauna or abiotic systems (Narayanan2011).

In the modern world, as the population grows, there is increasing exposure to noise pollution, which has profound public health implications. For example, noise pollution is one of the major problems for developing countries, but the problem is not equally recognized by all countries (Oyedepo and Abdullahi 2009). Urban noise pollution produces direct and cumulative adverse health effects by degrading residential, social, working, and learning environments with corresponding real and intangible losses. Nowadays, children experience a key part of their childhood in their school, and it forms one of their principal social activities and setting (Alsubaie 2014). Environmental challenges vary considerably among schools around the world, across countries, and within communities (WHO 2014).

The environmental noise levels in learning in institutions have a significant relationship with the academic achievement of students. In less developed countries (LDCs) like Cameroon, many children do not have access to a serene or ideal learning environment. Noise control in the school environment is a real public challenge. A significant increase in the population of urban centers has been witnessed in Cameroon in the last decade. This increase has influenced the lifestyle of the citizenry, contributing to the increase in noise pollution. Urbanization and industrialization have contributed to noise pollution in recent times without adequate consideration of its effects on the future (SemieMemunaSama 2014). Even though the World Health Organization (1980) maintains that to hear and understand spoken messages in the classrooms, the background sound level should not exceed 35dB (A) LAeq during teaching sessions. For outdoor playgrounds, the sound level of noise from external sources should not exceed 55 dB (A) LAeq. In most developing countries, poor urban planning also plays a vital role. For example, congested houses, large families sharing small spaces, and fighting over basic amenities lead to noise pollution, which may disrupt the environment of society.

In Bamenda II municipality, schools are exposed to different noise pollution sources with respectively indoor and outdoor noise levels in primary and secondary schools. Bamenda II Municipality accommodates the Central Business District (CBD) of the city of Bamenda and it is the focus of major business activities that either emit noise or are vulnerable to it. Several unregulated activities within the Municipality are contributing factors to unregulated noise. Unplanned urbanization and land use are undeniable threshold factors to various forms of pollution in the study area. There is an unplanned location of academic institutions vis-à-vis travel agencies within the study area. The location of schools has not been a concern to the authorities running them. Planning and location of schools by the proprietors have not taken noise pollution as a threat to pupils/students and staff. There is an encroachment on many school areas within the study area by noise from various activities. For instance, it is common to find schools located nearby commercial and other noise-generating activities such as Bus stations (Commuter Agencies) along Sonac Street where Saint Agnes Nursery and Primary school shares a boundary with Moghamo Travel Agency, distracting the concentration of learners. In the neighborhoods where school pupils/students live, there are encroaching bars as well. Markets, wielding workshops, and other unplanned business ventures in most parts of the Bamenda II Council Area are common practices. These educational institutions suffer from noises of various forms and hence perturbing school activities such as teaching, learning, and discussion sessions (Sop Sop et al. 9).

Therefore, to investigate the Effects of Noise Pollution on Schools in Bamenda II Municipality; the research question of this study is the perceived effects of noise pollution on the teaching/learning process in schools within the study area? The goal of this paper is to assess the perceived effects of noise pollution on the teaching/learning process in schools within Bamenda II municipality.

2   Materials and Methods

Study Area
The Bamenda II Council area has an estimated population of 211,556 inhabitants (Bamenda II CDP, 2012). Out of this population; the majority live in the urban areas, 60.9% (130,313 persons). The population comprises natives of the villages of Mankon, Chomba, Mbatu, and Nsongwa including migrants from neighboring villages like Bafut, Bali Nyonga, and other rural areas of the North-West and West Region, especially the Bamilekes and the Ibos from Nigeria. The surface area is estimated at 165.605 km^2 giving a population density of about 127.747 persons per km^2. This population is not

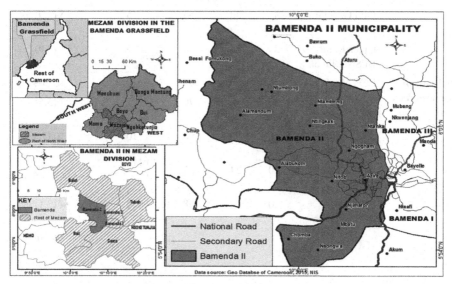

Fig. 1. Location of Bamenda II municipality in Mezam division of the Northwest Region of Cameroon. Source: Administrative units of Cameroon; Geo-database, 2015, NIS Yaoundé, Fieldwork, 2018.

evenly distributed as the urban areas are more densely populated than the rural areas. Bamenda II Council Area is between latitude 5° 6$^{//}$ and 5° 8$^{//}$ North and latitude 10° 9$^{//}$ and 10° 11$^{//}$ East of the Greenwich Meridian. The spatial location of some of these neighborhoods is stated in Fig. 1.

Study design

This study is a cross-sectional survey, conducted from October 2018 to January 2019. We use experimental research with a quantitative approach.

Target population and sample size

In the framework of our study, our target population comprised all people living in Bamenda II municipality; our sampling size was estimated at Sample Size = 0.1 × 1271(Target Population) = 127 pupils/students under study (Table 1).

Table 1. Institution/number of respondents from sampled schools.

School location	Name of the school	Pri 5	Pri 6	Total population	Administered	Retrieved (%)
Schools within Residential Areas	Step-by-Step BPSNtarinkon	35	60	95	9	9 (7.1)
	GPS Atuakom II	15	20	35	4	4 (3.1)
	GBSS Ngomgham	100	132	232	23	23 (18.1)
	Sacred Heart CollegeMankon	60	90	150	15	15 (11.8)
	GBHS Nitob	50	120	170	17	17 (13.4)
	GPS GMI Group IIA	35	20	55	5	5 (3.9)
	Green Light BPSNtarinkon	24	24	48	5	5 (3.9)
Schools in Commercial Areas	LCC Mankon	40	60	100	10	10 (7.9)
	Rosy BPS Old Town	30	40	70	7	7 (5.5)
	Saint Agnes PSSonac Street	40	60	100	10	10 (7.9)
	Alfred Saker BPS	20	24	45	5	5 (3.9)
	Blessed BPSNchuboh	20	18	38	4	4 (3.1)

(continued)

Table 1. (*continued*)

School location	Name of the school	Pri 5	Pri 6	Total population	Administered	Retrieved (%)
Schools Along Main Road Axis	GPS Mulang I	10	13	23	2	2 (1.6)
	GPS Old Town II	20	30	50	5	5 (3.9)
	Pledge PSAtuazire	30	30	60	6	6 (4.7)
Total		**529**	**742**	**1,271**	**127**	**127 (100.0)**

Source: Field Work, February 2019

The fieldwork covered four phases: direct observation, interviews, cross-sectional questionnaire survey, and measurement of noise level using a Sound Level Meter EXTECH Model 407732 (SLM) and GPS ETREX 10 was used to record the coordinates for the sampled schools. The investigations took place in various schools in Bamenda II municipality. All participants responded orally to a structured questionnaire provided by the investigating team. Data collected included socio-demographic characteristics (age, gender, marital status). Data on noise pollution were collected from the students and teachers in schools.

The investigations and experimentations took place in the various schools in Bamenda II Municipality by the research team trained for the Principal Investigator (PI). The students and teachers willing to take part in this study were interviewed respectively during a class break (10: am to 10:30) and closing time (2 pm to 2:30). Whereas Decibels were recorded from 7 to 8 am, 9–10 am, and 1–2 pm. Noise measurements were carried out during these periods to evaluate noise pollution levels in unoccupied classrooms, occupied classrooms during teaching, and playgrounds of the school premises.

The geographical coordinates of the schools of all participants were determined during fieldwork using a GPS. Free software such as Quantum SIG® (version 1.6) has made it possible to refer all schools in the study area. Secondary data were got from different sources, such as articles, reports, dissertations, and open access journals related to noise pollution. The data collected was coded, processed, and analyzed using Statistical Package for Social Sciences (SPSS 21) statistical software. The processing and the graphical presentation of the results were made with word processing software and Excel.

Ethical consideration: The protocol of this study was independently reviewed and approved by the Ethics Committee of the University of Bamenda. Informed consent was got from all participants included in the study. They were then invited to take part voluntarily in the study. They were informed that the study is confidential and that their participation will not affect their care. In addition, the investigation team informed the participants about their rights to withdraw from the study during the study period.

3 Results

3.1 Environmental Noise at Sampled Schools

Recordings and analyzes of noise levels in classrooms took place in all the selected schools. Noise measurements were carried out to evaluate noise pollution levels in the sampled schools. Readings and noise measurement averages were done at different points; unoccupied classrooms occupied classrooms during teaching and playgrounds on the school premises. Field observations revealed that most of the schools in the study area were within noisy areas. The schools are located close to commercial areas or along main road axes and within residential areas. The period the noise level reaches its peak varies with the different sampled schools depending on several factors, such as time of the day and the activities taking place (Table 2).

Table 2. Average noise levels in decibels (dB) in 15 sampled schools in the Bamenda II municipality

S/N	Location	7–8 am unoccupied classroom	10–11 am occupied classroom	1–2 pm playground
1	ASBPSAlakuma	65.82	64.96	71.44
2	BBPSNchuboh	55.46	64.05	68.3
3	GBHS Nitob	62.07	54.72	63.65
4	GBS GMI GP II A	63.26	67.68	64.24
5	GBSS Ngomgham	46.41	57.07	56.8
6	GPS Atuakom II	57.94	54.94	58.33
7	GPS Mulang I	48.06	54.51	61.93
8	GPS Old Town	60.24	65.12	68.33
9	GBPS Ntarinkon	60.56	65.34	56.01
10	LCC MankonMusang	57.25	58.99	58.71
11	PPSAtuazire	45.18	57.47	69.18
12	RBPSOld Town	55.99	61.52	68.96
13	SAHECO Mankon	37.66	37.06	49.16
14	SAPSSonac Street	59.93	65.17	67.52
15	SSEC PS Ntarinkon	50.46	62.86	66.29
Average	**55.09**	**59.43**	**63.26**	

Source: Fieldwork, 2019

Table 2 displays the distribution of average noise levels in decibels recorded for 15 schools at different time intervals. Schools such as ASBPS, BBPS, GBHS, GBS GMI, GPS Old Town, GBPS, SAPS, and SSECPS have extremely higher noise values, while SAHECO has the lowest noise values. The average equivalent noise level (Leq) is ranged between 37.66 dB (A)–65.82 dB (A) during 7–8 am, between 37.06 dB (A) and 67.68 dB (A) during the hours of 9–10 am, and ranging between 49.16 dB (A) and 71.44 dB (A) during the time interval of 1–2 pm. The mean equivalent noise level (Leq) is 55.09dB (A) with standard deviation of 7.63 dB (A) during 7-8am, 59.43 dB (A) with standard deviation of 7.36 dB (A) during 9–10am and 63.26dB (A) with standard deviation of 6.08dB (A) during 1–2pm.

3.2 Level of Awareness of Noise Pollution by Respondents

Regarding students' perception of noise pollution levels and noise awareness, 61.4% of them consider their school environments to be sometimes noisy, 37.0% consider the school environment to be noisy always while 1.6% hold firm grounds that their school environments are never noisy as stated in Table 3.

Table 3. Students' perception of noise levels in the environment

Variables	Perceptions	(%)	Total
Noisy school environment	Never	2 (1.6)	127
	Sometimes	78 (61.4)	
	Always	47 (37.0)	
Noise pollution awareness	Highly aware	54 (42.5)	127
	Relatively aware	72 (56.7)	
	Not aware	1 (0.8)	
The noise produced daily	Yes	100 (78.7)	127
	No	27 (21.3)	

Source: Fieldwork, 2019

The analysis in Table 3 shows that most of the respondents covering 56.7% are relatively aware of noise pollution, 42.5% show that they are highly aware; while 0.8% maintain neutrality, meaning, not aware of noise pollution in and around the school environment. Over 78.7% of the students report that noise within and around the school environment is generated daily while only 21.3% say that noise is not produced daily.

3.3 Effects of Noise Pollution on Teaching in Selected Schools in Bamenda II

Exposure to prolonged or excessive noise has been shown to cause a range of health problems, ranging from stress, poor concentration, productivity losses, communication difficulties, cognitive impairment, hearing loss, cardiovascular diseases, headaches, and fatigue.

This study reveals the effects of noise in the sampled schools. Both teachers and students unanimously agreed that noise pollution from the different sources hampers significantly teaching and learning in the selected schools. Teachers and students responded as discussed subsequently regarding the effects of noise pollution on the teaching-learning process in schools. In assessing the perception of teachers on the effects of noise on the teaching process, 50 (68%) of the teachers report being highly aware that external noise affects teachers' concentration in the delivery of lessons, as shown in Fig. 1. Also,13 (18%) of the teachers know relatively that noise affects teaching while 10 (14%) maintain that they are not aware of any effects of noise pollution concerning their teaching process as they only consider it a nuisance during sleeping hours. This, among other reasons, could be blamed on a lack of adequate awareness of its effects on humans and a dearth of data, as reported by some of the sampled teachers (Fig. 2).

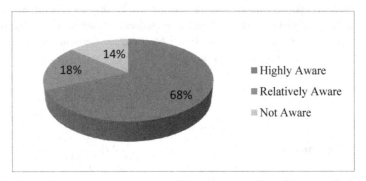

Fig. 2. Teachers' Perception on awareness of the adverse effect of noise pollution. Source: Fieldwork, 2019

Some respondents were further interrogated on their personal experiences as concerns noise impact as reported by a headteacher in the following except.

"The classrooms are no longer conducive for learning due to noise pollution from different sources. This has even encouraged naughty learners to often misbehave during lessons".

Another teacher explained that:

"It irritates me when I'm teaching, and noisy people are walking on the road next to the classrooms and cars keep hooting. Sometimes, I stop teaching to allow the noise to settle before I continue with teaching"

This affects the teaching-learning process as those uttered sessions impact work coverage and eventually affect children's academic performance, as noted.

Table 4 reveals the multi-faceted problems that plague educational institutions within the study area due to environmental noise pollution. 53.4% of respondents and 65.8% agree that communication interference and voice masking respectively between teachers and learners affect the teaching process. In the same vein, 52.1% of the respondents

Table 4. Effects of noise pollution on teaching in sampled schools in Bamenda II

Perceived noise effects on teachers	SA	A	IN	D	SD
Interference in communication between students and teachers	34 (46.6)	39(53.4)	-	-	-
Causes reduction in social interaction	10(13.7)	36 (49.3)	5 (6.8)	20 (27.4)	2 (2.7)
Teachers experience voice masking	23 (31.5)	48 (65.8)	2 (2.7)	-	-
Causes school children to be fatigued	30 (41.1)	43 (58.9)	-	-	-
Teachers' concentration is adversely affected by external noise	38 (52.1)	20(27.4)	-	15(20.5)	-
Hearing impairments or disturbances	21 (28.8)	30 (41.1)	2 (2.7)	10 (13.7)	10(13.7)
Impaired task performance (being unproductive)	18 (24.7)	31 (42.5)	5 (6.8)	19 (26.0)	-
Voice stress causes tiredness/fatigue	43 (58.9)	30 (41.1)	-	-	-
Causes annoyance and aggressiveness	17 (23.3)	40 (54.8)	1 (1.4)	10 (13.7)	5(6.8)
Naughty learners Misbehaving during teaching	20(27.4)	40(54.8)	11(15.1)	1(1.4)	1(1.4)

Source: Fieldwork, 2019

strongly agree that external noise adversely affects teachers' concentration, hindering effective delivery of lessons, as well as making them get tired quickly (58.9%). This implies that noise pollution significantly affects teaching in the selected schools in Bamenda II. This is because noise impedes the extent of the teacher's voice, is an object of distraction to teachers and learners, and impairment to learners' listening/hearing capacity. Noise has been identified by students as a harmful factor that interrupts the free flow of information in teaching and learning. The results presented in Table 5 show a summary of noise's effect on students' learning ability.

Any unwanted sound that our ears have not been built to filter can cause problems within the body and cause hearing problems. Man-made noises such as jackhammers, horns, machinery, and vehicles can be too loud for our hearing range. Constant exposure to loud levels of noise can easily result in the damage of our eardrums and loss of hearing, causing tinnitus or deafness. It also reduces our sensitivity to sounds that our ears pick up unconsciously to regulate our body's rhythm. Excessive noise pollution in classrooms can influence psychological health. Occurrences of aggressive behavior, disturbance of sleep, constant stress, fatigue, depression, anxiety, hysteria, and hypertension can be linked to excessive noise levels. The level of irritation increases with increased noise. Noise affects brain responses and students' ability to focus, which can lead to low-performance levels. It is also poor for memory, making it hard to study. High decibel noise can affect free communication between teachers and students, it may lead to misunderstanding.

The data in Table 5 reveals that most of the respondents (99.2%) acknowledge that external noise affects their concentration level, causing their reading (98.4%) and listening ability (97.7%) to reduce. In like manner, the students reported tiredness/fatigue (88.2%) and oral communication interference (97.6%) as well as headache (94.5%) as

Table 5. Effects of noise pollution on learning in some schools in Bamenda II

Opinion on noise effects	SA	A	IN	D	SD
External noise reduces the rate of concentration, assimilation, and performance	87 (68.5)	39 (30.7)	1 (0.8)	–	–
Affects reading ability	57 (44.9)	68 (53.5)	1 (0.8)	–	1 (0.8)
Decreases student's listening ability (hearing difficulty)	50 (39.4)	74 (58.3)	–	3 (2.4)	–
Pupils/Students feel stressed up or aggressive due to high noise	44 (34.6)	73 (57.5)	6 (4.7)	4 (3.1)	–
Reduces social interaction	18 (14.2)	60 (47.2)	8 (6.3)	28 (22.0)	13 (10.2)
Pupils/Students experience headaches due to exposure to noise	38 (29.9)	82 (64.6)	4 (3.1)	2 (1.6)	1 (0.8)
Causes stress	36 (28.3)	85 (66.9)	3 (2.4)	2 (1.6)	1 (0.8)
Oral communication is impeded by noise	70 (55.1)	54 (42.5)	1 (0.8)	–	2 (1.6)
Causes negative effects on behavior	20 (15.7)	50 (39.4)	28 (22.0)	21 (16.5)	8 (6.3)
Causes tiredness/fatigue	87 (68.5)	25 (19.7)	7 (5.5)	5 (3.9)	3 (2.4)

Source: Fieldwork, 2019

some effects of noise pollution they experience in the learning process. Once concentration is affected, this will lower students' interest in the classroom and their level of participation in classroom activities.

3.4 Perception of a Medical Practitioner on Noise Pollution Effects

The adverse effects of noise pollution in educational institutions of the Bamenda II Municipality are further explained by a medical practitioner from the Bamenda Regional Hospital along the following lines.

That we cannot see it, or smell it, does not mean noise pollution cannot harm us. The most common victims of noise pollution are our children. Many diseases, birth defects, and immune system changes are traced back to environmental noise pollution.

As per the information got from the expert on the impact of regular noise exposure on school-going children, the explanation from the authority is that noise can pose a serious threat to a child's physical and psychological health, including learning and behavior. Regular exposure to noise-related pollution in educational institutions compromises learners' auditory processing and can lead to speech or reading complications. "Just as children continue to grow physically as they get older, so too they continue to develop their speech perception capabilities as they develop into their teenage years". This implies that children are vulnerable to the effects of noise because of its potential to interfere with learning at a critical development stage.

For example:

Noise can interfere with speech and language; repeated exposure to noise during critical periods of development may affect a child's acquisition of speech, language, and language-related skills, such as reading and listening.

Impair hearing; tinnitus, often described as a ringing or buzzing sound in the ear, is a symptom associated with many forms of hearing loss.
Impair learning; the inability to concentrate in a noisy environment can affect a child's capacity to learn.

As part of remedial actions that can be taken to ease noise pollution, the official suggested the Government can help by establishing regulations that include preventive and corrective measures. The mandatory separation between learning institutions and sources of noise, fines for exceeding noise limits. Better urban planning can help create 'No-Noise' zones, where excessive noise is not tolerated. Primarily, bars, nightclubs, and restaurants should not be allowed to run a business around schools and hospitals. If it becomes necessary, there should be strong enforcement to use sound suppressing technology that makes the noise remain within the room. Parents, as well as school authorities, should create a quiet learning and sleeping environment. Has children's hearing tested if they are routinely engaged in noisy activities/places?

4 Discussion of Results

This study assessed the effects of noise levels in selected primary and secondary schools in the Bamenda II Municipality. It was revealed that the mean equivalent noise level in the morning (classrooms) was 55.09 and 59.43 dB, which are 20.09 and 24.43 dB (A) respectively above the prescribed noise limits for the silent area category (community learning environments). Similarly, the mean equivalent noise level in the afternoon (playgrounds) is 63.26dB (A) which also is well above the prescribed noise limits of 55 dB (A) by 8.26 dBA for the prescribed area category. The sampled schools, therefore, are highly noise-polluted institutions as all schools exceed the tolerance level of noise pollution, which shows that the environment is not suitable for the teaching-learning process. Noise levels measured are high due to noise from hooting by cars/riders, from scrapping sounds from tables and chairs, as observed at the time of noise recording. Also, reported and identified outdoor sources and the people (students and staff) themselves when they are learning indoors or playing outdoors. Noise levels in all the sampled classrooms are higher than the recommended standards by WHO (1980). This concurs with the study of the Accredited Standard Committee (2000) which affirms that Leq in an unoccupied classroom should not exceed 30–35 dBA. These high noise levels in the classrooms can be attributed to the poor acoustic conditions of most of the classrooms. The high levels are also due to their proximity to main road axes such as RBPS, BBPS, and ASBPS. The roads link other neighborhoods within the Municipality and other council areas within Bamenda city. The sources of noise pollution in Bamenda II municipality are near to what Puja (2015) in his study identified. According to him, the major sources of noise can be broadly divided into two classes, specifically indoor and outdoor noise pollution. Indoor sources are those sources of noise pollution that occur within or at a particular place. They are the unwanted sound caused by domestic appliances like television and radio, dog barking, or children at play. In opposition, common sources of outdoor noise arise from transportation systems such as aircraft, buses, cars, and trains; social centers such as churches, markets, mosques, and temples. Social centers near residential areas can cause annoyance, discomfort, and irritation to the residents exposed to the noise that is inevitably produced. Like any normal day, it is difficult or almost impossible not to encounter pollution from one of these sources. In Bamenda II municipality, students' perception of noise pollution level and noise awareness, 61.4% of them consider their school environments to be sometimes noisy, 37.0% consider the school environment to be noisy always while 1.6% hold firm grounds that their school environments are never noisy. In the perception of teachers on the effects of noise on the teaching process, 50 (68%) of the teachers reports being highly aware that external noise affects teachers' concentration in the delivery of lessons. Noise has been identified by students as a harmful factor that interrupts the free flow of information in teaching and learning. Most of the respondents (99.2%) acknowledge that external noise affects their concentration level, causing their reading (98.4%) and listening ability (97.7%) to reduce. In like manner, the students reported tiredness/fatigue (88.2%) and oral communication interference (97.6%)as well as headache (94.5%) as some effects of noise pollution they experience in the learning process. Once concentration is affected, this will lower students' interest in the classroom and their level of participation in classroom activities. This study is almost like what Ana et al. (2009) carried on the effects of noise in some secondary schools in Ibadan. The report shows that tiredness and lack of concentration are the most prevalent noise-related problems. According to the authors, over 60% of the respondents report vehicular traffic as the major source of noise, and over 70% complain of being disturbed by noise.

5 Conclusion

This study concludes that the mean equivalent noise level (Leq) is 55.09 dB (A) with a standard deviation of 7.63 dB (A) during 7–8 am, 59.43 dB (A) with a standard deviation of 7.36 dB (A) during 9–10 am and 63.26dB (A) with a standard deviation of 6.08 dB (A) during 1–2 pm. Therefore, it affects the teachers by preventing effective communication between teachers and students, making the teachers shout while teaching so that students could hear. These results in teachers developing headache/fatigue, loss of voice and concentration during teaching, and disruption of ongoing lessons. It also affects the students by preventing them from hearing the teacher, reducing their rate of concentration, and assimilation. Noise pollution can't, therefore, be seen as an unwanted sound that makes the teaching and learning environment impure by contaminating and distorting the teaching/learning process, having adverse psychological and health effects on teachers and students. In a nutshell, the study confirmed that noise affects teaching-learning outcomes in various schools. However, there is little attention from the government and the municipal council in enforcing the existing laws and regulations to reduce noise pollution from within and outside the school premises. Therefore, efforts must be made to abate and curb this urban menace to have an effective process of teaching and learning in schools. Further studies can be carried on finding effective mitigation strategies for noise pollution in school environments.

References

Accredited Standards Committee: American National Standard: Acoustical Performance Criteria, Design Requirements, and Guidelines for Schools (ANSI S12.60). Acoustical Society of America, USA (2002)

Alsubaie, A.S.R.: Indoor noise pollution in elementary school of eastern province. J. Res. Environ. Sci. Toxicol. 3(2), 25–29 (2014)

Ana, G.R.E.E., Shendell, D.G., Brown, G.E., Sridhar, M.K.C.: Assessment of noise and associated health affects at selected secondary school in Ibadan Nigeria. J. Environ. Pub. Health **2009**, 739502 (2009). https://doi.org/10.1155/2009/739502

Makinde, O.O.: Influences of socio-cultural experiences on residents' satisfaction in ikorodu low-cost housing estate, Lagos state Nigeria. Environ. Dev. Sustainab. 17(1), 173–198 (2015)

Narayanan, P.: Environmental Pollution Principles, Analysis, and Control. CBS Publishers & Distributors PVT Ltd, New Delhi, India (2011)

Oyedepo, O.S., Abdullahi, A.S.: A comparative study of noise pollution levels in some selected areas in Ilorin Metropolis Nigeria. Trends Appl. Sci. Res. 3(3), 253–266 (2009)

Puja, M.: Noise pollution: definition, sources, and effects of noise pollution. http://www.yourartic lelibrary.com/speech/noise-pollutiondefinition-sources-and-effects-of-noise-pollution/28295/ (2015)

SemieMemunaSama: Essential Readings in Environmental Law; IUCN Academy of Environmental Law. University of Ottawa, Canada. www.iucnael.org (2014)

Sop Sop, M.D., Fombe, L.F., Tizi, N.M.: Noise pollution on schools in Bamenda II municipality, Northwest Region of Cameroon. In Mélanges offerts au professeur Mougoue Benoit, In press (2021)

WHO-World Health Organization: Environmental Health Criteria of Noise (1980). Accessed 20 October 2018

WHO-World Health Organization: School and Youth Health. What is a Promoting School? (2014) http://www.google.com.ng/search?q=WHO.%20. Accessed 5 December 2018

Hydro-Meteorological Trends and Thermal Comfort of Khartoum Sudan

Mubarak Mohammed Osman[1], Mustafa Ergil[2], Iyendo Onosahwo Timothy[3]([envelope]) [ORCID], and Hassan Nasir Hassan[4]

[1] University of Bahri, Bahri, Sudan
[2] Department of Civil Engineering, Eastern Mediterranean University, Via Mersin 10, Gazimağusa, Northern Cyprus, Turkey
[3] Department of Architecture, Faculty of Engineering, Nile University of Nigeria, Abuja, Nigeria
timothy.iyendo@nileuniversity.edu.ng
[4] Wadmedani Ahlia University, Wad Madani, Sudan

Abstract. This study looked at the trends in hydro-meteorological parameters (relative humidity, temperature, rainfall, and wind speed) in Khartoum, Sudan, from 1965 to 2020. The hydro meteorological data used in this study were obtained from the Khartoum Meteorological Station. The above parameters were statistically investigated, and their trends were established using Microsoft excel. The thermal comfort details for Khartoum were also analyzed on a monthly and seasonal basis. The trends of hydro-meteorological parameters and the analysis of the thermal comfort results revealed that Khartoum has experienced global warming, which causes a drop in thermal comfort.

Keywords: Khartoum · Rainfall · Relative humidity · Temperature · Thermal comfort · Wind speed

1 Introduction

The relevance of hydrological data in climate studies cannot be overstated. Hydrological resources, on the other hand, cannot be effectively managed without knowledge about their location, quantity, quality, and likelihood of availability in the foreseeable future. Water management and modelling, climate change research, flood modelling and forecasting, and other hydrological research activities all require hydrological data records. Due of the prevailing conflict in developing countries such as Sudan, gathering hydrological data is challenging. As a result of inadequate documentation and poor data archive management, large amounts of data are lost. It has been extensively reported that monitoring of the Earth's hydrology declined in the late twentieth century. The World Meteorological Organization (WMO) performed research in 2006 that demonstrated widespread international concern about the status of historical data records and the necessity for data rescue initiatives in virtually all countries (Fry 2010). The Khartoum meteorological station has been a major source of concern for climate researchers because of this

A. D. Mambo et al. (Eds.): InterSol 2022, LNICST 449, pp. 16–28, 2022.
https://doi.org/10.1007/978-3-031-23116-2_2

hydro-meteorological data trend analysis. Furthermore, the city has experienced many extreme climatic incidents in recent years (Osman & Sevinc 2019).

Since the previous century, many researchers exploring the built environment have focused their attention on the evaluation of weather indicators. Thermal comfort is an important consideration in building research since it has a significant impact on the overall quality of a building. On the other hand, hydro-meteorological data collected in the intended design location has a significant impact on thermal comfort. A thermally comfortable built environment necessitates careful consideration of hydro-meteorological data.

Temperature, relative humidity, and rainfall are some of the climatic variables that are examined in climate change research, which can lead to frequent and extreme weather events (Ahmed et al. 2014). Policymakers throughout the world have used research findings from meteorological station data to develop long-term planning and prevent calamities. When evaluating the hydrology of earlier years, time series analysis provides a tremendous advantage (Mirza et al. 1988; Shi & Xu 2008; Ahmed et al. 2014).

Temperature, rainfall, and wind speed data patterns were analysed in the first half of this study whereas Khartoum city thermal comfort details were analysed in the second phase of this study. From 1965 to 2020, linear trends were drawn for all hydro-meteorological parameters examined in this study to identify their increasing or decreasing tendency based on seasonal changes in the year. The computer-based programme Climate Consultant 6.0 is used to undertake a thermal comfort assessment for Khartoum. This computer software requires the energy plus weather (EPW) file. The relevant computations were performed using the available weather files between 1965 and 2020, which were typically based on hourly values. In this study, because the Khartoum Metrological Station does not keep track of hourly climatic data, the EPW file was created using average data imported from the Meteonorm 7.2 programme (Meteonorm 2018). Furthermore, two thermal comfort models are employed to calculate the thermal comfort zone for Khartoum: the adaptive comfort model and the ASHRAE Standard 55 with its current handbook of fundamental models.

2 Study Area

Khartoum is the capital of the Republic of Sudan, and it is in the central part of the country, where the White and Blue Niles converge and flow into the Mediterranean Sea, much like the Nile River does in Egypt. The two rivers meet in the shape of an elephant's trunk (al-Khartûm – elephant's trunk in Arabic), as shown in Fig. 1 (Osman & Sevinc 2019). The data for this study was obtained from the Khartoum meteorological station, which is located at 15°33′06″ N latitude and 32°31′56″ E longitude and has an average height of 380 m above mean sea level (Shakurov et al. 2016).

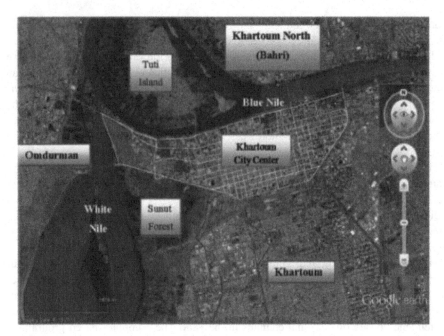

Fig. 1. The geographical location of Khartoum City Center (Osman & Sevinc, 2019).

2.1 Climatic Condition of the Region

Khartoum's summer climate is hot and dry, with low relative humidity during the hot period, interrupted by scanty light rain showers. During the dry season (winter), temperatures are normally cold in the early morning and warm at midday, with low relative humidity.

Khartoum is classified as having a hot-arid climatic zone by the Köppen climate classification. Earlier research conducted by Elagib and Mansell (2000), classified the city's climate into three seasons: (1) the dry season (winter) consists of the months of November, December, January, and February, (2) the summer season begins in March and ends in May, and (3) the wet season (autumn) lasts from June through October.

2.2 Thermal Comfort

Thermal comfort, a critical aspect of building design since human life began (Iyendo et al. 2016), has been defined as the state of mind that reflects satisfaction with the thermal environment and is subjectively judged (ANSI/ASHRAE 2017). People nowadays spend between 80% and 90% of their daily time indoors (Rupp et al. 2015; Kuchen 2016). This brings the importance of thermal comfort to the attention of building and environmental researchers. However, global population growth has coincided with an increase in urban densities, resulting in significant thermal stress and health risks. These circumstances need the development of a long-term or sustainable measure of thermal comfort. Such a measure can assist building designers in designing climate-responsive buildings that lessen dependency on fossil fuels (Hirashima et al. 2018). The goal of our research is to calculate the thermal comfort zone of Khartoum using two thermal comfort models: the adaptive comfort model and the ASHRAE Standard 55 with its current handbook of essential models (ANSI/ASHRAE 2017).

Thermal Comfort Model
Climate Consultant 6.0 was used to calculate the thermal comfort of Khartoum city (EPW), using the Energy Plus Weather File. The EPW file was calculated using the average climate data for the city from 1996 to 2020. Most weather data are based on hourly climatic parameter values. There are no records of hourly climate data at the Khartoum Metrological Station. As such, the average data was imported into the Meteonorm 7.2 program to generate an EPW file using the following procedure: Meteonorm takes the long-term monthly averages of the parameters. With a stochastical process (Markov Chains), daily and then hourly values are synthetically generated. For the derived radiation parameters, diffuse and direct irradiance, are calculated using the Perez model to split the global radiation value into the diffuse and direct part (Albatayneh et al. 2017; Meteonorm 2018).

ASHRAE Standard 55 with Current Handbook of Fundamental Model
With the current handbook of thermal comfort model, the American Society of Heating, Refrigerating, and Air-Conditioning Engineers (ASHRAE) Standard 55 considers dry bulb temperature, clothing level (clo), metabolic activity (met), air velocity, humidity, and mean radiant temperature (MRT). The Predicted Mean Vote (PMV) model is used to determine or calculate the comfort zone for most people. Furthermore, the adaptive comfort model indicates that in residential buildings, which are mostly naturally ventilated, people adjust their apparel to match seasonal conditions and feel at ease in greater air velocities. Accordingly, they have a greater range of comfort than those in buildings with central air conditioning (Altahir 1988).

3 Results and Discussions

A trend analysis technique was evaluated for climate data from 1965 to 2020 to observe seasonal and monthly fluctuations in climatic factors. Appropriate months that define Khartoum's seasons are categorised, and seasonal long-term averages of hydro-meteorological data (relative humidity, dry bulb temperature, rainfall, and wind speed) are considered.

3.1 Season-Based Trends Analysis

Dry Season (Nov, Dec, Jan, and Feb)
The winter (dry season) in Khartoum is marked by extremely low relative humidity (RH), which ranges between 8 and 10%. As seen in Fig. 2, the RH has been falling by about 0.02% annually during the Dry Season.

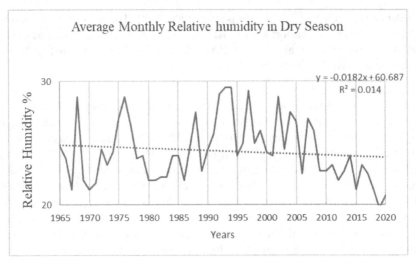

Fig. 2. Linear trends analysis of relative humidity of dry season, Khartoum Sudan for 1965–2020.

On the other hand, as shown in Fig. 3, the seasonal temperature rises by 0.03 °C/year based on linear trend analysis.

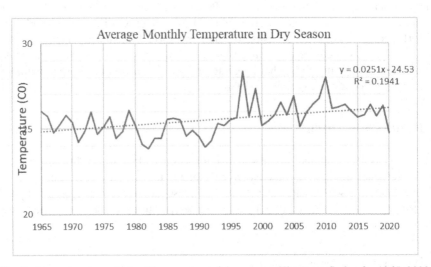

Fig. 3. Linear trends analysis of temperature of dry season, Khartoum Sudan for 1965–2020.

According to Tahir and Yousef (2013), plant cover reductions accounted for both the drop in RH and rainfall. However, it was discovered in this study that seasonal rainfall decreased by 0.005 mm/year during the study period, as seen in Fig. 4.

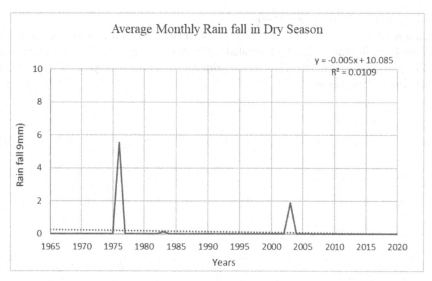

Fig. 4. Linear trends analysis of rainfall of dry season, Khartoum Sudan for 1965–2020.

The Dry Season in Khartoum has traditionally been marked by northern winds passing through the greater desert, followed by dust and sandstorms. Dust and sandstorms are more often than ever before, demonstrating the effects of climate change. Similarly, as shown in Fig. 5, a trend analysis of wind speed revealed an annual rise of 0.003 m/s.

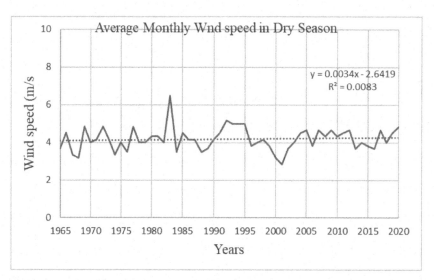

Fig. 5. Linear trends analysis of wind speed of dry season, Khartoum Sudan for 1965–2020.

Hot Season (March, April, and May)

Khartoum's hot (summer) season features low relative humidity, with temperatures reaching 40 °C in some areas. As illustrated in Fig. 6, this study's trend analysis revealed a 0.3% yearly decrease in RH. There is a significant reduction in the year 1975, showing strong climate fluctuations.

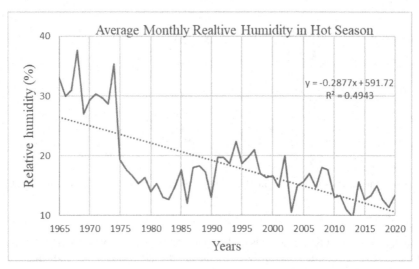

Fig. 6. Linear trends analysis of relative humidity of hot season, Khartoum Sudan for 1965–2020.

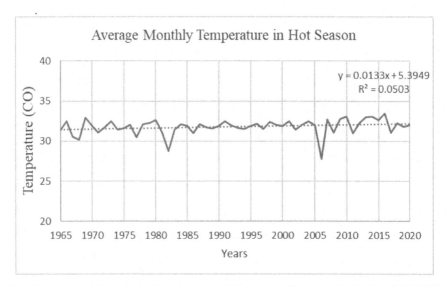

Fig. 7. Linear trends analysis of temperature of hot season, Khartoum Sudan for 1965–2020.

As seen in Figs. 7, 8, and 9, there is an annual rise of 0.01 °C in temperature, 0.0003 mm in rainfall, and 0.003 m/s in wind speed throughout this season. These findings show that there has been a climatic shift during the hot seasons from 1965 to 2020, which is consistent with Yousif and Hashim (2013) who revealed that Khartoum was the hottest city in the world in 2009 (Osman & Sevinc 2019).

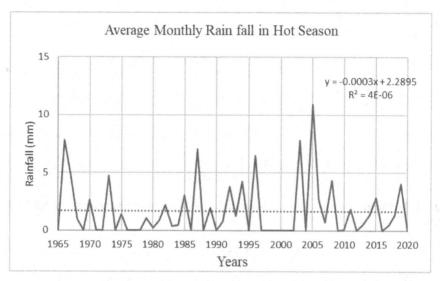

Fig. 8. Linear trends analysis of rainfall of hot season, Khartoum Sudan for 1965–2020.

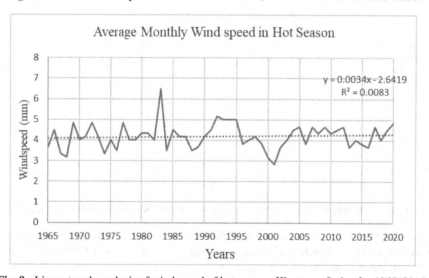

Fig. 9. Linear trends analysis of wind speed of hot season, Khartoum Sudan for 1965–2015.

Wet Season (June, Jul, Aug, Sept, and Oct)
The wettest month in Khartoum is August, which falls during the autumn (wet) season. As seen in Fig. 10, there was a 0.06% annual rise in RH. This may be considered a sign of climate change on its own, but Khartoum also saw an annual temperature increase of 0.01 °C over this period, as seen in Fig. 11.

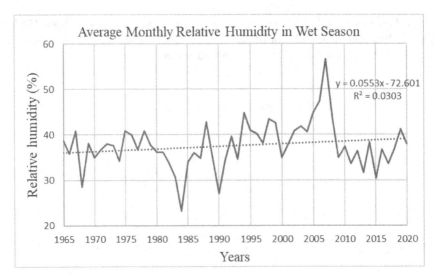

Fig. 10. Linear trends analysis of relative humidity of wet season, Khartoum Sudan for 1965–2020.

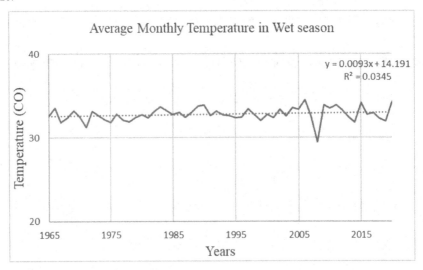

Fig. 11. Linear trends analysis of temperature of wet season, Khartoum Sudan for 1965–2020

Despite a 0.12 mm decrease in annual rainfall during this season, as seen in Fig. 12, the area experienced significant floods due to high rainfall events in 1988, 2003, 2007, and 2009. Despite the decrease in rainfall, there was a 0.01 m/s annual rise in wind speed, as seen in Fig. 13. These findings are consistent with Altahir (1988), and Tahir and Yousif's (2013) investigations.

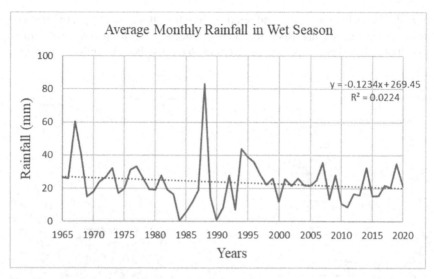

Fig. 12. Linear trends analysis of rainfall of wet season, Khartoum Sudan for 1965–2020

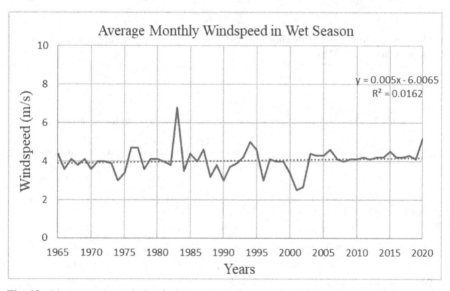

Fig. 13. Linear trends analysis of wind speed of wet season, Khartoum Sudan for 1965–2020

3.2 Thermal Comfort of Khartoum

Without the use of mechanical cooling systems, it is impossible to attain 100% thermal comfort. Even with thermal-comfort strategies and a mechanical cooling system, Khortum can only achieve 72.9% thermal comfort (i.e., 6385 h out of 8760 h), as shown in Fig. 14. The adaptive comfort model raised the comfort range from 21.3% to 24.2%. The little differences gained via this research are due to the contribution given to global horizontal solar radiation control and relative humidity alteration using a thermal comfort model. It should be emphasised that, in recent decades, the drop in relative humidity as a result of reduced plant cover in the city may have also been an influencing factor.

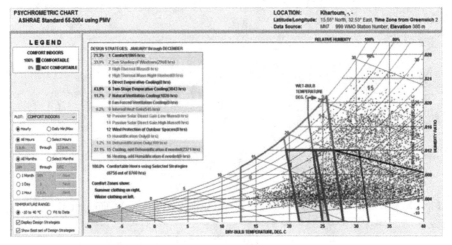

Fig. 14. Psychometric chart with climate-responsive design strategies applied to the city of Khartoum (Meteonorm 2018)

Table 1. Design strategies of seasons based a whole day data for Khartoum

Seasons (months)	Time schedule	Temperature (min-max °C)	Humidity (min-max %)	Thermal comfort without applying design strategies (hours/ year; %)
Dry (Nov, Dec, Jan& Feb)	6 am–12 noon	12.7–38.5	18–56	43.5%
	12 noon–6 pm	19.2–40.6	10–59	15.7%
	6 pm–12 midnight	13.5–36.3	10–34	52.6
	12 midnight–6 am	12.5–30.3	13–47	53.8%
Hot (March, Apr & May)	6 am–12 noon	17–43.5	17–46	53.8%
	12 noon–6 pm	20.2–45.4	10–43	23.4%
	6 pm–12 midnight	20.2–41.2	10–20	0.2%
	12 midnight–6am	16.6–35.1	11–34	13.7%
Wet (Jun, Jul, Aug, Sep & Oct)	6 am–12 noon	22.7–43.9	20–99	4.6%
	12 noon–6 pm	26.3–43.9	12–93	0%
	6 pm–12 midnight	24.9–43.9	11–88	1.1%
	12 midnight–6 am	21.5–42.4	18–84	13.2%

Table 1 shows the thermal comfort for a complete day in Khartoum on a seasonal basis, Table 2 shows the monthly fluctuations, and Table 3 shows the season-based thermal comfort for Khartoum.

Table 2. Monthly based thermal comfort for Khartoum

Months	Comfort (%)	Comfort hours	Total hours
January	28.4	211	744
February	27.8	187	672
March	28.1	209	744
April	26.4	190	720
May	6.3	47	744
June	0	0	720
July	18.1	135	744
August	33.2	247	744
September	30.8	222	720
October	30	223	744
November	32.9	237	720
December	28.4	211	744
Annual	24.2	2119	8760

Table 3. Seasonal based thermal comfort for Khartoum

Design strategies	Dry season	Hot season	Wet season
Thermal Comfort	41.7% (1200 h)	22.9% (506 h)	4.3% (159 h)

4 Conclusion

In this study, the average monthly values were used to conduct a seasonal trend analysis of Khartoum's hydro-meteorological data sets from 1965 to 2020. The following findings emerged from the analysis: Relative humidity (RH) decreases in the dry and hot seasons while increasing in the rainy (wet) season. Temperatures rise in all three seasons of the year, but rainfall decreases in all three seasons as well. Khartoum's thermal comfort level in these seasons is usually reduced when humidity drops in the dry and hot seasons. Although wind speed rises throughout the year, it may be beneficial for improving thermal comfort, but it may not contribute much to increasing the degree of thermal comfort.

The greatest thermal comfort in Khartoum, Sudan is 41.7% (1200 h) during the dry season, while the lowest is 4.3% during the wet season (159 h). As a result, the dry season is regarded as the most pleasant of Khartoum's climatic seasons. Conclusively, it should be highlighted that the Khartoum climatic region has seen climate change in these time series (1965–2020) as temperature increases, rainfall decreases, and more frequent sand-dust storms and floods. They would undoubtedly diminish the region's thermal comfort.

References

Ahmed, A.S.F., Khan, K.M.M.K., Rasul, R.M.G.: Selection of suitable passive cooling strategy for a subtropical climate. Int. J. Mech. Mater. Eng. 9(1), 14 (2014)

Albatayneh, A., Alterman, D., Page, A., Moghtaderi, B.: Thermal assessment of buildings based on occupants behavior and the adaptive thermal comfort approach. Energy Procedia 115, 265–271 (2017)

Altahir, E.A.: Testing for the suspected trend in annual rain fall series in Central and West Sudan. In: The Sudan Engineering Society Journal. Issue 30. Department of Civil Engineering, University of Khartoum, Sudan (1988)

ANSI/ASHRAE: Standard 55–2017, Thermal environmental conditions for human occupancy. American National Standards Institute, American Society of Heating, Refrigerating and Air-Conditioning Engineers, Atlanta, GA, USA (2017)

Elagib, N.A., Mansell, M.G.: Recent trends and anomalies in mean seasonal and annual temperatures over Sudan. J. Arid Environ. 45(3), 263–288 (2000)

Fry, M.: Hydrological Data Rescue–The Current State of Affairs. IAHS-AISH Publication, pp. 459–464 (2010)

Hirashima, S.D.S., Katzschner, A., Ferreira, D.G., De Assis, E.S., Katzschner, L.: Thermal comfort comparison and evaluation in different climates. Urban Clim. 23, 219–251 (2018)

Iyendo, T.O., Akingbaso, E.A., Alibaba, H.Z., Özdeniz, M.B.: A relative study of microclimate responsive design approaches to buildings in Cypriot settlements. ITU A| Z. 13(1), 69–81 (2016)

Kuchen, E.: Variable thermal comfort index for indoor work space in office buildings: a study in Germany. Open J. Civil Eng. 6(04), 670 (2016)

Meteonorm 7.3: Handbook part II: theory version 7.3 (2018). https://meteonorm.com/en/meteon orm-documents/. Accessed 16 July 2019

Mirza, M.Q., Warrick, R.A., Ericksen, N.J., Kenny, G.J.: Trends and persistence in precipitation in the Ganges, Brahmaputra and Meghna River Basins. Hydrol. Sci. J. 43, 845–858 (1998)

Osman, M., Sevinc, H.: Adaptation of climate-responsive building design strategies and resilience to climate change in the hot/arid region of Khartoum Sudan. Sustain. Cities Soc. 47(2019), 101429 (2019)

Rupp, R.F., Vásquez, N.G., Lamberts, R.: A review of human thermal comfort in the built environment. Energy Build. 105, 178–205 (2015)

Shakurov, I., Elamin A., Zebilila M.: Development and metabolism of the city of Khartoum (Republic of Sudan): spatial designing of the coastal territory of the Blue and White Nile. In: E3S Web of Conferences, vol. 6. EDP Sciences (2016)

Shi, X., Xu, X.: Interdecadal trend turning of global terrestrial temperature and precipitation during 1951–2002. Prog. Nat. Sci. 18(11), 1383–1393 (2008)

Tahir, H.M., Yousif, T.A.: Modeling the effect of urban trees on relative humidity in Khartoum State. J. For. Prod. Ind. 2(5), 20–24 (2013)

Community Water Projects Sustainability for Climate Change Resilience and Adaptation in Suam Catchment Area of West Pokot County, Kenya

Kennedy W. Nyongesa[✉]

Department of Mathematics and Applied Sciences, Kitale National Polytechnic,
P.O Box 2132-30200, Kitale, Kenya
kennyongesa@yahoo.com
http://www.kitalenationalpolytechnic.ac.ke/

Abstract. Managing water resources still remains a challenge to most of the players in the water sector. This is even made worse by climate change impacts that are experienced globally in the recent past. It is evident in most parts of the African continent that women and young children shoulder the burden of providing water to the family. This leaves them with little time for other demanding day-to-day assignments. The study sought to analyze how Integrated Water Resources Management (IWRM) advances the Sustainability of Community water projects in the Suam Catchment area of West Pokot County. The study looked at the governance structure, steps that are taken in developing capacities in Community water projects, mechanisms that are used in monitoring and implementing Community water projects in relation to sustainability in the Suam Catchment Area of West Pokot County. The sample was drawn from the staff of Kerio Valley Development Authority, Ministry of Water, Environment and Natural Resources, County Government of West Pokot, Water Resources Management Authority, Kapenguria Water and Sanitation Company, Ministry of Agriculture, Water Resources Users Associations, and local people all are stakeholders. Purposive sampling, as well as simple random sampling, was used. The sample composed of 96 respondents, the sample was evenly distributed with 12 persons per group. The study found that the leadership and management of community water projects were vested in appointed/elected leaders (45%) and water officers (16%). The findings indicated that 60% of the respondents had been trained on water usage and management. It was also clear that 53.8% of the respondents had never had access to IWRM policy documents even though 61.3% had been involved in the monitoring and implementation of community water projects in the area. In the ranking of the Integrated Water Resource Management policy factors, consideration of climate resilience and adaptation was ranked first (3.28), water-related information gathering was ranked second (3.14), monitoring and evaluation were ranked third (3.13), engagement with local communities was ranked fourth (3.08). The study recommends that there is an urgent need for community sensitization on climate change, climate resilience, and adaptation in the context of sustainability of the Community water projects.

A. D. Mambo et al. (Eds.): InterSol 2022, LNICST 449, pp. 29–48, 2022.
https://doi.org/10.1007/978-3-031-23116-2_3

Keywords: Climate change · Climate adaptation · Climate resilience · IWRM · Water resource

1 Introduction

Access to water resources remains a daily challenge to most families across the globe even though it is one of the basic fundamental rights of human existence. Water is essential and has a very significant role in the well-being and development of the eco-systems (Brauman 2015), supports life forms including various animal species and vegetation. It is also imperative to point out that the human community, various local economies and natural systems solely rely on water resources for their normal functioning; thus, destructive and non-sustainable measures normally practiced towards the use of water resources destroy ecosystems (UNICEF 2012). This has set a pace for the adoption of the Integrated Water Resources Management (IWRM) policy across the globe (Savenije 2008). This has also seen many players in the Water sector fronting several mechanisms that aim at full implementation and realization of the policy mandates and objectives. Pegram (2013) asserts that in Europe, the Water Framework Directive provides a high-level legal framework within which the Member States are responsible for developing river basin-based approaches for meeting good ecological status for all waters. Similarly, in Canada, the South Saskatchewan River Basin (SSRB) provides an example of river basin governance,the situation here is characterized by decentralized, multilevel assigned water licenses as asserted by Hurlbert and Diaz (2013). In developing countries, IWRM has been carried out with the objective of empowering people, poverty alleviation, improving livelihoods, and promoting economic growth (Merrey *et al.* 2005). In Zimbabwe, IWRM sought to bring together fragmented water institutions and users into integrated planning, allocation, and management framework (Chifamba 2013). According to Sokile and Koppen (2004) Tanzania's Integrated Water Resources Management has demonstrated a bias towards the formal state-based institutions for water management resulting in an escalation of state-based formal institutional arrangements through which Water Resources Users Associations (WRUAs) are formed besides providing frameworks for water allocation. A number of countries that have attempted to develop reform processes based on Integrated Water Resources Management principles have faced significant challenges (Pegram 2013). As Jiang (2009) posits, water resource management has been inefficient,which has led to an increased vulnerability to increasingly severe water scarcity. Moreover, water resources management challenges have increased ranging from flash floods, poor water quality, reduced water quantity, catchment degradation, lack of community participation and involvement, and increased water- related conflicts (Pegram *et al.* 2013). Yet, as a framework for managing water resources, Galli *et al.* (2012) argue that IWRM has helped nations to develop integrated systems and approaches that can best inform decision-making hence, best practices implemented.

In Kenya, Integrated Water Resources Management has informed water resource management practices aimed at achieving the goal of access to clean, safe, and increased water availability, which is a key determinant of health (Plummer 2015). Water is a key resource in Kenya, critical to the conservation of ecosystems and the development of agriculture, industry, power generation, livestock production, and other important economic activities (Mango *et al.* 2011). Climate change has led to increased water resources vulnerability and demand precipitating difficulty in allocating water, given the limited water resources (Baker *et al.* 2015). Consequently, Suam River Basin is one of the major catchment areas that were intended to be impacted by the Integrated Water Resources Management policy. However, since the time policy document on water management through the water act, of 2016 of Kenya, there have been limited studies to assess how plans developed for Integrated Water Resources Management, particularly relating to Suam Catchment Area, have succeeded or failed to meet the objectives set out.

1.1 Statement of the Problem

Unforeseen factors such as climate change related conditions are expected to increase the pressure exerted on water resources in most of these regions. Kenya being a developing nation has implemented various water reforms that have targeted the water sector starting with the Water Act 2002 and now Water Act 2016. However, various issues remain which include but are not limited to health concerns that are still on the rise: distance and time covered to water points, which remains worryingly lengthy, prolonged queuing at water sources by the communities, and ever-skyrocketing costs. These often make water inaccessible. In the instances of glaring water challenges, communities and other local stakeholders have come up with adaptive mechanisms and local water provision projects to ensure the smooth provision and sustainability of water management. However, despite the initiation and implementation of these water projects, their relative success hardly lasts to complete a cycle and achieve the expected goals. This situation has been attributed to factors such as inadequate funding, low community participation, ineffective management support systems, and unfavorable climatic conditions that have affected the sustainable operations of water supply projects.

1.2 The Rationale of the Study

This research sought to analyze how Integrated Water Resource Management (IWRM) advances the sustainability of community water projects in the Suam Catchment Area of West Pokot County in Kenya in light of climate change. This assessment was important because the findings shall have both practical and theoretical benefits to various water stakeholders, policymakers, planners, donor agencies, and relevant government agencies in formulating relevant policies. Secondly, the communities in the Suam Water Catchment Area will gain a lot from the findings as they will be sensitized to the importance of environmental conservation in the context of water sustainability and this may lead to low environmental degradation. Thirdly the communities will be sensitized about climate change resilience and adaptation.

1.3 Purpose of This Study

The purpose of this study was to assess how Integrated Water Resources Management (IWRM) advances the Sustainability of Community Water Projects in the Suam Catchment Area of West Pokot County in Kenya; as a tool for climate change resilience and adaptation.

1.4 Specific Objectives

The following were the specific objectives:

1) To examine the governance structures of the Community Water Projects in relation to water sustainability in the Suam Water Catchment Area of West Pokot County.
2) To evaluate whether there are efforts to develop capacities among the local people on Community Water projects in relation to water sustainability in the Suam Water Catchment Area of West Pokot County.
3) To analyze mechanisms used to monitor and implement Community Water projects in relation to water sustainability in the Suam Water Catchment Area of West Pokot County.

1.5 Scope of the Study

The assessment involved the study of the Suam River Basin in North Pokot Sub-County, West Pokot County comprising surface water, particularly river discharge. Secondly, only residents and water managers in the said area were the respondents. This assessment attempted to investigate various ways that have been developed in the catchment area to find out whether they have resulted in reduced water stress on the riverine ecosystem and improved climate change resilience and adaptation. The assessment highlights measures to be undertaken to place greater focus on legal, institutional, economic, social, and ecological factors that have lived up to or alternatively failed to meet expectations as far as Sustainability of Community Water projects is concerned in light of climate change.

2 Literature Review

2.1 Climate Change in Perspective

According to IPCC's (2014) fifth assessment report (AR5), the climate in a wider sense is the state, including a statistical description of the climate system of the atmosphere, observed over comparable time periods. There is a distinction between climate change attributable to human activities altering the atmospheric composition, and climate variability attributable to natural causes. Climate change directly interrupts natural capital, and thus the resource base for human livelihood (ACCESS/IUCN 2014).

2.2   Climate Change Resilience and Adaptation

Resilience refers to the ability of a system to stand up to shocks or changes and maintain an acceptable level of function and performance (Folke 2006; Nelson et al. 2007); likewise, adaptation refers to adjustments to limit the negative effects, or take advantage of the positive effects of climate change. Adaptation is especially important in developing countries since those countries are predicted to bear the brunt of the effects of global warming (Farber 2007; Cole 2008). Thus, the capacity and potential for humans and other natural systems to adapt are unevenly distributed across different regions and populations, and developing countries generally have less capacity to adapt (Schneider et al. 2007). Furthermore, the degree of adaptation relates directly to the situational focus on environmental issues (Nyongesa et al. 2016). Adaptive capacity is closely linked to social and economic development (Ruth and Ibarrarian 2009). The adaptation challenge grows with the magnitude and the rate of climate change (IPCC 2007). Figure 1 explains the relationships between risk, hazard mitigation, resilience, adaptation, and climate cha*nge*.

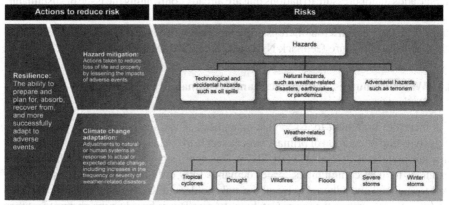

Source: GAO analysis of Presidential Policy Directive 8, previous GAO work, and National Oceanic and Atmospheric Administration data. | GAO-16-454

Fig. 1. The relationships between Risk, Hazard mitigation, Resilience, Adaptation, and Climate change. Source: GAO report: www.gao.gov/products/ GAO-16-454 CLIMATE CHANGE.

Governments have approached adaptation through Laws and Long-Term Plans. Another response to climate change is known as climate change mitigation (Verbruggen 2007). Even the most effective reductions in emissions, however, would not prevent further climate change impacts, making the need for adaptation unavoidable (Klein 2007). Nyongesa et al. (2016) concluded that in the absence of mitigation efforts, the effects of climate change would reach such a magnitude as to make adaptation impossible for some natural ecosystems. Others are concerned that climate adaptation programs might interfere with the existing development programs and thus lead to unintended consequences for vulnerable groups (Misra 2016). For human systems, the economic and social costs of unmitigated climate change would be very high (Opperman et al. 2009).

2.3   Climate Change Impacts on Water Resources in Africa

Many countries in Africa live under water stress; defined as those using more than 20% of their renewable water resources while withdrawals of over 40% implies serious water stress (Pittock 2007). For example, reports show that water withdrawal in Nigeria during the 1990s was 28 cubic meters per person per year (Gleick 2000; World Bank 2003). The Dialogue on Water and Climate (2004) noted that water stress would increase significantly in those regions that are already relatively dry (such as sub-Saharan Africa). About 25% of the contemporary African population experiences water stress, while 69% live under conditions of relative water abundance (Vorosmarty et al. 2005), but abundance does not necessarily mean availability. Over time, human activities such as forest clearing, deforestation, and agriculture, among others have disturbing influences on the water cycle including vapor-transpiration, flow regimes, groundwater table, and sea level (Stolberg et al. 2003). In addition, human activities influence cloud formation via the emission of aerosols and their gaseous precursors (Kruger and Gracie 2002), change in the CO_2 absorption by the oceans and other carbon sinks increases in extreme precipitation events (Stolberg et al. 2003). According to UNEP (2003), climate, water resources, biophysical and socio-economic systems are interconnected in complex ways, so a change in any one of these induces a change in another. Anthropogenic climate change adds major pressure to nations that are already confronting the issue of sustainable water resource use in Africa. This can be in a form not often recognized, namely as water vapor from the transpiration of crops and evaporation from natural and man-made lakes which is called moisture feedback Nyongesa et al. (2016).

2.4   Water Resources Management and Sustainability of Community Water Projects

It is therefore important to assert that enactment of various policies that promote the inclusivity and integration of primary water users in the management and implementation of water projects is critical (UNDP 2017). This approach will make the available water resources to meet communities' water demands fully even in dry seasons,this is if it is well formulated and adhered to by all the stakeholders in Kenya and especially in water catchment areas such as the Suam Catchment Area. This is based on the abstract fact that having several community water projects by various actors may reduce stresses related to inadequate supply. There is a growing global concern over the future of the world's water resources due to the increasing human pressure on the intricate and finite water resources. The water resource is not only a basic need but is also a centerpiece of sustainable development and a crucial part of poverty alleviation (Foch and Thiemann 2004). The Dublin principles and the Earth Summit's Agenda 21, also emphasize the need for integrated water management, recognizing water as one of the natural resource elements that need to be managed in a sustainable manner (Figueres et al. 2003). Many parts of the world, markedly the Middle East and sub-Saharan Africa (SSA) are experiencing intense competition over water resources due to management failures (Taha 2007).

In this context, water is a precious resource on which all dimensions of an extended security concept (food security, economic security, and livelihood security) depend (Liu et al. 2010). This is in the wider context of human safety. This study on sustainable utilization of regional water resources in China indicates that water resources are one of the most important factors hindering the sustainable development of the world economy and society. This makes water resources one of the main factors restricting local sustainable development. This, therefore, calls for tilting in Water Resources Management

(WRM) from raindrops to rivers and lakes, a strategy that would widen the prioritization of water management and policy options (UN 2017). Access to water resources still remains a daily challenge to most families across the globe even though it is one of the basic fundamental rights of human existence. Water plays a very significant role in the well-being and development of ecosystems (Brauman 2015). However, as observed by Kalbus (2012) and UNICEF (2012) more than 0.9 billion people across the globe do not have access to safe drinking water and about 2.6 billion people are living without adequate sanitation. Meanwhile, an increasing number of countries continue to experience water crises with most river basins having non-existent or unsatisfactory mechanisms and institutions to manage the available water resources (Biswas 2012). This, therefore, means that in order to attain sustainable development, improving water resources management should be considered fundamental to realizing social and economic growth as well as providing environmental services that are sustainable oriented. Biswas (2012) alludes that there have been rising concerns that management of water resources is inhibited by various constraints that are dynamic and complex hence requiring an integrated water resources management approach that involves all stakeholders. As a result of this, the United Water Conference held in 1977 in Mar del Plata, Spain formally coined and ratified the concept of IWRM as the only way to correctly tackle and solve most water resource management-related issues (Rahaman 2005). The population at risk of increased water stress in Africa is projected to be 75–250 million and 350–600 million people by the 2020s and 2050s, respectively (Arnell 2004).

Similarly, Annan (2000) noted that about one-third of the world's population already live in countries considered being water-stressed, where consumption exceeds 10% of the total supply. Yet, as a framework for managing water resources, IWRM can help develop integrated ecosystem approaches that can potentially best inform decision-makers in tackling multiple issues while attempting to meet the needs of various sectors concurrently (Cai et al. 2003). Similarly, it can help with the integration of technical, economic, environmental, social, and legal aspects into a coherent analytical framework. According to Plummer (2015) in Kenya, Integrated Water Resources Management has informed water resource management practices aimed to achieve the goal of access to clean, safe and increased water availability, which is a key determinant of health water as a critical resource in Kenya. Kenya as a water-scarce country in Arid and Semi-Arid Lands (ASALs) has an annual average rainfall of about 630 mm with a population of nearly 40 million people that is rapidly expanding (Plummer 2015). In addition, climatic changes have led to increased water resources vulnerability. Consequently, Suam River Basin is one of the major catchments that were intended to be impacted by the Integrated Water Resources Management implementation. However, since the inception of the policy framework through the passing of the Water Act 2016, there have been limited studies to assess how plans developed for Integrated Water Resources Management, particularly relating to Suam Catchment Area, have succeeded or failed to meet the objectives set out. Kenya being one of the developing nations, there has been various water reforms that have targeted the water sector starting with the Water Act of 2002.

2.5 Theoretical Framework

This study used the Complex Adaptive System (CAS) theory to guide it. Complex Adaptive System (CAS) theory is a theoretical basis for analyzing the dynamics of social-ecological systems (Rammel et al.2007). A Complex Adaptive System (CAS) is a nonlinear, interactive system that has the ability to adapt to a changing environment. In this study, the components of the study that will be considered comprise governance structures, capacity development, and monitoring of the implementation process. Accordingly, governance structures represent the acknowledgment of the essential role of institutions (legal frameworks, cultural norms) of individual and collective actors (governmental and non-governmental). This will help highlight the conditions for the success and failure of governance arrangements. According to Pahl-Wostl (2009), polycentric and adaptive governance systems are particularly complex, and therefore to reduce problems of fit between administrative and biophysical boundaries new formal institutions ought to be initiated in line with the world hydrological principles.

2.6 Conceptual Framework

The conceptual framework presented in Fig. 2 shows a schematic representation of the link between the variables. The independent and dependent variables are likely to be moderated by Government policy, Project financing and Climate Change, Climate Change Resilience, Mitigation, and Adaptation.

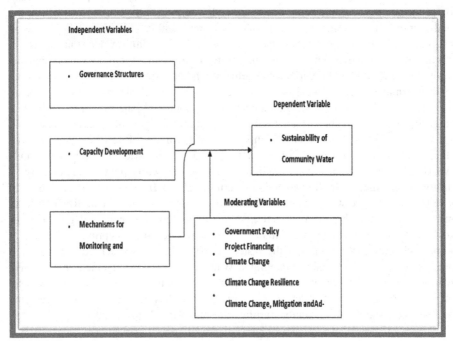

Fig. 2. Conceptual Framework Showing Interrelationships between variables in the study.

3   Methodologies

3.1   Research Design

A descriptive survey research design was used in the study which attempted to describe the phenomenon under study in terms of behavior, attitudes, knowledge and perceptions as far as sustainability of community water projects and Integrated Water Resources Management was concerned.

3.2   Target Population of the Study

The target population of the study comprised of key stakeholders who are people associated with the Suam River Basin management and development. This included Water Resources Users Associations (WRUAs), local organizations, community members, employees of Kerio Valley Development Authority; Ministry of Interior and Coordination of National Government employees, Water Resources Management Authority employees, Ministry of Water, Environment and Natural Resources employees, County government officials; Kapenguria Water and Sanitation Company employees, Ministry of Agriculture; and the Local communities along the Suam River Basin.

3.3   Sample Size, Sampling Techniques and Data Collection Tools

Purposive and simple random sampling techniques were used. Simple random sampling was used to select 12 respondents from stakeholder groups. Consequently, a sample size of 12 people from each sampling group ensured adequate data from each sampling group. The total sample size was 96 respondents. Data for this study was collected using questionnaires and interview schedules.

4   Results

4.1   Governance Structures in Relation to Sustainability of Community Water Projects

Leidel (2012) observes that good water governance always includes aspects of democracy where decisions are made based on the agreed modes from each and every community member affected by the community water projects. Dietz et al. (2013) observe that, there exist visible imbalances in governance among various stakeholders and decisions on water resource allocation, development, management and protection. The researcher ascertained whether the various leaders were democratically elected and appointed or not. This is illustrated in Table 1.

Table 1. People in-charge are democratically elected

	Frequency	Valid%	Cumulative%
Yes	12	15	15
No	68	85	10
Total	**80**	**100**	

As illustrated in Table 1, most of the leadership and management of community water projects were not democratically appointed or selected. The study ranked various water governance issues and factors that resonate with Integrated Water Resources Management principles. A Likert scale type of question was used where 1 represented Strongly Disagree, 2 Disagree, 3 Neutral, 4 Agree and 5 Strongly Agree. Table 2 shows the Factors, Mean, Standard Deviation and the Rank of the factors respectively.

Table 2. Ranking of governance matters

Factors	Mean	S.Dev	Rank
1. Some members of the governing council are hostile and prejudiced	3.03	1.147	1
2. The governance of community water projects is rational	2.83	1.111	2
3. The respondents will highly accept to be part of the governance council	2.76	1.183	3
4. The governance of water projects is drawn from community members	2.31	1.239	4
5. Individuals charged with the management of community water are knowledgeable	2.58	1.3	5
6. There is all-inclusive governance of community waters	2.1	1.323	6

As illustrated in Table 2, the study revealed that the respondents sampled disagreed with the notion that "there was an all-inclusive governance of community water projects in the area". This report concurs with the democracy approach in terms of governance of integrated water resource management how it adopts a bottom-up structure. The one-way ANOVA test on whether governance of community water projects had any significant relationship with the sustainability of the said water projects reveals that, the F-value (46.347) was found to be significant at a 0.002 significance level with a degree of freedom of 1% as illustrated in Table 3.

Table 3. ANOVA test for governance structure

	Sum of squares	d.f	Mean square	F	Signifant difference
Between Groups	31.322	1	21.222	46.347	0.002
Within Groups	69.254	176	0.449		
Total	**100.576**	**177**			

As illustrated in ANOVA Table 3, it is clear that the significance value is 0.002 is below 0.05, and there is a statistically significant difference in the mean of governance structures put in place and the sustainability of community water projects within the Suam water catchment areas of West Pokot County.

4.2 Development of Capacities and Sustainability of Water Projects

The second objective of the study was to ascertain whether there are efforts to develop capacities among the communities on Community Water projects in relation to sustainability. This analysis ascertained whether the respondents sampled had ever been trained on how to effectively and efficiently use water resources in the and this was mainly to validate the whole issue of sustainability of the existing community water projects in the area. This is illustrated in Table 4, which shows the Frequency, Valid Percent and the Cumulative Percent respectively.

Table 4. Training on how to effectively and efficiently use Water Resources

	Frequency	Valid percent	Cumulative percent
Yes	48	60	60
No	32	40	100
Total	80	100	100

Table 4 clearly shows that (60%) of respondents had training on how to effectively and efficiently use water resources with (40%) de-affrming. It was also revealed that most of the target population of this study was individuals working in the water sector and in one way or the other had qualifications in water management. Kalbus (2012) observes that successful implementation and monitoring of community water projects under Integrated Water Resources Management solely depends on the capacity development of staff and other personnel working in the field of water resources management. This study noted that this will ensure that various strategies and mechanisms put in place are clearly followed and implemented as far as the realization of the Integrated Water Resources Management is concerned. This was basically to assess the need for water knowledge among the water users and managers given the dynamics surrounding the water sector. This is illustrated in Table 5.

Table 5. The Rate at which Refresher Courses on Water use need to be conducted

Duration	Frequency	Valid%	Cumulative%
Annually	24	30	30
Quarterly	15	18.8	48.8
Monthly	25	31.3	80
As need maybe	16	20	100
Total	**80**	**100**	

Table 5 shows that there were varied views in regard to the frequency of conducting refresher and/or other trainings. Leidel (2012) found out that there was need to enable and support practical implementation of Water Resources management capacities which may include knowledge transfer and development of resources for implementation, particularly in terms of technical, financial, and administrative capacities. Capacity building and development should be tailored to the catchment conditions in order to increase impact. This was necessary as it was the main agenda of this research study. This is illustrated in Table 6.

Table 6. Access to integrated water resource management policy

	Frequency	Valid%	Cumulative%
Yes	37	46.3	46.3
No	43	53.8	100
Total	80	100	

As illustrated in Table 6, (53.8%) of the respondents were not familiar with the Integrated Water Resource Management Policy. 46.3% of the respondents had accessed the IWRM policy. In the ranking of these sentiments on a Likert scale question as used in Table 2 and 9, the mean and standard deviation was used in answering as illustrated in Table 7.

Table 7. Issues relating to IWRM policy

Factor	Mean	S.Dev	Rank
Consideration of Climate Resilience and Adaptation	3.28	1.396	1
Water related information gathering	3.13	1.267	2
Monitoring and evaluation	3.08	1.491	3
Engagement with local communities	2.98	1.441	4
Implementation of basin strategies	2.94	1.215	5
Transparency in water allocation	2.81	1.284	6
Managing water quality	2.53	1.396	7
Provision of Water is a basic right	2.51	1.432	8
Protection of the Riparian Areas	2.48	1.449	9

Table 7 shows that in ranking of the Integrated Water Resource Management policy issues, factors consideration of Climate Resilience and Adaptation was ranked first (3.28),"Water related information gathering" was ranked second (3.14), "Monitoring and evaluation" was ranked third (3.13), "Engagement with local communities" was ranked fourth (3.08), "Existence and implementation of basin strategies" was ranked fifth (2.98), "Transparency in water allocation" was ranked sixth (2.94), "Managing water quality" was ranked seventh (2.81), "Provision of Water is a basic right" was ranked eight (2.53), "Protection of the Riparian areas" was ranked ninth (2.51) and "Distribution of Functions, responsibilities and authority across levels" was ranked tenth (2.48). Further probing on this revealed that there were Water Users Committees that were formed and were concerned with the collection of information relating to water use and management. These committees were basically drawn from the local people. The finding that agrees with Ruiter (2015) who sees that sensitizing common water users about how to mitigate water challenges is the first step in enhancing the capacity of the local community and the nation whose water resource conservation practices ensure water resources are sustainably handed down to future generations.

4.3   Mechanisms Used to Monitor and Implement Community Water Projects

The third objective of the study was to establish mechanisms used to monitor and implement Community water projects in relation to sustainability in the Suam Water Catchment Areas of West Pokot County. The sampled respondents were asked to state whether they had ever been involved in the implementation and monitoring of community water projects in the area. This was basically to assess whether in one way or the other they are involved in the matters affecting the communities they serve or reside as this was part of the main agenda of this research. This is illustrated in Table 8.

Table 8.   Involvement in monitoring and implementation of water projects

	Frequency	Valid%	Cumulative%
Yes	49	61.3	60
No	31	38.8	100
Total	**80**	**100**	

Table 8 shows that most people (61.3%) of the respondents in the study had in one way or the other been involved in the monitoring and implementation of community water projects in the area. This clearly shows how community members are valued and called upon by the water implementers to offer their services in the projects that affect their livelihood at large; and that Integrated Water Resources Management requires adaptive capacities where resource governance and management systems, processes, and structural elements are transformed as a response to experienced or expected changes in the environment, internal as well as external, societal and natural. In the rating of the factors that relate to monitoring and implementation of community water projects and their sustainability, a Likert scale question was used as in Table 2 and 7.

Table 9. Ranking of monitoring and implementation factors

Factors	Mean	Std. D	Rank
Knowledge sharing and training	3.93	1.439	1
Existence of adaptation Strategy	3.76	0.984	2
Availability and creation of knowledge for Climate adaptation	3.71	1.017	3
Resources capacity Financial	3.56	0.966	4
Sustainability	3.56	1.157	5
Protection against droughts	2.48	1.067	6
Protection against floods	2.46	1.158	7
Construction and operation of water storage facilities	2.31	1.228	8
Enlisting of women in water governance	2.3	1.237	9
Maintenance of environmental quality	2.15	0.969	10

As illustrated in Table 9, it's clear that the respondents rated "Knowledge sharing and training "as first (3.93), "Existence of adaptation Strategy" second (3.76), "Availability and creation of knowledge for adaptation" third (3.71), "Human Resources capacity" fourth (3.56), "Financial Sustainability" fifth (3.56), "Protection against droughts" sixth (2.48), "Protection against floods" seventh (2.46), "Construction and operation of water storage facilities" eighth (2.31), "Enlisting of women in water governance" ninth (2.30) and "Maintenance of environmental quality" tenth (2.15). Thus, among these factors emphasis on knowledge sharing and training of the individuals charged with water management was majorly agreed by majority of the respondents. This analysis found it eminent to identify the people charged with the management of community water projects in Suam catchment areas of West Pokot County and this was basically to identify the authority behind the community water monitoring and implementation. This is illustrated in Table 10.

Table 10. People charged with monitoring and implementation of projects

People responsible	Frequency	Valid%	Cumulative%
Local leaders	40	50	50
Area Provincial Administrators	35	43.75	93.75
Appointed/Elected Local Residents	5	6.25	100
Totals	**80**	**100**	

5 Conclusion

The study makes conclusions that there is community water projects in the Suam water catchment area of West Pokot County and that in one way or the other, the local community members are involved in the management of the same water projects. The study established that 85% of the sampled respondents held views that the management and leadership of the said community water projects were not democratically elected and/or appointed. This analysis concludes that the leadership of the community water projects in the area is imposed on the people without their input and this greatly dims the hopes for the sustainability of the same projects and hence their use for climate change resilience and adaptation. The study also found out that 60% of the sampled respondents had actually had training on how to effectively and efficiently make use of water resources. The study, therefore, makes conclusions that there are efforts by the people concerned with water management to continuously and effectively train the community members on how to manage and use the water resources in the catchment area. The study further established that 53.8% of the sampled population was not familiar with the Integrated Water Resource Management Policy. The study makes conclusions that most of the water managers in the area are not following the IWRM principles and thus they are not very familiar as far as policy statements are concerned. An ability to recognize sustainable practices and the attainment of sustainability goals will require a well-designed measuring system (Emerson et al. 2012). As a result, there is a need for monitoring and evaluation of management practices and outcomes for the Suam Catchment Area and the Community Water Projects to enhance their sustainability in the context of climate change resilience and adaptation.

6 Recommendations for Policy Action

Based on the findings, the study offers the following recommendations: 1) There is an urgent need for the ministry of water and natural resources to avail the necessary materials, personnel, and IWRM policy documents to water officers in the area as this will greatly aid in the conservation of the water catchment zone. 2) The entire population residing in the Suam Water Catchment area should be sensitized and be trained on effective and efficient water usage.3) There is also an urgent need for the election of the water management committees and those involved in the monitoring and implementation of community water projects in the Suam Water Catchment areas of West Pokot County to involve the community members in identifying them through an open and democratic process.

Moreover, it is increasingly recognized that inadequate governance structures and especially the gap between existing and necessary capacities, rather than technical challenges, are constraints for enhanced water resources management. IWRM must deal with complex and dynamic adaptive systems that comprise political, economic, social, environmental, and technical factors and their interactions (Leidel et al. 2012). This makes capacity development a key issue in river basin management in community projects such as Suam Water Catchment Area in West Pokot County. The operation is at three levels including human capacity development level such as enhancing trained actors,organizational capacity development level, including improving processes within organizations; and capacity development level involving creating an enabling environment through legislative, administrative, judicial, and organizational arrangements.

7 Suggestions for Further Research

This study proposes that a similar studies need to be developed on the importance of implementing correctly the Integrated Water Resource Management policy drawing from the cases resulting from conflicts on available scarce water resources in the area, the local pastoralist communities are forced to crossover to neighboring Uganda for the search of the commodity. The study also suggests that where possible a descriptive survey on the effective methods of capacity building of the rural communities, especially in arid and semi-arid areas should be carried out with the main purpose of aiding the entire process of IWRM implementation.

Appendix 1

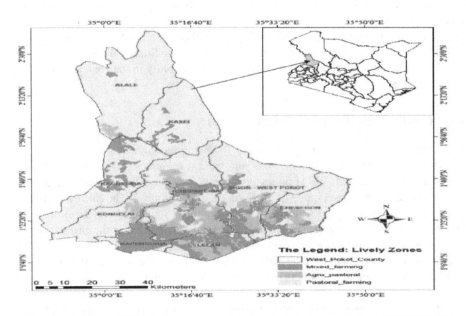

Diagram 1. Map-of-West-Pokot-County and its Location in Kenya. Source: UNDP (2017).

Appendix II

Diagram 2. Trans boundary Location of the Suam Region Between Kenya and Uganda. Source: UNDP (2017).

References

ACCESS/IUCN: An overview of climate change and adaptation in Tropical Mountain Ecosystems. In: Olago, D.O., Odada, E.O., Ochola, W., Olaka, L. (eds.) Prepared by African Collaborative Centre for Earth System Science (ACCESS), iii+11p (2014).

Annan, K.: We the peoples: the role of the United Nations in the 21st century. In: Report prepared for the Millennium Summit (2000)

Arnell, N.W.: Climate change and global water resources: SRES emissions and socio-economic scenarios. Glob. Environ. Change **14**, 31–52 (2004)

Ayenew, T.: Water management problems in the Ethiopian rift: Challenges for development. J. Afr. Earth Sci. **48**, 222–236 (2007)

Bartlett, J.E., II, Kotrlik, J.W., Higgins, C.: Organizational research: determining appropriate sample size for survey research. Inform. Technol. Learn. Perform. J. **19**(1), 43–50 (2001)

Bedřich, M.E.: How to understand and measure environmental sustainability: indicators and targets. Ecol. Ind. **17**, 4–13 (2012). https://doi.org/10.1016/j.ecolind.2011.04.033

Biswas, A.: Integrated water resources management: is it working? Water Res. Dev. 5–22 (2012)

Borchardt, D.: Management of water in a changing world: lessons learnt and innovative. In: Dresden International Conference on Integrated Water Resources Management, Dresden, Germany (2011)

Brauman, K.: Hydrological ecosystem services: linking ecohydrologic process to human well-being in water research and watershed management. Wires Water. **2**(4), 345–358 (2015)

Butterworth, J., Warner, J., Moriarty, P., Smits, S., Batchelor, C.: Finding practical approaches to integrated water resources management. Water Alternat. **3**, 68–81 (2010)

Cernea, M.M., Schmidt-Soltau, K.: National parks and poverty risks: is population resettlement the solution? In: World Parks Congress. Durban, South Africa, pp. 1–31 (2003)

Soltau, K.: National parks and poverty risks: is population resettlement the solution? In: World Parks Congress. Durban, South Africa, pp. 1–31 (2003)

Cosgrove, W., Rijsberman, F.: World water vision: making water everyone's business. World Water Council, Earthscan, London (2000)

Dialogue on Water and Climate: Climate Changes the Water Rules. www.waterandclimate.org/report.htm (2004)

Dietz T.E, et al.: The struggle to govern the commons. Science. **302**, 1907–1912 (2013)

Folke, C.: Resilience: the emergence of a perspective for social-ecological systems analyses. Glob. Environ. Chang. **16**(3), 253–267 (2006)

Emerson, K., Nabatchi, T., Balogh, S.: An integrated framework for collaborative governance. J. Public Adm. Res. Theory **22**(1), 1–29 (2012)

Farber, D.A.: Adapting to climate change: who should pay. Fla. St. U. J. Land Use & Envtl. L. **23**(1), 8 (2007)

Fraenkel, J.R., Wallen, N.E.: How to Design and Evaluate Research in education. McGraw-Hill Inc, New York (1990)

Figuaeres, C., Rockstreonm, J., Tortajada, C.: Rethinking Water Management: Innovative Approaches to Contemporary Issues. Earthscan Publications (2003)

Förch, G., Thiemann, S.: Lake Abaya research symposium proceedings. Catchment and Lake Research (2004)

Kalbus, E.K.: Integrated water resource management under different hydrological, climatic and socio-economic conditions. Environ. Earth Sci. **65**, 1363–1366 (2012)

GAO Report: Climate change: governments have approached adaptation through laws and long-term plans. www.gao.gov/products/GAO-16-454 (2010)

Gleick, P.H. The world's water 2000–2001. In: The Biennial Report on Freshwater Resources. Island Press, Washington, DC (2000)

Goetz, J.P., Le Compte, M.D.: Ethnography and Qualitative Design in Educational Research. Academic Press, New York (1984)

Google: Google Map (2017). Retrieved from Pokot South Sub County. www.kenyans.co.ke/constituency/pokot-south. Accessed 15 April 2017

Grigg, N.S.: Water infrastructure planning process. In: Integrated Water Resources Management. Palgrave Macmillan, UK, pp. 241–250 (2016)

GWP: GWP toolbox: integrated water resource management (2017). Retrieved from GWP Toolbox. http://www.gwptoolbox.org or http://www.cap-net.org

Harvey, P.A., Reed, R.A.: Community-managed water supplies in Africa: sustainable or dispensable? Commun. Dev. J. **42**(3), 365–378 (2006)

Huntjens, L.P.-W.: Institutional design propositions for the governance of adaptation to climate change in the water sector. Glob. Environ. Chang. **22**, 67–81 (2012)

IPCC: Adaptation and mitigation options. In (book section): Summary for Policymakers. In: Climate Change 2007: Synthesis Report. Contribution of Working Groups I, II and III to the Fourth Assessment Report of the Intergovernmental Panel on Climate Change. Core Writing Team, Pachauri, R.K., Reisinger, A. (eds.)). Rint version: IPCC, Geneva, Switzerland. This version: IPCC website. ISBN 978-92-9169-122-7 (2007)

IPCC: Working Group II (WGII) assesses the Vulnerability of socio-economic and natural systems to climate change, potential negative and positive consequences, and options for adapting to it. In: The Fifth Assessment Report (AR5) Cycle Spanned 2008–2014, (published in 2014) (2014)

Kerlinger, F.N.: Foundations of Behavioral Research, 2nd edn. Rinehart and Winston Inc., New York (1983)

Klein, R.J.T.: Executive summary. In (book chapter): Inter-relationships between Adaptation and Mitigation. In: Climate Change 2007: Impacts, Adaptation and Vulnerability. Contribution of Working Group II to the Fourth Assessment Report of the Intergovernmental Panel on Climate Change (M.L. Parry et al. (eds.)) (2007)

Krüger, O., Graßl, H.: The indirect aerosol effect over Europe. Geophys. Res. Lett. **29**(19), 1925 (2002)

Leidel, M., Niemann, S., Hagemann, N.: Capacity development as a key factor for integrated water resources management (IWRM): improving water management in the Western Bug River Basin Ukraine. Environ. Earth Sci. **65**(5), 1415–1426 (2012)

Leidel, M.N.: Capacity development as a key factor for development of integrated water resources management: improving water management in Western Bug River Basin, Ukraine. Environ. Earth Sci. **65**(5), 1415–1426 (2012)

Liu, C., Zhang, K., Zhang, J.: Sustainable utilization of regional water resources: experiences from the Hai Hua ecological industry pilot zone project in China. J. Clean. Prod. **18**, 447–453 (2010)

IUCN: Water Vision to Action: Catalyzing Change Through the IUCN Water & Nature Initiative. International Union for Conservation of Nature, Gland, Switzerland (2011)

Marshall, A.: Water Issues in Developing Countries. World Bank, Geneva (2010)

Misra, M.: Smallholder agriculture and climate change adaptation in Bangladesh: questioning the technological optimism. Clim. Dev. **0**(4), 337–347 (2016). ISSN 1756-5529

Molle, F.: River-basin planning and management: the social life of a concept. Geoforum **40**(3), 484–494 (2009)

Morelli, J.: Environmental sustainability: a definition for environmental professionals. J. Environ. Sustainab. **1**(1), 2–9 (2011)

Mugenda, O.M., Mugenda, A.G.: Research Methods. ACTS Press, Nairobi, Kenya (1999)

Nelson, D.R., Adger, W.N., Brown, K.: Adaptation to environmental change: contributions of a resilience framework (PDF). Annu. Rev. Environ. Resour. **32**, 395–419 (2007)

Nyongesa, K.W., Omuya, B.S., Sitati, N.W.: Impacts of climate change on ecosystems and biodiversity and implications on sustainable development. the cradle of knowledge. Afr. J. Educ. Soc. Sci. **3**(1) (2016)

Pahl-Wostl, C.: A conceptual framework for analyzing adaptive capacity and multi-level learning processes in resource governance regimes. Glob. Environ. Chang. **19**(3), 354–365 (2009)

Pallett, J.: Sharing Water in Southern Africa. Desert Research Foundation of Namibia, Windhoek (1997)

Pegram, G.Y.: Understanding enabling capacities for managing the "wicked problem" of nonpoint water solution in catchment: a conceptual framework. Environ. Manag. **128**, 441–452 (2013)

Pittock, A.B.: Climate Change: Turning Up the Heat, p. 316. Australia, Earthscan (2007)

Plummer, R.L.: A systematic review of water vulnerability assessment tools. Water Res. Manag. **26**(15), 4327–4346 (2015)

Preskill, H., Boyle, S.: A multidisciplinary model of evaluation capacity building. Am. J. Eval. **29**(4), 443–459 (2008)

Rahaman, M.: Integrated water resource management: evolution, prospects and future challenges. Sustain. Sci. Pract. Policy. **1**, 15–21 (2005)

Ruiters, C.: Water institutions and governance models for the funding, financial and management of water infrastructure in South Africa. Water SA. **41**(5), 660–676 (2015)

Opperman, J.J., Galloway, G.E., Fargione, J., Mount, J.F., Richter, B.D., Secchi, S.: Sustainable floodplains through large-scale reconnection to rivers. Science **326**(5959), 1487–1488 (2009)

Rammel, C., Stagl, S., Wilfing, H.: Managing complex adaptive systems: a co-evolutionary perspective on natural resource management. Ecol. Econ. **63**(1), 9–21 (2007)

Ruth, M., Ibarrarian, M.E.: Distribution Impacts of Climate Change and Disasters: Concepts and Cases. Edward Elgar, Northampton (2009)

Saravanan, V., McDonald, G., Mollinga, P.: Critical review of integrated water resources management: moving beyond polarized discourse. Nat. Res. Forum. **33**(1), 76–86 (2009). Blackwell Publishing Ltd

UNDP: Integrated water resources management. Retrieved from United Nations Development Programme. http://www.undp.org/content/undp/en/home/ourwork/environmentandenergy/foc usareas/waterandoceangovernance/integrated-water-resources-management.html (2017)

UNICEF: A Snapshot of Drinking Water and Sanitation in Africa. Geneva (2012)

UN: World Water Development Report 2017. Retrieved from UN Water. http://www.unwater.org/publications/worldwater-development-report-2017/ (2017)

Savenije, H.: Integrated water resource management: concepts and issues. Phys. Chem. Earth. **33**(5), 290–297 (2000)

Savenije, H.H.G., van der Zaag, P.: Water as an economic good and demand management, paradigms with pitfalls. Water Int. **27**(1), 98–104 (2002)

Schneider, S.H., et al.: Executive summary. In (book Chapter): Chapter 19: Assessing Key Vulnerabilities and the Risk from Climate Change. In: Climate Change 2007: Impacts, Adaptation and Vulnerability. Contribution of Working Group II to the Fourth Assessment Report of the Intergovernmental Panel on Climate Change (M.L. Parry, O.F.Canziani, J.P. Palutikof, P.J. van der Linden and C.E. Hanson, Eds.) (2007)

Stålnacke, G.D.: Integrated water resources management. Irrig. Drain. Syst. **24**(3–4), 155–159 (2010)

Stolberg, F., Borysova, O., Mitrofanov, I., Barannik, V., Eghtesadi, P.: Caspian Sea. In: GIWA Regional Assessment 23. Global International Waters Assessment (GIWA) (2003)

Taha, F.: Water Scarcity Leading to International Conflict: The Case of the Nile Basin Department of History, Faculty of Arts, University of Khartoum, Guest Researcher Nile Basin Research Program, University of Bergen, Jan–June 2007 (2007)

Turner, J., Müller, R.: On the nature of the project as a temporary organization. Int. J. Project Manage. **21**(1), 1–8 (2003)

United Nations Environment Programme, UNEP (ed.): GEO-Global Environmental. UN (2017, March 22). World Water Development Report 2017 (2003). Retrieved from UN Water

Verbruggen, A. (ed.): Glossary J-P. In (book section): Annex I. In: Climate Change 2007: Mitigation. Contribution of Working Group III to the Fourth Assessment Report of the Intergovernmental Panel on Climate Change (B. Metz et al. (Eds.)). Print version: Cambridge University Press, Cambridge, UK, and New York, N.Y., U.S.A. This version: IPCC website. ISBN 978-0-521-8801 (2007)

Vörösmarty, C.J., Douglas, E.M., Green, A.A., Ravenga, C.: Geospatial indicators of emerging water stress: an application to Africa. Ambio **34**(3), 230–236 (2005)

World Bank: World Development Report (2003). Sustainable Development in a Dynamic World Transforming Institutions, Growth, and Quality of Life. World Bank (2003)

The Nigerian HealthCare Facilities: Need for Adopting Evidence-Based Design as an Innovative Approach for Improved Health and Wellbeing

Iyendo Onosahwo Timothy[1,2]([✉]) [ID], Patrick Chukwuemeke Uwajeh[1], and Adenike Bamisaye[1]

[1] Department of Architecture, Faculty of Engineering, Nile University of Nigeria, Abuja, Nigeria
timothy.iyendo@nileuniversity.edu.ng
[2] Department of Architecture, Faculty of Architecture, Near East University, Northern Cyprus, Via Mersin 10, Nicosia, Turkey

Abstract. As a result of innovative design technological approaches and practices, healthcare design has dramatically improved over the years. This has resulted in the emergence of new domains in the design of healthcare facilities. One facet of these domains is "evidence-based design" (EBD) practices, which have left indelible imprints on healthcare design and the built environment by focusing on end-users. EBD has become a beneficial trend in healthcare design and is predominantly applied in the United States and Europe. However, this design practice has not been significantly utilized in the design of Nigerian healthcare facilities. Therefore, this paper examines the level of awareness, uptake, and prevalence of EBD factors in five selected healthcare facilities (general hospitals) in Lagos and Abuja, Nigeria. It also highlights the function, design aspects, principles, process, and stages of EBD in the healthcare design process. A qualitative research design was adopted for the present study. A structured checklist was distributed to patients (N = 25) and staff (N = 25) to obtain their views on the EBD intervention at selected general hospitals. The researcher's observation was used to collect other additional data. The results show that incorporating EBD elements into the design of healthcare facilities in Nigeria will significantly reduce stress, increase job satisfaction, and improve overall health outcomes.

Keywords: Evidence-based design · Healthcare facilities · Design factor · Wellbeing

1 Introduction

There has been a significant transformation in the design of healthcare facilities in recent years. This includes the application of innovative design approaches that have created

A. D. Mambo et al. (Eds.): InterSol 2022, LNICST 449, pp. 49–65, 2022.
https://doi.org/10.1007/978-3-031-23116-2_4

new domains within the healthcare milieu, such as user-centered design and evidence-based design (EBD) (Reay et al. 2017; Quan et al. 2017), Djukic and Marić 2017). These design approaches take into consideration the needs of users and introduce novel ways of improving the health care landscape. The EBD is one component of this approach, which has been defined as "the purposeful attempt to base design decisions on credible evidence from research in order to improve design outcomes and critically evaluate post-occupancy results" (Zimring et al. 2004). In the same vain, Oladejo et al. (2015), recommends that healthcare facilities require the consideration and measurement of user needs and expectations to achieve optimal design. This can be done by communicating vital information to the design team and others working towards the effectiveness of the organization.

Pioneering establishments and industries have adopted the knowledge of EBD approaches in the last few decades and have integrated them into their context (Smith 2007). This approach has been applied in various building types, however have been widely utilized in healthcare facilities (Hamilton and Watkins 2009). Fundamentally in EBD approach, it is required that design strategies and evidence need to be incorporated into different phases of the building process. To achieve this, the EBD procedure needs to be broken down into steps that would correspond with the conventional design stages.

The Center for Health Design (CHD) documents the EBD process into eight steps, namely: (1) define evidence-based goals and objectives; (2) find sources for relevant evidence; (3) critically interpret relevant evidence; (4) create and innovate evidence-based design concepts; (5) develop a hypothesis; (6) collect baseline performance measures; (7) monitor implementation of design and construction; and (8) measure post-occupancy performance results (CHD 2012; Rashid 2013). Incorporating these steps into practice requires team work between healthcare organizations, researchers, and the design team.

Fig. 1. Integration of the evidence-based design process in project stages (Adapted from CHD 2012; Rashid 2013; Martin 2009)

A schematic wheel showing the stages of integrating the eight-evidence-based design process into various phases of a project from start to finish is show in Fig. 1. It is important for designers to note that adopting EBD approach is not a rejection of creativity but a means to improve their design solutions (Martin 2009). Similarly, Fig. 2. Highlights the integration of EBD steps as it relates to various project designs phase as stated by the Center for Health Design.

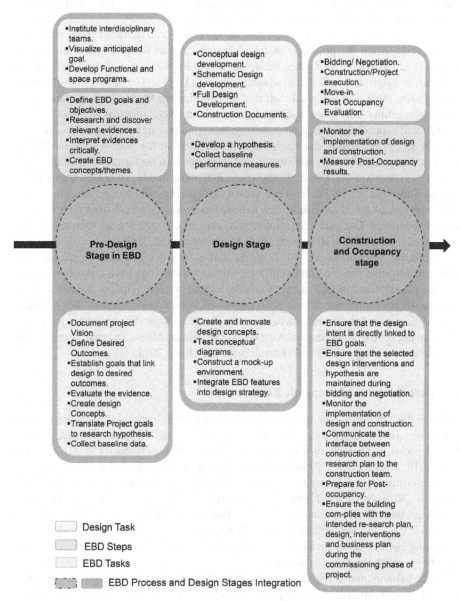

Fig. 2. EBD process and their integration in design stages (Adapted from CHD 2012; Rashid 2013; Martin 2009)

1.1   Describing the Evidence-Based Design (EBD) Concept in Healthcare Settings

The EBD concept was adapted from evidence-based medicine (EBM), which is a medical practice approach that emphasizes the use of evidence from well-designed and conducted research to improve decision-making. EBM is "the conscientious, explicit, and judicious use of current evidence in making decisions for clinical treatments and outcomes of patients" (Sackett et al. 1996). This involves gathering reliable imperial evidence from research and using the evidence to develop the basis for clinical procedures and treatment programs (Molzahn 2007; Sackett et al. 1996, 1997).

However, the origins of evidence-based design (EBD) can be traced all the way back to the 1860s, when the provision of fresh air was cited as the first canon for linking the physical environment of a healthcare facility to improved patient and staff safety, wellness, and satisfaction. With the advances made in EBD and technology development in the 1970s, there was a gradual shift that transformed the healthcare landscape into a "medical machine" that promoted social, physical, and psychological wellness.

The EBD approach is based on gathering data from research and project evaluations in order to design therapeutic spaces that are restorative for patients and healthcare workers, encourages family involvement and improves staff performance, (Smith 2007), as well as to improve the design, management, and policymaking of healthcare facilities (Sigma Theta Tau 2010). Studies have shown that patients who looked out into a brick wall experienced less discomfort when exposed to a view of nature from their hospital rooms, consumed less pain medication, and were discharged sooner than those who looked out onto a brick wall (Ulrich 1984; Malenbaum et al. 2008).

Similarly, Mackrill et al. (2017) stated that a well-designed healthcare environment can improve patients' and staff's experiences as well as have a positive impact on their physical and mental status. To achieve these positive impacts, a range of non-pharmacological approaches have been employed in healthcare settings. For instance, therapeutic gardens and healing gardens as non-pharmacological interventions have been shown to improve wellness and reduce the levels of pain, agitation, and anxiety of patients in healthcare settings (Gillis and Gatersleben 2015; Jiang 2014).

1.2   Describing the Therapeutic Environment

Patients, their families, and healthcare workers frequently perceive healthcare settings as stressful. However, if they are structured to promote beneficial physiological, psychological, social, and behavioral effects, they can be therapeutic (Iyendo et al. 2016; Linden et al. 2016; Uwajeh et al. 2019) (see Fig. 3). Previous research has backed up this theory, demonstrating the necessity to create healing settings that increase user experience (Ghazali and Abbas 2017; Iyendo 2017; Altimier 2004). Other effective interventions include art therapy (Kometiani 2017), music therapy (Goldstein 2016), music medicine (Iyendo 2016), and horticulture therapy (Detweiler et al. 2012). While the advantages of healing environments have been explored, there is still a need to delve more into the specific elements of these environments.

Both patients and caregivers benefit from therapeutic surroundings because they foster a shared environment that promotes self-healing. In other words, the healing environment should mirror the patients' values, beliefs, and philosophies. Hence, the integration of EBD strategies into the healthcare environment has created a sustainable and ecological healthcare ecosystem (Anåker et al. 2017) that improves clinical outcomes (Ulrich et al. 2008; Iyendo 2016), economic performance, and job satisfaction (Pati et al. 2008).

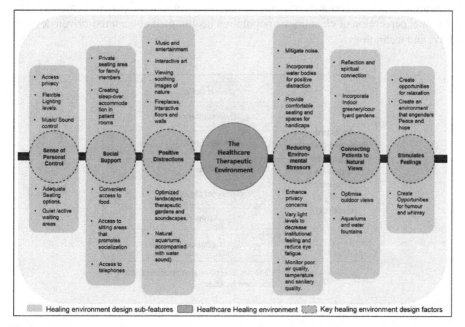

Fig. 3. A model for understanding the therapeutic environment (Adapted from Linden et al. 2016; Uwajeh et al. 2019).

2 Research Methods

A qualitative research design was adopted for the present study. A structured checklist was distributed to patients (N = 25) and staff (N = 25) to obtain their views on the EBD intervention at selected general hospitals in Lagos and Abuja, Nigeria. Twenty-two males (N = 22) and twenty-eight females (N = 28) participated in the study. The researchers also collected additional data through observation. The authors designed the structured checklist employed in this investigation. To ensure content validity, items were adapted from prior relevant studies (CHD 2012; Iyendo et al. 2016) and modified to fit within our current investigation.

The information was gathered over an eight-week period in September and October 2021.The checklist covered four sections, including demographic characteristics of respondents; the staff and patients' awareness of EBD factors; the staff rating of EBD factors; and the patient rating of EBD factors.

3   Literature Review of Related Works

As shown in Fig. 4, the Center for Health Design (CHD) categorizes health and design strategies for improving healthcare environments into fourteen (14) major topics: behavioral and mental health; clinical design; communication; emergency department throughput; healthcare reform; impact on ageing; infection control; noise; patient-centered medical home; perception of cleanliness; population health; patient-centered-driven design; safety; and technology.

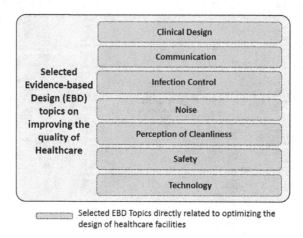

Selected EBD Topics directly related to optimizing the design of healthcare facilities

Fig. 4. Main EBD topics on healthcare improvement (Adapted from CHD 2012)

3.1   Clinical Design

The various physical aspects of healthcare environments can either positively or negatively impact patient experiences. For example, when considering an ambulatory design, renovation, or improvement to the physical space, what a patient goes through from the time they enter a community clinic to the time they leave the building or clinic parking lot should always be considered during the design process. Significant evidence demonstrates that user-centered data acquired from evidence-based studies has been used to improve the physical environment and patient safety in hospitals through architectural design (Selami Cifter and Cifter 2017; Ulrich et al. 2008; Calkins and Cassella 2007; Dettenkofer et al. 2004), improved staff outcomes (Bayramzadeh and Alkazemi 2014; Weinel 2008; Miller et al. 2006; Chhokar et al. 2005; Keir and MacDonell 2004; Nelson et al. 2003) as well as other factors, including Landscape, gardens and nature-based views (Iyendo et al. 2016; Beyer et al. 2014, Thompson et al. 2014; Lottrup et al. 2013; Ulrich et al. 2008; Kearney and Winterbottom 2005; Ulrich 1984), Table 1 presents studies that highlight the positive architectural impacts of well-designed clinical environments and their effect on user's outcome.

Table 1. Studies on EBD interventions related to Clinical Design.

EBD factor(s) and references	Findings	EBD Interventions
Design impact: Selami Cifter and Cifter 2017; Reay et al. 2017; Ulrich et al. 2008; Calkins and Cassella 2007; Dettenkofer et al. 2004)	• Patients may experience stress in inadequate design clinical settings that restrict them privacy • Inadequately constructed and located nursing stations might increase nurses' stress levels and degrade care quality • Stress-free hospital surroundings promote patient well-being and the healing process	• Patient-care unit floor design should have corridors structured around a central nursing station, where medications and charts are centrally situated to prevent staff fatigue and maximise time for treatment • Private patient rooms enable greater operational and administrative freedom and have a beneficial therapeutic impact on patients • Infections such as influenza, tuberculosis (TB), measles, and chickenpox can be prevented by housing patients in single rooms
Improved staff outcomes: (Bayramzadeh and Alkazemi 2014; Weinel 2008; Miller et al. 2006; Chhokar et al. 2005; Keir and MacDonell 2004; Nelson et al. 2003)	• Using ceiling-lift technology for patient handling increases patient safety and dignity • Staff stress levels are increased in intensive care units by blinking lights, alarms, and equipment noise	• When comparing ceiling lifts to floor lifts, evidence indicates that caregivers sustain less musculoskeletal injuries • Lifting and transferring patients using a ceiling lift places less strain on the trunk and shoulder muscles than lifting and transferring patients with a floor lift • The installation of assistive equipment helps to reduce back injuries among healthcare workers
Landscape, gardens, and nature-based views: (Iyendo et al. 2016; Beyer et al. 2014; Thompson et al. 2014; Lottrup et al. 2013; Ulrich et al. 2008; Kearney and Winterbottom 2005; Ulrich 1984)	• Patients undergoing heart surgery reported feeling less anxious and stressed when shown a landscape scenario with trees and water bodies • Residents of hospitals prefer windows with abundant views of nature over those with limited views of nature • In healthcare, exposure to nature can help alleviate symptoms of sadness, anxiety, and stress • Patients who recover in a hospital with a view of trees have shorter hospital stays, use less pain medication, and have better outcomes than patients who recover in a hospital with a view of a brick wall	• Garden design that incorporates water bodies, natural noises such as bird song, and the sound of the breeze results in healing spaces that contribute to overall wellbeing • Introduce indoor plants to detoxify the air and to reflect, diffract, or absorb certain frequencies of sound • Certain plants are said to be as good as carpeting in reducing high-frequency sounds in rooms with hard surfaces • Integrating natural green or land-scape aspects into the healthcare ecosystem to improve patient outcomes and to foster a positive atmosphere for visitors and healthcare providers • Relaxing nature scenes might help deflect unpleasant thoughts

3.2 Communication

There are several examples of the consequences of poor communication in the literature: avoidable hospital admissions (Vermeir et al. 2015; Garåsen and Johnsen 2007) and readmissions (Walraven et al. 2002; Moore et al. 2003). Hospital admissions have been observed to be reduced when interventions to increase communication and coordination are implemented (Peikes et al. 2009). Other avoidable problems of inadequate communication in healthcare have been shown to have an economic impact. These include unnecessary testing, polypharmacy-inappropriate referrals, and recurrent recommendations for concerns that were not satisfactorily addressed during the first visit. (Gandhi et al. 2000; Epstein 1995).

3.3 Infection Control

In most institutions today, healthcare-associated infections and other easily transmissible diseases are a substantial concern. Implementing some of the most current healthcare design best practices can help to mitigate their impact. As seen in Table 2, EBD findings and interventions from research literature, case studies, interviews, and other materials to provide an overview of the topic of infection control are highlighted (Prussin and Marr 2015; Allegranzi and Pittet 2009; Ulrich et al. 2008; Ulrich and Wilson 2006; Griffiths

Table 2. Studies on EBD interventions related to Infection Control.

EBD factor(s) and references	Findings	EBD Interventions
Infection Control: [Prussin and Marr 2015; Allegranzi and Pittet 2009; Ulrich et al. 2008; Ulrich and Wilson 2006; Mineshita et al. 2005; Griffiths et al. 2005; Blanc et al. 2004; Conger et al. 2004; Sehulster et al. 2004)	• Showers, sinks, aerators, faucets, and toilets are all common places for pathogenic bacteria to congregate • Faucets should not be directed directly into the sink trap, as this may result in splashing • In healthcare environments, patients, employees, and visitors often carry pathogens from ill patients or other airborne sources • In patient rooms, placing sinks near the entrance encourages hand washing, but placing them away from the bed prevents splashes from reaching the patient • Environmental services personnel's work can be made easier and faster by designing rooms with furniture and surfaces that can be easily cleaned with only one or two products	• Using a variety of control methods during the construction or remodelling process, such as effective filters, appropriate ventilation systems, and air change rates • Installation of high-efficiency particulate air filters in acute healthcare settings, particularly ambulatory care facilities and operating rooms, is recommended to remove particles as small as 0.3 μm in diameter, such as (Aspergillus spores), 2.5 μm to 3.0 μm in diameter • Infection transmission between patients and caregivers is reduced by placing hand-washing basins with continuous impermeable surfaces near staff mobility pathways • Healthcare facilities should keep cold water below 68°F (20 °C), hot water above 140°F (60 °C), and circulate hot water with a minimum return temperature of 124°F (51 °C)

et al. 2005; Mineshita et al. 2005; Sehulster et al. 2004) (Blanc et al. 2004; Conger et al. 2004).

3.4 Noise

Noise has an impact on the safety and health of patients and is a significant component of their experience. Patients frequently complain about noise levels while in the hospital, but there are a variety of treatments that can help to create a healthier and more comfortable environment (Iyendo 2016; Iyendo 2017; Iyendo et al. 2016; Hofhuis et al. 2012; Gardner et al. 2009; Akansel and Kaymakçi 2008; Ulrich et al. 2008; Cmiel et al. 2004; Baldock 2003; Mazer 2012; Orellana et al. 2007) (Table 3).

Table 3. Studies on EBD interventions related to Noise.

EBD factor(s) and references	Findings	EBD Interventions
Noise: [Iyendo 2016; Iyendo 2017; Iyendo et al. 2016; Hofhuis et al. 2012; Gardner et al. 2009; Akansel and Kaymakçi 2008; Ulrich et al. 2008; Cmiel et al. 2004; Baldock 2003; Mazer 2012; Orellana et al. 2007)	• Noise is associated with medical and nursing errors, as well as tracking and monitoring activities • Patient anxiety can be exacerbated by noise from physicians' and nurses' paging devices • Ambient noise contributes to sleep deprivation and confusion, which can result in increased prescription use and patient constraint • Noise has a significant impact on employee stress and irritation levels, perceived job pressure, burnout, and emotional tiredness • Noise impairs memory, aggravates agitation, aggressive behaviour, sadness, and anxiety, and exacerbates communication difficulties	• Utilizing sound-absorbing materials to reduce noise can assist in minimising distractions, reducing stress and medical mistakes, and improving sleep and general staff job performance • Implementation of new technologies to mitigate the noise generated by physicians' and nurses' paging devices, as well as fall alarm sensors put on patient beds • The use of pleasant natural sound interventions, such as singing birds, soft breeze, and ocean waves, indicated advantages that contribute to patients' and staff's reported restoration of attention and stress recovery • When compared to silence, listening to calming music has been demonstrated to lower stress, blood pressure, and post-operative trauma

3.5 Perception of Cleanliness

In terms of infection prevention, environmental cleanliness has an impact on patient experience, satisfaction, perceived service quality, and real service quality. To achieve specified degrees of cleanliness, an interdisciplinary strategy is required, which includes building design, operational and regulatory modifications, personnel education, and organizational culture changes (CHD 2012).

3.6 Safety

The design industry and healthcare owners have often taken distinct approaches to safety. Designers frequently consider fire and life safety, whereas healthcare owners and caregivers may consider safety in terms of serious reportable occurrences and hospital-acquired disorders. However, adverse outcomes such as healthcare-associated infections, prescription errors, damage from patient handling, self-harm (or aggression against others), security breaches, and falls can all be exacerbated by poorly built and operated hospital environments. Healthcare safety is complicated and necessitates a methodical approach that includes a grasp of organizational aspects, people, and the often-overlooked environment (CHD 2012).

3.7 Technology

Healthcare facilities can improve diagnosis and treatment, as well as patient outcomes, by utilizing cutting-edge technologies such as electronic health record systems, robotic surgery, remote video connections, and pharmaceutical safety systems. These advances can support cost-effective and efficient patient-centered care, all of which should be carefully integrated into the details of the layout and design. Recent studies reveal the advantages of medical robotics, wearables, and autonomous systems in healthcare during the novel coronavirus pandemic. Robots, for example, might be employed to help limit the spread of COVID-19 or assist in large-scale COVID-19 screening. By allowing frontline healthcare providers to assess, evaluate, monitor, and treat patients from a safe distance, digital health solutions, such as telehealth and telepresence technologies, can greatly minimize the risk of infectious disease transmission (Tavakoli et al. 2020; Parimbelli et al. 2018; Weinstein et al. 2014). The healthcare system has been able to conduct emergency minimally invasive surgeries using telerobots, lowering the risk to the physician during the pandemic. For example, Intuitive's daVinci Surgical Robot has been widely adopted in hospitals around the world (See Fig. 5). A clinician controls the daVinci's patient-side manipulators through a surgical console. While the surgical console is usually situated in the same operating room as the patient, plastic sheets or tents might be utilized to totally segregate the surgeon from COVID-19 patients with minimum changes to existing clinical practice (Tavakoli et al. 2020).

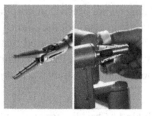

Your surgeon is with you in the operating room, seated at the da Vinci system console. The console gives your surgeon control of the instruments he or she uses to perform your surgery.

The da Vinci vision system delivers 3D high-definition views, giving your surgeon a crystal clear view of the surgical area that is magnified 10 times to what the human eye sees.

Your surgeon uses tiny instruments that move like a human hand but with a far greater range of motion. The system's built-in tremor-filtration technology helps your surgeon move each instrument with smooth precision.

Fig. 5. The daVinci surgical robot by intuitive (da Vinci Systems 2021).

4   Results and Discussion

4.1   Socio-Demographic Characteristics of the Respondents'

Combined data on the distribution of respondents by gender indicates that 22 (44%) are male and 28 (56%) are female (Fig. 6).

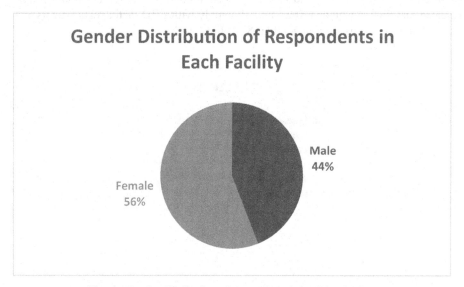

Fig. 6. Gender distribution of respondents in each institution.

4.2   Staff and Patient Awareness of EBD Factors in the Selected Hospitals

Table 4 presents the level of awareness about EBD among staff and patients. The findings found that just a small percentage of staff (10%) in each of the five hospitals reported being aware of EBD in hospitals. This was especially noticeable among employees who traveled outside of the country and visited hospitals in other countries, such as the United Kingdom and the United States. On the contrary, most patients (90%) stated that they were unaware of EBD in their hospitals. This is because EBD is not implemented at the hospitals where they are admitted.

Table 4. Checklist for staff and patient awareness of EBD Factors in the selected healthcare facilities

EBD Factors	Number of Respondents	Classification of response	Awareness level (%)
Staff	25	Aware	10%
Patients	25	Oblivious	90%

4.3   Staff Rating of EBD Factors in the Selected Hospitals

Considering the extent to which the selected hospitals use EBD, most of the staff (90%) claimed that noise levels within the hospitals were a major complaint and concern, followed by "safety" (84%) and lack of "infection control" (66%). The findings also revealed that most hospitals (70%) did not comply with EBD factor requirements and that technology was used inefficiently (68%) (Fig. 7).

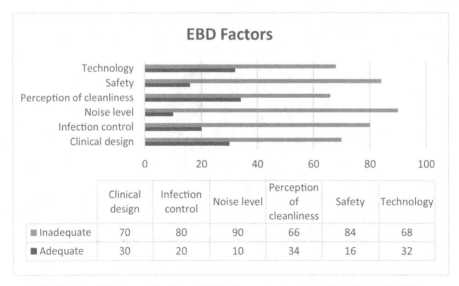

	Clinical design	Infection control	Noise level	Perception of cleanliness	Safety	Technology
■ Inadequate	70	80	90	66	84	68
■ Adequate	30	20	10	34	16	32

Fig. 7. Checklist for staff rating of EBD Factors in the selected healthcare facilities

4.4 Patient Rating of EBD Factors in the Selected Hospitals

As provided in Fig. 8, in terms of patient perceptions of EBD use, results from the five hospitals studied revealed that most patients (90%) believe that a lack of safety is their primary issue, which could be attributable to ineffective staff care. This is unsurprising given that most patients concur that hospital designs (82%) are inadequate, and noise levels (78%) within hospitals remain a significant patient complaint, followed by a lack of infection control (76%). A slight majority (64%) believed that technology was underutilized in hospitals and that it should be fully employed to improve health and well-being.

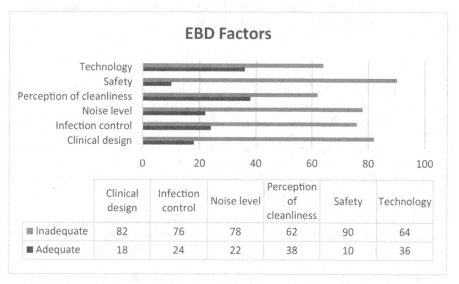

Fig. 8. Checklist for patient rating of EBD Factors in the selected healthcare facilities

5 Conclusion

The results of our research show how patients and staff in Nigerian general hospitals feel about the use of EBD. It also yielded important data for increasing patient knowledge and insight into the use of EBD. The staff and patients' ratings on EBD factors revealed that safety issues should be prioritized, followed by noise levels, infection control, and clinical design. According to our findings, both patients and staff believe that proper implementation or application of EBD in Nigerian hospitals would improve their health and well-being as well as the hospital physical environment for better outcomes. As a result, more research is needed to determine how much EBD factor support patients and staff should receive, as well as how much they should rely on other aspects of EBD factors for productive outcomes.

5.1 Limitations and Directions for Future Research

Although our study was limited to only five hospitals, this appears to be a restriction in terms of the findings' wider transferability and generalizability. Nonetheless, because our research is based on real-life staff and patient experiences, it adds to the empirical research findings that are useful for informing EBD practice in hospital settings. There is also a lack of thorough statistical analysis. We have argued, however, that interpretive research, such as this investigation, is not suitable for extensive statistical analysis because it is based solely on reporting perception. Nonetheless, a longitudinal and ethnographic study in which a researcher spends a significant amount of time observing staff and patients' perceptions and ratings of EBD factors in use in various Nigerian hospitals would be beneficial in providing richer insights into how EBD affects patients' health and wellbeing, as well as staff performance in general.

References

Akansel, N., Kaymakçi, Ş: Effects of intensive care unit noise on patients: a study on coronary artery bypass graft surgery patients. J. Clin. Nurs. 17(12), 1581–1590 (2008)

Allegranzi, B., Pittet, D.: Role of hand hygiene in healthcare-associated infection prevention. J. Hosp. Infect. 73(4), 305–315 (2009)

Altimier, L.B.: Healing environments: for patients and providers. Newborn Infant. Nurs. Rev. 4(2), 89–92 (2004). https://doi.org/10.1053/j.nainr.2004.03.001

Anåker, A., Heylighen, A., Nordin, S., Elf, M.: Design quality in the context of healthcare environments: a scoping review. HERD: Health Environ. Res. Des. J. 10(4), 136–150. (2017). https://doi.org/10.1177/1937586716679404

Baldock, C.: More attention must be paid to sleep. Bri. J. Nursing 13(6), 296 (2003)

Bayramzadeh, S., Alkazemi, M.F.: Centralized versus decentralized nursing stations: An evaluation of the implications of communication technologies in healthcare. HERD: Health Environ. Res. Des. J. 7(4), 62–80 (2014)

Blanc, D.S., Nahimana, I., Petignat, C., Wenger, A., Bille, J., Francioli, P.: Faucets as a reservoir of endemic Pseudomonas aeruginosa colonization/infections in intensive care units. Intensive Care Med. 30(10), 1964–1968 (2004)

Calkins, M., Cassella, C.: Exploring the cost and value of private versus shared bedrooms in nursing homes. Gerontologist 47(2), 169–183 (2007)

CHD (Center for Health Design).: Evidence-Based Design Accreditation and Certification. Author, Concord, CA (2012). http://www.healthdesign.org/edac/about

Chhokar, R., Engst, C., Miller, A., Robinson, D., Tate, R.B., Yassi, A.: The three-year economic benefits of a ceiling lift intervention aimed to reduce healthcare worker injuries. Appl. Ergon. 36(2), 223–229 (2005)

Cmiel, C.A., Karr, D.M., Gasser, D.M., Oliphant, L.M., Neveau, A.J.: Noise control: A nursing team's approach to sleep promotion: Respecting the silence creates a healthier environment for your patients. Am. J. Nurs. 104(2), 40–48 (2004)

Conger, N.G., et al.: Mycobacterium simiae outbreak associated with a hospital water supply. Infect. Control Hosp. Epidemiol. 25(12), 1050–1055 (2004)

da Vinci Systems, I.: Robotic-Assisted Surgery as a Minimally Invasive Option (2021). https://www.davincisurgery.com/

Dettenkofer, M., Wenzler, S., Amthor, S., Antes, G., Motschall, E., Daschner, F.D.: Does disinfection of environmental surfaces influence nosocomial infection rates? A systematic review. Am. J. Infect. Control 32(2), 84–89 (2004)

Detweiler, M.B., et al.: What is the evidence to support the use of therapeutic gardens for the elderly? Psychiatry Investig. **9**(2), 100–110 (2012). https://doi.org/10.4306/pi.2012.9.2.100

Djukic, A., Marić, J.: Towards socially sustainable healthcare facilities–the role of evidence-based design in regeneration of existing hospitals in Serbia. Procedia Environ. Sci. **38**, 256–263 (2017)

Epstein, R.M.: Communication between primary care physicians and consultants. Arch. Fam. Med. **4**, 403–409 (1995)

Gandhi, T.K., Sittig, D.F., Franklin, M., Sussman, A.J., Fairchild, D.G., Bates, D.W.: Communication breakdown in the outpatient referral process. J. Gen. Intern. Med. **15**(9), 626–631 (2000)

Garåsen, H., Johnsen, R.: The quality of communication about older patients between hospital physicians and general practitioners: A panel study assessment. BMC Health Serv. Res. **7**(1), 1–7 (2007)

Gardner, G., Collins, C., Osborne, S., Henderson, A., Eastwood, M.: Creating a therapeutic environment: A non-randomised controlled trial of a quiet time intervention for patients in acute care. Int. J. Nurs. Stud. **46**(6), 778–786 (2009)

Ghazali, R., Abbas, M.Y.: Paediatric wards: Healing environment assessment. Asian J. Environ.-Behav. Stud. **2**(3), 77–87 (2017).

Gillis, K., Gatersleben, B.: A review of psychological literature on the health and wellbeing benefits of biophilic design. Buildings **5**(3), 948–963 (2015). https://doi.org/10.3390/buildings5030948

Goldstein, B.: The Secret language of the heart: How to use music, sound and vibration as tools for healing and personal transformation. Hierophant Publishing (2016)

Griffiths, W.D., Bennett, A., Speight, S., Parks, S.: Determining the performance of a commercial air purification system for reducing airborne contamination using model micro-organisms: A new test methodology. J. Hosp. Infect. **61**(3), 242–247 (2005)

Hamilton, D.K., Watkins, D.H.: Evidence-based design for multiple building types. John Wiley & Sons (2009)

Hofhuis, J.G., Langevoort, G., Rommes, J.H., Spronk, P.E.: Sleep disturbances and sedation practices in the intensive care unit: A postal survey in the Netherlands. Intens. Crit. Care Nurs. **28**(3), 141–149 (2012)

Huisman, E.R.C.M., Morales, E., Van Hoof, J., Kort, H.S.M.: Healing environment: A review of the impact of physical environmental factors on users. Build. Environ. **58**, 70–80 (2012)

Iyendo, T.O.: Exploring the effect of sound and music on health in hospital settings: A narrative review. Int. J. Nurs. Stud. **63**, 82–100 (2016). https://doi.org/10.1016/j.ijnurstu.2016.08.008

Iyendo, T.O.: Sound as a supportive design intervention for improving health care experience in the clinical ecosystem: A qualitative study. Complement. Ther. Clin. Pract. **29**, 58–96 (2017).

Iyendo, T.O., Uwajeh, P.C., Ikenna, E.S.: The therapeutic impacts of environmental design interventions on wellness in clinical settings: A narrative review. Complement Ther. Clin. Pract. **24**, 174–188 (2016)

Jiang, S.: Therapeutic landscapes and healing gardens: A review of Chinese literature in relation to the studies in western countries. Front. Architect. Res. **3**(2), 141–153 (2014). https://doi.org/10.1016/j.foar.2013.12.002

Kearney, A.R., Winterbottom, D.: Nearby nature and long-term care facility residents: Benefits and design recommendations. J. Hous. Elder. **19**(3/4), 7–28 (2005)

Keir, P., MacDonell, C.: Muscle activity during patient transfers: A preliminary study on the influence of lift assists and experience. Ergonomics **47**(3), 296–306 (2004)

Kometiani, M.K.: Creating a vital healing community: A pilot study of an art therapy employee support group at a pediatric hospital. Arts Psychother. **54**, 122–127 (2017). https://doi.org/10.1016/j.aip.2017.04.012

Mackrill, J., Marshall, P., Payne, S.R., Dimitrokali, E., Cain, R.: Using a bespoke situated digital kiosk to encourage user participation in healthcare environment design. Appl. Ergon. **59**, 342–356 (2017). https://doi.org/10.1016/j.apergo.2016.08.005

Malenbaum, S., Keefe, F.J., Williams, A.C., Ulrich, R., Somers, T.J.: Pain in its environmental context: Implications for designing environments to enhance pain control. Pain **134**, 241–244 (2008). https://doi.org/10.1016/j.pain.2007.12.002

Martin, C.S.: The challenge of integrating evidence-based design. Health Environ. Res. Des. J. **2**(3), 29–50 (2009)

Mazer, S.E.: Creating a culture of safety: reducing hospital noise. Biomed. Instrum. Technol. **46**(5), 350–355 (2012)

McCullough, C.S. (Ed.): Evidence-Based Design for Healthcare Facilities. Sigma Theta Tau. (2010)

Miller, A., Engst, C., Tate, R.B., Yassi, A.: Evaluation of the effectiveness of portable ceiling lifts in a new long-term care facility. Appl. Ergon. **37**(3), 377–385 (2006)

Mineshita, M., Nakamori, Y., Seida, Y., Hiwatashi, S.: Legionella pneumonia due to exposure to 24-hour bath water contaminated by Legionella pneumophila serogroup-5. Intern. Med. **44**(6), 662–665 (2005)

Molzahn, E.J.: Revealing Attributes of Supportive Healing Environments in Interior Design: Staff Perceptions in Healthcare Design. Doctoral dissertation. Colorado State University Libraries, Colorado (2007)

Moore, C., Wisnivesky, J., Williams, S., McGinn, T.: Medical errors related to discontinuity of care from an inpatient to an outpatient setting. J. Gen. Intern. Med. **18**(8), 646–651 (2003)

Nelson, A., Lloyd, J., Menzel, N., Gross, C.: Preventing nursing back injuries: Redesigning patient handling tasks. AAOHN J. **51**(3), 126–134 (2003)

Oladejo, E., Umeh, O., Ogbuefi, J.: An examination of impact of tertiary healthcare facility design on user needs and satisfaction in South East Nigeria. J. Environ. Earth Sci. **5**(5), 35–43 (2015)

Orellana, D., Busch-Vishniac, I.J., West, J.E.: Noise in the adult emergency department of Johns Hopkins Hospital. J. Acoust. Soc. Am. **121**(4), 1996–1999 (2007)

Parimbelli, E., et al.: Trusting telemedicine: a discussion on risks, safety, legal implications and liability of involved stakeholders. Int. J. Med. Informatics **112**, 90–98 (2018)

Pati, D., Harvey Jr. T. E., Barach, P.: Relationships between exterior views and nurse stress: An exploratory examination. HERD: Health Environ. Res. Des. J. **1**(2), 27–38, (2008). doi:https://doi.org/10.1177/193758670800100204

Peikes, D., Chen, A., Schore, J., Brown, R.: Effects of care coordination on hospitalization, quality of care, and health care expenditures among Medicare beneficiaries: 15 randomized trials. JAMA **301**(6), 603–618 (2009)

Prussin, A.J., Marr, L.C.: Sources of airborne microorganisms in the built environment. Microbiome **3**(1), 1 (2015)

Quan, X., Joseph, A., Nanda, U.: Developing evidence-based tools for designing and evaluating hospital inpatient rooms. J. Inter. Des. **42**(1), 19–38 (2017). https://doi.org/10.1111/joid.12091

Rashid, M.: The question of knowledge in evidence-based design for healthcare facilities: Limitations and suggestions. HERD: Health Environ. Res. Des. J. **6**(4), 101–126 (2013)

Reay, S., Collier, G., Kennedy-Good, J., Old, A., Douglas, R., Bill, A.: Designing the future of healthcare together: prototyping a hospital co-design space. CoDesign **13**(4), 227–244 (2017). https://doi.org/10.1080/15710882.2016.1160127

Wouden, H.: Evidence-based medicine. Tijdschrift voor praktijkondersteuning **10**(1), 11–12 (2015). https://doi.org/10.1007/s12503-015-0008-9

Sackett, D.L., William M.C. Rosenberg, J.A. Muir Gray, Haynes, R.B., Richardson, W.S.: Evidence-based medicine: What it is and what it isn't: It's about integrating individual clinical expertise and the best external evidence. BMJ: Br. Med. J. **312**(7023), 71–72 (1996)

Sehulster, L.M., Chinn, R.Y.W., Arduino, M.J., Carpenter, J., Donlan, R., Ashford, D., et al.: Guidelines for Environmental Infection Control in Health-care Facilities. Recommendations from CDC and the Healthcare Infection Control Practices Advisory Committee (HICPAC).

American Society for Healthcare Engineering/American Hospital Association, Chicago, IL (2004).

Selami Cifter, A., Cifter, M.: A review on future directions in hospital spatial designs with a focus on patient experience. Des. J. **20**(sup1), S1998–S2009 (2017)

Smith, J.: Health and nature: The influence of nature on design of the environment of care. In: The Center for Health Design, pp. 1–19 (2007)

Tavakoli, M., Carriere, J., Torabi, A.: Robotics, smart wearable technologies, and autonomous intelligent systems for healthcare during the COVID-19 pandemic: An analysis of the state of the art and future vision. Adv. Intell. Syst. **2**(7), 2000071 (2020)

Ulrich, R.S.: View through a window may influence recovery from surgery. Science **224**(4647), 420–421 (1984). http://www.jstor.org/stable/1692984

Ulrich, R.S., Wilson, P.: Evidence-based design for reducing infection. Public Serv. Rev. Health **8**, 24–25 (2006)

Ulrich, R.S., Zimring, C., Zhu, X., DuBose, J., Seo, H. B., Choi, Y.S., Joseph, A.: A review of the research literature on evidence-based healthcare design. HERD: Health Environ. Res. Des. J. **1**(3), 61–125, (2008)

Uwajeh, P.C., Iyendo, T.O., Polay, M.: Therapeutic gardens as a design approach for optimising the healing environment of patients with Alzheimer's disease and other dementias: A narrative review. EXPLORE (2019)

Van der Linden, V., Annemans, M., Heylighen, A.: Architects' approaches to healing environment in designing a Maggie's Cancer Caring Centre. Des. J. **19**(3), 511–533 (2016). https://doi.org/10.1080/14606925.2016.1149358

Van Walraven, C., Seth, R., Austin, P.C., Laupacis, A.: Effect of discharge summary availability during post-discharge visits on hospital readmission. J. Gen. Intern. Med. **17**(3), 186–192 (2002)

Vermeir, P., et al.: Communication in healthcare: a narrative review of the literature and practical recommendations. Int. J. Clin. Pract. **69**(11), 1257–1267 (2015)

Watkins, N., Keller, A.: Lost in translation: Bridging gaps between design and evidence-based design. HERD: Health Environ. Res. Des. J. **1**(2), 39–46 (2008).

Weinel, D.: Successful Implementation of Ceiling-Mounted Lift Systems. Rehabil. Nurs. **33**(2), 63–66 (2008)

Weinstein, R.S., et al.: Telemedicine, telehealth, and mobile health applications that work: opportunities and barriers. Am. J. Med. **127**(3), 183–187 (2014)

Zimring, C., Joseph, A., Choudhary, R.: The Role of the Physical Environment in the Hospital of the 21st Century: A Once-in-a-Lifetime Opportunity. The Center for Health Design, Concord, CA (2004)

Artificial Intelligence (AI) and Machine Learning (ML) for Development

An E-Nose Using Metal Oxide Semiconductor Sensors Array to Recognize the Odors of Fall Armyworm Pest for Its Early Detection in the Farm

Manhougbé Probus A. F. Kiki[1]([⊠]), Sèmèvo Arnaud R. M. Ahouandjinou[2],
Kokou M. Assogba[1], and Yves N. Sama[3]

[1] Ecole Polytechnique d'Abomey-Calavi, Université d'Abomey-Calavi, Cotonou, Bénin
kprobus2005@gmail.com
[2] Institut de Formation et de Recherche en Informatique, Université d'Abomey-Calavi,
Cotonou, Bénin
[3] Institut Lafayette, 2 Rue Marconi, 57070 Metz, France

Abstract. Considerably decrease hunger and food insecurity in the world is one of sustainable development goals of the horizon 2030. Agriculture, which is one of most countries main sector and the only factor in the diet of the world's population, is challenged by pest attack. Technology tools offer real opportunities to better protect farms from many damages caused to crops. In this work, an e-nose system using Metal Oxide Semiconductor sensors for early detection of fall armyworm (FAW) pest is proposed. This is based on a special architecture designed to have an affordable and efficient e-nose. Detailed investigations were carried out to identify sensors with potential sensitivity to FAW odors. Then, the sensors were used in a sensor matrix as electronic nose. An electronic acquisition card was achieved to interface the electrical output of the array of seven metal oxide semiconductor gas sensors exposed to an odor diffusion system with the computer. A LabVIEW program was developed for data analysis. The system was successfully exploited to study the response of the sensor array to volatile organic compounds (VOC) released by FAW and for optimizing the data acquisition, as well as signal pre-processing, storage, and wave forms presentation. Experiments were carried out using real FAW. The results and analysis presented in this paper show evidence of discrimination of Fall armyworm's VOC signature, thus the first detection of FAW presence by e-nose system.

Keywords: E-nose · Odors recognition · Pest monitoring · Fall armyworm detection

1 Introduction

Sub-Saharan Africa has favorable climate and soils for agriculture. Thanks to this agricultural potential, most of the countries of this region are massively engaged in both

© ICST Institute for Computer Sciences, Social Informatics and Telecommunications Engineering 2022
Published by Springer Nature Switzerland AG 2022. All Rights Reserved
A. D. Mambo et al. (Eds.): InterSol 2022, LNICST 449, pp. 69–81, 2022.
https://doi.org/10.1007/978-3-031-23116-2_5

export (cocoa, coffee, cotton) and local agricultural activity (many seeds such as cowpeas, maize, rice, pineapples, palm nuts, yam). Therefore, agriculture is the main vector of development of these countries. Nevertheless, this vital development sector faces various challenges such as global warming, invasion of insect pests. In the specific case of invasion of insect pests, one of the most devastating is fall armyworm (FAW) that can cause more than 70% of yield losses. So, concrete solutions are required to deal with the problem of invasion of insect pests and secure the yield of agricultural activity. The intuitive solution is the use of chemicals to kill the insects. But this approach, if it does not have drawbacks in environmental terms, still requires to be well managed for efficiency and economic viability. Moreover, in many sub-Saharan African countries, the detection of FAW by smallholder farmers is synonymous with the onset of an invasion of their maize fields. At this stage, the spread of invasion is difficult to counter, even with the support of government organizations in terms of phytosanitary treatment. Therefore, early detection of the presence of FAW before its spread may be a crucial information to take appropriate actions at the right time.

Intelligent data collection and processing systems are widespread and have several applications fields such as industry, building, road control, safety, health, etc. These smart systems, often based on smart sensors, could bring a significant advancement in specific agriculture [1]. This work focused on data collection system especially an e-nose coupled with data analysis tools for FAW early detection in crop fields. Biological studies of life cycle and behavior of FAW named scientifically Spodoptera frugiperda provides this important information that FAW has odorous sex-pheromones containing (Z) -9-tetradecenyl acetate (Z-9–14: OAca) [2]. These odorous sex-pheromones can be detected thanks to a suitable e-nose [3]. Making an e-nose specially designed for the detection of this particular type of odor is not easy. Therefore, a concisely review of the artificial olfaction technology as well as experimental tests to identify potentially sensitive materials and sensors for FAW odor were carried out. The main contribution of this work is to provide an alternative (approach) to the lack of specific sensors dedicated to FAW detection.

The paper presents the design and achievement of an affordable system for FAW data collection and preliminary results, based on judiciously identified commercial sensors. It is a first step of smart monitoring system for early detection of FAW in farm fields. Such a detection method can contribute to the establishment of an effective control protocol against fall armyworm as soon as it is detected around a monitored environment. This should reduce the use of plant protection products, pesticides, and Genetically Modified Organisms (GMOs) [4]. In sum, the system provides additional resources that can be involved in ecological management of the fall armyworm problem.

The paper is organized as follows. Section 2 presents a short review on Electronic Nose, Metal Oxide Semi-Conductor Sensors, and their applications. In Sect. 3, the proposed electronic nose for early detection of FAW is described. Section 4 is devoted to experiments, results, and discussion.

2 Review on Electronic Nose and Metal Oxide Semi-conductor Sensors

2.1 Survey on Electronic Nose

E-noses are sensor systems that are designed to mimic the mammalian nose. This critical artificial function offers the possibility to recognize different olfactory signatures in correlation with a range of fields, including environment monitoring, disease diagnosis, public security affairs, agricultural production, food industry, etc. [5]. The first work on the development of a device truly capable of measuring odors dates back to the 1960s [6, 7]. However, the term electronic nose did not appear in the literature until twenty years later following research at the University of Warwick in Great Britain by the group of Dodd and Persaud [8]. E-noses are composed of an array of non-specific sensors that respond to either individual or classes of chemical volatiles [9]. As presented in Fig. 1, the odorant molecules to be studied are carried with a controlled concentration towards the E-nose using sampling or pre-concentrating technique. When the odorant land on the sensor array and interact with the sensing materials, a reversible change in a chemical or physical property is induced. These changes are transduced into an electrical signal. Due to the non-specificity of the electric signal about the chemical identity, the output of the sensor array is further processed by machine learning algorithms to correctly identify, classify, and quantify the analytes (VOC). Pattern recognition in electronic noses is a dynamic and fast developing field, due to the constant need to adapt the theory or methodology to the specific complexity or conditions of data acquisition [10–16].

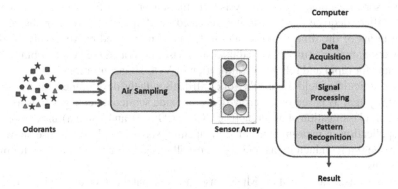

Fig. 1. Concept of E-Nose System Operation Principle [17]

Different sensing techniques have been use in the constructing of e-noses, which include surface acoustic wave (SAW) [18], quartz crystal microbalance (QCM) [19], metal oxides [20–22] conducting polymers [23, 24], carbon nanotubes (CNTs) [25], or a combination of multiple techniques [26].

In summary, many technologies of gas sensor exist, and several have already received attention for electronic nose applications. It is worthwhile noting that each of the technologies has favorable and critical points in terms of selectivity, sensitivity, response time, stability regarding environmental conditions (such as humidity and temperature). Metal oxide semiconductor (MOS) sensors are particularly useful for monitoring VOCs which are organic chemical compounds that evaporate easily at room temperature. Even though most of these sensors suffer the lack of selectivity towards VOCs from similar chemical classes, they are a promising technology within the framework of our experimental objectives which consist of detecting FAW odorous sex-pheromones ($C_{16}H_{30}O_2$) whose chemical nature is VOCs-type [27].

2.2   Survey on Electronic Nose

Metal oxide semiconductor (MOS) gas sensors are used in a variety of application fields. They are relatively inexpensive compared to other sensing technologies, robust, lightweight, long lasting and benefit from high material sensitivity and quick response times [28].

MOS sensor is the most widely used technology for e-noses, and the most common sensing materials of MOS are semi-conducting or metal-oxides including, iron oxides, titanium di-oxide, tin dioxides, zinc oxides, nickel oxide, cobalt oxide etc. The sensing materials are put on a ceramic substrate, like alumina. Generally, the device also has a heating element [29]. Working of this sensor depends on the types of the sensing materials (reduction or oxidization). When analytes collect upon the surface of these materials certain reactions occur resulting in electron transfer from the analytes to the conducting materials, which trigger changes in the electrical signals. Sambemana's works [28] have led to the adaptation of an electronic nose to the essential oils intensities detection. Detection of volatilized substances was achieved using a network of commercial metal oxide sensors. Response signals analysis from the sensors to different concentrations of the oils, after adequate digital filtering, revealed good cross-sensitivity of the sensors both in terms of the time response and in terms of its derived curve. Analysis using classification methods (unsupervised then supervised) revealed the best combination of parameters for rapid and reliable identification of VOCs concentrations.

In the agriculture field, Kanade's work [30] deals with the development of an artificial olfactory system as based on an array of metal oxide semiconductor gas sensors to be used for the classification of different fruits (Guava, Orange and Banana) and exploration of its application in measurement of fruit ripening stages. Study of E-nose show that Metal oxide semiconductor Gas sensors are usually used in e-nose technology for many applications.

The main disadvantage of the MOS sensor array is that the devices require to operate at temperatures between 250 and 450 °C [31]. Therefore, they consume a significant amount of energy and need a relatively long time for heating before they are ready to take measurements.

A typical structure of a MOS sensor is given in Fig. 2. The semiconducting layer oxidizes the sample compound. Gas concentration is detected by measuring the resistance change of the Metal Oxide sensing layer. The resistance change is related to the effect of oxidizing or reducing reaction at the surface and in grain boundaries area, which results in the modulation of the potential barrier, thus electrons flow in the circuit. The sensitivity of the sensor can be tuned by adjusting the operation temperature or by using noble metals as catalytic dopants.

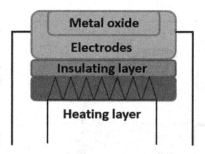

Fig. 2. Scheme of a metal oxide sensor

Two families of metal oxides exist, p-type and the n-type. N-type sensors which respond mainly to reducing compounds (e.g. CO, H_2, CH_4, C_2H_5 or H_2S), and p-type sensor which respond mainly to oxidizing compounds (O_2, NO_2, and Cl_2). The reactions occurring between these sensing materials and gases are described in Eqs. (1), (2):

$$\frac{1}{2}O_2 + e^- \rightarrow O^-(g) \tag{1}$$

$$R(s) + O^-(g) \rightarrow RO(s) + e^- \tag{2}$$

where e is an electron from the oxide, $R(s)$ is the reducing gas, s is the sensing materials, and g is gas. In the first step, oxygen from the environment is incorporated in the surface semiconductors lattice of the sensor, setting its electrical resistance to a stable state. During the measurement, target volatile molecules near the surface of the sensing material react (oxidation/reduction) with the incorporated oxygen species causing a change of the electrical properties, such as capacitance and resistance of the device [13].

SnO$_2$ is one of the most widely used metal oxide (N-type) gas-sensing material because of its high sensitivity and simple fabrication. This family of metal oxide gas sensor is available in commercial version as MQ sensors and still used in recent applications for odor detection [32, 33].

3 Proposed Sensor Based on Electronic Nose for Early Detection of FAW

3.1 Monitoring and Detection of FAW

A bibliographic review of the different methods of fighting against FAW [3] shows that it is a very current research subject which is still under investigation. Indeed, no solution at present offers a full protection of crop guarantee to farmers against FAW attacks. In this work, an original and new tool based on E-nose is proposed for a FAW monitoring strategy in order to early detect its presence in the corn fields.

The idea is to contribute to the development of a new and ecological approach in the fight against FAW. In this work, the objective is not the measurement of fall armyworm VOCs concentration but their detection and at the end, two architectures of the E-nose are explored (Fig. 3).

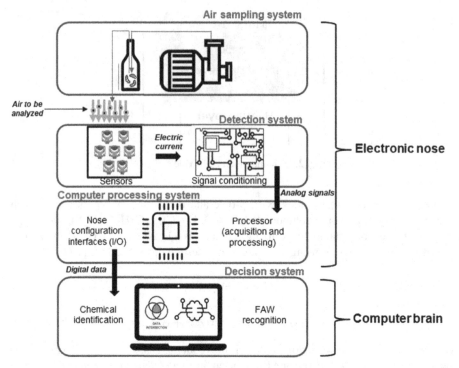

Fig. 3. E-nose's Structure for FAW detection

This architecture uses a classical air sampling method at the air collecting stage. It is divided into four main parts. The proposed architecture for FAW detection is detailed as follows:

- **The air collecting system (The air sampling system)** is the first part of the E-nose, through which the air to be analyzed is carried to the sensors. This stage is the mechanical part of the system. It consists of a glass enclosure connected to a solenoid valve and a pump to convey the air to be analyzed in the measuring enclosure.
- **The detection system** is based on a matrix of sensors and signal conditioning circuits that are the reactive parts of the e-nose. It is mainly based on semiconductor type metal oxide transducers that are installed in the measurement enclosure. Their electrical parameters (conductivity, resistivity) are modified as soon as they enter into contact with volatile substances such as FAW's odor.
- **The computer processing system** has microcontroller (Arduino MEGA 2560 micro-controller board) as the main component of this part. When the sensors detect a volatile substance, a specific response (Voltage) corresponding to the digital measurement of each of the sensors is filtered, recorded and accessible in a memory.
- **The decision system** (Informatique brain) part has two main roles. Firstly, it treats the data from the e-nose and displays them in a usable form for analysis and secondly, it compares the data from the e-nose with specific signatures of FAW's volatile

substances. Different methods such as Support Vector Machine (SVM) or Linear Discriminant Analysis (LDA) can be used to realize pattern recognition. In our case signal profile recognition was used.

3.2 Metal Oxide Device

SnO2 semiconductor based MQs were used in our experiments. This type of MQ has low conductivity in clean air. In the presence of a detectable gas, the sensor's conductivity increases (for reducing reaction) depending on the gas concentration in the air. A simple electrical circuit can convert the change in conductivity to an output signal which corresponds to the gas concentration. The change of Vo the output voltage of the e-nose obeys the following equations:

Equation (3). Change of V_0 through to use V_C and metal oxide sensor conductivity (GMOS) with the resistor R_L.

Equation (4). Based on GMOS estimation through the use V_C and V_0 with the resistor R_L by.

$$V_0 = \frac{R_L}{R_L + \frac{1}{G_{MOS}}} \bullet V_c \tag{3}$$

$$G_{MOS} = \frac{1}{R_L} \bullet \frac{V_0}{V_C - V_0} \tag{4}$$

$$R_{MOS} = R_L \bullet \left(\frac{V_C}{V_0} - 1\right) \tag{5}$$

With GMOS the conductivity of the Metal oxide sensor.

For instance, in contact with a reducing gas, an SnO2-MOS sensor fixes more electrons, which increases its conductivity, thus decreasing its resistance. Inserted in a voltage divider bridge structure as shown in Fig. 4, the reduction reaction causes an increase in the voltage Vo (Eq. (3)). A Metal oxide sensor conductivity (Eq. (4)) or resistor (Eq. (5)) can also be estimate to appreciate chemical reaction.

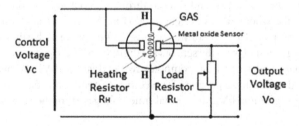

Fig. 4. Electronic diagram of the conditioning circuit of a metal oxide gas sensor

3.3 Sensor Array Module

This In our experiment, the sensor array was mainly composed of SnO2 based commercial MQs. This choice was guided by the olfactory nature of FAW. Studies and research on FAW show that female species naturally release sex pheromones which are closely-related analogue of (Z)-9-tetradecenyl trifluoromethyl ketone (Z9–14:TFMK) [34] with the chemical formula $C_{16}H_{30}O_2$. This chemical formula is an organooxygen compound like a number of substances which are detected by the sensors used in this work and presented in Table 1.

Table 1. MQ series metal oxide gas sensors choose for e-nose's array sensor

Sensor No	Sensor model	Target Gas sensitivity
1	MQ2	Alcohol, CH4
2	MQ3	Alcohol, Solvent vapors
3	MQ4	LPG, CH4
4	MQ5	LPG, Natural gas, Coal gas
5	MQ6	LPG, Propane
6	MQ7	Carbon Monoxide (CO)
7	MQ8	Alcohol, H2

The air temperature and relative humidity data were collected during the experiments, thanks to a temperature and humidity sensor (DHT22). The objective is to study how these factors might affect the response of the sensor array.

3.4 Experimental Tools

In accordance with proposed architecture, experimental setups were explored. In what follow, the results from the two setups are evaluated. Figure 5 presents the experimental tools.

Here, ambient air is pumped and filtered through a coal tube before being brought to the olfactive tube where FAWs are captured (Fig. 5). The air is charged by FAW's volatile organic compound and enters the sensor array enclosure with a dynamic flow. The electrical signals generated from the sensors are digitally filtered, processed with Arduino MEGA 2560 board and sent to the computer for analysis. LabVIEW instrumentation software was used to develop a program for electronics control and data acquisition from the e-nose. The programmed VI Shows real time voltages from the sensor array.

4 Experimental Results and Discussion

4.1 Measurement Protocol

Proper use of MQ sensor begins with the preheating phase. MQ sensors have their own heating element. Prior to experimental measurements, the sensor matrix is powered and

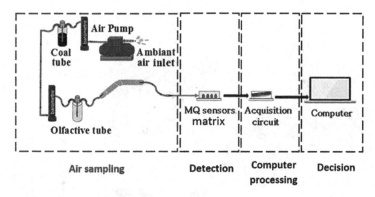

Fig. 5. Experimental setup for the detection of FAW based on e-nose.

brought to the operating temperature. During the preheating of the sensors, the temperature inside the chamber increases and stabilizes in the range 55 °C–58 °C (experimental measurement). The measured relative humidity in the chamber during the experiments was stable around 60%.

The procedure is to put adult female FAW (which produces sex pheromones) in a sealed chamber with two ports (input-output) for controlled air circulation. Input is filtered air which is pumped from ambient. The air that passes through the FAW's chamber becomes charged with VOCs and goes out to the measurement enclosure. The measurements are carried out over periods of 10 min [35], taking into account the recovery time of the sensors. The data are displayed and saved on LabVIEW VI for analysis. Figure 6 shows the experimental setup.

5   Results and Discussion

The characteristics of the sensor's matrix in the air sampling classic e-nose setup are depicted on Fig. 7. Figure 7(a) shows the output signal of the sensors during the preheating phase and when the sensors are exposed to ambient air. It may be seen that around t = 550 s, the output signal is disturbed by the adsorption of ambient chemical species. Then, after about 500 s exposure (beyond t = 1100 s) sensor's response are stable, which is a favorable situation for the detection of chemical elements other than those constituting the ambient air. Afterwards, similar experiments were carried out with the presence of FAW inside the sealed chamber. Figure 7(b) shows the resulting output signals, first with 10 FAWs and then with 20 FAWs. The first observation to underline is the low signal-to-noise ratio (SNR). Nevertheless, small variations of the output voltage are noticed with sensors MQ2 and MQ3 over a long period of measurement. This variation shows that the sensors resistance decreases through a reduction reaction on the Metal oxide transductors. Further increase of the number of FAWs did not increase the output signal, which may be explained by the logarithmic increase of odor intensity with a given quantity of VOCs. The other MQs show the same light variation of the signal, but the signal gradually decreases and reaches initial level after about 350 s. This

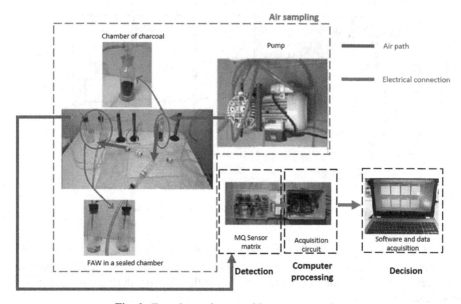

Fig. 6. Experimental setup with e-nose procedure.

phenomenon which resembles an adsorption/desorption mechanism, reflects a very low sensitivity of these sensors to FAW.

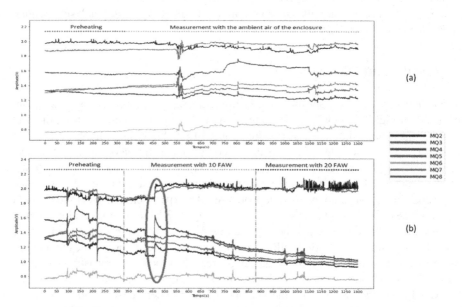

Fig. 7. Sensors array signals with FAW's data collected with e-nose

For all the sensors, the variation of the output signal (in red circle) begins 120 s after the presence of FAW in sealed chamber. This delay may be due to the fact that FAWs do not produce VOC immediately after they are introduced into the sealed chamber. This delay can also be explained by the high dilution of FAWs pheromones by ambient air.

Due to the low SNR ratio of the measurements results, the signals should be filtered to give more information. And data analysis tools should be developed to extract automatically the FAW's parameters for its detection.

6 Conclusion and Future Work

In this work, we have revised the current state of e-noses, focusing on MOS sensors and its ability to be used for versatile applications. To ecologically monitor Fall armyworm Pest, we proposed an electronic nose to detect and collect Fall armyworm VOC data. The air collecting systems were explored. This first FAW detection in laboratory experiment is very promising for further improvement and deployment for an automatic and real time detection in agricultural fields. Future work will be devoted to noise filtering of the sensors signal data analysis tools to perform accurate FAW detection and making a custom-built air concentration system to have more sensibility performance compared to the classic air sampling system.

Acknowledgement. The authors would like to thank International Institute of Tropical Agriculture (IITA) of Benin Republic for its helpful assistance during the experimental work. Especially for the stock farming of the fall armyworm pest. Without it, this work could not be achieved.

References

1. Kiki, M. P. A. F., Ahouandjinou, S. A. R. M., Assogba, K. M.: Towards a smart farming for early detection of fall armyworm pest. In: 2019 International Conference on Smart Applications, Communications and Networking (SmartNets), Sharm El Sheik, Egypt pp. 1–5 (2019). https://doi.org/10.1109/SmartNets48225.2019.9069756
2. Batista-Pereira, L.G., et al.: Isolation, identification, synthesis, and field evaluation of the sex pheromone of the brazilian population of *Spodoptera frugiperda*. J. Chem. Ecol. **32**(5), 1085 (2006). https://doi.org/10.1007/s10886-006-9048-5
3. Ahouandjinou, S.A.R.M., Kiki, M.P.A.F., Amoussouga Badoussi, P.E.N., Assogba, K.M.: A multi-level smart monitoring system by combining an E-nose and image processing for early detection of FAW pest in agriculture. In: Thorn, J.P.R., Gueye, A., Hejnowicz, A.P. (eds.) InterSol 2020. LNICSSITE, vol. 321, pp. 20–32. Springer, Cham (2020). https://doi.org/10.1007/978-3-030-51051-0_2
4. Fatoretto, J. C., Michel, A. P., Silva Filho, M. C., Silva, N.: Adaptive potential of fall armyworm (Lepidoptera: Noctuidae) Limits Bt Trait Durability in Brazil. *J. Integr. Pest Manag.* **8**(1) (2017) https://doi.org/10.1093/jipm/pmx011
5. Hu, W., Wan, L., Jian, Y., Ren, C., Jin, K.: Electronic noses: From advanced materials to sensors aided with data processing. *Adv. Mater. Technol.* 1800488 (2018). https://doi.org/10.1002/admt.201800488
6. Gardner, J.W., Bartlett, P.N.: A brief history of electronic noses. Sens. Actuators B Chem. **18**(1–3), 210–211 (1994). https://doi.org/10.1016/0925-4005(94)87085-3

7. Moncrieff, R.W.: An instrument for measuring and classifying odors. J. Appl. Physiol. **16**(4), 742–749 (1961). https://doi.org/10.1152/jappl.1961.16.4.742

8. Persaud, K., Dodd, G.: Analysis of discrimination mechanisms in the mammalian olfactory system using a model nose. Nature **299**(5881), 352–355 (1982). https://doi.org/10.1038/299 352a0

9. Li, C.W., Wang, G.D.: The research on artificial olfaction system-electronic nose. J. Phys. Conf. Ser. **48**, 667–670 (2006). https://doi.org/10.1088/1742-6596/48/1/125

10. E. Garcia-Breijo, J. Atkinson, L. Gil-Sanchez, R. Masot, and J. Ibañez.: A comparison study of pattern recognition algorithms implemented on a microcontroller for use in an electronic tongue for monitoring drinking waters. *Sens. Actuators Phys.* **172**(2), 570–582 (2011). https://doi.org/10.1016/j.sna.2011.09.039

11. Zhang, W., Liu, T., Ye, L., Ueland, M., Forbes, S.L., Su, S.W.: A novel data pre-processing method for odour detection and identification system. Sens. Actuators Phys. **287**, 113–120 (2019). https://doi.org/10.1016/j.sna.2018.12.028

12. Liu, T., Cao, J., Li, D., Chen, Y., Yang, T., Zhu, X.: Active instance selection for drift calibration of an electronic nose. Sens. Actuators Phys. **312**, 112149 (2020). https://doi.org/10.1016/j.sna.2020.112149

13. Tan, J., Xu, J.: Applications of electronic nose (e-nose) and electronic tongue (e-tongue) in food quality-related properties determination: A review. Artif. Intell. Agric. **4**, 104–115 (2020). https://doi.org/10.1016/j.aiia.2020.06.003

14. Hai, Z., Wang, J.: Electronic nose and data analysis for detection of maize oil adulteration in sesame oil. Sens. Actuators B Chem. **119**(2), 449–455 (2006). https://doi.org/10.1016/j.snb.2006.01.001

15. Maschenko, A.A., Musatov, V., Varezhnikov, A.S., Kiselev, I., Sommer, M., Sysoev, V.V.: On the feasibility to apply a neural network processor for analyzing a gas response of a multisensor microarray. Sens. Actuators Phys. **190**, 61–65 (2013). https://doi.org/10.1016/j.sna.2012.11.016

16. Breijo, E.G., Pinatti, C.O., Peris, R.M., Fillol, M.A., Martínez-Máñez, R., Camino, J.S.: TNT detection using a voltammetric electronic tongue based on neural networks. Sens. Actuators Phys. **192**, 1–8 (2013). https://doi.org/10.1016/j.sna.2012.11.038

17. S. Li: Recent developments in human odor detection technologies. *J. Forensic Sci. Criminol.* **1**(1) (2014). https://doi.org/10.15744/2348-9804.1.S104

18. Jha, S. K., Yadava, R. D. S.: Statistical pattern analysis assisted selection of polymers for odor sensor array. In: 2011 International Conference on Signal Processing, Communication, Computing and Networking Technologies, Thuckalay, Tamil Nadu, India, 575–580 (2011). https://doi.org/10.1109/ICSCCN.2011.6024617

19. Shafiqul Islam, A. K. M., Ismail, Z., Ahmad, M.N., Saad, B., Othman, A.R.: Transient parameters of a coated quartz crystal microbalance sensor for the detection of volatile organic compounds (VOCs). *Sens. Actuat. B Chem.* **109**(2), 238–243 (2005). https://doi.org/10.1016/j.snb.2004.12.116

20. Borowik, P., Adamowicz, L., Tarakowski, R., Siwek, K., Grzywacz, T.: Odor detection using an e-nose with a reduced sensor array. Sensors **20**(12), 3542 (2020). https://doi.org/10.3390/s20123542

21. Ahmadou, D., Losson, E., Siadat, M., Lumbreras, M.: Optimization of an electronic nose for rapid quantitative recognition. In: 2014 International Conference on Control, Decision and Information Technologies (CoDIT), Metz, France, pp. 736–741 (2014). https://doi.org/10.1109/CoDIT.2014.6996988

22. Faleh, R., Bedoui, S., Kachouri, A.: Review on smart electronic nose coupled with artificial intelligence for air quality monitoring. Adv. Sci. Technol. Eng. Syst. J. **5**(2), 739–747 (2020). https://doi.org/10.25046/aj050292

23. Le Maout, P., Laquintinie, P.S., Lahuec, C., Seguin, F., Wojkiewicz, J-L., Redon, N., Dupont, L.: A low cost, handheld E-nose for renal diseases early diagnosis. In: 2018 40th Annual International Conference of the IEEE Engineering in Medicine and Biology Society (EMBC), Honolulu, HI, pp. 2817–2820 (2018). https://doi.org/10.1109/EMBC.2018.8512847

24. Wilson, A., Oberle, C., Oberle, D.: Detection of off-flavor in catfish using a conducting polymer electronic-nose technology. Sensors 13(12), 15968–15984 (2013). https://doi.org/10.3390/s131215968

25. Johnson, A.T.C., Khamis, S.M., Preti, G., Kwak, J., Gelperin, A.: DNA-coated nanosensors for breath analysis. IEEE Sens. J. 10(1), 159–166 (2010). https://doi.org/10.1109/JSEN.2009.2035670

26. Haddad, R., Medhanie, A., Roth, Y., Harel, D., Sobel, N.: Predicting odor pleasantness with an electronic nose. PLoS Comput. Biol. 6(4), e1000740 (2010). https://doi.org/10.1371/journal.pcbi.1000740

27. PubChem: (Z)-9-Tetradecenyl acetate. https://pubchem.ncbi.nlm.nih.gov/compound/5364714

28. Fine, G.F., Cavanagh, L.M., Afonja, A., Binions, R.: Metal oxide semi-conductor gas sensors in environmental monitoring. Sensors 10(6), 5469–5502 (2010). https://doi.org/10.3390/s100605469

29. Burgués, J., Marco, S.: Low power operation of temperature-modulated metal oxide semiconductor gas sensors. Sensors 18(2), 339 (2018). https://doi.org/10.3390/s18020339

30. A. Kanade and Dr. A. D. Shaligram: Development of an E-nose using metal oxide semiconductor sensors for the classification of climacteric fruits. *Int. J. Sci. Eng. Res.* 5(2), 467–472 (2014). https://doi.org/10.14299/ijser.2014.02.003

31. A. S. Yuwono and P. S. Lammers: Odor pollution in the environment and the detection instrumentation: p. 33.

32. Ward, R.J., Jjunju, F.P.M., Griffith, E.J., Wuerger, S.M., Marshall, A.: Artificial odour-vision syneasthesia via olfactory sensory argumentation. IEEE Sens. J. 21(5), 6784–6792 (2021). https://doi.org/10.1109/JSEN.2020.3040114

33. Estakhroyeh, H.R., Rashedi, E., Mehran, M.: Design and construction of electronic nose for multi-purpose applications by sensor array arrangement using IBGSA. J. Intell. Rob. Syst. 92(2), 205–221 (2017). https://doi.org/10.1007/s10846-017-0759-3

34. Malo, E.A., Rojas, J.C., Gago, R., Guerrero, Á.: Inhibition of the responses to sex pheromone of the fall armyworm. Spodoptera frugiperda. J. Insect Sci. 13(134), 1–14 (2013). https://doi.org/10.1673/031.013.13401

35. Sambemana, H., Siadat, M., Lumbreras, M.: Gas sensor characterization at low concentrations of natural oils. Chem. Eng. Tran. 23, 177–183 (2010)

Prediction of Process Failure Approach Using Process Mining

Diahame Mamadou$^{(\boxtimes)}$ and Camara Mamadou Samba

Ecole Supérieur Polytechnique, Université Cheikh Anta Diop de Dakar (UCAD),
Dakar, Senegal
{diahame.mamadou,mamadou.camara}@esp.sn

Abstract. Events log are a collection of events that concern a business process. In them, we may find cases where its output is different from what expected. These differences are considered as failure and many publications usually propose prediction model to improve the business model. But existing approach of prediction rarely take into account the loops. The aim of this work is to propose a prediction of business process failure while considering loops as failure. So, in order to introduce the loop, we need first to determine how to implement the loop in existent event log. We propose some machine learning model in order to do the prediction. And then, compare the prediction model in order to get the best one. The prediction model is made by using the event log's dataset of a loan application performed in a financial institution.

Keywords: Process failure · Process mining · Event log · Event loop · Machine learning

1 Introduction

Nowadays with the boom of data, we easily find massive data that can be used. The generation of those data are mostly related to event. These events are collected and organized into event log with which we can determine the process model of a system [1]. A process instance may contain some error that can be consider as failure. Sometimes, during a given case or instance, we can find excessive repetitions (>3) of an or multiple event(s). this repetition can be seen as failure because it can affect the performance of the business process.

Differentiating the terms fault, error and failure is significant in the context of business process failure prediction. In present literature, they have a well-defined semantic by [2] as follow:

– A fault is the adjudged or hypothesized cause of an error.
– An error is the deviation of the system from its desired state.
– Finally, a failure occurs when the system is not able to deliver its output as it is supposed to, leading to an undesirable outcome.

A. D. Mambo et al. (Eds.): InterSol 2022, LNICST 449, pp. 82–95, 2022.
https://doi.org/10.1007/978-3-031-23116-2_6

The aim of this work is to propose a prediction of business process failure while considering loops as failure. So, in order to introduce the loop, we need first to determine how to implement the loop in existent event log. We propose some machine learning model in order to do the prediction. The prediction model is made by using the event log of a loan application performed in a financial institution.

The remainder of this paper is organized as follows: Sect. 2: we present the related work. Section 3: the description of the loan application data. Section 4: describe the pre-processing step. Section 5: define the metric that are going to be used for the comparison. Section 6: describe the learning model technique that are used. Section 7: Comparison of the result.

2 Related Work

2.1 Process Failure

There are publications that address the process failure in different angle. For [3], they propose the PreMiSE (PREdicting failures in Multi-tIer distributed SystEms) which according to them is a novel approach that can accurately predict failures and precisely locate the responsible faults in multi-tier distributed systems. In order to identify the failure, they use a Key Performance Indicators (KPI) for instance CPU utilization for each CPU processor in the system. For [4], the goal of their paper is to examine the exploitation of events in order to find errors and predict potential failures during (distributed) process execution. They use artificial neural network for the prediction model. In [5], they use the local outlier factor (LOF) algorithm which is an unsupervised fault detection algorithm with rule-based monitoring approaches. They used the LOF with the KNNI prediction algorithm for the prediction of abnormal termination of a real-time business process. For [6], they propose a novel method for predicting the next process event and also a novel application for deep learning methods. This application consists of using the Long Short-Term Memory (LSTM) which is a Recurrent Neural Network (RNN) architecture.

2.2 Loop

There are documents that talk about the loop. For [7, 8], a loop causes a task to be executed multiple times during a given case. In [8] and [9], they define two types of loops:

- Basic loops: which according to [10] can be compared to WHILE loops.
- Arbitrary loops: which are like the GOTO statements according to [11].
  According to [7, 8], in order to defined a representation of loops inside the event log, one can add the element task_instance. We used a similar representation of the loops where we named it "Iteration". In [10], they try to address the loop failure by proposing a methodology based on the CRISP-DM (Cross Industry Standard Process for Data Mining). Their methodology consists of a number of Step based on the 6 phases of the CRISP-DM process [12] which are: Business understanding, Data understanding, Data preparation, Modeling, Evaluation and Deployment.

2.3 Critics

For [3–6], they use some predictive model for different objective and did not treat the loop issue. Their propositions show different ways to identify the failure of a business process. In [10] even if they made a proposition of methodology, there wasn't an implementation of it. For the [7–9], they made a good explanation for the loop but since then there are not much publication that take it into account.

3 Data Description

The dataset used is from the BPIC 2017 [13]. This dataset is from a financial institution. The event log provided contains all loan applications filed in 2016 and their subsequent handling up to February 2nd 2017. The characteristic of the dataset is as follow:

– Number of variables: 19. Among them, we have 11 categorical variables, 6 numerical and 2 Booleans
– Number of observations (events): 1,202,267: These observations represent the event of the application process
– Number of instances (cases): 31,509 cases it is represented by the variable 'case:concept:name'

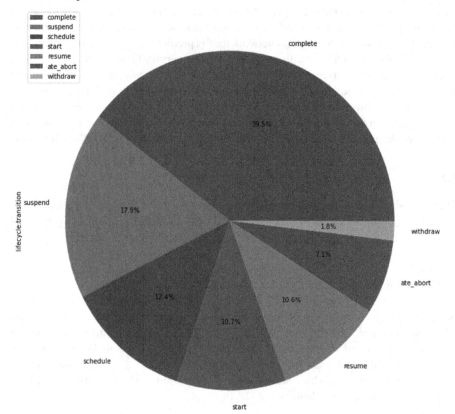

Fig. 1. Distribution of the lifecycle:transition value

The variable that contains the event is named "concept:name" which can take 26 different values. These values will be referred in the document as event's types. We can see a disparity between the number of instances and the number of observations. The variable that concerns the failure of a business process is the lifecycle:transition. In fact, it can take a total of 7 value which are represented in the Fig. 1.

The Fig. 1 represent the status of the execution of an event. In fact, based on the figure, we can see that, after the execution of an event during a trace, the status of it can take different values like: 'complete', 'resume', 'suspend', 'ate_abort'. Among these values, the value that can represent a business process failure is "ate_abort".

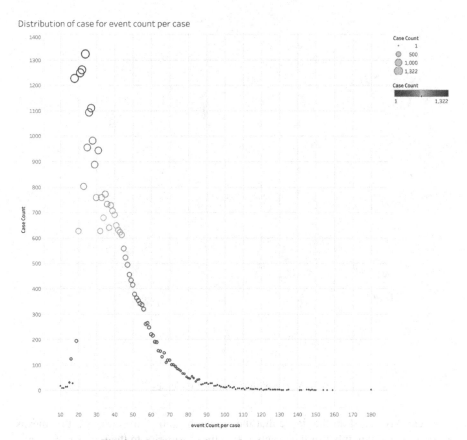

Fig. 2. Distribution of cases for the event count per case

In the Fig. 2 we have the distribution of the case that have the same number of events. The figure permits us to see the relation between the number of events for a case and how much cases have the same number. The Abscissa represent the number of events per cases. We can see that the smallest number of events for a case is 10 and the maximum number of events is 180. The ordinate represents the count of the cases that have the same number of events. We can say that the count is between 1 and 1322. The most common number of events is around 24 events which has a total of 1322 related cases.

We can also see a trend as the number of events increase, there is less likely cases that have the same number of events.

Therefore, considering the loop as failure (>3) can have a valuable effect in the business process. In order to show it in a more detail way, we have the Fig. 3 which show the ratio of repetition of a case. The ratio is obtained by doing the relation between the number of event's types in a case and the number of events that are in that same case.

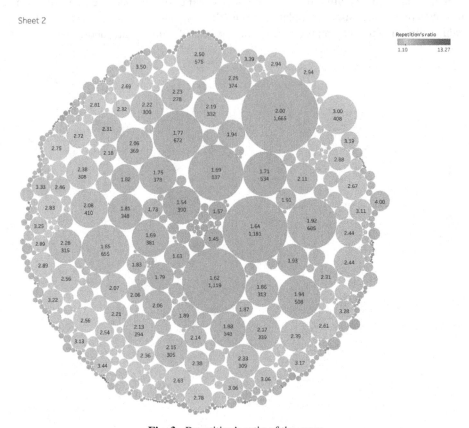

Fig. 3. Repetition's ratio of the cases

We can say based on the figure that the common ratio of the case is 2 that means that for a case, the number of the events is two times superior to the number of event's types. Therefore, for that ratio, there are 1665 cases that have the same ratio. The Fig. 3 shows that in the dataset that we use, there are some case where predicting loops can have a great impact in the quality of the business process model.

There are some documents that made an advance analysis of the dataset [14–16].

4 Preprocessing

Based on the analysis of the data, we find that there no variable that materialize the loop inside an instance. In order to materialize the loop inside the dataset, we added a new variable named "iteration" which count each event during the execution of a process. We also decide to delete the variable that has high number of unique values. Those variables are:

- EventID
- time: timestamp

Then, we have to also find the variable that have high correlation with our prediction variables ("lifecycle:transition", "iteration"). The first one represents the final state of an event. The ladder counts each event during the execution of a process. In order to do so, we first need to determine the correlation between the variable. That correlation is show in the Fig. 4 through a heatmap chart.

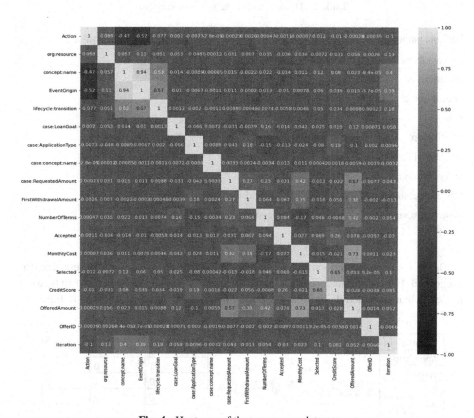

Fig. 4. Heatmap of the preprocess dataset

According to the heatmap, we can determine that the variable that have high correlation to our prediction variable are:

- concept:name
- EventOrigin

- Org:resource
- Selected
- CreditScore
- NumberOfTerms
- OfferedAmount
- Case:RequestedAmount
- Case:LoanGoal

This selection is motivated by all variable that has a correlation superior to 0.01 to the prediction variable which are "lifecycle:transition", "iteration". The specificity of those variables is described in the Table 1.

Table 1. Description of the selected variable

Variable name	Type	Number of unique value
concept:name	Categorical	26
EventOrigin	Categorical	3
Org:resource	Categorical	149
Selected	Boolean	2
CreditScore	Numerical	520
NumberOfTerms	Numerical	147
OfferedAmount	Numerical	663
Case:RequestedAmount	Numerical	701
Case:LoanGoal	Categorical	14

Based on our selected variables, we can see that there are some of them that are categorical. For those categorical variables, we need to encode them in order to be used inside the learning model. To do that we use the OneHotEncoder explained in Fig. 5.

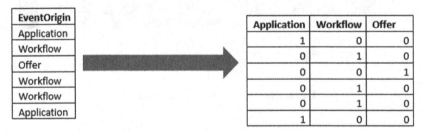

Fig. 5. How OneHotEncoder work

As for the prediction model, our target is when the "lifecycle: transition" is equal to "ate_abort" and when the "iteration" is superior or equal to 3.

Then we split the data into training data and test data with a 0.8 ratio. Which mean that the training data will have 80% of the total data and the test data will have 20%. We didn't do the shuffle because that won't represent the execution of a process.

5 Metric

In order to compare the predictions models, we need a uniform metric to compare them to. There is a common metric that usually permit to determine the others metrics. That metric is known as confusion matrix and is show in the Table 2. The matrix is composed of 4 values. According to [4], the terms "positive" and "negative" refer to the classifier's prediction, and the terms "true" and "false" refer to whether that prediction corresponds to the external judgment (correspond to the observation). The Table 2 represent the confusion matrix.

Table 2. Confusion matrix

		Prediction value	
		Positive	Negative
Observation	True	True Positive (TP)	False Negative (FN)
	False	False Positive (FP)	True Negative (TN)

The metrics used are the accuracy, the precision, the recall, the F1 score [17] and the ROC graph [18].

6 Prediction Model

With the popularization of learning technique, there are a lot more that are discover. For our prediction model we decide to limit our self to 4 prediction model. The prediction that we use are the Random Forest Classifier (RF), the Decision Tree Classifier (DT), the Logic Regressor (LR) and the Multi-Layer Perceptron Classifier (MLP). Among these models, we can say that the first 3 are machine learning algorithm and the last one use neural network for the prediction. To facilitate the learning, we decide to use pipeline. In the pipeline, we decide to use the column transformer parameter with the OneHotEncoder. This encoder concerns the following columns: 'org:resource', 'lifecycle:transition', 'EventOrigin', 'concept:name', 'case:LoanGoal'.

Since we split the date into train part and test part, we use a 80% ratio for the split for the train dataset. Therefore, the training dataset is a total of 961,813 events.

7   Result

In order to get the result, we need to test the predictive model with the test dataset. This test dataset consists of 240,454 events. The result we obtained are displayed in this section. So, in this section, we will first display the confusion matrix of each predictive model then, we will show a comparative ROC graph.

As described earlier, based on the confusion graph, we can determine others metrics like accuracy, precision etc. So, after we show the confusion graph, we will also display the other metric into a table named classification report. The classification report shows the precision, recall and f1-score metrics through a table. The percentage obtain in the confusion matrix is based on the number of events for the test dataset which is equal to 240,454.

7.1   Random Forest Classifier (RF)

The Fig. 6 represent the confusion matrix of the random forest classifier.

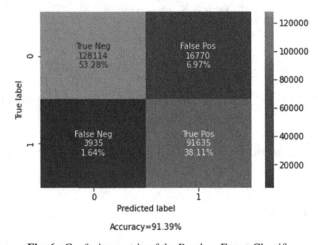

Fig. 6. Confusion matrix of the Random Forest Classifier

In the figure above, we have the confusion matrix for the Random Forest Classifier. In it, we can see that the True Negative is equal to 53.36% where the True Positive is 38.07%. As for the accuracy, it is equal to 91.39%. The Table 3 show the classification report of the RF.

Table 3. Classification report of RF

		Precision	Recall	f1-score	Support
Observation	0	0.88	0.97	0.93	132049
	1	0.96	0.85	0.90	108405
Average		0.92	0.91	0.91	240454

7.2 Decision Tree Classifier (DT)

The Fig. 7 represent the confusion matrix of the decision tree classifier.

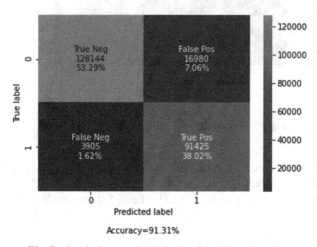

Fig. 7. Confusion matrix of the Decision Tree Classifier

In the figure above, we have the confusion matrix for the Decision Tree Classifier. In it, we can see that the True Negative is equal to 53.29% where the True Positive is 38.02%. As for the accuracy, it is equal to 91.31%. The Table 4 show the classification report of the DT.

Table 4. Classification report of DT

		Precision	Recall	f1-score	Support
Observation	0	0.88	0.97	0.92	132049
	1	0.96	0.84	0.90	108405
Average		0.92	0.91	0.91	240454

7.3   Logistic Regression (LR)

The Fig. 8 represent the confusion matrix of the logistic regression.

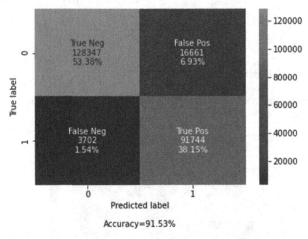

Fig. 8. Confusion matrix of the Logistic Regression

In the figure above, we have the confusion matrix for the Logistic Regression. In it, we can see that the True Negative is equal to 53.38% where the True Positive is 38.15%. As for the accuracy, it is equal to 91.53%. The Table 5 show the classification report of the LR.

Table 5. Classification report of LR

		Precision	Recall	f1-score	Support
Observation	0	0.89	0.97	0.93	132049
	1	0.96	0.85	0.90	108405
Average		0.92	0.91	0.91	240454

7.4   Multi-Layer Perceptron Classifier (MLP)

The Fig. 9 represent the confusion matrix of the Multi-Layer Perceptron classifier.

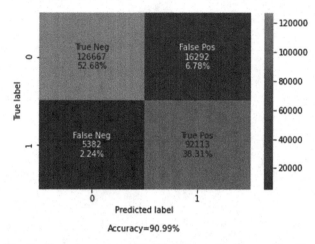

Accuracy=90.99%

Fig. 9. Confusion matrix of the Multi-Layer Perceptron Classifier

In the figure above, we have the confusion matrix for the Multi-Layer Perceptron Classifier. In it, we can see that the True Negative is equal to 52.68% where the True Positive is 38.31%. As for the accuracy, it is equal to 90.99%. The Table 6 show the classification report of the MLP.

Table 6. Classification report of MLP

		Precision	Recall	f1-score	Support
Observation	0	0.89	0.96	0.92	132049
	1	0.94	0.85	0.90	108405
Average		0.92	0.91	0.91	240454

7.5 ROC Graph

The roc graph does a comparison of the different model use early.

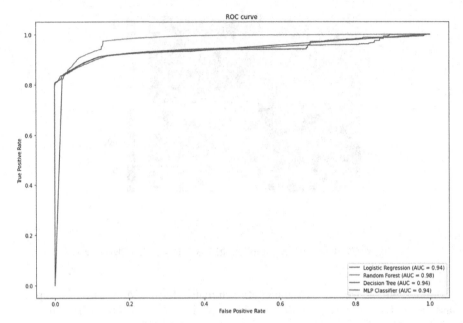

Fig. 10. ROC curve which compares the LR, RF, DT, MLP

The Fig. 10 represent the ROC graph which compares the different prediction model named earlier. In it, we can see the evolution of the False Positive Rate compare to the True Positive Rate during the training. According to [18], the Area Under ROC Curve (AUC) of a classifier is equivalent to the probability that the classifier will rank a randomly chosen positive instance higher than a randomly chosen negative instance. So, in our ROC curve, we can see that the RF score an AUC of 0.98 while the other prediction model has 0.94. However, it cannot determine clearly the final accuracy of the prediction model.

8   Conclusion

The prediction of business process failure is always useful for improving the efficiency of a business process. Therefore, taking into account the loop can be benefiting for a process model. Because it can reduce the number of repetitive events into an efficient one. In our process, with the applied data, we conclude that the logistic regression algorithm fit the best for the prediction with an accuracy of 91.53%. There may be better algorithm for the prediction. The hole process of prediction and analysis has been made by using the IBM cloud service. A comparison to other cloud service can be made to determine the one with best performance. Even if in our proposition we didn't use the timestamp, it may affect the final state of a process case or it can be the cause of loops.

References

1. Van der Aalst, W.: Process mining software. Process Min., 325–352 (2016). https://doi.org/10.1007/978-3-662-49851-4_11
2. Avizienis, A., Laprie, J.-C., Randell, B., Landwehr, C.: Basic concepts and taxonomy of dependable and secure computing. IEEE Trans. Dependable Secur. Comput. **1**, 11–33 (2004). https://doi.org/10.1109/TDSC.2004.2
3. Mariani, L., Pezzè, M., Riganelli, O., Xin, R.: Predicting failures in multi-tier distributed systems (2019).
4. Borkowski, M., Fdhila, W., Nardelli, M., Rinderle-Ma, S., Schulte, S.: Event-based failure prediction in distributed business processes. Inf. Syst. (2017) https://doi.org/10.1016/j.is.2017.12.005
5. Kang, B., Kim, D., Kang, S.H.: Real-time business process monitoring method for prediction of abnormal termination using KNNI-based LOF prediction. Expert. Syst. Appl. **39**(5), 6061–6068 (2012) ISSN 0957-4174. https://doi.org/10.1016/j.eswa.2011.12.007
6. Evermann, J., Rehse, J.R., Fettke, P.: A deep learning approach for predicting process behaviour at runtime, pp. 327–338 (2017). https://doi.org/10.1007/978-3-319-58457-7_24
7. van der Aalst, W.M.P., Weijters, A.: Process mining: a research agenda. Comput. Ind. **53**(3), 231–244 (2004)
8. van der Aalst, W., Dongen, J., Herbst, B.F.V., Maruster, G.W., Schimm, L.: Workflow mining: a survey of issues and approaches. Data Knowl. Eng. **47**(2), 237–267 (2003)
9. van der Aalst, W.M.P.: Process Mining: Discovery. Springer, Conformance and Enhancement of Business Processes (2011)
10. Camara, M.S., Fall, I., Mendy, G., Diaw, S.: IEEE 2015 19th International Conference on System Theory, Control and Computing (ICSTCC)—Cheile Gradistei, Romania (2015.10.14–2015.10.16). 2015 19th International Conference on System Theory, Control and Computing (ICSTCC)—Activity failure prediction based on process mining, pp. 854–859 (2015). https://doi.org/10.1109/ICSTCC.2015.7321401
11. van der Aalst, W.M.P., Hofstede, A.H.M.T., Kiepuszewski, B., Barros, A.P.: Workflow patterns. Distrib. Parallel Databases **14**(1), 5–51 (2003)
12. Chapman, P., Clinton, J.: Crisp-dm 1.0. SPSS Inc, Tech. Rep. (2000)
13. https://doi.org/10.4121/uuid:5f3067df-f10b-45da-b98b-86ae4c7a310b
14. Povalyaeva, E., Khamitov, I., Fomenko, A.: From the Moscow Higher School of Economics, with their submission entitled: Density Analysis of the Interaction with Client
15. Blevi, L., Robbrecht, J., Delporte, L.: From KPMG Technology Advisory, Belgium, with their submission entitled: Process mining on the loan application process of a Dutch Financial Institute
16. Rodrigues, A et al.: From Pontifícia Universidade, with their submission entitled: STAIRWAY TO VALUE: Mining the loan application process
17. Metrics and scoring: quantifying the quality of predictions—Scikit-learn 0.24.2 documentation 2021/09/10
18. ROC Graphs: Notes and Practical Considerations for Researchers Tom Fawcett March 16, 2004.

An AI-Based Model for the Prediction of a Newborn's Sickle Cell Disease Status

Souleymane Bosso Farota[1], Al Hassim Diallo[2], Mouhamadou Lamine Ba[1],
Gaoussou Camara[1(✉)], and Ibrahima Diagne[2,3]

[1] LIMA, Université Alioune Diop, B.P. 30, Bambey, Senegal
gaoussou.camara@uadb.edu.sn
[2] Université Gaston Berger, B.P. 34, Saint-Louis, Senegal
[3] Centre de Recherche et de Prise en Charge Ambulatoire de la Drépanocytose,
Université Gaston Berger, Dakar, Senegal

Abstract. Sickle cell disease remains a global public health problem. In Senegal, a neonatal screening and early follow-up program is conducted at the CERPAD. Such a program, started in April 2017, implements the strategy of systematic screening at birth and concerns children born in the maternity wards of the CHRSL as well as from the reference health center of the city of Saint-Louis. However, out of 18 257 newborns screened since the beginning of the program, only 49 (less than 0.5%) are pathological (SS, SC, etc.) which is extremely low compared to the cost in terms of human resources, working time and use of laboratory consumables. To mitigate the impacts of these limitations of the actual early detection and follow-up approach, we therefore propose in this paper a new approach to targeted screening based on artificial intelligence. We tested and compared the performances of five machine learning algorithms for the prediction of sickle cell status. The preliminary results are promising for the task of whether or not a given newborn has a potentially pathological profile, with the majority of the models showing a high prediction accuracy.

Keywords: AI · Machine learning · Predictive model · Neonatal screening · Targeted screening · Sickle cell · Senegal

1 Introduction

Sickle cell disease is a genetic disease with severe health implications on the daily life of the persons that suffer from it. It is estimated that each year over 300 000 babies with severe forms of these diseases are born worldwide, the majority in low and middle income countries.[1] Unfortunately, most of the children born with sickle cell disease in low-income or/and developing countries are still dying at an early age. For instance, without proper management of SS form, 50% of children die before the age of 5 [1]. As

---

[1] https://www.afro.who.int/health-topics/sickle-cell-disease.

© ICST Institute for Computer Sciences, Social Informatics and Telecommunications Engineering 2022
Published by Springer Nature Switzerland AG 2022. All Rights Reserved
A. D. Mambo et al. (Eds.): InterSol 2022, LNICST 449, pp. 96–104, 2022.
https://doi.org/10.1007/978-3-031-23116-2_7

a result, sickle cell disease remains nowadays a serious public health issue, particularly in Sub-Saharan Africa.

In Senegal, the Center of Research and Ambulatory Care for Sickle Cell Disease (CERPAD) is concerned about this state of affairs and has set itself the general objective of contributing to the fight against sickle cell disease in Senegal, mainly through fundamental and applied research programs. Its ambition is to collect and analyze epidemiological, clinical and socio-anthropological data in collaboration with other research teams at the University Gaston Berger by proposing an efficient model for neonatal screening and early management of sickle cell disease adapted to the public health system in Senegal. CERPAD has adopted the strategy of a systematic screening at birth since April 2017. Since then, out of 18,257 newborns screened, only 49 (less than 0.5%) are pathological (SS, SC, etc.). This is in contrast with the expensive cost of the screening program in terms of human resources, working time and use of laboratory consumables. Finding a sustainable funding of such a screening program in the medium and long term is very difficult, particularly in low-income countries. Therefore, in this paper, we propose a new targeted screening approach based on a machine learning model for sickle cell status prediction. The preliminary results, obtained by evaluating five standard machine learning algorithms on real data, are promising with the majority of the models showing a high prediction accuracy; accuracy value equals 100% and AUC close to 1.

The rest of the paper is organized as follows. Section 2 summarizes the state-of-the-art while Sect. 3 describes the dataset. The methodology will then be introduced in Sect. 4, followed by the presentation of our results and their discussion in Sect. 5. We conclude in Sect. 6.

2   Review of the Literature

There are several research projects which have been developed for healthcare settings based on machine learning approaches and especially for sickle cell disease. These works could be classified according to the different phases of the evolution of the disease (crisis, complications, etc.) or the management process (screening, biological and radiological analysis, treatment, hospitalization). However, we offer a few examples of recent work that highlight the use of artificial intelligence (or machine learning) in this field. For instance, [2] developed a collection of 14 models with genetic risk score composed of different numbers of SNPs and used the ensemble of these models to predict HbF in patients with sickle cell anemia. The models were trained in 841 patients with sickle cell anemia and were tested in 3 independent cohorts. [3] developed a model to predict the severity of a patient's case, to determine the clinical complications of the disease, and to suggest the correct dosage of the treatment(s). They also presented similar work that attempted to estimate the severity of SCD in diagnosed patients to aid medical professionals in prescribing drugs. [4] propose Machine-learning algorithms for predicting hospital readmissions in sickle cell disease. In [5], image processing and machine learning techniques are used to automate the process of detection of sickle cells in microscopic images then classify the RBC into three shapes: circular, elongated (sickle cell) and other shape. The machine learning classifier random forest, logistic regression naïve baye and support vector machine were used in this research. [6] implements a powerful and efficient Multi-Layer Perceptron (MLP) classification algorithm that distinguishes Sickle

Cell Anemia (SCA) into three classes: Normal (N), Sickle Cells(S) and Thalassemia (T) in red blood cells. An Automated screening of sickle cells technique using a smartphone-based microscope and deep learning is proposed in [7]. An automated diagnosis model of sickle cell anemia using SVM classifier is proposed in [8] based on images.

To the best of our knowledge our work is the first in Sub-Saharan African that investigates the efficiency of machine learning approaches for the prediction of human sickle cell status at birth.

3 Materials

Our study concerns newborns screened and followed at the CERPAD. These newborns come from the maternity wards of the CHRSL and the reference health center of the city of Saint-Louis. Newborns are monitored during visits. They also receive emergency care for acute attacks or other complications related to the disease. Data management is done through an electronic patient record management system of the National Medical Information System for Senegal (SIMENS) [9, 10]. The system currently registers over 18,257 sickle cell patients screened.

Table 1. Description of the attributes of the Sickle Cell dataset

Attribute/variable	Type	Description
Weight	Real	The weight of the child at birth
Height	Real	The size of the child at birth
PC	Real	Cranial perimeter of the child at birth
Full term birth	Boolean	Birth at term of pregnancy
Premature	Boolean	If the child is premature or not
Number of WA	Integer	The number of weeks amenorrhea
Multiple pregnancy	Integer	The number of fetuses in pregnancy
Fetal distress	Boolean	Birth complications
Transfused	Boolean	Whether the mother received a blood transfusion
Sickle cell disease	Boolean	Pathological sickle cell status

In this study, a sickle cell disease dataset containing 5,732 individuals were extracted from the 18,257 records to design our expected model. There were several attributes in this dataset. Only 10 attributes were considered according to the domain experts' recommendation after many exchanges on features selection (see Table 1).

4 Methods

4.1 Overview of Our Approach

Machine Learning plays an important role in disease prediction [11]. Machine Learning algorithms are mainly divided into four categories: Supervised learning, Unsupervised learning, Semi-supervised learning, and Reinforcement learning [12]. In this paper, we use supervised learning techniques to predict patient status. Our problem is to classify patients into a given class (sick or healthy). It is a priori difficult to know which of the existing classification algorithms is the best for our dataset. It is therefore necessary to test different algorithms, then to compare their performance and to deduce the best one for our case of study. The following are the procedural steps of the designed methodology applied in this research. The dataset presented above and including the attributes mentioned in Table 1 are provided as input to the different machine learning algorithms. The input dataset is divided into 80% for the training dataset and the remaining 20% for the test dataset. In this paper, we focus on five classifiers: AdaBoost, Logistic Regression (LR), Support Vector Machine (SVM), k-nearest neighbors (KNN) and Random Forest (RF), described here [13].

The objective of this study is to effectively predict whether the patient suffers from sickle cell disease or not. In this step, we will first define the evaluation measures that we will use to evaluate our models. The most important evaluation metric for this problem area is sensitivity, specificity, accuracy, F1 measure.

4.2 Experimental Performance Evaluation

We tested and compared the performance of the aforementioned machine learning algorithms (see Sect. 4.1) using our Sickle Cell real dataset presented in Sect. 3. For the performance evaluation purposes, we relied on the precision, recall (or sensitivity), specificity, F1-measure (also known as F1-score), accuracy, and AUC (Area Under the Curve) metrics. We sum up in Table 2 the definition, as well as the formula, of each of these performance evaluation metrics. Recall that these metrics are computed based on the confusion matrices obtained from the results of the testing phase of each machine learning algorithm on the test set.

The precision metric estimates the ability of the model to predict the correct classes of the individuals in the positive class. When it is necessary to determine the number of positive predictions, given predictions in both classes, that can be accurately predicted, recall is another useful evaluation measure, representing the proportion of positives successfully categorized. The F1-score provides a good balance between the precision and the recall when evaluating the performance of a classifier, particularly in the presence of unbalanced data.

AUC provides an aggregate measure of performance across all possible classification thresholds. One way of interpreting AUC is as the probability that the model ranks a random positive example more highly than a random negative example. AUC ranges in value from 0 to 1. A model whose predictions are 100% wrong has an AUC of 0.0; one whose predictions are 100% correct has an AUC of 1.0.

Table 2. Description of the performance measures

Characteristic	Formula	Description
True Positive (TP)	no formula	Number of positive cases correctly screened
True Negative (TN)	no formula	Number of negative cases correctly detected
False Positive (FP)	no formula	Number of negative cases incorrectly screens as positive
False Negative (FN)	no formula	Number of cases that could not be detected
Precision	$\frac{TP}{TP+FP}$	Proportion of positive identifications that were actually correct
Recall	$\frac{TP}{TP+FN}$	Proportion of actual positives that were identified correctly
Specificity	$\frac{TN}{TN+FP}$	It measures the proportion of negatives correctly identified as such
Accuracy	$\frac{TN+TP}{TN+FN+TP+FP}$	It is the ratio of correct prediction given the total number of cases
F1-score	$2 * \frac{Precision*Recall}{Precision+Recall}$	Its value is equal to the harmonic mean of the precision and the recall

4.3 Evaluation Setting up

For the purpose of our comparative evaluation study, we used Scikit-Learn, a popular Python library that provides an implementation of the most popular existing machine learning algorithms. All the experiments have been performed on Jupyter notebook 6.4.5 and Orange3.

4.4 Segmentation of the Dataset

For fitting and evaluating each algorithm, the Sickle Cell Dataset has been divided into two parts as follows.

- A training set representing 80% of the entire dataset
- A test set representing 20% of the entire dataset

To avoid being biased we randomly select the individuals to include in the training and the testing set. A k-fold cross validation with k = 10 has been also performed during the training step.

4.5 Cross Validation Phase

To be safe against overfitting or underfitting, we introduced a cross validation step during the setting up of each model. To this end, we used Orange which is an open-source data visualization, machine learning, and data mining toolkit. It features a visual programming front-end for exploratory data analysis and interactive data visualization, and can also be used as a Python library.

Figure 1 shows the k-fold cross validation pipeline with Orange using no over or under sampling. Our reasoning is that if we model a problem with 10% positive classes, we should not train the model with a 80:20 class distribution, as this will not reflect real life. Using Orange, we can balance the class distribution and perform k-fold cross-validation during the fitting of the learning model.

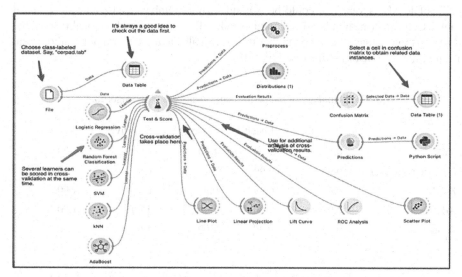

Fig. 1. K-fold cross-validation in Orange Tool

4.6 Selection of the Hyper-parameters of the Algorithms

A random stratification procedure has been used on the Sickle Cell data to produce 10 unique training datasets. The performance was good for each classification and the same training and test datasets were used to train and test the five classifiers under the same conditions and in the same environment, thus allowing the relative performance and consistency of the algorithms to be assessed for prediction. The conditions under which the classifiers were trained and tested were varied according to the evaluation of the criteria.

5   Results and Discussions

The performance measures of our five tested algorithms, depicted in Table 3 and Fig. 2, are obtained using the confusion matrix based on the results of the experiments conducted on the patient sickle cell dataset.

Results on Table 3 shows that all the models present very good performance regarding the different metrics. Indeed, excepting the precision of SVM and Random Forest which is equal to 0.54 and 0.95 respectively, the values of the metrics for the algorithms are either to 0.99 or 1. In order to validate those results, we further conducted a k-fold cross validation of the models in order to mitigate the overfitting or underfitting problems that might bias the performances by providing no repeatable results.

Figure 2 gives the AUC values, *i.e.* the true positive rate versus the false positive rate, of the compared algorithms. While K-NN AUC value is close to 0.5, the other classifiers (SVM, LR, AdaBoost, RF) show very high AUC. This confirms the promising performances, depicted in Table 3, of SVM, LR, AdaBoost, and RF. The fact that the AUC of K-NN is very low could be explained by the unbalanced nature of the used Sickle Cell Data (the number of individuals that suffer from the pathological form of the disease is much lower than the number of individuals having either a non-pathological form of the disease or not the disease at all).

Table 3. Summary of the performance measures of the algorithms

	Precision	Recall	F1-score	Sensitivity	Accuracy
SVM	0.54	1.00	1.00	1.00	1.00
Logistic regression	0.95	0.99	0.99	0.99	0.95
K-NN	0.99	0.99	0.99	0.99	1.00
AdaBoost	0.99	1.00	1.00	1.00	1.00
Random Forest	0.95	0.99	1.00	1.00	1.00

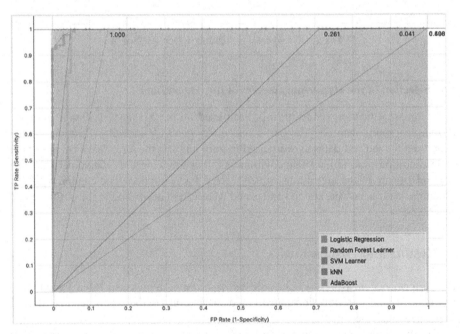

Fig. 2. AUC (Area Under the ROC Curve) of the compared algorithms

6   Conclusion

In this paper, we proposed an approach to neonatal screening for sickle cell disease targeting only children potentially carrying the sickle cell gene. For this purpose, we proposed a machine learning model built and trained on data collected in maternity wards on children at birth. Our model is based on the combination of five classification algorithms (AdaBoost, Logistic Regression, Support Vector Machine, k-nearest neighbors and Random Forest). The evaluation of our prediction model gives us an accuracy of 0.95 (LR) and 1 (the other classifiers). However, except K-NN all the tested classifiers have an AUC close to 1. We envision collecting and including data on parental sickle cell profiles in order to further boost the performances of our learning algorithm.

In the future, we plan to explore a probabilistic approach, e.g. by trying to infer the probability level of having potentially a pathological form of the disease, by considering our study as a regression problem. Furthermore, we also intend to extend our model to be able to predict directly the sickle cell profile (AA, AS, AC, SC, SS, etc.) of the newborns.

References

1. Thiam, L., et al.: Profils épidemiologiques, cliniques et hématologiques de la drépanocytose homozygote SS en phase inter critique chez l'enfant à Ziguinchor, Sénégal. Pan Afr. Med. J. **28**, 208 (2017). https://doi.org/10.11604/pamj.2017.28.208.14006
2. Milton, J.N., Gordeuk, V.R., Taylor, J.G., Gladwin, M.T., Steinberg, M.H., Sebastiani, P.: Prediction of fetal hemoglobin in sickle cell anemia using an ensemble of genetic risk prediction models. Circ. Cardiovasc. Genet. **7**, 110–115 (2014). https://doi.org/10.1161/CIRCGENETICS.113.000387
3. Alharbi, N.H., Bameer, R.O., Geddan, S.S., Alharbi, H.M.: Recent advances and machine learning techniques on sickle cell disease. Future Comput. Inform. J. **5**, 4(2020). https://doi.org/10.54623/fue.fcij.5.1.4
4. Patel, A., et al.: Machine-learning algorithms for predicting hospital re-admissions in sickle cell disease. Br. J. Haematol. **192**, 158–170 (2021). https://doi.org/10.1111/bjh.17107
5. Sen, B., Ganesh, A., Bhan, A., Dixit, S., Goyal, A.: Machine learning based Diagnosis and classification of Sickle Cell Anemia in Human RBC. In: 2021 Third International Conference on Intelligent Communication Technologies and Virtual Mobile Networks (ICICV). pp. 753–758 (2021). https://doi.org/10.1109/ICICV50876.2021.9388610
6. Yeruva, S., Varalakshmi, M.S., Gowtham, B.P., Chandana, Y.H., Prasad, P.K.: Identification of Sickle Cell Anemia Using Deep Neural Networks. Emerg. Sci. J. **5**, 200–210 (2021). https://doi.org/10.28991/esj-2021-01270
7. de Haan, K., et al.: Automated screening of sickle cells using a smartphone-based microscope and deep learning. Npj Digit. Med. **3**, 1–9 (2020). https://doi.org/10.1038/s41746-020-0282-y
8. Wahed, F.F., Juliette, A.A., Sinthia, P., Mary, G.A.A.: Detection of sickle cell anemia using SVM classifier. In: AIP Conference Proceedings, vol. 2405, pp. 020006 (2022). https://doi.org/10.1063/5.0074138
9. Camara, G., Diallo, A.H., Lo, M., Tendeng, J.-N., Lo, S.: A national medical information system for Senegal: architecture and services. Stud. Health Technol. Inform. **228**, 43–47 (2016)
10. Diallo, A.H., et al.: Towards an information system for sickle cell neonatal screening in Senegal. Stud. Health Technol. Inform. **258**, 95–99 (2019)

11. Jayatilake, S.M.D.A.C., Ganegoda, G.U.: Involvement of machine learning tools in healthcare decision making. J. Healthc. Eng., 6679512 (2021). https://doi.org/10.1155/2021/6679512
12. Mohammed, M., Khan, M.B., Bashier, E.B.M.: Machine Learning: Algorithms and Applications. CRC Press, Boca Raton (2016). https://doi.org/10.1201/9781315371658
13. Sarker, I.H.: Machine learning: algorithms, real-world applications and research directions. SN Comput. Sci. 2(3), 1–21 (2021). https://doi.org/10.1007/s42979-021-00592-x

Study of an Approach Based on the Analysis of Computer Program Execution Traces for the Detection of Vulnerabilities

Gouayon Koala[1]([✉]), Didier Bassolé[1], Télesphore Tiendrébéogo[2],
and Oumarou Sié[1]

[1] Laboratoire de Mathématiques et d'Informatique, Université Joseph Ki-Zerbo,
Ouagadougou, Burkina Faso
gouayonkoala1@gmail.com
[2] Laboratoire d'Algèbre, de Mathématiques Discrètes et d'Informatique,
Université Nazi Boni, Bobo-Dioulasso, Burkina Faso
http://www.ujkz.bf, http://www.univ-bobo.gov.bf

Abstract. Malicious attacks exploit software vulnerabilities to violate
key security features in computer systems. In this paper, we review the
related works of studies that propose mechanisms for detecting software
vulnerabilities or ways to protect application data. The aim is to analyse
how these mechanisms are exploited to detect software vulnerabilities
and secure data via applications. Then, we present tracing techniques
to understand the behaviour of applications. Finally, we present an approach based on the analysis of program execution traces that allows the
detection of vulnerabilities.

Keywords: Detection · Vulnerabilities · Tracing · Attacks

1 Introduction

Digital technology (devices, systems, connected objects) increasingly offers multiple benefits and a variety of services to businesses and individuals. This has
increased usage and apps are an important part of this digital boom. Competition
between application developers has brought much innovation. However, many of
these applications are increasingly vulnerable. Exploitable vulnerabilities in software can pose potential threats to the functioning of IT systems, impacting mil-
lions of users on a daily basis. To reduce malware, researchers have proposed protection and control mechanisms (firewalls, intrusion detection systems, web scan-
ners, etc.) to secure data. Despite these efforts, cybercriminals are using more
sophisticated and innovative evasion techniques that hamper efforts to secure
data. No system is spared from the malicious actions of attackers. In addition,
vulnerabilities in applications are increasing in number and intensity, facilitating

© ICST Institute for Computer Sciences, Social Informatics and Telecommunications Engineering 2022
Published by Springer Nature Switzerland AG 2022. All Rights Reserved
A. D. Mambo et al. (Eds.): InterSol 2022, LNICST 449, pp. 105–115, 2022.
https://doi.org/10.1007/978-3-031-23116-2_8

attacks in many systems [1–3]. To counter threats and attacks, several methods and techniques have been proposed by researchers [1, 4–9].

Studies based on these approaches have made it possible to propose solutions for the detection of vulnerabilities on the one hand and data protection mechanisms on the other. Despite all the efforts made, the search for effective protection against threats and attacks is still ongoing. Vulnerabilities and anomalies in applications therefore constitute a threat to their users (individuals or companies). To find solutions capable of effectively improving data protection become therefore essential [10]. The first step to improve this protection is to be able to detect threats and attacks on software. This study therefore reviews approaches based on analysis methods for detecting vulnerabilities. The objective is to propose an approach to detecting vulnerabilities in applications by exploiting these existing methods.

The rest of this document is organized as follows: in the Sect. 2 we present the Background of Study and the problematic of this study. The Sect. 3 defines the concepts used in our study and the Sect. 4 deals with related work and identified shortcomings. In the Sect. 5, we present our approach for analysing execution traces. We conclude by presenting a synthesis of our contribution and our perspectives in Sect. 6.

2   Background of Study

The digital market is growing at a rapid pace. From 2016 to 2020, we have gone from 2 billion objects to 200 billion connected objects, an increase of 200% [11]. This growth is due to the presence of digital technology in all sectors of activity such as education, health, finance, entertainment, home, energy, smart cities, tourism and transport [12–15]. Users are more concerned with innovations and benefits and rarely pay attention to the safety and security of the applications that offer them services. The use of certain applications can have consequences with regard to the protection of the data that passes through them. Thus, negligence in data protection can put users at risk and disrupt computer systems. For example, cybercriminals can take control of a computer system and cause panic among citizens[1].

Consequently, software security became an important strategic issue [1]. Thus, several research projects have been carried out and solutions proposed to solve these security problems. Despite these research efforts, the number of vulnerabilities in computer systems continues to increase [3]. Also, malicious actions to exploit these vulnerabilities continue to increase and some actions can cause serious problems such as loss of revenue, disruption of critical operations within an organisation, ... Despite the complexity of today's IT systems, hackers are adapting to the evolution to succeed in their attacks. Recent years have shown that attack scenarios are evolving and becoming more and more complex. These attacks target both hardware components and applications. Indeed, many

---

[1] https://www.voaafrique.com/a/une-cyberattaque-cause-des-p%C3%A9nuries-de-carburant-aux-usa/5888344.html.

applications contain multiple vulnerabilities that can be exploited by hackers. Most of these attacks rely on software-related attack vectors, in particular on use of software (privilege escalation, information leakage, denial of service ...) or on exploiting software implementation errors (buffer overflows).

Although proposals for solutions exist in the literature, it is difficult to propose security solutions applicable to all applications in particular. In order to reduce security vulnerabilities in software, several methods and analysis techniques are used to detect their vulnerabilities. When the source code of an application is accessible, we can obtain information that can help improve the detection of vulnerabilities and propose solutions to protect data. Indeed, such analysis is only possible if the source code is available and understandable. Hence the need to explore application tracing techniques in this study. These techniques have been used in the literature on monitored machines to detect anomalies in systems. Few works have focused on application traces, which can be valuable for improving the quality of vulnerability detection. With this study, we wish to analyse the traces to examine and even detect precursor behaviours of attacks. Thus, it is essential to know how programs work through their traces, and to ensure their correct behaviour. This problem constitutes the main subject of our work.

We will begin by recalling some basic terminology and concepts associated with computer security. This then allows us to understand the vulnerabilities, threats and attacks that undermine data protection.

3 Concepts

3.1 Vulnerability

A vulnerability is an accidental or intentional fault (with or without intent to harm) in the specification, design or configuration of the system, or in the way it is used [8,16]. Applications may have security holes. This is all the more serious as these applications sometimes handle confidential data (passwords, bank card numbers) and are generally exposed to the public. These security flaws exist on all operating systems because several flaws are due to programming errors in the application [17,18].

Thus, the increasing complexity of the technologies used for application development coupled with the neglect of security by application developers can largely explain the presence of recurring vulnerabilities. There is a wide variety of vulnerabilities targeting applications. However, some are more well-known and dangerous than others. Several databases list these vulnerabilities with statistics indicating their relative importance. For example, databases such as CVE[2] (Common Vulnerabilities and Exposures), NVD[3] (National Vulnerability Database) or VUPEN[4] (Vulnerability Penetration testing) list all types of vulnerabilities, including those targeting applications.

---

[2] https://www.cvedetails.com/.

[3] https://nvd.nist.gov.

[4] http://www.vupen.com.

The increase in vulnerabilities and attacks has led many researchers to focus more on security in applications in order to improve data protection [1,4,6,7, 10,19,20]. Work in this context has resulted in the proposal of taxonomies and classifications for the most common vulnerabilities and attacks [3,17,21–23]. Also, the vulnerability can be exploited to create an intrusion.

3.2 Attack and Intrusion

Attack is a malicious interaction to violate one or more security properties. It is an external fault created with the intention to harm. An attack may or may not be carried out by automatic tools [17,23].

Intrusion is an internal, but externally generated malicious act resulting from an attack that successfully exploited a vulnerability. Intrusion is any penetration of a computer system with the aim of undermining its confidentiality, integrity or availability. Intrusion detection brings together all the techniques implemented to alert the users of the computer system targeted by an attacker [1,17,21].

3.3 Execution Trace

A trace is a constitution of imprints left in an environment as a result of a process [24]. Any process can produce more or less persistent footprints. Just as a fingerprint is linked to something, a trace is always associated with an activity. Thus, the digital trace is a constitution of digital footprints left in a computer environment on the occasion of computer processes [18,24]. Over the years, the computer trace has become an object to be protected like other resources available in the computerised environment. Through web applications, many digital traces are constructed via the digital footprints left behind. We consider an execution trace as a reference to a mechanism that mainly collects information. This data can be analysed to detect sources of errors in software systems [25,26]. Thus, the execution traces of applications provide relevant data on the internal state of these applications.

4   Related Work

In this section we review the work relating vulnerabilities detection and proposed solutions. This allows us to understand the vulnerabilities, threats and attacks that compromise data protection and to discuss different ways of classifying them.

The widespread use of software is visible worldwide. Users are being targeted by cyber attacks that have exposed critical flaws in IT systems. Information security has become a major concern [4,11,27]. The danger posed by vulnerable applications affects information security and threatens the entire digital world by exploiting vulnerabilities. The scanning techniques used for vulnerability detection can be categorised into static, dynamic and hybrid approaches.

Static approach techniques (rule-based or model-based analysis, code similarity detection, etc.) rely on source code analysis [19,20]. The techniques of the dynamic approach (fuzz tests, analysis of spots or alterations, etc.) are performed during the execution of the programme [9,28]. Limitations in accessibility and understanding of the source code and poor code coverage have led to the hybrid analysis approach. The techniques of this approach combine static and dynamic analysis techniques to reduce the limitations of both approaches [5,6,21,29].

In the field of connected objects, various techniques have been proposed for vulnerability detection. Several papers have provided reviews on software vulnerability detection from different perspectives. For example, Chaabouni et al. [27], compared several techniques in the literature to detect and prevent new attacks in connected objects. In their review, they classified the threats and security challenges in connected objects (Fig. 1).

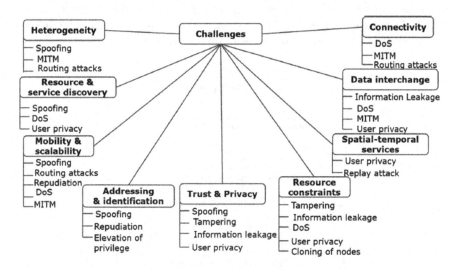

Fig. 1. Classification of threats in computer systems (Chaabouni et al. [27])

Their study reveals DDoS attacks that have compromised data availability. Their analysis notes that security attack vectors have evolved in terms of bot complexity and diversity. Although their work focuses on the characteristics of the attacks. They concentrate on network intrusion detection systems (NIDS). Nevertheless, we deduce that from these sequences of possible attacks in a computer system, there are attacks related to the programs that interest us in this work.

In [4], authors focused on the efforts made for intrusion detection in connected objects. In this review, Benkhelifa et al. made a set of proposals on the architecture of connected objects in order to improve data protection.

In [30], Braiek et al. examined fault detection in data and/or machine learning models in their review. The work of Zhang et al. in [2] provide a survey of machine learning testing by bringing together aspects of work that have dealt specifically with software testing. In their review, authors have simultaneously covered all the types of machine learning approaches that have so far been addressed using testing. They thus identify the problems and challenges associated with software testing techniques and machine learning testing problems. This review provides a comprehensive study with a primary focus on machine learning testing.

Lin et al. [1], in their literature review discussed deep learning/neural network approaches to vulnerable code learning and neural networks for software vulnerability detection. In this review, authors examined neural techniques for learning and understanding code semantics to facilitate vulnerability discovery.

For mobile apps, a recent study on vulnerability detection techniques in Android was done by Qamar et al. [31]. Authors have provided taxonomies of malware detection approaches based on the analysis techniques used, platforms and data. In addition, this review presents the different attacks on mobile applications by providing a taxonomy on malware attack vectors. This taxonomy allowed them to examine the threat groups and vulnerabilities. This allowed them to identify their impact on users as presented in Fig. 2.

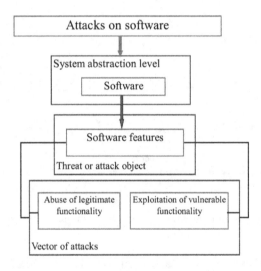

Fig. 2. Diagram of software attacks in a computer system (Qamar et al. [31])

All these techniques have shortcomings and some are sometimes ineffective in practice [5]. So far, the rapid increase in the number of vulnerabilities disclosed after the release of software products suggests that current software vulnerability detection techniques need to be improved in terms of efficiency and effectiveness [3,21]. Thus, an approach based on program execution traces can be used in research to study the behaviour of applications. Despite the problem of some application traces being very large (compression problems), the interest in traces is gaining importance as more and more researchers study the dynamic activities of computer systems. Unfortunately, approaches based on execution traces are specific, hence a global approach.

We will provide an up-to-date overview of existing methods used for vulnerability detection, which includes a description of each method, its strengths and weaknesses, and its resistance to malware evasion techniques. In addition, we include an overview of studies on machine learning techniques used to improve vulnerability detection in software. Although various approaches and/or techniques for vulnerability detection are proposed in the literature, the changing digital environment with cloud computing, connected objects leads to new software vulnerabilities and thus new exploits such as ransomware.

Malware authors can use techniques such as code obfuscation, dynamic code loading, encryption or packaging to evade static analysis and even signature-based antivirus tools. Furthermore, static scanning techniques are limited by the understanding of the programming language used for application development.

Dynamic scanning techniques, on the other hand, can provide a greater understanding of the code being scanned. It thus provide better results in detecting vulnerabilities in software. It can be deduced that dynamic scanning is more robust than static scanning. However, existing dynamic analysis tools and techniques are imperfect. Moreover, no single tool can cover all aspects of malware behaviour and thus effectively detect vulnerabilities. This has led to the analysis of applications with methods of a hybrid approach that combines both approaches (static and dynamic). These techniques use machine learning algorithms to detect vulnerabilities and reduce malware.

Unfortunately, these techniques are used separately and lack a public reference data set for exchange. Such a set could allow a reliable and practical comparison of different machine learning detection techniques. This shortcoming may allow some vulnerabilities to escape detection.

These limitations show the importance of implementing experiments to evaluate the effectiveness of software vulnerability detection techniques by subjecting applications to different analysis approaches and different attack scenario assumptions. The knowledge gained from these experiments will also be useful in identifying ways to improve the design of systems for data protection.

5 Methodology

One of the most important needs for the security of the data to be processed is the improvement of the software vulnerability detection strategy. Although tracing techniques have already been used to detect anomalies on different systems, especially with the help of system calls made on a monitored machine [18,25,32]. Few works have focused on the set of information available in the events. The arguments of the system calls can prove invaluable in improving the quality of vulnerability detection. The Fig. 3 shows our model for studying application execution traces.

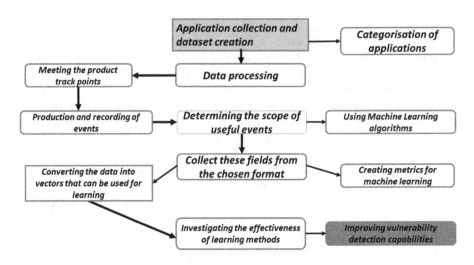

Fig. 3. The stages of transformation of the events collected with the tracing techniques

A tracepoint is a piece of code added to the execution of the traced program. When it is executed, it makes a call to the plotter so that the latter records the event associated with the tracepoint. An event contains information about the system to time of execution when the associated trace point was encountered. It can contain various information with a time stamp and contains information about the system when it was generated, such as the name of function where the tracepoint was present.

The purpose of tracing an application is to obtain accurate information about its state of operation. To obtain this information, tracing relies on events that are captured when the system reaches certain states. The collection is fast and does not change the behaviour of the system very much. The events are generated using tracepoints. These tracepoints can be added statically to an application or dynamically during its execution. Tracepoints are small pieces of code that have the function of making a call, containing information about the state of the system, at the time they are encountered by the processor. We will use all the information gathered by the tracer points to improve the quality of vulnerability detection. The tracer is the software responsible for collecting events as they occur and storing them in an orderly fashion in the trace. Therefore, it must be less disruptive to the system while it is running so that the information collected is relevant and valid. We will then analyse this information in detail to identify vulnerabilities which we will then classify. Thus, we will identify the challenges of our analysis with a view to proposing software countermeasures to improve data protection. Then, we will make a choice of implementation that could improve the results of vulnerability detection and thus reduce the risks related to the exploitation of such an attack vector.

Traces as computer objects are managed by the computer environment in a trace base. This base is a digital device known to collect, organize and provide services on the traces thus managed. In the perspectives of our study, we plan to further refine our analysis approach. We are interested in logging, which refers to a mechanism for collecting information to support the normal operation of a system. To analyse the execution traces of programs, several analysis tools or tracers are proposed. Thus, we will comprehensively evaluate the tracer tools for the implementation of our approach. This evaluation assumes a set of test data that we have to choose. We will also discuss runtime trace analysis tools as a means of protection against attacks. In addition, we will compare our results with previous studies on software vulnerabilities. Finally, we will reconstruct the semantics of a program from its execution trace.

6 Conclusion

The IT environment is constantly changing with a proliferation of malware. The level of complexity of malware is increasing every day, prompting the exploration of new analysis methods, machine learning techniques, etc. This paper explored the notion of modelled digital traces. It developed the possibilities of exploiting them to build a vulnerability detection model on the one hand and to improve the detection of application vulnerabilities on the other. We have studied techniques and methods for detecting software vulnerabilities. Research efforts have been made with different approaches to detect software vulnerabilities. We have presented a state of art of studies on vulnerability detection and data protection in applications. The focus is on detection methodologies and threats addressed, results and shortcomings. In addition, we presented our approach to analysis based on program execution traces. We have shown that the analysis of execution traces of application can provide relevant and valuable information about the impact of this application on data security according to the predefined rules of the method. From the terminologies associated with traces and the study of digital traces, we have presented the strategies adopted and identified the strengths of this approach.

The continuation of our work can be divided into three main areas. Firstly, we will study the tools for analysing execution traces in order to select those best suited to our approach, depending on the platforms. Second, we will analyse the application traces of our dataset and evaluate our results. Finally, we will reconstruct the semantics of a program from its execution trace.

References

1. Lin, G., Wen, S., Han, Q-L., Zhang, J., Xiang, Y.: Software vulnerability detection using deep neural networks: a survey. In: Proceedings of the IEEE, May 2000. https://doi.org/10.1109/JPROC.2020.2993293
2. Zhang, J.M., Harman, M., Ma, L., Liu, Y.: Machine learning testing: survey, landscapes and horizons. IEEE Trans. Softw. Eng. **48**, 1 –36 (2022). https://doi.org/10.1109/TSE.2019.2962027

3. Chakkaravarthy, S.S., Sangeetha, D., Vaidehi, V.: A Survey on malware analysis and mitigation techniques. Comput. Sci. Rev. **32**, 1–23 (2019). https://doi.org/10.1016/j.cosrev.2019.01.002.,

4. Benkhelifa, E., Welsh, T., Hamouda, W.: A Critical review of practices and challenges in intrusion detection systems for IoT: towards universal and resilient systems. IEEE Commun. Surv. Tutor. PP(99), 1 (2018)

5. Yamaguchi, F., Golde, N., Arp, D., Rieck, K.: Modeling and discovering vulnerabilities with code property graphs. In: IEEE Symposium on Security and Privacy, pp. 590–604, May 2014

6. Liu, L., De Vel, Q., Han, Q.-L., Zhang, J., Xiang, Y.: Detecting and preventing cyber insider threats: a survey. IEEE Commun. Surv. Tuts. **20**(2), 1397–1417, 2nd Quart. (2018)

7. Sun, N., Zhang, J., Rimba, P., Gao, S., Zhang, L.Y., Xiang, Y.: Data-driven cybersecurity incident prediction: a survey. IEEE Commun. Surveys Tuts. **21**(2), 1744–1772 (2019)

8. Ghaffarian, S.M., Shahriari, H.R.: Software vulnerability analysis and discovery using machine-learning and data-mining techniques: a survey. ACM Comput. Surv. **50**(4), 1–36 (2017)

9. Newsome, J., Song, D.X.: Dynamic taint analysis for automatic detection, analysis, and signature generation of exploits on commodity software. In: Proceedings of NDSS, pp. 3–4 (2005)

10. Li, Z., et al.: Vuldeepecker: a deep learning-based system for vulnerability detection. In: Proceedings of NDSS, pp. 1–15 (2018)

11. U. N.: IDC, Intel, "A Guide to the Internet of Things Infographic." February 2015. https://www.intel.com/content/www/us/en/internet-of-things/infographics/guide-to-iot:html

12. Vermesan, Q., Friess, P.: Internet of Things Applications - From Research and Innovation to Market Deployment Book. River Publishers, Jun. 2014. http://www.internet-of-thingsresearch.eu/pdf/IERC_Cluster_Book_2014_Ch.3_SRIA_WEB.pdf

13. Chen, C., Seff, A., Kornhauser, A., Xiao, J.: Deepdriving: learning affordance for direct perception in autonomous driving. In: Proceedings of the IEEE International Conference on Computer Vision, pp. 2722–2730 (2015)

14. Litjens, G., et al.: A survey on deep learning in medical image analysis. Med. Image Anal. **42**, 60–88 (2017)

15. Pei, K., Cao, Y., Yang, J., Jana. S.: Deepxplore: automated whitebox testing of deep learning systems. In: Proceedings of the 26th Symposium on Operating Systems Principles, pp. 1–18. ACM (2017)

16. Sestili, C.D., Snavely, W.S., VanHoudnos, N.M.: Towards security defect prediction with AI (2018). arXiv:1808.09897. http://arxiv.org/abs/1808.09897

17. Akrout, R.: Analyse de vulnérabilités et évaluation de systèmes de détection d'intrusions pour les applications Web. Thesis, Institut National des Sciences Appliquées de Toulouse (INSA Toulouse) (2013)

18. Meresse, S., Muratet, M., Yessad, A.: Analyse de traces d'exécution de programmes informatiques : application au jeu sérieux Prog&Play", ORPHEE-RDV, atelier: Méthodologies et outils pour le recueil, l'analyse et la visualisation des traces d'interaction, January 2017, Font-Romeu, France. hal-01515783

19. Kim, S., Woo, S., Lee, H., Oh, H.: VUDDY: a scalable approach for vulnerable code clone discovery. In: Proceedings of Symposium on Security and Privacy, pp. 595–614, May 2017

20. Jang, J., Agrawal, A., Brumley, D.: ReDeBug: finding unpatched code clones in entire OS distributions. In: IEEE Symposium on Security and Privacy, pp. 48–62, May 2012

21. Votipka, D., Stevens, R., Redmiles, E., Hu, J., Mazurek, M.: Hackers vs. testers: a comparison of software vulnerability discovery processes. In: Proceedings of IEEE Symposium on Security and Privacy (SP), pp. 374–391, May 2018

22. Sang, F.L.: Protection des systèmes informatiques contre les attaques par entrées-sorties. Thesis, Institut National des Sciences Appliquées de Toulouse(INSA Toulouse) (2013)

23. Benali, F.: Modélisation et classification automatique des informations de sécurité" (2009)

24. Mille, A.: Des traces à l'ère du Web. Intellectica **59**, 7–28 (2013)

25. Galli, T., Chiclana, F., Siewe, F.: Quality properties of execution tracing, an empirical study. Appl. Syst. Innov. **4**, 20 (2021). https://doi.org/10.3390/asi4010020

26. Savary, A.: "Détection de vulnérabilités appliquée à la vérification de code intermédiaire de Java Card", Université de Limoges (2016)

27. Chaabouni, N., Mosbah, M., Zemmari, A., Sauvignac, C., Faruki, P.: Network intrusion detection for IoT security based on learning techniques. IEEE Commun. Surv. tutor. **21**, 2671 –2701 (2018)

28. Pewny, J., Schuster, F., Bernhard, L., Holz, T., Rossow, C.: Leveraging semantic signatures for bug search in binary programs. In: Proceedings of the 30th Annual Computer Security Applications Conference (ACSAC), pp. 406–415 (2014)

29. Wu, Z., Pan, S., Chen, F., Long, G., Zhang, C., Yu, P.S.: A comprehensive survey on graph neural networks (2019). arXiv:1901.00596. http://arxiv.org/abs/1901.00596,

30. Braiek, H., Khomh, F.: On testing machine learning programs (2018). arXiv preprint arXiv:1812.02257

31. Qamar, A., Karim, A., Chang, V.: Mobile malware attacks: review, taxonomy & future directions. Futur. Gener. Comput. Syst. **97**, 887–909 (2019). https://doi.org/10.1016/j.future.2019.03.007

32. Hojaji, F., Mayerhofer, T., Zamani, B., Hamou-Lhadj, A., Bousse, E.: Model execution tracing: a systematic mapping study. Softw. Syst. Model **18**, 3461–3485 (2019)

ICT for Development

Comparative Evaluation on Sentiment Analysis Algorithms

Aman Kumar$^{(\boxtimes)}$, Manish Khare🆔, and Saurabh Tiwari

Dhirubhai Ambani Institute of Information and Communication Technology (DA-IICT),
Gandhinagar, Gujarat, India
{201911018,manish_khare,saurabh_t}@daiict.ac.in

Abstract. Classifying texts based on sentiments present in the text is called Sentiment Analysis. There are many Sentiment Analysis Techniques available. In this paper, we have addressed the problem of sentiment analysis and compared many different machine learning and deep learning algorithms to perform sentiment analysis based on their accuracy. We extracted useful features to feed them in our classifier to generate results. Also, we have used the majority vote ensemble method to achieve more accurate results.

Keywords: Sentiment analysis · Natural language processing · Machine learning · Deep learning · Comparison

1 Introduction

Sentiment Analysis is one of the functional problems used for quantifying the sentiments and emotions from neutral texts. It refers to obtaining sentiment data from the source, processing it using an algorithm, and generating positive, negative, and neutral sentiments [1]. Sentiment Analysis helps industries to analyze thousands of product reviews in mere seconds. Sentiment Analysis involves four steps: Step 1 is Gathering data, which involves gathering data to analyze and use, for Example, GitHub comment logs. Step 2 is Preparing data for processing, and here the data undergoes a few steps to make it for processing. These steps involve Tokenisation, Lower Casing, Stemming, Removing punctuation, and stop words. Step 3 is the significant step for Sentiment Analysis which is Applying Classifier. We select a classifier that will classify the text into sentiments. Step 4 is the Visualisation of results. In this step, we visualize the results to understand the outcome of the analyzed data.

This paper has compared many machine learning algorithms used for Sentiment Analysis. These algorithms are NLTK, Decision Trees, Random Forest, Support Vector Machine (its kernels, i.e., Linear Kernel, Polynomial Kernel, Gaussian Radial Basis (RBF) Kernel, Sigmoid Kernel), Convolutional Neural Network (CNN), Long Short Term Memory (LSTM) and Ensemble Techniques.

The organization of the paper is as follows. Section 2 contains the discussion about sentiment analysis and the various literature survey related to sentiment analysis.

© ICST Institute for Computer Sciences, Social Informatics and Telecommunications Engineering 2022
Published by Springer Nature Switzerland AG 2022. All Rights Reserved
A. D. Mambo et al. (Eds.): InterSol 2022, LNICST 449, pp. 119–131, 2022.
https://doi.org/10.1007/978-3-031-23116-2_9

Section 3 presents the methodology, dataset creation, pre-processing, and tool selection. Section 4 presented the result analysis and discussion. Section 5 presents the conclusions and future work of the study.

2   Sentiment Analysis

Sentiment Analysis is the management of sentiments, subjective texts, and opinions. The sentiments can be categorized into negative, positive, and neutral. Sentiment analysis is used to determine the emotion of the user automatically. Sentiment analysis is an important research area due to the massive number of daily posts on social media; extracting people's opinions is challenging. Sentiment Analysis allows us to sort large data sets and automatically detect each text's polarity, which saves time and resources [2]. Some Examples of Sentiment Analysis are given in Table 1.

Table 1. Examples of sentiment analysis

Text	Sentiments
I am very happy today	Positive
I have to complete this	Neutral
The weather is terrible	Negative
Dataset is a mixture of words	Neutral

2.1   Advantage of Sentiment Analysis

The advantage of Sentiment Analysis is that it can analyze vast amounts of data quickly, which can be a hassle to do manually. Real-Time Analysis: Industries use it to monitor real-time data and make changes or improvements wherever needed. Consistent Criteria: Analysing sentiment is a subjective task that can be perceived differently when done by two-member and results will probably be biased.

2.2   Related Work

Several authors have conducted several studies on sentiment analysis. An essential aspect in approaching Sentiment analysis is presented in Feldman [3]. The author discussed the techniques to perform sentiment analysis and the various sentiment analysis applications that help us solve real-world problems. The author also discussed how sentiment analysis techniques could solve complex problems that some industries face and simplify their sentiment analysis problems.

Beigi et al. [4] discussed the application of sentiment analysis on disaster relief and the overview of sentiment analysis in social media. The author talks about how sentiment analysis is not limited to politics, business intelligence, and other issues. The author studied the reaction of the local crowd and used such information to improve disaster management. Dolianiti et al. [5] presented the applications of sentiment analysis in education. The author discussed how recognition and emotions are involved in every learning process and how student profiles can enhance information regarding the effective state. The author explored many different ways in which sentiment analysis can apply in the educational domain.

Das et al. [6] discussed real-time stock prediction by analysing the sentiment of Twitter streaming data in their study. The author attempts to make decisions related to finance, such as stock market prediction, to predict a company's stock prices. To perform this task, Twitter streaming data has been considered for scoring the impression carried for a particular firm.

3 Methodology

This study performs a comparative study on different sentiment analysis algorithms. The overall methodology adopted for sentiment analysis is divided into three different parts. First, the data is collected from the dataset used. Second, the sentiment analysis is conducted on the artefacts. Finally, the tool is selected for performing sentiment analysis.

3.1 Dataset

We have used sentiment140[1] dataset. Graduate students of Stanford University create Sentiment140. It contains 1,600,000 pre-classified tweets extracted using Twitter API. The tweets have predefined sentiments (0 = negative, 4 = positive) that have been used for sentiment analysis. It contains six fields target and that is: it is the predefined polarity of the tweet, ids: it is an id assigned to a tweet, date: the date on which tweet is written, flag: query of the tweet, user: the user who has written the tweet, text: Textual content of the tweet. Many other datasets can be used for Sentiment Analysis, but this is the most common dataset.

3.2 Sentiment Analysis

Sentiment analysis contains six different steps: Tokenisation, Lower casing, removing punctuation, removing stop words, stemming, and word embedding. These steps are explained in Fig. 1, and details about these steps are given below.

1) Tokenisation.

Tokenisation is converting a piece of text into tokens. It is the task of converting sentiments into words, called tokens. Tokens are the building blocks of the Natural Language. The common ways of processing raw text happen at the token level. We have used functions of the list to tokenise the text [7].

2) Lower Casing.

The lower casing is converting the tokens into lower case letters. We converted all texts into lowercase so that the processing algorithm does not recognise capital letters and lowercase letters separately. We have used the lower method of string in python for lower casing the text [8].

---

[1] http://help.sentiment140.com.

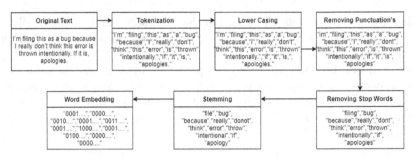

Fig. 1. Steps of data pre-processing for sentiment analysis

3) Removing punctuation.

It helps us optimise text so that the processing algorithm works more efficiently because punctuation does not add more value to sentiment data. We have removed punctuation from the text using a punctuation variable from the string in python [8].

4) Removing Stop Words.

Stop words are words that do not contribute to sentiment analysis. These stop words are a set of commonly used words that carry very little information. Stop words such as: I, am, the, etc. We have used nltk.corpus[2] library to remove stop words from text [8].

5) Stemming.

It is a process of gaining the root word of a word by removing affixes and suffixes. Some examples of stemming are like for word 'confirmed' the stemmed word is 'confirm'. We have used WordNetLemmatizer from nltk.stem[3] library to perform word-stemming [8].

6) Word Embedding.

It represents words in the form of a vector that encodes the value of the word. Word2Vec [9] for Word Embedding allows us to represent each word in unique vectors and represent the relationship between them. We have used Word Embedding for Machine Learning Algorithms such as SVM, CNN and LSTM.

3.3   Tool Selection

After pre-processing data and making it fit our sentiment analysis algorithm, we use different classifiers and algorithms to classify our text into sentiments [10–12]. We used different Sentiment Analysis Algorithms.

1) Natural Language Toolkit (NLTK).

The central concept behind NLP is that we must analyse the dataset by accepting the dataset and reading the data. We read the data and compare it with the dictionary of

---

[2] https://www.nltk.org/api/nltk.corpus.html.
[3] https://www.nltk.org/api/nltk.stem.html.

words to check whether the word is already defined in the dictionary or not. NLP has two main approaches [13].

- Rule-Based Approach—We use a supervised learning algorithm based on a dictionary of words and rules.
- Machine Learning-Based Approach—We use unsupervised data. In this, we use training data as trained data to generate our model.

We are using a Rule-based approach for sentiment analysis. We are using Sentiment Intensity Analyser of nltk.sentiment.vader[4] library. The sentiment IntensityAnalyzer assigns a sentiment score to each token which determines the polarity of the word. Then we take the overall sum of each tweet; if the sum is positive, it is assigned as a positive tweet, but if the sum is zero, then the tweet is assigned as a neutral tweet, or else it is assigned as a negative tweet. The process of sentiment analysis is given in Fig. 2.

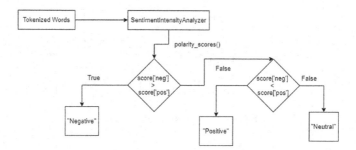

Fig. 2. Process of Natural Language ToolKit (NLTK)

2) **Decision Tree.**

It is a classifier model in a tree where each node represents a feature, and every child node represents an outcome. It uses labels to form a decision tree. The data division is done until the leaf node contains specific minimum numbers of recursion records used for classification [14]. We use categorical variable decision trees as sentiment is divided into three classes positive, neutral and negative. First features are extracted from the text, which acts as nodes in a decision tree. Then the data is fed to a DecisionTreeClassifier from sklearn[5] library, which gives us the polarity of the text. The process is given in Fig. 3.

3) **Random Forest.**

---

[4] https://www.nltk.org/api/nltk.sentiment.html.
[5] https://scikit-learn.org/stable/modules/generated/sklearn.tree.DecisionTreeClassifier.html.

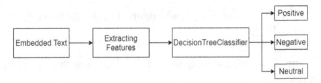

Fig. 3. Process of decision tree

It is an ensemble technique that can use for classification problems. It is a Bagging Problem. It includes Bootstrapping and Aggregation. Bootstrapping is selecting random samples and creating Decision Trees.

Aggregation is the voting of the classifier by checking each Decision Tree and noting the maximum frequency result [14]. We are creating many different decision trees and applying a voting classifier to the predictions of all the trees. The process of applying random forest is given in Fig. 4.

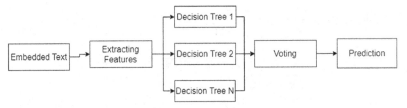

Fig. 4. Process of random forest

4) **Support Vector Machine.**

SVM is a linear classifier that gives non-probabilistic binary values. It is sparse, so it is ideally suited for text classification. In SVM, for a training set of points, we want to find a maximum-margin hyper-plane. The equation of hyper-plane is

$$w^T.x + b = 0 \qquad (1)$$

where $x, w \in R^n, b \in R$
    we need to maximise the margin [14]

$$\min_{w,b,\xi_i} \frac{1}{2} w^T w + \sum_{i=1}^{l} \xi_i \qquad (2)$$

Subject to,

$$y_i(w^T x_i + b) \geq 1 = \xi_i \qquad (3)$$

$$\xi_i \geq 0, i = 1, 2, 3, ..., l$$

Here l is the number of training point

Our approach has experimented with four different kernels used in SVM [14, 15]. The formula for all these kernels are given below:

- Linear Kernal

$$K(x_i, x_j) = x_i^T x_j \tag{4}$$

- Polynomial Kernal

$$K(x_i, x_j) = (x_i^T * x_j + 1)^d \tag{5}$$

- Gaussian Radial Basis Kernal (RBF)

$$K(x_i, x_j) = \exp(-\gamma ||x_i - x_j||^2) \tag{6}$$

- Sigmoid Kernal

$$K(x, y) = \tanh(\alpha x^T y + c) \tag{7}$$

We have first extracted all the embedded text features and then applied an svm classifier from sklearn library. In the classifier, we have used different kernels of SVM to get more accurate results. The process of applying SVM is given in Fig. 5.

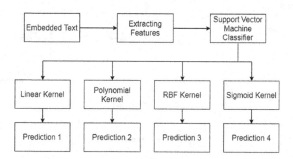

Fig. 5. Process of Support Vector Machine

5) Convolutional Neural Network.

CNN is a Deep Learning algorithm that can take input in the form of matrices and can differentiate one from another by assigning importance to various factors. To extract specific features from the data convolutional layers have many filters known as kernels. As we want to analyse sequential data, we are using temporal convolution. We have used Keras with Tensorflow to implement the CNN model. From Word Embedding, we received the vocabulary of the top 90,000 tweets represented by a 200-dimensional vector. We have trained 2 CNN based models [16–18].

- 3 Layer Convolutional Neural Network—First Layer is a Dropout Layer with parameter 0.4, which drops out 40% of the data from the Word Embedding Layer. Then we have used a CNN Layer with 600 filters of kernel size 3 with zero paddings with a relu activation function. After the Convolutional layer, we have applied a max pool layer. Similarly, two more CNN Layers with 300 and 150 filters, respectively. Then we have used Flatten Layer to flatten the vectors. Then we have used a dense layer with parameter 600, which have a dropout layer with parameter 0.5, which drops out 50% of the output. Then we have used a dense layer with a sigmoid activation function to get the model's output. The process of the 3-Layer Convolutional model is shown in Fig. 6.
- 4 Layer Convolutional Neural Network—First Layer is a Dropout Layer with parameter 0.4, which drops out 40% of the data from the Word Embedding Layer. Then we have used a CNN Layer with 600 filters of kernel size 3 with zero paddings with a relu activation function. After the Convolutional layer, we have applied a max pool layer. Similarly, three more CNN Layers with 300, 150 and 75 filters, respectively. Then we have used Flatten Layer to flatten the vectors. Then we have used a dense layer with parameter 600, which have a dropout layer with parameter 0.5, which drops out 50% of the output. Then we have used a dense layer with a sigmoid activation function to get the model's output. The process of the 4-Layer Convolution model is shown in Fig. 7.

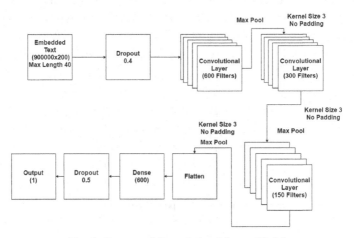

Fig. 6. Process of Convolution 3 Layer Model

6) **Long Short Term Memory (LSTM).**

LSTM is based on RNN architecture used in the deep learning field, and it has feedback connections. It can also process an entire sequence of data points. The core concept of LSTM's is the cell states and their various gates. Information is passed through various gates, which are composed of point-wise multiplication operation and sigmoid layer. The gates can learn what information to keep and forget during training [19–21].

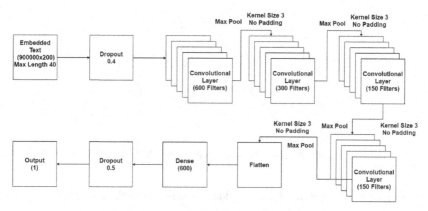

Fig. 7. Process of Convolution 4 Layer Model

We have used Keras with Tensorflow to implement the LSTM model. From Word Embedding, we received the vocabulary of the top 90,000 tweets represented to be a 200-dimensional vector. First Layer is a Dropout Layer with parameter 0.4, which drops out 40% of the data from the Word Embedding Layer. Then we have used an LSTM layer with parameter 128 with relu activation function. Then we have used Flatten Layer to flatten the vectors. Then we have used a dense layer with parameter 600, which have a dropout layer with parameter 0.5, which drops out 50% of the output. Then we have used a dense layer with a sigmoid activation function to get the model's output. The process of the LSTM model is shown in Fig. 8. At the same time, essential components of the LSTM network model are given in Fig. 9.

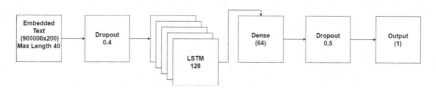

Fig. 8. Process of LSTM Model

- Sigmoid—It is the activation function that gives values ranging from 0 to
- Forget gate—It decides whether to keep the information or forget the formation based on the output of a sigmoid function.
- Input gate—It is used to update cell state. It generates values between 0 and 1 and provides the importance of data.
- Cell State—we can calculate cell state by multiplying cell state by forgetting vector.

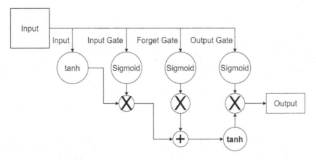

Fig. 9. An essential component of the LSTM Model

• Output gate—It determines the next hidden state for prediction.

7) **Ensemble Technique.**

In the quest to improve accuracy, we have developed a simple ensemble model. We have developed several models and used those models with a Majority vote Ensemble to get the result favoured by most models. We have developed three models for ensemble techniques. They are as follows [22].

• LSTM
• 3-Layer Convolutional Neural Network
• 4-Layer Convolutional Neural Network

we have used a majority vote ensemble to get the final sentimental score. In the Majority vote, we can choose the option coming from a maximum number of models. For example, if we have 3 model ensemble techniques in which two models are giving True, and one model is giving False. So we choose True as a majority of the models are giving True as an answer. The ensemble model is given in Fig. 10.

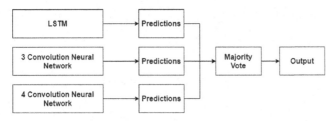

Fig. 10. Process of ensemble model

4   Result Analysis and Discussion

The dataset's data contains some emoticons, URLs, user mentions, symbols, and hashtags, so we need to pre-process the data before using sentiment analysis algorithms. We have implemented several machine learning and deep learning algorithms. Our dataset contains 800,000 negative and 800,000 positive tweets in text format. So for machine learning algorithms, we have converted them in suitable format by using Word2Vec as a Word Embedding Technique [5]. Figure 11, shows a comparison of different machine learning algorithms for sentiment analysis. From Fig. 11, one can be observed that NLTK has a minimum accuracy of 61.2%, whereas the ensemble model has the highest accuracy of 83.88%. Also, in SVM, RBF Kernel has the most accuracy among all the Kernels, as shown in Fig. 11.

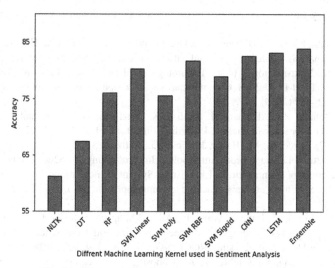

Fig. 11. Comparison of sentiment analysis algorithms

5 Conclusions and Future Work

The Research deals with the different sentiment analysis algorithms we can use and compare their results to get the most accurate results. From our results, we can say that Recurrent Neural Networks like LSTM works best for text classification. We have also created an ensemble model that gives the best results using the majority vote ensemble on three models. For our future work, we can extend the application of our sentiment analysis algorithms. For example, we can use sentiment analysis algorithms to gain knowledge about reviews from Twitter.

For future work, we can extend the application of our sentiment analysis algorithms, for example, sentiment analysis algorithms, to gain knowledge about reviews from Twitter. We can also use it for research purposes like developing a project that can get any topic from twitter and review the topic. For example, in COVID-19, we can gain knowledge about the world's sentiment by analysing tweets. We can also implement Sentiment Analysis algorithms so that they can work with different languages.

References

1. Vinodhini, G., Chandrasekaran, D.: Sentiment analysis and opinion mining: a survey. Int. J. Adv. Res. Comput. Sci. Softw. Eng. **2**(6), 282–292 (2012)
2. Ain, Q.T., Riaz, A., Noureen, A., Kamran, M., Hayat, B., Rehman, A.: Sentiment analysis using deep learning techniques: a review. Int. J. Adv. Comput. Sci. Appl. **8**(6), 424–433 (2017)
3. Feldman, R.: Techniques and applications for sentiment analysis. Commun. ACM **56**(4), 82–89 (2013)
4. Beigi, G., Hu, X., Maciejewski, R., Liu, H.: An overview of sentiment analysis in social media and its applications in disaster relief. In. Pedrycz, W., Chen, S.M. (eds.) Sentiment Analysis and Ontology Engineering. Studies in Computational Intelligence, vol. 629, pp. 313–340 (2016)
5. Dolianiti, F.S., Iakovakis, D., Dias, S.B., Hadjileontiadou, S., Diniz, J.A., Hadjileontiadis, L.: Sentiment analysis techniques and applications in education: a survey. In: Tsitouridou, M., Diniz, J. A., Mikropoulos T. (eds.) Technology and Innovation in Learning, Teaching and Education. TECH-EDU 2018. Communications in Computer and Information Science, vol. 993, pp. 412–427 (2019)
6. Das, S., Behera, R.K., Kumar, M., Rath, S.K.: Real-time sentiment analysis of Twitter streaming data for stock prediction. Procedia Comput. Sci. **132**, 956–964 (2018)
7. Manning, C., Surdeanu, M., Bauer, J., Finkel, J., Bethard, S., McClosky, D.: The Stanford CoreNLP natural language processing toolkit. In: Proceedings of 52nd Annual Meeting of the Association for Computational Linguistics: System Demonstrations, pp. 55–60 (2014).
8. Kawade, D.: Sentiment analysis: machine learning approach. Int. J. Eng. Technol. **09**, 2183–2186 (2017)
9. Wang, J. H., Liu, T.W., Luo, X., Wang, L.: An LSTM approach to short text sentiment classification with word embeddings. In: Proceedings of the 30th Conference on Computational Linguistics and Speech Processing (ROCLING 2018), pp. 214–223 (2018)
10. Jongeling, R., Datta, S., Serebrenik, A.: Choosing your weapons: on sentiment analysis tools for software engineering research. In: proceeding of IEEE International Conference on Software Maintenance and Evolution (ICSME), pp. 531–535 (2015).
11. Ramakrishnan, U., Shankar, R., Krishna, G.: Sentiment analysis of Twitter data: based on user-behaviour. Int. J. Appl. Eng. Res. **10**(7), 16291–16301 (2015)
12. Varsha, S., Vijaya, S., Apashabi, P.: Sentiment analysis on Twitter data. Int. J. Innov. Res. Adv. Eng. **1**(2), 2349–2163 (2015)
13. Pletea, D., Vasilescu, B., Serebrenik, A.: Security and emotion: sentiment analysis of security discussions on Github. In: Proceedings of the 11th Working Conference on Mining Software Repositories, pp. 348–351 (2014)
14. Rahman, M.A., Seddiqui, M.H.: Comparison of classical machine learning approaches on bangla textual emotion analysis. https://arxiv.org/abs/1907.07826 (2019)
15. Goyal, M., Gupta, N., Jain, A., Kumari, D.: Smart government e-services for Indian railways using Twitter. In: Sharma, D.K., Balas, V.E., Son, L.H., Sharma, R., Cengiz, K. (eds.) Micro-Electronics and Telecommunication Engineering, pp. 721–731 (2020)
16. Santos, C.D., Gatti, M.: Deep convolutional neural networks for sentiment analysis of short texts. In: Proceeding of 25th International Conference on Computational Linguistics, pp. 69–78 (2014)
17. Zhang, L., Wang, S., Liu, B.: Deep learning for sentiment analysis: a survey. WIREs Data Min. Knowl. Discov. **8**(4), e1253 (2018)
18. Kim, Y.: Convolutional neural networks for sentence classification. In: Proceedings of the International Conference on Empirical Methods in Natural Language Processing (EMNLP), pp. 1746–1751 (2014)

19. Tang, D., Qin, B., Liu, T.: Document modeling with gated recurrent neural network for sentiment classification. In: Proceedings of the International Conference on Empirical Methods in Natural Language Processing, pp. 1422–1432 (2015)
20. Tholusuri, A., Anumala, M., Malapolu, B., Lakshmi, J.: Sentiment analysis using LSTM. Int. J. Eng. Adv. Technol. (IJEAT) **8**(6S3), 2249–8958 (2019)
21. Kurniasari, L., Setyanto, A.: Sentiment analysis using recurrent neural network. In: Journal of Physics: Conference Series, vol. 1471, p. 012018 (2020)
22. Wang, X., Jiang, W., Luo, Z.: Combination of convolutional and recurrent neural network for sentiment analysis of short texts. In: Proceedings of 26th International Conference on Computational Linguistics, pp. 2428–2437 (2016)

A New Wavelet Based Steganography Method for Securing Medical Data

Aminata Ngom[1(✉)], Sidoine Djimnaibeye[1], Ndeye Fatou Ngom[2], Samba Sidibé[2], and Oumar Niang[2]

[1] Laboratoire LACGAA, Université Cheikh Anta Diop de Dakar, Dakar, Senegal
myangoma@gmail.com

[2] Laboratoire LTISI, Ecole Polytechnique de Thies, Thiés , Senegal

Abstract. The transmission of confidential information over an open communication channel is susceptible to many threats like copyright infringement, eavesdropping and hacking. In this paper, we propose a solution combining data encryption techniques and multiscale signal analysis for securing patients' confidential data. Discrete Wavelet Transform (DWT) is first applied to an ECG signal. The confidential patient information and the electrocardiogram (ECG) signal are then encrypted with the Advanced Encryption Standard (AES) method. Finally, the output of the encryption is hidden in an image to form the stego image and transferred to a medical server. While cryptography ensures the confidentiality of the data modified by the encryption process, steganography enhance the security. The evaluation of the proposed system was performed with real data and quantitative parameters such as Percent Residual Difference (PRD), Mean Squared Error (MSE) and Peak Signal to Noise Ratio (PSNR). The experimental results show the proposed scheme has a good encryption effect and a strong ability to resist detection compared with the existing methods.

Keywords: Wavelet transform · ECG · Steganography · Cryptography · Image processing

1 Introduction

With the advent of telecare medical information systems, data exchanges over insecure support such as the internet become frequent. The security of personal information is one of the most important factors to ensure when it needs to be transmitted between two parties over an unsecured channel. Existing solutions includes cryptography and steganography [9, 16]. Cryptography scrambles the information while steganography conceals the existence of the information in another medium so that the secret information is imperceptible. To address the challenges of transmitting users' personal data in the medical domain, data related to the diagnosis of the patients can be integrated in biometric supports such as electrocardiogram (ECG) signals [8, 14, 22]. To protect personal data, several solutions based on cryptography, watermarking and steganography have been proposed [17, 20, 23]. In watermarking, the secret information is hidden in the host signal by an encryption process using the confidential key and the new signal called

A. D. Mambo et al. (Eds.): InterSol 2022, LNICST 449, pp. 132–143, 2022.
https://doi.org/10.1007/978-3-031-23116-2_10

stego is sent to the receiver via the Internet. The receiver extracts the secret information from the signal by a decoding process using the same secret key. In steganography, the original information is hidden in another cover (images, video, and audio) and forms the embedded message. The embedded message is transmitted to the authorized person via the internet and the latter extracts the real information from the alternative cover. *Ibaida et al.* [14] proposed a steganography algorithm to hide patient information inside ECG signal with five-level wavelet decomposition. They used a scrambling matrix to find the correct embedding sequence with the user-defined key before determining steganography levels for each subband by experimental methods. *Priya and Suganya* [19] made a survey on various steganography methods, in which patient details and diagnosis reports are embedded into ECG signals. They observed that transform domain was mostly used since the spatial domain is prone to attacks such as noise or lossy compression attacks and it may be easily modified by the third party. Recently, several solutions with satisfying results based on information hiding and wavelets transform have been proposed [17,23]. Hybrid methods encrypt confidential information and then hide the encryption data in an image to increase the security level. Among these methods, we have the medical image steganography scheme using individual and double pixel's allocation scheme, three random function and Bit Invert System (BIS) proposed by *Hashim et al.* [10]. *Hureib and Gutup* proposed a method combining elliptic curve cryptography with Image steganography [12]. Recently, a bit mask oriented genetic algorithm based secure medical data transmission mechanism is proposed by *Hari Mohan Pandey* [16].

In this paper, we propose a new data exchange method that combines cryptography and stenography. The proposed approach uses the frequency domain through the discrete wavelet transform (DWT) and the least significant bit based steganography method. Beyond the fact that our solution protects the signal thanks to the DWT method, we have added an AES encryption on the DWT signal and the patient's personal data to make the solution more robust. We have hidden information in an image that will be sent to the medical server. This allows us to make the message sent over the network imperceptible. While cryptography ensures the confidentiality of the data modified by the encryption process, DWT compression ensures a good reconstruction of the ECG signal and steganography ensures imperceptibility of the information sent over the network. To reinforce the security of our proposal, we assume that a mutual authentication protocol [24] between the different users of the medical system (medical staff and patients) is set up. This protocol will allow to have a session key which will be used in our architecture as AES encryption key. We evaluate the effectiveness of the proposed solution for real data and quantitative parameters such as Percent Residual Difference (PRD), Mean Squared Error (MSE), and Peak Signal to Noise Ratio (PSNR). Comparative analysis and experimental results show the proposed scheme has an efficient encryption effect and a strong ability to resist detection.

The rest of the paper is organized as follows. Section 2 presents the proposed methodology. Section 3 presents the experimental results and the performance analysis. Section 4 draw concluding remarks and future scopes.

2   Methodology

In this the section, we highlight our contribution, present the proposed framework, describe the DWT algorithm and present the encryption technique.

2.1   Contribution

Several solutions based on cryptography and stenography have been proposed for securing data [4, 11, 13]. Most of them propose methods that directly apply the coding of the patient's personal information on the support (signal, image, etc.). In this paper, the proposed solution is different because the signal is first compressed using discrete wavelet method before applying encryption and stenography operations. We assume that a mutual authentication protocol between the server and the personal device is set up [24]. This protocol will allow generation of a session key that will be used to encrypt patient personal data. We also take a cover image and apply AES (Advanced Encryption Standard (AES)) encryption to the original signal and the patient's personal data for added security. The steps proposed in [20] were used for preprocessing operation and wavelet coding coefficients. After applying the different steps, we obtain as output the DWT compression of the ECG signal and the patient's personal data that have not yet been transformed. At this level, we use two elements: AES encryption and a cover image. The compressed signal and the patient data are first grouped and encrypted. Then, the LSB (Least Significant Bit) method is used to hide the already encrypted signal and the patient's personal data in an image that will be sent to the medical server (Fig. 2). To obtain information on the patient, the doctor will have to retrieve the stego image (from the server), apply the LSB method to obtain the encrypted personal data of the patient and the compressed ECG signal (DWT). He will then have to decrypt the result obtained (AES) and finally decompress the ECG signal to finally gather all the elements necessary for his consultation (Fig. 3).

2.2   Proposed Framework

The proposed framework first collects the patient's ECG signals using various body sensors. The signals are then sent to the smartphone via Bluetooth, on which the patient's confidential data is stored. Then, on the smartphone, the signals are firstly decomposed using the Discrete Wavelet Transform (DWT), and the AES encryption is applied to the discrete wavelet transformed signal and to the patient's personal data. And finally the output of the AES encryption is encoded into the cover image using the LSB (Least Significant Bit) method and returns the stego image. The LSB method is applied to the stego image to obtain the encrypted information (DWT signal and the patient's personal data). The encrypted information is recovered and decrypted to get the patient's personal data and the DWT signals. Inverse of the DWT (IWT) is applied to the signals to recover the original signals.

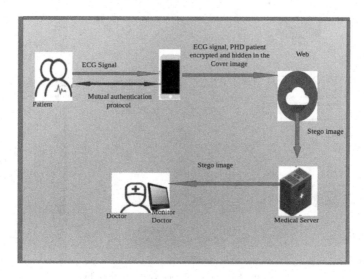

Fig. 1. Workflow

Figure 1 summarizes the different phases of data exchange on the network. The first step corresponds to the sending of the patient's data to the medical server and the second step corresponds to the exchange between the medical server and the medical staff.

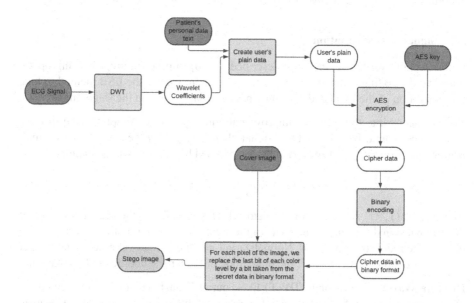

Fig. 2. Block diagram of sender stenography

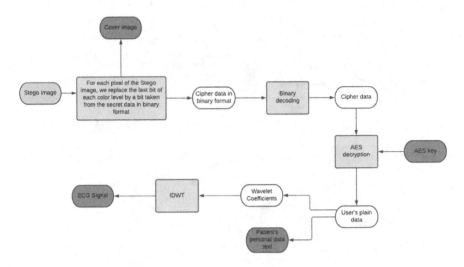

Fig. 3. Block diagram of receiver Stenography

Figure 2 summarizes transformation steps performed on the ECG signal and the patient's personal data (encryption, cover image) from a data collection (at the sensor) to storage (at the medical server). Figure 3 is the reverse process of Fig. 2. This step retrieves the initial ECG signal information and patient personal data that has been encrypted and hidden in a cover image.

2.3 Signal Transformation

In this section, we follow the steps described in [20] to perform preprocessing operations and the coding of the wavelet coefficients. Then, we use the LSB method to hide the encryption of the ECG and the user's personal data to obtain the stego image.

The prepocessing step aims to improve data quality before computing the discrete wavelet coefficient. If x_i is the ECG signal, then the signal y_i generated after normalization, mean removal and zero padding is described by the following equation:

$$yi = [zeros(1, M)(\frac{x_i}{A_m}) - m_x zeros(1, M)] \tag{1}$$

where $zeros(1, M)$ represent a row vector of M zeros, A_m is the maximum value of the original signal, and m_x is the mean of the signal which is normalized. Zero padding reduces the reconstruction error. Normalization and mean removal reduce the number of wavelet coefficients and make the magnitude of the largest coefficient less than one.

Discrete Wavelet Transform (DWT) like Fourier Transfrom (DFT) are method for converting an image from the spatial domain to the frequency domain. However, unlike the DFT which represents a signal in just frequency domain, the DWT can give simultaneous space and frequency representation. In continuous wavelet, the signal is separated into scaled and translated versions $(\psi_{a,b}(t))$ of a single function $\psi(t)$ known as the mother wavelet [7]:

$$(\psi_{a,b}(t)) = \frac{1}{\sqrt{|a|}} \psi(\frac{t-b}{a}) \tag{2}$$

where a and b are the scale and translation parameters with $a, b \in \mathbb{R}$ and $a \neq 0$. The DWT uses a sampling with parameters a and b based on powers of two: $a = 2^j, b = k2^j$ with $j, k \in \mathbb{Z}$. DWT could be written as:

$$d_{j,k} = \int_{-\infty}^{\infty} s(t) 2^{-\frac{j}{2}} \psi^*(2^{-j}t - k) d(t) = (s(t), \psi_{j,k}(t)) \tag{3}$$

The ECG signal is decomposed by DWT up to the fifth levels. The decomposition of the signal is achieved by rotating the signal with a pair of high-pass and low-pass analysis filters to form Quadrature Mirror Filters (QMFs). The output of each filter is sampled by a factor of two. The scale wavelet coefficients are calculated by recursively applying a low-pass signal sampled from the previous scale by a pair of analytical filters. The inverse transformation is obtained starting from the top layer, where the wavelet coefficients are over-sampled by a factor of two, and then filtered using a QMF composite pair. The determination of the decomposition band threshold is done by removing all coefficients lower than a threshold T. The thresholds are selected on the basis of Energy Packing Efficiency (EPE) defined as:

$$EPE_{Di} = \frac{\bar{E}_{CDI}}{E_{CDI}} \times 100 \tag{4}$$

where $\bar{E}_{CDI}$ is the total energy in the detail coefficients of level i after thresholding and E_{CDI} is the total energy in the detail coefficients of level i before threshold determination. The computation of a threshold based on a EPE, is done with the following steps:

1. compute the total energy in the wavelet coefficients X: $E = \sum X^2$,
2. compute the desired retained energy E' and the thresholded coefficients,
3. form the sequence $X_x[K]$ by sorting the magnitudes of the wavelet coefficients in descending order.

Coding the Wavelet Coefficients: The significant coefficients are grouped together in a separate file before being compressed using a variable-length code based on run-length encoding. The code uses 1 bit to identify the run type, 4 bits to represent the number of bits needed to code the run length and represents the binary equivalent of the run length. The header information consists of 64 bits. The first 20 bits are used to store the number of wavelet coefficients, the next bits are used to store the index value of the last significant coefficients, the next 12 bits are used to store the magnitude of the original signal, and the last 12 bits are used to store the mean of the normalized signal.

Least Significant Bit (LSB): LSB steganography is a technique in which least significant bit of pixel is replaced with secret data bits. It has the advantage to be easy to implement and give stego image that contain embedded data without major perceptible distortions. The pixels choice or the order of embedding capacity may be determined by a stego key. General operations of data hiding by using the LSB substitution method are described in [6]. Let C be the original 8-bit grayscale cover-image of $M_c \times N_c$ pixels represented as:

$$C = (x_{ij} | 0 < i < M_c < j < N_c, x_{ij} \in (0, 1, ..., 255)) \tag{5}$$

Suppose that the n-bit secret message M is to be embedded into the k LSBs of the cover-image C. Firstly, the secret message M is rearranged to form a conceptually k_bit virtual image M represented as:

$$M' = (m'_i | 0 < i < n', m'_i \in (0, 1, ..., 2^k - 1)), \tag{6}$$

where $n' < M_c \times N_c$. The mapping between the $n - bit$ secret message $M = m_i$ and the embedded message. $M' = m'_i$ can be defined as follows:

$$m'_i = \sum_{j=0}^{k-1} m_i \times k + j \times 2^{k-1-j} \tag{7}$$

A subset of n pixels $(x_{li1}, x_{li2}, ...x_{ln'})$ is selected from cover-image C in a predefined sequence. The embedding process is completed by replacing the k LSBs of x_{li} by m'_i. The pixel value x_{li} of the chosen pixel for storing the $k - bit$ message m'_i is modified to form the stego-pixel x'_{li} as follows:

$$x'_{li} = x_{li} - x_{li} mod 2^k + m'_i \tag{8}$$

In the extraction process, given the stego-image S, the embedded messages can be readily extracted without referring to the original cover-image. Using the same sequence as in the embedding process, the set of pixels $(x'_{li1}, x'_{li2}, ...x'_{ln'})$ storing the secret message bits are selected from the stego-image. The k LSBs of the selected pixels are extracted and lined up to reconstruct the secret message bits. The embedded message bits m'_i can be recovered by:

$$m'_i = x'_{li} mod 2^k \tag{9}$$

2.4   Data Encryption

Asymmetric cryptography is an encryption algorithm that uses the concept of a key pair. Thus, in asymmetric cryptography, encryption and decryption are performed with different keys. In contrast, symmetric cryptography is an encryption algorithm in which encryption and decryption are performed with the shared key. This shared key is calculated by each party through a mutual authentication and key exchange protocol. *Abd Elminaam and al.* presents a performance evaluation of some symmetric encryption algorithms: AES, DES, 3DES, RC6, Blowfish and RC2 [2]. Following the analysis of the experimental results, they conclude that AES is faster and more resource-efficient.

AES [3] is symmetric-key block encryption with 128, 192 or even 256 bit keys. AES comprises a series of linked operations, some of which involve replacing inputs by specific outputs (substitutions) and others involve shuffling bits around (Fig. 4). AES performs all its computations on bytes rather than bits and treats the 128 bits of a plaintext block as 16 bytes. These 16 bytes are arranged in four columns and four rows for processing as a matrix.

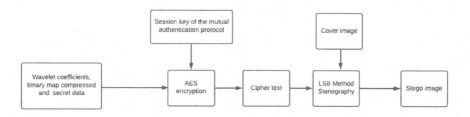

Fig. 4. AES encryption method

3 Performance Measure and Experimental Results

3.1 Data Considered

In this work, we used data from the physioNet apnea-ECG database [1, 18]. The data consist of records varying in length from slightly less than 7 h to nearly 10 h each. The study also considers AES-128 encryption and cover image of size $384 \times 800 \times 3$.

3.2 Assessing the Multiscale Analysis Quality

The compression algorithm was tested on 10 records from the MIT-BIH arrhythmia database. The PSNR (Peak Signal to Noise Ratio), PRD (Percent Residual Difference), and (mean squared error) are used as quantitative performance measures. The results were obtained by first encoding and decoding the real signal file and the compressed signal file (DWT). Figure 5a and 5b give illustrations of the results obtained. We can observe on Fig. 5a the results of the first 5 signals obtained before and after the compression of the signal. We can notice that the PRD varies from 12.3, 12, 11.7, 12.5, 11.9. Figure 5b represents the results of the last 5 signals before and after the compression, and we can observe a variation of the PRD of 11.9, 11.8, 11.3, 10.9, 10.8. The compressed signal is recovered with the personal data of the patient to be encrypted and encoded again in an cover image to form the stego image.

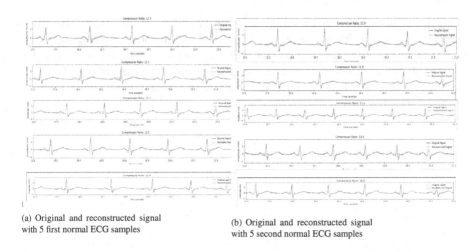

(a) Original and reconstructed signal
with 5 first normal ECG samples

(b) Original and reconstructed signal
with 5 second normal ECG samples

Fig. 5. Original and reconstructed signal with 10 normal ECG samples

3.3   Assessing Effects of the Encryption Process

Comparing stego images with cover image results requires measuring image quality. To evaluate the proposed model, the performance of the proposed technique is measured by using Peak Signal to Noise Ratio (PSNR), Percent Residual Difference (PRD), and the Mean Squarred Error (MSE). PSNR provides information about signal and noise levels. It is a good measure to compare restoration results for the same image. If the image has a high PSNR, it means that the received signal has little interference effect and is therefore faithfully restored. PSNR value shows the peak signal to noise ratio of the original signal and stego image. PSNR is defined as:

$$PSNR = 10 \times log(\frac{P^2}{MSE}) \tag{10}$$

where $P = max(C(i,j), S(i,j))$ is the peak signal value of the cover-image. MSE is the cumulative squared error between the compressed and original image, while PSNR is a measure of the maximum error. A low MSE value corresponds to a low error. MSE is the mean pixel-by-pixel squared difference between the cover image and the hidden image. MSE is defined as:

$$MSE = \frac{1}{M * N} \sum_{i=1}^{M} \sum_{j=1}^{N} [C(i,j) - S(i,j)]^2 \tag{11}$$

where x_i is the original signal obtained from the ECG record, y_i is the reconstructed signal ,and N denotes the number of bits in the input signal [5]. Where, M and N are the rows and columns of the cover image respectively, and $C(i,j)$ and $S(i,j)$ mean the pixel value at position (i,j) in the cover image and the corresponding stego-image, respectively. The distortion between original signal and reconstructed signal is measured by the PRD. PRD is defined through Eq. 12 as follows:

$$PRD = \sqrt{\frac{\sum_{i=1}^{N}(x_i - y_i)^2}{\sum_{i=1}^{N}(x_i)^2}} \tag{12}$$

Table 1 shows the results of the performance of the system by using PRD, MSE and PSNR values for 10 normal ECG. We evaluated the quality of the signal recovered with the PRD and the quality of the image obtained with the PSNR. According to the analysis of *Nemcová et al.* [15], a PRD between [0–4.33] is an excellent result, a PRD between [4.33–7.8] is a very good result, a PRD between [7.8–11.59] is a good result. We can see in Table 1 that our PRD is between [0.11–0.13] where it was observed that the PRD value of Bashar A Rajoub proposal produced 1.06%. We can therefore conclude that we have a satisfactory result of signal compression.

Table 1. Performance analysis

Sample No	PRD %	MSE (db)	PSNR (db)
1	0.13	0.29	53.53
2	0;12	0.30	53.51
3	0.11	0.29	53.48
4	0.12	0.29	53.45
5	0.11	0.30	53.40
6	0.12	0.30	53.40
7	0.11	0.30	53.28
8	0.11	0.30	53.33
9	0.11	0.30	53.31
10	0.12	0.30	53.40

The signal to noise ratio (PSNR) is a measure of the fidelity of a stego image. PSNR is the estimation of the degree of distortion caused in the stego image compared to the original cover image. *Ratnakirti et al.* [21] classified the visual fidelity scale into three groups. For a value of PSNR < 40, the fidelity is low. If $40 < PSNR < 60$, the fidelity is medium. And finally if $PSNR > 60$, then the fidelity is high. For our architecture we have satisfactory results since our PSNR > 50 db.

One significant requirement to certify the security of the encryption method is that a slight change in a plain image should result in a noticeable change in the cipher image. To observe the impact of the encoding on the image we displayed the histogram of the cover image before the encoding process (Fig. 6a) and the histogram of the image (stego) after the encoding process (Fig. 6b) and compared the results of the two histograms before and after the encoding. And we have satisfactory results since there is no remarkable difference between the two images and the two histograms.

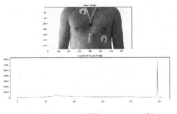

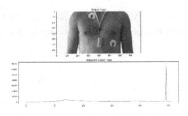

(a) Input image and Histogram of input image

(b) Output image and Histogram of output image

Fig. 6. Output image before and after the encoding process

4   Conclusion

This paper proposes a transmission system based on a combination of encryption approaches (cryptography, steganography) and multiscale signal analysis techniques. The experimental results show the proposed scheme has a good encryption effect and confirmed its performance and its efficiency compared with the existing methods. Future research will focus on using machine learning techniques to choose the region of interest for embedding patients' information and network analysis as an optimization mechanism to secure image information through canal transmission. Another challenge will be using blockchain to better secure data transmission.

References

1. Apnea-ECG Database. www.physionet.org/content/apnea-ecg/1.0.0/. Accessed 9 Nov 2021
2. Abd Elminaam, D.S., Abdual-Kader, H.M., Hadhoud, M.M.: Evaluating the performance of symmetric encryption algorithms. Int. J. Netw. Secur. **10**(3), 216–222 (2010)
3. Abdullah, A.: Advanced encryption standard (AES) algorithm to encrypt and decrypt data, June 2017
4. Abdur Razzaq, M., Shaikh, R., Adnan, M., Ahmed, A.: Digital image security: fusion of encryption, steganography and watermarking. Int. J. Adv. Comput. Sci. Appl. **8** (2007). https://doi.org/10.14569/IJACSA.2017.080528
5. Bhardwaj, R., Sharma, V.: Image steganography based on complemented message and inverted bit LSB substitution. Procedia Comput. Sci. **93**, 832–838 (2016). https://doi.org/10.1016/j.procs.2016.07.245, www.sciencedirect.com/science/article/pii/S1877050916314879
6. Chan, C.K., Cheng, L.: Hiding data in images by simple LSB substitution. Pattern Recogn. **37**, 469–474 (2004). https://doi.org/10.1016/j.patcog.2003.08.007
7. jin Chen, D., Wan, S., Xiang, J., Bao, F.S.: A high-performance seizure detection algorithm based on discrete wavelet transform (DWT) and EEG. PLoS ONE **12**, e0173138 (2017)
8. Cheng, L.T., Yang, C.Y.: High performance electrocardiogram steganography based on fast discrete cosine transform. Int. J. Inf. Control Comput. Sci. **11**(7) (2018). https://doi.org/10.5281/zenodo.1317262
9. Elhoseny, M., Ramírez-González, G., Abu-Elnasr, O.M., Shawkat, S.A., Arunkumar, N., Farouk, A.: Secure medical data transmission model for IoT-based healthcare systems. IEEE Access **6**, 20596–20608 (2018). https://doi.org/10.1109/ACCESS.2018.2817615

10. Hashim, M., Taha, M.S., Aman, A.H.M., Hashim, A.H.A., Rahim, M.S.M., Islam, S.: Securing medical data transmission systems based on integrating algorithm of encryption and steganography. In: 2019 7th International Conference on Mechatronics Engineering (ICOM), pp. 1–6. IEEE (2019)

11. Hashim, M., Taha, M., Aman, A., Hashim, A., Rahim, M., Islam, S.: Securing medical data transmission systems based on integrating algorithm of encryption and steganography. In: 2019 7th International Conference on Mechatronics Engineering (ICOM), pp. 1–6, October 2019. https://doi.org/10.1109/ICOM47790.2019.8952061

12. Hureib, E., Gutub, A.A.: Enhancing medical data security via combining elliptic curve cryptography and image steganography. Int. J. Comput. Sci. Netw. Secur. **20**(8), 1–8 (2020)

13. Hureib, E., Gutub, A.: Enhancing medical data security via combining elliptic curve cryptography and image steganography, Vol. 20, pp. 1–8 , August 2020

14. Ibaida, A., Khalil, I.: Wavelet-based ECG steganography for protecting patient confidential information in point-of-care systems. IEEE Trans. Bio-med. Eng. **60** (2013). https://doi.org/10.1109/TBME.2013.2264539

15. Nemcová, A., Smisek, R., Maršánová, L., Smital, L., Vitek, M.: A comparative analysis of methods for evaluation of ECG signal quality after compression. BioMed Res. Int. **2018** (2018). https://doi.org/10.1155/2018/1868519

16. Pandey, H.: Secure medical data transmission using a fusion of bit mask oriented genetic algorithm, encryption and steganography. Fut. Gene. Comput. Sys. **111** (2020). https://doi.org/10.1016/j.future.2020.04.034

17. Pawar, K., Naiknaware, D.: AES encrypted wavelet based ECG steganography. Int. J. Eng. Tech. **4** (2018)

18. Penzel, T., Moody, G., Mark, R., Goldberger, A., Peter, J.: The apnea-ECG database. In: Proceedings of Conference Computers in Cardiology 2000, vol. 27, pp. 255–258 (2000). https://doi.org/10.1109/CIC.2000.898505

19. Priya, J., Suganya, R.: Steganography techniques for ECG signals: a survey. In: 2016 11th International Conference on Industrial and Information Systems (ICIIS), pp. 269–273 (2016). https://doi.org/10.1109/ICIINFS.2016.8262949

20. Rajoub, B.: An efficient coding algorithm for the compression of ECG signals using the wavelet transform. IEEE Trans. Bio-med. Eng. **49**, 355–362 (2002). https://doi.org/10.1109/10.991163

21. Roy, R., Changder, S.: Quality evaluation of image steganography techniques: a heuristics based approach. Int. J. Secur. Appl. **10**, 179–196 (2016)

22. Edward Jero, S., Ramu, P., Ramakrishnan, S.: Discrete wavelet transform and singular value decomposition based ECG steganography for secured patient information transmission. J. Med. Syst. **38**(10), 1–11 (2014). https://doi.org/10.1007/s10916-014-0132-z

23. Santiago, A.M., et al.: Lightweight security hardware architecture using dwt and AES algorithms. IEICE Trans. Inf. Syst. **E101.D**(11), 2754–2761 (2018). https://doi.org/10.1587/transinf.2018EDP7174

24. Zhang, Y., Xie, K., Ruan, O.: An improved and efficient mutual authentication scheme for session initiation protocol. PLoS ONE **14**, e0213688 (2019). https://doi.org/10.1371/journal.pone.0213688

A Dual Ring Architecture Using Controllers for Better Load Balancing in a Fog Computing Environment

Birane Koundoul[1]([✉]), Youssou Kasse[1], Fatoumata Balde[1], and Bamba Gueye[2]

[1] University of Bambey, Bambey, Senegal
{birane.koundoul,youssou.kasse,fatoumata.balde}@uadb.edu.sn
[2] University of Dakar, Dakar, Senegal
bamba.gueye@ucad.edu.sn

Abstract. Fog Computing is a paradigm that extends cloud computing by bringing network and cloud resources closer to the edge. This means that points of presence are placed close to end users for easy access and to enable delay-sensitive applications to have minimal response times. This Fog layer preprocesses data as close to the sensors as possible. However, with the increasing demand of IoT, even when close to sensors, fog nodes tend to be overloaded, compromising the response times of latency-restricted IoT (Internet of Things) applications, and therefore also compromising the quality of user experience. However, the limited storage and processing capacity leads us to ask the question: wouldn't load balancing be an asset in the Fog Computing environment to avoid overwhelming some fog nodes? It is in this sense that we will exploit load balancing in the Fog Computing environment. We will propose an algorithm for selecting the fog node with the best resource (BRFC) to handle the request. A controller node is placed at each zone to manage data access and placement. This will prevent some nodes from being overloaded or underloaded in order to improve response time, system performance, throughput, cost and even energy consumption.

Keywords: Fog computing · Load balancing · IoT · Quality of service · System performance

1 Introduction

Fog Computing is a geographically distributed paradigm, brings network power and computing to the edge of the network, closer to end users and IoT devices, as it is supported by widespread fog nodes [1]. This technology consists of a set of nodes that are heterogeneous in terms of storage, processing resources. However, these resources are very limited compared to the cloud. Cloud Computing with its almost unlimited storage and processing capacity requires load balancing of physical and virtual servers to better manage system performance. Since

A. D. Mambo et al. (Eds.): InterSol 2022, LNICST 449, pp. 144–154, 2022.
https://doi.org/10.1007/978-3-031-23116-2_11

the emergence of Fog Computing, the goal is to solve some of the problems that Cloud Computing faces. The latter with its almost unlimited processing and storage capacity can handle any type of task with any size. However, with the advent of the Internet of Things, some time-sensitive applications require a minimum response time. This is a hindrance for the traditional cloud. Fog computing was not born to replace cloud computing.

Most of the data requiring analysis, processing and storage is transmitted to the cloud. This can have a negative influence on latency, security, mobility, and reliability because with the existence of delay-sensitive applications, the reduction of response time is necessary. In [2,3], the authors showed that the proximity of the Fog layer to Internet of Things (IoT) devices can remarkably reduce latency and meet the requirements of extremely low latency.

However, as the volume of data sent by these connected objects continues to increase, this results in a reduction in system performance. As a result, load balancing in the Fog Computing environment is a necessity for a better quality of service.

In this paper, we will propose a solution somewhat similar to [4], but we will place a controller at each zone, responsible for managing the load balancing in each zone. This prevents underloading and overloading of some nodes. This controller node stores all the objects of the nodes in the zone.

The rest of the paper is structured as: in Sect 2 presents a summary of related work in the literature. In Sect. 3, we will discuss our model to better understand the load balancing in each zone managed by the controller node. In Sect. 4, we will represent our model as a graph to better understand the role of the controller node. In Sect. 5, we will show the experimental results obtained compared with those of Mostafa et al. Finally, we end the paper in Sect. 6 with a conclusion and propose some directions for future work.

2   Related Work

With the era of big data, the amount of data sent continues to increase exponentially. This is why researchers have tried to provide solutions by proposing algorithms, architectures, etc. to make systems more efficient. It is in this sense that Masip-Bruin et al. have proposed a new Fog to Cloud (F2C) architecture [5], to facilitate the communication between the Fog layer and the cloud layer. They also proposed a management system that allows them to discover the set of fog nodes and choose the best node among the others. This solution, the task can be divided into individual function and in turn also divided according to the fog layers. In addition, this solution, the authors did not explain how the task will be divided into individual functions or even specify the criteria for selecting the most optimal fog node to process the task.

In [4], Mostafa et al. proposed a solution for load balancing in Fog Computing. In their solution, they proposed an algorithm for fog resource selection (FResS) and also enables automatic fog selection and allocation for IoT systems. It is a solution that predicts the execution time using logs. A new module is placed between the Fog layer and the IoT devices. This module consists of a task scheduler, a task manager, a resource selector and a history analyzer. These modules perform various tasks related to resource selection, predictions and history management. In this new module, if a task arrives, they check the logs if the task has been once executed to predict the execution time, waiting times in the queues and data transfer times. Otherwise the task scheduler sends the task description to the task manager to find similar tasks in order to predict the execution time and the resources needed to execute the task. This will lead to the task selector component until logging.

According to Xu et al. in [6], load balancing is one of the key factors to achieve resource efficiency and avoid bottlenecks, overloading or underloading of nodes and low load. In this paper, Xu et al. . proposed a corresponding resource allocation method in a fog environment through static resource allocation and dynamic service migration to achieve load balancing for Fog Computing systems. In this paper, the authors did not consider the negative impact of service migration, including traffic for different types of compute nodes, cost of service migration, performance degradation for service migration, and data transmission cost.

The paper [7], banerjee et al. proposed a distributed resource allocation protocol algorithm to achieve load balancing in a large-scale distributed network. With their algorithm, the response time and resource utilization could be significantly improved over FIFO. However, some preferred to use graph partitioning theory to balance the loads dynamically. This allows us to study the problem of trade-off between energy consumption and delay in F2C scenarios [8,9].

In [10], Souza et al. modeled the service allocation problem as a multidimensional knapsack problem (MKP) aiming at optimal service allocation considering delay, load balancing and energy consumption. It is an algorithm to solve the combinatorial optimization problem. Load balancing is an essential mechanism in the cloud as well as in Fog Computing. Load balancing helps to make networks more efficient. It distributes processing and traffic evenly across a network, ensuring that no device is overwhelmed. Several research works are interested in load balancing to make the system more efficient in terms of storage, processing, network traffic.

Mostafa et al. in [4] have addressed this same load balancing topic at the Fog Computing level. They introduced a new module to interact the fog layer and IoT devices. The role of this module is to predict the execution time of a task in order to reduce latency and manage balancing dynamically in the fog. The module consists of a task scheduler in charge of retrieving the task before sending the information about the task itself to the selector. However, several limitations are to be noted such as: 1) the fault tolerance is not fully ensured with the interconnection of zones. Because if a link between two zones fails, communication between some zones will be possible via the cloud. 2) In addition the bus topology applied in its architecture. This means that the performance decreases according to the number of zones and also if the central link fails, all its network will fail. 3) The location of FResS is not specified in relation to the different zones, which means that it can be a bit far from some zones. This can lead to a long response time. 4) A lack of precision of the duration of the archived data.

Although work is progressing to solve load balancing in cloud computing or fog computing, our proposal allows to manage the load of tasks in the fog to avoid some nodes underloaded or overloaded. Our method is somewhat similar to that of [4], but we will place in each zone a controller node. The controller will schedule, select, and even store objects from the nodes storing the tasks. We will detail in Sect. 3 the placement and access of information according to the controller node.

3 Description of Our Approach with a Controller Node for Load Balancing

In our architecture [11], we proposed a model with three layers. At the Fog layer, interconnected zones in double ring mode are applied Fig. 1. This allows to manage fault tolerance. The controller node manages the placement and reading of data. If a new task arrives, the controller node consults its table to find the location of the task. However, if the task is not present in its zone, with inter-zone communication (A2A), the controller node transfers the task to a neighboring zone. This transfer does not happen randomly because the controller nodes communicate stored objects with each other via messages and an update message is sent after each new task stored or task location changed from one node to another.

In addition, we have represented our model as a graph with the controller node as its vertex. The controller node is connected to all other nodes either directly or indirectly to manage load balancing. All user tasks are redirected to the controller node, knowing the location of all objects stored by the nodes. However, it is still challenging to achieve load balancing for compute nodes in the fog environment when running IoT applications. Considering this challenge, a dynamic resource allocation method managed by a controller node for load balancing in a fog environment is proposed in this paper.

The controller node has some information about the other nodes, such as storage capacity, free memory space, CPU capacity, and RAM capacity. This allows it to select the best node for storing the task. With each new task that arrives, this controller node checks its table (DB) to determine the node with the necessary resources capable of storing the task. In addition to this, the controller node has the ability to transfer data from some nodes to other nodes to handle load balancing. This load balancing makes the system more efficient. According to Xu et al. in [11], due to the diversity of runtime and specifications of compute nodes in the fog, the resources could not be fully utilized. This makes it important to migrate data between nodes.

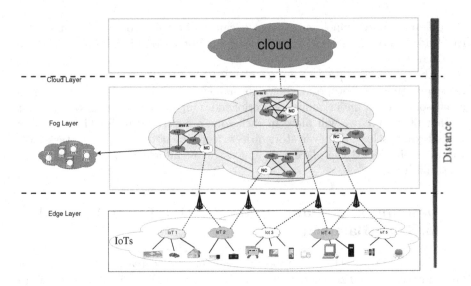

Fig. 1. Architecture for load balancing with the controller node.

3.1 Overview of the Load Balancing Method

Our method consists of four main steps, namely checking the table (database -
DB) to select the node with more available resources (step 2) in order to transfer
the task in this detected node (step 3). In this method, step 1 is to first check the
DB containing all the information of the different nodes. To judge if a node is
able to store the new task, it is necessary to detect the available space of all the
compute nodes (see Fig. 2 of the sequence diagram). The returned information
will allow the controller node to redirect the task to the selected node. Two or
more nodes can be returned and in this case the controller node selects the best
node among the others according to the storage capacity, the bandwidth but also
the number of hops. Another step (step 4) is used for data migration between
nodes. The controller node has the ability to move data from one node to another.
In addition, some workloads from compute nodes with higher resource utilization
are migrated to compute nodes with low resource utilization. Figure 3 illustrates
the migration of data between the different areas performed by the controller
node. Each area is connected to two other areas that they communicate through
the controller nodes. Each task received by the controller node, a check will be
made at the level of its table to select the best zone to transfer the task. After
receiving and processing the task, a message is sent to the original controller
node to update its table.

3.2 Determination of the Shortest Path

In this section, we will explain the method used at the controller node to determine the shortest path. All nodes are connected to the controller node. The

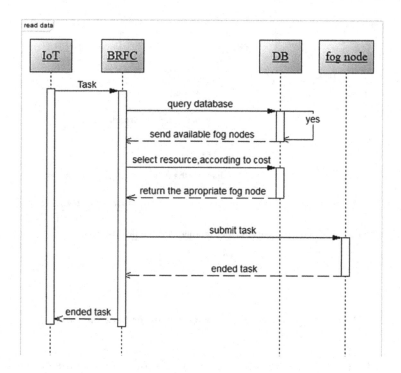

Fig. 2. Diagram for selecting the best fog to handle a task.

shortest path problem is one of the most classical problems in graph theory and the most important in applications especially for optimization problems. If we consider an area as a directed graph G (X, U, L), we associate to each arc u(i, j) a real number l(u) where lij, called the length or weight of the arc. This weight of the arc between two vertices s (source vertex or origin vertex) and d (destination vertex) of the graph allows to determine all the paths from s to d. A path is noted u* whose total length l(u*) is minimal.

Node a is considered the controller node. It is connected to all nodes directly or indirectly. The greedy algorithm is applied, which seeks to build a solution step by step by respecting certain conditions:

- never go back on a decision
- taking at each step the solution that seems to be the best locally
- hoping also to obtain an optimal solution.

Many computer techniques are likely to provide an exact or approximate solution to problems such as determining the minimum and maximum with respect to a function, determining the shortest path between two points, giving change from a vending machine, etc. The glutton algorithm is a possible method for solving these types of problems. It is an algorithm that allows for fast computation time and easy implementation but does not guarantee optimisation.

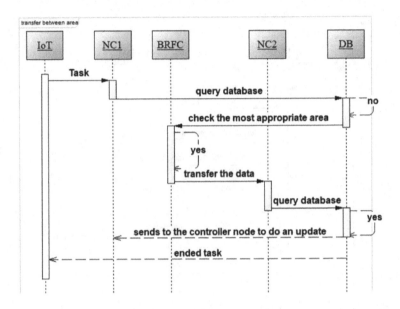

Fig. 3. Sequence diagram for data transfer between areas.

Let e_i be the set of nodes, nb_j = the weight of the arc and s the distance between two vertices (nodes). The algorithm will sort the arc weights in descending order, thus maximising the number of arc weights chosen.

4   Results and Experiments

After simulation with the GridSim tool, we have a better result compared to the proposal of Mostafa et al. in [4]. We used the same parameters to compare our two algorithms. One cloud storage site, three fog storage sites, and 150 IoT devices were defined by the simulator, 500 to 2000 task requests, and varying bandwidth connectivity from 500 MB/S to 2000 MB/S.

Depending on the number of tasks, the result in Fig. 6 shows that our algorithm is better in terms of response time. We see that our algorithm tries to minimize the request agreement time by redirecting some tasks to the neighboring zones. The choice of the zone always depends on the task because the controller nodes communicate the information they store with each other. Each time data is stored, the controller node records the location of the object and sends an update to the controller nodes. This facilitates the redirection of the request in case it is not present in the host area. Table 1 shows the set of cloud computing parameters and fog layer areas and Table 2 shows the characteristics of the tasks.

Table 1. Characteristics of the fog and cloud zones.

Settings	Fog	Cloud
Number of area	3	1
Number of nodes per area	6	12
Latency	[50–100] between area	≈200
CPU MIPS	[500–2000]	[3000–10000]
Bandwidth	500 Mo/s	2000 Mo/s

Table 2. Characteristics of the tasks

Properties	Values
Storage capacity (MB)	[1–10]
Bandwidth (MB/s)	[0,5–1]

The latency between fog nodes in a zone is 10 ms.

The results presented in Fig. 4 show that the adopted BRFC model outperforms the FReSS model, so that the task response time was reduced by 19.10%. In Fig. 5, we have the cost according to the number of users. The *BRFC* model is even better. Of course, as the number of users increases, the cost also increases. However, with our model, we were able to reduce the cost by 28.18% compared to the FReSS model.

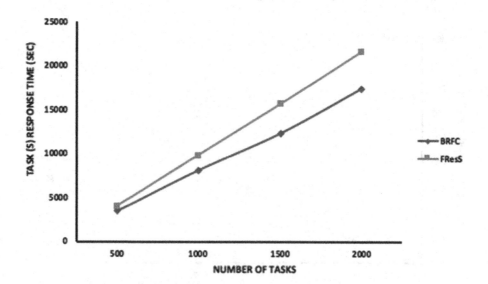

Fig. 4. Response time as a function of the number of tasks.

Finally in Fig. 6, we used the bandwidth to compare the two models. The bandwidth is a very important factor that influences the response time according to the number of users but also according to the number of tasks. The higher the bandwidth is, the more the execution time decreases. The results obtained in Fig. 6 show that we could reduce the total execution time of the tasks by 35.05% compared to the FResS model.

Table 3. Task turnaround time of our BRFC approach compared to the FResS approach.

Number of tasks	500	1000	1500	2000	Total
BRFC	3450	8070	12300	17400	41220
FResS	4000	9780	15600	21570	50950
Between	550	1710	3300	4170	9730

4.1   The Limits of My Model

After simulation with the GridSim tool, we found that our model is better compared to that of Mostafa et al. in [4]. However, some limitations are to be noted in our model such as the trade-off between the storage capacity and the number of objects to be stored. As the number of objects becomes larger, the capacity also increases. In addition, with only one controller node, if the latter fails, inter-zone communication will no longer be possible. This is why we considered

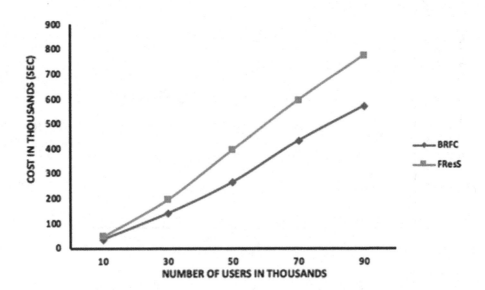

Fig. 5. The cost according to the number of users.

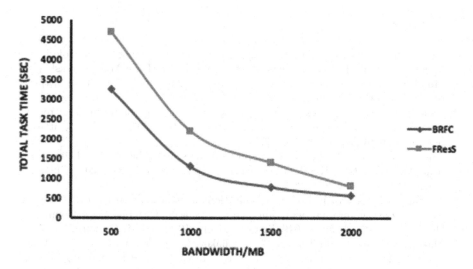

Fig. 6. Total working time depending on the variant bandwidth.

proposing a new model with two controller nodes (a primary node and a secondary node). The data will be redirected to the secondary node if the queue threshold has been reached. In addition to handle the optimization problems with the glutton algorithm, we will use a particular structure named matroid to design an optimal glutton algorithm.

5   Conclusion

Fog computing is an infrastructure that has emerged to solve some of the problems encountered by cloud computing. With the birth of the Internet of Things, load balancing is necessary to avoid overwhelming some fog nodes. In this article we have proposed a model with a controller node in each zone. The role of this controller node is to manage the placement and location of data. Unlike with the model of Mostafa et al. in [4] where a module is placed between the fog environment and the IoT devices to predict task execution times. However, after simulation with GridSim tool, we found our BRFC algorithm better compared to FResS. As the results show. We have reduced 19.10% of the task response time, 28.18% of the cost and 35.05% of the total task execution time. This means that we have a better model compared to FResS.

In addition, with the agreement times increasing with the number of requests. In future work, we plan to improve our model by adding two controller nodes (a primary controller node and a secondary controller node). The new secondary controller node will process new tasks if the threshold set for the agreement queue is reached at the primary controller node. In addition, we will also improve our glutton algorithm to handle the optimization. Finally, we also plan in future work to take into account the number of fog nodes at each zone in an incremental way.

References

1. Bonomi, F., Milito, R., Zhu, J., Addepalli, S.: Fog computing and its role in the internet of thing. In: Proceedings of the first Edition of the MCC Workshop on Mobile Cloud Computing, Helsinki, Finland, août 2012, pp. 13–16 (2012). https://doi.org/10.1145/2342509.2342513

2. Yousefpour, A., et al.: All one needs to know about fog computing and related edge computing paradigms: a complete survey. arxiv180805283vr (2019) https://doi.org/10.1016/j.sysarc.2019.02.009

3. Auluck, N., Azim, A., Fizza, K.: Improving the schedulability of real-time tasks using fog computing. IEEE Trans. Serv. Comput. **15**, 372 –385 (2019). https://doi.org/10.1109/TSC.2019.2944360

4. Mostafa, N.: Cooperative fog communications using a multi-level load balancing. In: 2019 Fourth International Conference on Fog and Mobile Edge Computing (FMEC), pp. 45–51, June 2019. https://doi.org/10.1109/FMEC.2019.8795325

5. Masip-Bruin, X., Marín-Tordera, E., Tashakor, G., Jukan, A., Ren, G.-J.: Foggy clouds and cloudy fogs: a real need for coordinated management of fog-to-cloud computing systems. IEEE Wirel. Commun. **23**(5), 120–128 (2016). https://doi.org/10.1109/MWC.2016.7721750

6. Xu, X., et al.: Dynamic resource allocation for load balancing in fog environment. Wirel. Commun. Mob. Comput. **2018**, e6421607 (2018). https://doi.org/10.1155/2018/6421607

7. Banerjee, S., Hecker, J.P.: A multi-agent system approach to load-balancing and resource allocation for distributed computing. In: Parrend, P., Bourgine, P., Collet, P. (eds.) First Complex Systems Digital Campus World E-Conference 2015. SPC, pp. 41–54. Springer, Cham (2017). https://doi.org/10.1007/978-3-319-45901-1_4

8. Ningning, S., Chao, G., Xingshuo, A., Qiang, Z.: Fog computing dynamic load balancing mechanism based on graph repartitioning. China Commun. **13**(3), 156–164 (2016). https://doi.org/10.1109/CC.2016.7445510

9. Deng, R., Lu, R., Lai, C., Luan, T.H., Liang, H.: Optimal workload allocation in fog-cloud computing toward balanced delay and power consumption. IEEE Internet Things J. **3**(6) , 1171–1181 (2016). https://doi.org/10.1109/JIOT.2016.2565516

10. Souza, V.B., Masip-Bruin, X., Marin-Tordera, E., Ramirez, W., Sanchez, S.: Towards distributed service allocation in fog-to-Cloud (F2C) scenarios. In: 2016 IEEE Global Communications Conference (GLOBECOM), déc. 2016, pp. 1–6. https://doi.org/10.1109/GLOCOM.2016.7842341

11. Koundoul, B., Kasse, Y., Balde, F., Gueye, B.: Leveraging cloud inter-zone architecture for response time reduction. In: Faye, Y., Gueye, A., Gueye, B., Diongue, D., Nguer, E.H.M., Ba, M. (eds.) CNRIA 2021. LNICST, vol. 400, pp. 87–97. Springer, Cham (2021). https://doi.org/10.1007/978-3-030-90556-9_8

12. Xu, X., et al.: Dynamic resource allocation for load balancing in fog environment . Wirel. Commun. Mob. Comput. **2018**, e6421607 (2018). https://doi.org/10.1155/2018/6421607

Recommendation System for Carbon Reduction

Umar Adam Ibrahim$^{(\boxtimes)}$ (ID) and Djadjiti Namla (ID)

Nile University of Nigeria, Abuja, Nigeria
umaradamibrahim@nileuniversity.edu.ng

Abstract. Nigeria is one of the country's most vulnerable to carbon emission (CO_2). A basic understanding of public perception on vulnerability, attitude and the risk in relation to Carbon Emissions and health provide strategic directions for government policy, adaptation strategies and development of guidelines. The aim of this research was to collect data on people's knowledge and perception about Carbon Emissions and their impact on health. A cross-sectional survey was conducted online from 20th to 31 August 2021. A structured questionnaire was used to collect data among 129 people online. This research revealed that respondents had a low and inconsistent understanding of climate change and its impact on health. To reduce carbon emission, we built a carbon emission recommender system, which would calculate carbon emitted by individuals and industries and then suggest alternative resources that can be used to reduce or mitigate carbon emission.

Keywords: Carbon emissions · Footprint · Awareness

1 Introduction

Nigeria is a country in West Africa bordered by Cameroon, Nigeria, Chad, and Benin [1]. Nigeria is the most populous country in Africa, with a population of over 211 million. This huge population has also contributed hugely to the greenhouse gases emitted in Nigeria. According to [2] F gases, Nitrous oxide (N_2O), Methane (CH_4) are non-CO_2 gases emitted while Land-use (LULUCF), Non-Combustion, Building, Transport, Industry and Power & heat are CO_2 emitted in Nigeria. Furthermore, industries have also contributed to the emission of gas in Nigeria. Lack of stable electricity has also pushed the majority of the population to depend on fuel, coal and other high carbon emitted processes of generating power.

At this point let's look at carbon emission: which was defined by [3] as the release of carbon into the atmosphere. Carbon emission refers to greenhouse gas emissions. Additionally, carbon emission is a major contributor to climate change, which is also increasing global warming. Climate change has effect Nigeria in several ways such as high temperatures, floods, drought and changes in weather.

Human activity happens to be a huge contributor to climate change [3]. Human activities comprise greenhouse gas emissions. In addition, the major greenhouse emission is the emission of carbon dioxide. The emission of CO_2 is major caused by fuel-burning

A. D. Mambo et al. (Eds.): InterSol 2022, LNICST 449, pp. 155–162, 2022.
https://doi.org/10.1007/978-3-031-23116-2_12

activities. Human activities such as deforestation, transportation activities and industrial sector activities have increased carbon emission.

Climate changes affected both the humankind and environment; however, human health is impacted by the ecological condition. Climate changes affected human health in many ways such as Asthma, vector-borne diseases, repository disease. Evidence shows that human health and climate change are interrelated.

As a populous country, Nigeria is one of the countries that are vulnerable to climate change because of its geographical location [12]. The result in [12] shows that carbon emission is a major contributor to carbon dioxide and the use of dirty fuel. The huge populations' density, rely on agriculture for food and fuel, wood/coal for energy [2]. Drought, landslides and flooding are types of climate change hazards that have harmed Nigeria. Nigeria's carbon emission has increased by 270%. However, not all hope is lost as the Nigerian government pledged to reduce carbon emission by 20% by 2030 [2].

Pledging and promising to reduce carbon emission, is not the only and final solution. To speed up the process, there is a need to fully engage the citizens of Nigeria. Engaging the citizens will only be fruitful by knowing their level of knowledge and understanding of carbon emission. A survey is one of the methods used in understanding people's knowledge and understanding.

To develop an artificial intelligence solution for carbon reduction in the energy sector. We designed and developed a recommender system for carbon reduction. To achieve that we started by conducting a cross-sectional survey online. The result of the survey is presented in Sect. 3.

Our recommender system would help in monitoring individual/industries' carbon emissions. The system would now suggest to the individual and industries methods/alternative resources to utilize for reducing carbon emission. The contribution of this work can be summarized as follows:

- We ran an online survey to understand people's knowledge/awareness about carbon emission.
- We built an awareness website, where individuals and industries can learn more about causes, effects and solutions for mitigating carbon emission.
- We designed a recommender system for carbon reduction, the goal is to have a system that would track and suggest methods of reducing carbon emission to industries and individuals.
- We finally developed a recommender system for carbon reduction; the system will track industries/individual carbon emissions and hence recommend the necessary materials and equipment that would reduce carbon emission

The rest of this paper was organized as follows: Sect. 2 discusses the related work. Section 3 presented the survey. Section 4 presents the online survey result. Section 5 presents the proposed recommender system. Finally, Sect. 6 concludes the paper.

2   Related Work

According to [2] in 2015 Nigeria was the world's 17th largest greenhouse gas emitted. Moreover, it is Africa's largest oil producer and the world's 9th largest exporter. It is projected that Nigeria will overtake China in the nearest future to become the world's second-most populous country. Unfortunate more than a 3rd of Nigerians lack access to electricity and rather depend on wood, charcoal etc.

The aim of the paper [4] was to gather data on people's knowledge and perception about climate change and its effects on health. They conducted a cross-sectional survey among 7 vulnerable districts of Bangladesh. 6720 people participated who are from 224 rural areas. They used a structured questionnaire method with an observational checklist in collecting data from households. The research shows that 54.2% had some knowledge of climate change, however, 45.8% do not. The research also shows that educational qualification and monthly income, occupation and age is also associated with knowledge about climate change. The research concluded to emphasize the need for policy marker to introduce a climate change child centre education and training for health workers.

Paper [5] ran a cross-sectional study to understand the knowledge and awareness of adolescent people in Yogyakarta. The survey results show that the youths have less knowledge and awareness about climate change. Hence, the recommended that there is a need to improve adolescent knowledge of climate change. From the survey, they find out that only less than 15% of respondents believe that climate change is a very important problem. The majority of the respondents do not see climate change as an important problem. 50% of the respondents feel the climate change argument is not convincing. Participants do not also know that climate is caused by human activities. The above outcome suggested that there is a need to incorporate climate change in the curriculum of high education. This is to close the knowledge gap and also enhance adolescent knowledge about climate change.

Paper [6] also conducted a survey to investigate health risks in Nigeria caused by climate change. The research pointed out that climate change has greatly caused a serious health problem in Nigeria. These health risks are malaria, high blood pressure, skin cancer, cardiovascular respiratory disorder and other health issues. The research recommended that government should raise awareness of the adverse effect of climate change. The impact is among vulnerable groups such as children, women and people in rural areas.

According to [7] the China government adopted public awareness and understanding method to promote the development and deployment of Carbon dioxide Capture, Utilization and Geological Storage (CCUS) technology. This public awareness and understanding were done via a national survey. The aim of the survey is to understand the public awareness and understanding regarding the environmental impact & management of CCUS technology. The result indicated that the awareness of the high environmental impact of the technology by the public has negatively encouraged lower acceptance of the system by the public. It has also indicated that there are high expectations from the government department to play a major role in managing the environment. Finally, the ability to communicate and inform the public about the importance of CCUS technology via open lectures, traditional and media channels and government agencies can reduce the high negative assumed risk by the public, thus enhancing public acceptance of the technology.

The building sector has posed a lot of issues and challenges when it comes to the reduction of carbon emission [8]. The work presented solutions that can be adapted to control the urbanization of cities. These solutions include introducing standard policies, impact assessment of building processes and adopting low carbon technology and the reduction of energy utilization.

The work done by [9] explored whether using a health framework can encourage behavioural reductions of greenhouse gas in the US. To promote behavioural reductions of greenhouse gas emissions and adaption measures. The feels using the health frame will really motivate citizens to reduce the amount of carbon they emit. Using random digit dialing they conducted a cross-sectional survey in United State. The health threat from a personal perspective was explored. The data were analyzed via logistic regressions and path analysis. 771 people participated in the survey. 81% acknowledged that climate change was happening. Participants stated that they are ready to reduce energy consumption if they are convinced that climate change could affect their way of life.

In Nigeria to understand the awareness of climate change and sustainable development among undergraduates in two major universities in Oyo state Nigeria. Paper [10] primary aim was to improve the knowledge of climate among undergraduates. 300 undergraduates were selected randomly from these two universities. The data collected was analyzed using a simple percentage and T-test. The research presented that there is a high level of awareness on the concept of climate change. Education, personal experience and access to information were great influencer factors to the awareness. However, there is still a gap in awareness; the study recommended that climate education needs to be structured and integrated into school curricula at all levels.

To ascertain the level of awareness regarding climate change among tertiary institution students in Taraba state Nigeria. In [11] a descriptive survey was conducted among 225 students. A structured questionnaire was conducted among participants. The survey outcome indicated that 18.2% have never heard of climate change. While 81.8% heard about climate change, 89% do not even know what climate is all about, its causes, effects and mitigations measures. The study suggested that there is a need for a climate change awareness club in Jalingo tertiary institutions.

In [13] pointed out that with the huge amount of data and information on the internet. It is difficult for users to select or decide on what to buy. Hence, a recommender system is an intelligent computer-based system that predicts based on user usage and adoption and helps to suggest an item from a huge pool of items. Their major work centred on providing comprehensive research on recommender systems. They presented the approaches, associated issues and techniques used for information retrieval.

3 Survey

In this study, an online survey was conducted. Responses were collected from 20 August 31 August 2021. We used to google form to create an online survey term: Carbon Emission Awareness in Nigeria. The survey was divided into 3 sections, which are Sect. 1 basic information, section Climate change awareness and Sect. 3 Attitude towards climate change.

In Sect. 1 majority of the responders are male, and the majority are of age 15–20. Furthermore, the majority of the responders are residing in the north-central geopolitical zone, and generally, they stay in the federal capital. Finally, people with BSc-HND have the highest responders.

In Sect. 2, 97.7% believe climate change exists which is a good number. For the question that asked how well people understood what carbon emission is and how it affects the environment. The majority of responders have a piece of average knowledge about carbon emission and its effect. That means there is a need for more awareness and sensitization. 82.9% understand the causes of global warming. Finally, in Sect. 2 we have an open-ended question, which answers displayed in Fig. 1.

In Sect. 3, we asked about the attitude towards climate change, 30.7% of people are extremely concerned about climate change. While 29.9% are average concerned about climate change, which is a huge number. For mitigation, 72.4% agreed they would contribute to mitigating climate change if they had the information. We also have three open-ended questions which comments were shown in Fig. 2.

4 Result

This section presented the result pulled out from our survey. Due to limited time, we had to stop the survey. As stated, the above section comprises basic information, Sect. 2 awareness while Sect. 3 was the attitude towards climate change.

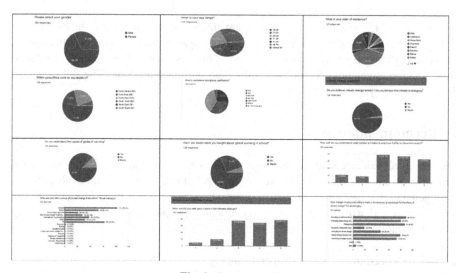

Fig. 1. Survey result

5 Calculator

Knowing the amount of carbon we emit based on our daily activities is called "carbon footprint" [14]. Knowing our carbon footprint would also help also in reducing the amount of carbon we emit and this is the current trend used for mitigating carbon emission. Scientists believe individuals are also a major contributor of emission based on their activities and fuel/power consumption and usage. According to [14] the bigger our carbon footprint the larger our carbon emission to the society. Family can also help by reducing their carbon footprint. However, we can only reduce our carbon footprint when we have knowledge of the amount of carbon we emit daily according to our activities.

There are many carbon footprint calculators, which are designed and developed, based on the situation in Europe and US. Meaning currently there is no official carbon emission calculator made for Nigeria. Based on our knowledge the closest work on carbon footprint was the research done in Lagos state [15]. However, they did their calculator manually, which is a tedious process and time-consuming method.

The calculator was integrated with a recommender system. The essence is for the recommender algorithm to suggest ways and processes that individuals and industries can use in reducing their carbon footprint.

6 Recommender System

According to [13] recommender system are intelligent computer that helps users in making a decision. The goal of our recommender system is to help in reducing carbon emissions. This system will calculate users'/industries carbon footprint. Then suggest another alternative for reducing and mitigating carbon emissions. The below image depict how the system would function.

7 Recommendation

Our survey shows that majority of the responders have little knowledge about carbon emission, its cause and impact. However, the level of education influenced this output. This generated a new question that is what about people that have less educational qualification and worst-case serious non-educated people. This led to the following recommendation

- There is a need to run a pen and pencil survey.
- There is a need to organize seminars, training and workshop in remote and rural areas
- There is a need for the government to engage individuals, NGOs and industries.
- There is a need to incorporate climate change education in all curricular rights from primary to tertiary institution.

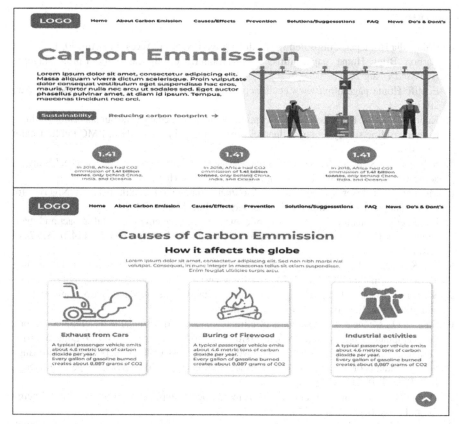

Fig. 2. Recommendation system

8   Conclusion

The awareness level of the survey responders on carbon emission was more than our assumption and perception of people on changing climatic factors and their impacts on health is higher. There is a need to run a physical survey for people in remote and rural areas. This is to ascertain the carbon emission knowledge level in these vulnerable areas. Further to protect our next generations a carbon emission education needs to include in our educational curriculum at all levels.

For future work to get an effective working recommender system there is a need to build a calculator based on Nigeria's reality and factors. This calculator can accurately monitor carbon emissions from individuals and industries. These would help the system in suggesting other alternatives to reduce carbon emission and ways to mitigate it.

Acknowledgement. This work was supported by Google Africa travel Grants. We would like to express our deep and sincere gratitude to all the participants.

References

1. Wikipedia Homepage. https://en.wikipedia.org/wiki/Nigeria. Accessed 1 Aug 2021
2. Carbon Brief Home page. https://www.carbonbrief.org/the-carbon-brief-profile-nigeria. Accessed 1 Aug 2021
3. Ecolife Home page http://www.ecolife.com/define/carbon-emission.html. Accessed 1 Aug 2021
4. Kabir, M.I., et al.: Knowledge and perception about climate change and human health: findings from a baseline survey among vulnerable communities in Bangladesh. BMC Public Health **16** (2016)
5. Sulistyawati, S., et al.: Assessment of knowledge regarding climate change and health among adolescents in Yogyakarta Indonesia. J. Environ. Public Health **2018** (2018)
6. Monday, I.F.: Investigating effects of climate change on health risks in Nigeria. In: Environmental Factors Affecting Human Health. IntechOpen (2019)
7. Li, Q., et al.: A national Survey of Public awareness of the environmental impact and management of CCUS technology in China. ScienceDirect, Energy Procedia **114**, 7237–7244 (2017)
8. Ali, K.A., et al.: Issues, impacts, and mitigations of carbon dioxide emissions in the building sector. Sustainability, **12**(18), 74727 (2020). www.mdpi.com/journal/sustainability
9. Semenza, J., et al.: Climate change and climate variability: personal motivation for adaptation and mitigation. Environ. Health **10**(1), 46 (2011)
10. Sola, A.O., Micheal, E.: Awareness of climate change and sustainable development among undergraduates from two selected Universities in Oyo State, Nigeria. World J. Educ. **6** (2016)
11. Oruonye, E.D.: An assessment of the level of awareness of the effects of climate change among students of tertiary institutions in Jalingo Metropolis, Taraba State Nigeria. J. Geogr. Reg. Plan. **4**(9), 513–517 (2011)
12. Ogundipe, A.A., et al.: CO_2 emission and environmental implication in Nigeria. Int. J. Energy Econ. Policy **10**(3), 317–324 (2019)
13. Isinkaye, F.O., et al.: Recommendation systems: principles, methods and evaluation. Egypt. Inform. J. **16**, 261–273 (2015)
14. www.energystar.gov
15. Bola-Popoola, A.G., et al.: Investigation and quantification of carbon footprint in Lagos megacity. Congent Eng. **6**, 1703470 (2019)

Engineering Impact on Sustainability Development

Assessment of Heavy Metal Concentrations of Municipal Open-Air Dumpsite: A Case Study of Gosa Dumpsite, Abuja

Djadjiti Namla[1]([⊠]) , George Mangse[1] , Peter O. Koleoso[2] ,
Chukwuma C. Ogbaga[1] , and Onyinye F. Nwagbara[1]

[1] Department of Biological Sciences, Microbiology and Biotechnology, Faculty of Natural and Applied Sciences, Nile University of Nigeria, Abuja, Nigeria
namla.djadjiti@nileuniversity.edu.ng

[2] Department of Computer Sciences, Faculty of Natural and Applied Sciences, Nile University of Nigeria, Abuja, Nigeria

Abstract. Heavy metals are among the major components of municipal solid wastes with a high atomic weight and a minimum density five times that of water. These metals pose serious environmental and health problems. This study was conducted to determine the concentrations of selected heavy metals- Lead (Pb), Cadmium (Cd), Copper (Cu), Zinc (Zn) and Manganese (Mn)- in a solid waste site, Gosa dumpsite, Abuja. These heavy metals were studied during the 2019 dry season using Atomic Absorption Spectroscopy. Six soil samples were collected from six different points from the main dumpsite. Soil samples were digested and the physicochemical parameters such as particle size, pH, Cation exchange capacity, exchangeable cations and analysis of the soils were carried out using standard procedures. The results revealed variations in the physicochemical parameters in the different study points. Notably, there was a high level of Pb (1.382 ± 1.223 mg/l), Cd (0.257 ± 0.022 mg/l) and Mn (0.615 ± 1.347 mg/l) which exceeded the WHO (Pb: 0.010 mg/l, Cd: 0.001 mg/l and Mn: 0.050 mg/l) and SON (Pb: 0.010 mg/l, Cd: 0.003 mg/l and Mn: 0.200 mg/l) limits for agricultural and industrial soils. However, Cu and Zn were within WHO and SON permissible limits. These results were similar in the soil samples obtained from the main dumpsite and the nearby study points within the Gosa village. The high levels of Pb, Cd and Mn may be attributed to the transfer and infiltration of leachate from the dissolved materials in solid waste from the dumpsite.

Keywords: Gosa village · Municipal solid waste · Open air dumpsite · Heavy metals

1 Introduction

Uncontrolled dumpsites in open-air areas are generally observed in many parts of the world, especially in developing countries—and Nigeria is a typical example [1]. Dumpsites attract flies and insects (which are eventually pathogenic vectors) that considerably

© ICST Institute for Computer Sciences, Social Informatics and Telecommunications Engineering 2022
Published by Springer Nature Switzerland AG 2022. All Rights Reserved
A. D. Mambo et al. (Eds.): InterSol 2022, LNICST 449, pp. 165–174, 2022.
https://doi.org/10.1007/978-3-031-23116-2_13

impact human health by causing diseases. Communities living near an open-air dump-site, particularly individuals commonly known as scavengers who always get in contact with wastes are susceptible to developing health disorders. But a landfill is properly designed and offers a great advantage over the open one [2]. It is a more efficient system that helps minimize environmental issues thereby reducing health risks [2]. Gosa inhabitants are fond of indiscriminate disposal of both liquid and solid municipal wastes. Thus, the Gosa dumpsite is characterized by drained sandy loamy and clay loamy soils from different locations of the site, mountainous heaps of solid waste and refuse packs dumped openly besides households mainly at the backyards of the village. Besides, the villagers openly dispose of solid wastes, including faeces, and any types of wastes close to their houses.

Heavy metals are among the major components of municipal solid wastes, found naturally with a high atomic weight and a minimum density five times that of water. Because of their toxic and tenacious nature, these metals pose serious environmental and ecological threats as a result of the poor disposal of solid wastes. Substantial heavy metals are created from two sources-natural and man-made. The natural source is a result of filtering of metal stores and standard rocks while the man-made sources incorporate metal refining, industrial effluents, and solid waste disposal [3]. For instance, Lead (Pb), and Nickel (Ni) which are man-made are derived from coal and gas, whilst Manganese (Mn), Cadmium (Cd), and Zinc (Zn) are obtained from batteries that are improperly disposed of [4].

Most of the metals get into the ground, form leachate and runoff into our waterways [5]. They either become volatilized or are tied up in the soil due to their ability to form volatile species through natural biogenic processes [6]. The soil is inhabited by many species and families of microorganisms such as the total heterotrophic bacteria (THB) and the rhizobia. These soil microbes are very important as they perform various functions in the soil which include improving soil structure and soil aggregation, recycling of soil nutrients and water recycling [6]. In fact, the soil is constantly infected through human activities through the unintentional launch of chemical substances or the wrong method of hazardous waste disposal. In addition, plants located on and or around the waste dumpsites have the tendency to accumulate heavy metals in their cells especially in the edible parts with potential health implications when consumed. Likewise, the high fixation levels of the metals hamper the physical, synthetic, and organic functionalities of the soil altering plant growth and soil microorganisms and can be toxic to humans [7].

On account of the environmental concerns, the fate and adverse effects of heavy metals have gained considerable interest in the past few years. Thus, this paper focuses on the determination of the concentrations of heavy metals in soil with emphasis on Gosa dumpsite, Abuja.

2   Materials and Methods

2.1   The Study Area and Samples Collection

Gosa village is among the dirtiest satellite towns in Abuja. It is located along the ever-busy Airport Road, opposite the popular Gosa market. The dumpsite at Gosa is one of the largest open-air and uncontrolled dumpsites in Abuja and is characterized by drained sandy loamy and clay loamy soils. The dumpsite also has mountainous heaps of solid waste and refuse packs dumped openly near households and mainly at the backyards of the village. The figure below shows the geographical representation of the Federal Capital Territory and the main Gosa dumpsite. The figure also shows the sampling points- the centre of the main dumpsite (9.0246320, 7.3390300), two meters (9.0256520, 7.3388750), four meters (9.0269286, 7.3389735), and six meters away from the centre (9.0275780, 7.3394782), then two randomly selected points from the main Gosa village (9.0324889, 7.3369012) and (9.0369600, 7.3396130). Soil samples were collected during the 2019 dry season at a depth of between 15–30 cm from each point using a soil auger. Collected soil samples were transferred into sterilized plastic containers and transported to the laboratory for chemical analyses (Fig. 1).

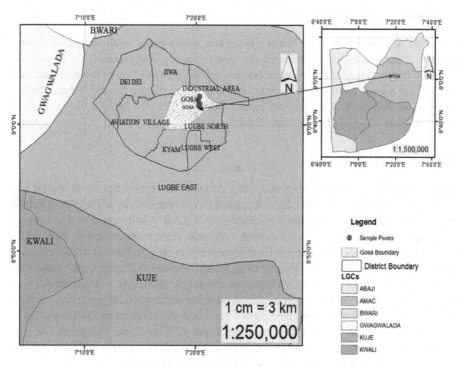

Fig. 1. Map displaying the Abuja districts and Gosa boundaries with the sampling points

2.2 Physicochemical Analysis

To evaluate the soil quality, physicochemical properties of the soil were determined. The percentages of sand, silt and clay as well as the texture of the collected soil samples were determined using the Jar test technique. Soil pH was determined at a ratio of 1 part soil to 5 parts potassium chloride solution, using a digital pH meter. Cation concentration of the soils was determined using the pH 7 ammonium acetate (NH$_4$OAc) method, as described by [8], which is a modified method of [9]. The Effective Cation Exchange Capacity (ECEC) was computed by the summation of exchangeable bases. While the base saturation (BS) was computed as the sum of basic cations expressed as a percentage of ECEC. The electrical conductivity of the soil was measured following the method of [10]. The digital conductivity meter was employed to measure the soil electrical conductivity, using the same soil solution that was used during the determination of the soil pH. Soil organic matter (SOM) was determined using the wet acid dichromate digestion and ferrous ammonium sulphate titration method of Walkley-Black measurements of soil organic carbon (SOC) following a modified procedure from [11]. The total Nitrogen was determined following a modified method of [10]. Phosphorus from the testing soil sample was measured with a spectrometer using the molybdenum blue colour method.

2.3 Digestion of Soils

The soils were sieved with a 2 mm sieve. Prior to the metal analysis, the remaining portion of each collected sample was digested following [10] method. 2 g of soil was weighed into a conical flask. 10 ml of Nitric acid (HNO$_3$) and 2 ml of hydrochloric acid (HCl) were added and the mixture was heated at 95 °C till the volume reduced before being allowed to cool. And then the cold solution was filtered using a filter paper and distilled water was added to make it 50 ml.

2.4 Heavy Metals Analysis

Heavy metal analysis was performed using Atomic Absorption Spectroscopy (iCE™ 3300 AAS, Thermo Scientific, MA, Boston, USA) connected to a Thermo Scientific SOLAAR™ software. The Thermo Scientific SOLAAR™ software contained pre-set spectrophotometer parameters for copper, cadmium, lead, manganese and zinc, which were used to measure the samples. Each measurement was performed in triplicate and the fast resample method was adopted to speed up the analysis. Copper, cadmium, lead, manganese and zinc stock standard solutions containing 1000 mg/L of these metals were diluted with a pre-mixed solution of deionized water and analytical grade concentrated nitric acid to provide working standards of various concentrations in 2% (w/v) HNO$_3$. The calibration blank solution used throughout was a 2% w/v HNO3 solution. The calibration curve was obtained using the calibration standards that were manually prepared. The method of quadratic least-squares fit was used for the calibration.

3 Results and Discussion

3.1 Soil Particles Size

The results for soil particles size were expressed in percentage (Table 1). Sand had the highest percentage in terms of soil particle size, across all the soil samples, with an average of 57.51%, higher than that of the control soil obtained from the botanical garden of Nile University of Nigeria. However, from all the collected soil samples, clay had the least percentage of particle size with 13.96%. These results are comparable to those of [8] and [12], using surface and middle slope soils respectively. The results from the physical properties of the soil samples indicate that sand is the prevalent soil particle, and the dominant soil texture is loamy-silt across all collected soil samples. According to [4] and [12], this texture limits the proliferation of microorganisms and the mineralization of natural matter.

Table 1. Percentage particle size fraction (%) of the soil samples

	Height of each layer (cm)				Percentage of particles		
	Sand	Silt	Clay	Total	% Sand	% Silt	% Clay
CT	3.50	1.30	0.80	5.60	62.50	23.21	14.29
2M	3.60	2.15	0.75	6.50	55.38	33.08	11.54
4M	4.20	1.55	1.00	6.75	62.22	22.96	14.81
6M	3.90	3.00	0.80	7.70	50.65	38.96	10.39
VP1	4.75	3.00	1.75	9.50	50.00	31.58	18.42
VP2	4.50	1.50	1.00	7.00	64.29	21.43	14.29
CON	3.3	1.8	1.5	6.6	50.00	27.30	22.70

CT = Centre, CON = Control area, 2M = 2 m, 4M = 4 m, 6M = 6 m, VP1 = first point from the village and VP2 = second point from the village
% Sand = (Height of sand)/(Total height) *100
% Silt = (Height of silt)/(Total height) *100
% Clay = (Height of clay)/(Total height) *100
Total height = height of the three particles

3.2 Soil Organic Matter (SOM)

The SOM results revealed that the soils from Gosa dumpsite have relatively low organic matter compared to the control soil (1490.00 mg/kg^{-1}) and to [13] standard (Table 2).

CT = Centre, CON = Control area, 2M = 2 m, 4M = 4 m, 6M = 6 m, VP1 = first point from the village and VP2 = second point from the village. The soils from this study area have a slightly high clay content (mainly from the central portion of the main dumpsite). This is due to the build-up of non-biodegradable substances over the last 35 years since the dumpsite became operational [14]. The non-biodegradable substances include clothes, papers, plastic bags, buckets, tin cans, sacks, glass bottles, water sachets and strong waste.

Also, the inordinate parts of natural matter in the soil from the Gosa dumpsite may also be due to different kinds of metropolitan solid wastes released inside the dumpsite, like paper, utilized batteries, electronic merchandise, wood, plastic paper, straws, containers, metal jars, snacks, garments, glass bottles, cotton fleece, food squander, leaves, organic product waste, medication bottles, froths, cinders, water sachets, cardboard, and human excreta [14]. Previous researchers attribute this high level of organic matter in

Table 2. Mean values of carbon, available Phosphorus (Av. P), azote, organic matter and C/N ratio of soil samples

Mg/kg^{-1}					AV. P
	SOC	SOM	TN	C\N	
CT	703.80	1210.50	83.00	8.50	89.50
2M	623.26	1072.00	79.00	7.90	71.12
4M	633.72	1090.00	88.00	7.20	43.12
6M	581.40	1000.00	108.00	5.40	40.00
VP1	546.50	940.00	62.00	8.80	65.00
VP2	610.47	1050.00	980.00	0.62	63.00
CON	866.28	1490.00	41.29	21.00	24.80

soils from a dumping site to the ubiquitous availability of non-fermentable materials present in the wastes, which are barely decomposed and therefore break down very slowly [12]. Also, the slow decay of soil natural matter is likely because of a reduced flow of oxygen in the dumpsite supported by [15].

3.3 Soil pH

The results from the concentration of the hydrogen ion analysis revealed that the soil pattern from the centre of the dumpsite is acidic. And as for the two randomly selected points from the Gosa village, the first point had a water pH of 6.90 while the second point revealed acidic pH. However, the pH variation (ΔpH = pHwater - pH KCl) of soil samples from the dumpsite soil was ΔpH <1, displaying excess acidity. Thus, the soil from the centre and soil collected at points located far away from the centre were strongly acidic, with the water pH ranging from 5.98 to 5.56.

According to [16], soils with an acidic pH (less than 6) have little amounts of Ca^{2+}, Na^+, Mg^{2+} and K^+ cations. Whereas, the soils possessing pH less than 5 have significant amounts of manganese concentrations.

The slight acidic content of the dumpsite soil could be due to the age of the waste, which is similar to the findings of [12]. According to their assertion, the pH - value of soil from a dumpsite diminishes consistently upon waste disposal. They likewise referenced that the impartial causticity (water pH = 6.90 and pHKCl = 6.20) of the open dumpsite soil can diminish the soil micronutrient accessibility for flora and favour the improvement of metallic accumulation.

3.4 Soil Cation Exchange Capacity

Cation exchange capacity (CEC) is defined as the fundamental soil property that helps predict plant nutrient availability. In this study, Calcium (Ca^{2+}) had the dominant basic cation within the complex, with a range of 1.0–4.5 cmol.kg^{-1}, followed by potassium (K^+) with a range of 0.25–3.34 cmol.kg^{-1}, Mg^{2+} (ranging from 0.15–2.15 cmol.kg^{-1}), and Na^+ (ranging from 0.04–0.73 cmol.kg^{-1}), across all collection points of the study site (Table 4). The value of the cation exchange capacity (CEC) of the soil diminishes with regards to proximity to the dumpsites. Our result is consistent with the findings of [12]. However, the first point selected from the village had the highest exchange value of 11.74 cmol.kg^{-1}. The difference in the Base Saturate (V) ranged from 57.39 to 87.22% between the study points. Also, the results showed that these soils were strongly desaturated ($58\% < V\% < 89\%$) with a high exchange acidity, regardless of the point of collection from the study site (Table 3).

Table 3. Mean values of pH, Cations (Ca^{2+}; Mg^{2+}; Na^+; K^+), cation exchangeable capacity (CEC) and saturation base (V%) of soil samples

	pH of soil samples			Cation concentration of soil (cmol/kg^{-2})				Total CEC (cmol/kg^{-2})	Base Saturate BS (v%)	
	pH (water)	pH (KCl)	Delta pH	K+	Ca++	Na+	Mg++	Meq /100 g	Total Base	V%
CT	6.90	6.20	0.70	0.56	2.00	0.06	0.24	4.36	2.86	65.39
2M	6.79	5.59	1.20	0.50	1.31	0.04	0.17	3.52	2.02	57.39
4M	5.98	5.00	0.98	0.75	1.75	0.73	0.25	4.98	3.48	69.90
6M	5.56	4.50	1.06	0.25	2.25	0.15	0.21	4.36	2.86	65.60
VP1	6.90	6.20	0.70	3.34	4.50	0.25	2.15	11.74	10.24	87.22
VP2	4.10	4.00	0.10	0.75	1.00	0.13	0.15	3.53	2.03	57.51
CON	6.73	6.00	0.73	4.50	3.97	0.30	2.00	12.15	10.26	87.56

CT = Centre, CON = Control area, 2M = 2 m, 4M = 4 m, 6M = 6 m, VP1 = first point from the village and VP2 = second point from the village.

3.5 Heavy Metals Analysis

Metal concentration levels in the soil varied from one point of the main dumpsite to another and to the points from the nearby vicinity (Gosa village). Lead had the highest concentration in all the samples collected from the main dumpsite with 0.473 mg/L, 1.382 mg/L and 3.249 mg/L as minimum, average and maximum concentrations respectively. The mean values of all heavy metals decreased with the distance away from the centre of the main dumpsite and this could be due to high amount of wastes at the center of the dumpsite. Only Zinc and the Manganese had widely distributed concentrations with strong standard deviations, higher than the mean value (Table 4).

Lead, Cadmium, and Manganese concentrations in all the soil samples (both from the main dumpsite site and Gosa village were above the permissible limits of WHO (Pb = 0.010 mg/kg^{-1}; Cd = 0.001 mg/kg^{-1} and Mn = 0.050 mg/kg^{-1}) and SON (Pb = 0.010 mg/kg^{-1}; Cd = 0.003 mg/kg^{-1} and Mn = 0.200 mg/kg^{-1}), except the concentrations of Copper and Zinc which were lower than the threshold limit across all the soil samples (Table 4). From four meters (4M) and six meters (6M) away to the centre of the main dumpsite, Zinc and Copper concentrations were below the detection limit of WHO and SON. However, our results showed that metal concentrations from soils in the main landfill were generally in much greater quantities than those of soils from the nearby vicinity (the Gosa village). Increasing from the centre then two meters away from the centre (Table 4).

This degree of natural matter presumably favours the sorption of metal as a result of SOM's assimilation characteristics [4]. Additionally, the excessive lead, cadmium and manganese content observed in the soil samples from the main dumpsite compared to those soils collected from the nearby Gosa village could be due to different sorts of municipal solid squanders from the dumpsite [17]. Consistent aggregation of various sources of metropolitan solid wastes, like electronic products, electroplating waste, painting waste, and utilized batteries could be the beginning of the metalloids observed in the soil from the dumpsite [14]. These outcomes are consistent with findings from other studies, which demonstrate that uncontrolled, free-access dumpsites address a critical source of heavy metal defilement in the ecosystem [18].

The abnormal concentrations of lead (1.382 mg/l), cadmium (0.257 mg/l), and manganese (0.615 mg/l) contents in soils from the dumpsite are above the limits recommended by the Standard Organization of Nigeria (SON) and the World Health Organization (WHO) [10], and are higher in the main dumpsite relative to the other points. Lower metal or metalloids in control soil relative to the study points suggests that the contaminated soils were human-induced. [8] reported that such human-induced contamination might be from wastes.

The contamination of the Gosa dumpsite soil with harmful metals or metalloids may present dangers and perils to the people and the biological system [12]. Also, Gosa dumpsite soil may experience an ecological danger if these metals relocate into the groundwater and plants.

Table 4. Heavy metal concentration from the soil from the Gosa dumpsite compared to WHO and SON standards

	Pb (mg/L)	Cd (mg/L)	Cu (mg/L)	Zn (mg/L)	Mn (mg/L)
CT	3.249 ± 0.000	0.287 ± 0.000	0.542 ± 0.000	0.164 ± 0.000	0.337 ± 0.000
2M	2.622 ± 0.000	0.282 ± 0.000	0.26 ± 0.000	BDL	BDL
4M	0.746 ± 0.000	0.250 ± 0.000	0.580 ± 0.000	BDL	BDL
6M	0.628 ± 0.023	0.246 ± 0.000	0.042 ± 0.000	BDL	BDL
VP1	0.473 ± 0.000	0.243 ± 0.000	1.178 ± 0.000	1.290 ± 0.000	BDL
VP2	0.571 ± 0.000	0.236 ± 0.000	0.718 ± 0.000	1.042 ± 0.000	3.351 ± 0.000
WHO	0.010	0.001	1.500	15.00	0.050
SON	0.010	0.003	2.000	3.000	0.200

In comparison to other locations in Nigeria and neighbouring African countries, the lead (1.382 mg/l) content in the soils from the Gosa dumpsite is less than that of

Oke-ogi dumpsite soil (91.67 mg/l) from Iree, Osun, Nigeria [19], Effiakuma-sekondi (5.11 mg/l) from Takoradi, Ghana [20]. The average amount of cadmium concentration (0.257 mg/l) detected in the soils from Gosa dumpsite was higher than that of soils from the Effiakuma-sekondi (0.050 mg/l) from Takoradi, Ghana [20]. But it was lower than that of the Lumberstewart dumpsite (0.400 mg/l) from Bulawayo, South Africa [21].

Additionally, the observed soils from the Gosa dumpsite have a manganese concentration of 0.615 mg/l, which is relatively higher than the permissible limits recommended by WHO (0.050 mg/l) and SON (0.200 mg/l) for agricultural soils; however, it is lower than the manganese content from Oke-ogi dumpsite soil (3.200 mg/l) from Ire, Osun, Nigeria [19].

The presence of heavy metals in the Gosa dumpsite and its close-by area (Gosa village) soils could be a significant ecological threat from the point of view of soil contamination [22]. If not, the interaction between metals and natural soil matter could prompt complex outcomes on the solvency, portability, and bioavailability of metals in the event that they are filtered into the encompassing zones [12]. This could cause soil weakening issues for agribusiness and nearby inhabitants in the closest area.

4   Conclusion and Recommendations

The results of this study indicate that soils from the main Gosa dumpsite are sandy-loam and that the loamy aspect of the soils decreases from the centre of the main dumpsite towards the nearby Gosa village. The centre of the dumpsite has soil with acidic pH and high organic matter content. However, the base saturation of these soils is relatively high across all soil samples collected from all points of collection. The heavy metal content investigation revealed that lead, cadmium and manganese concentrations were significantly higher than the permissible concentrations. This study was conducted during the 2019 dry season, thus, further studies during the rainy season are recommended, with the assumption that rain could increase the metal concentrations of the soils.

References

1. Vongdala, N., Tran, H.D., Xuan, T.D., Teschke, R., Khanh, T.D.: Heavy metal accumulation in water, soil, and plants of municipal solid waste landfill in Vientiane, Laos. Int. J. Environ. Res. Public Health **16**(1), 22 (2018)
2. Boumphrey, S.: World's fastest growing cities are in Asia and Africa. Euromonitor. (2010). http://www.euromonitor.com. Accessed 25 Aug 2020
3. Raymond, A.W., Felix E.O.: Heavy metals in contaminated soils: a review of sources, chemistry, risks and best available strategies for remediation. Ecology **2011**(402647), (2011)
4. Sebasthiar, E., Ammaiyappan, S., Kurian, J., Kandasamy, P.: Assessment of heavy metal species in decomposed municipal solid waste. Chem. Speciat. Bioavailab. **17**(3), 95–102 (2005)
5. Atiku, S., Ogbaga, C.C., Alonge, O.A., Nwagbara, O.F.: Comparative study of the physicochemical and bacteriological qualities of some drinking water sources in Abuja, Nigeria. Global J. Pure Appl. Sci. **24**(1), (2018)

6. Pécheyran, C., Quetel, C.R., Martin Lecuyer, F.M., Donald, O.F.X.: Simultaneous determination of volatile metal (Pb, Hg, Sn, In, Ga) and nonmetal species (Se, P, As) in different atmospheres by cryofocusing and detection by ICPMS. Analyt. Chem. **70**(13), 2639–2645 (1998)

7. Huang, Y., Wang, L., Wang, W., Li, T., Yang, Z.H.: Current status of agricultural soil pollution by heavy metals in China: a meta-analysis. Sci. Total Environ. **651**(2), 3034–3042 (2019)

8. Mohamed, S.S., et al.: Mapping of heavy metal contamination in alluvial soils of the Middle Nile Delta of Egypt. J. Environ. Eng. Landsc. Manag. **24**(3), 218–231 (2016)

9. Amos-Tautua, B.M., Onigbinde, A.O., Ere, D.: Assessment of some heavy metals and physicochemical properties in surface soils of municipal open waste dumpsite in Yenagoa, Nigeria. Afr. J. Environ. Sci. Technol. **8**(1), 41–47 (2014)

10. Chapman, H.D.: Cation-exchange capacity. In: Black, C.A., et al. (eds.), Methods of Soil Analysis, Part 2, Chemical and Microbiological Properties, pp. 891–901 Agronomy No. 9, Madison, WI, USA (1965)

11. Ukpong, E.C., Antigha, R.E., Moses, E.O.: Assessment of heavy metals content in soils and plants around waste dumpsites In Uyo Metropolis, Akwa Ibom State. Int. J. Eng. Sci. **2**(7), 75–86 (2013)

12. Roper, W.R., Robarge, W.P., Osmond, D.L., Heitman, J.L.: Comparing four methods of measuring soil organic matter in North Carolina soils. Environ. Sci. Soil Sci. Soc. Am. J. **83**, 466–474 (2019)

13. AEPB Homepage. https://bpe.gov.ng/abuja-environmental-protection-board-aepb. Accessed 24 June 2021

14. Devisme, A.B., BolouBi, E., Kassin, K., Balland, C.B.B., Gueable, Y.: Assessment of heavy metal contamination degree of municipal open-air dumpsite on surrounding soils: case of dumpsite of Bonoua, Ivory Coast. Int. J. Eng. Res. Gen. Sci. **6**(5), 28–42 (2018)

15. Aduayi, E.: Making the Soil Nutritious to Plants. Obafemi Awolowo University Press Limited, Ile-Ife (1985)

16. Aibor, M.S., Olorunda, J.O.: A Technical Handbook of Environmental Health in the 21st Century for Professional Students. His Mercy Publisher, Akure (2006)

17. Praveena, G.S., Prasada Rao, P.V.V.: Impact of leachate on soil properties in the dumpsite (A Case study of Greater Visakhapatnam). Int. J. Eng. Res. Gen. Sci. **4**(1), 235–241 (2016)

18. Ping, C.L., Michaelson, G.J., Stiles, C.A., González, G.: Soil characteristics, carbon stores, and nutrient distribution in eight forest types along an elevation gradient Eastern Puerto Rico. Ecol. Bull. **5**(4), 67–86 (2013)

19. Quenea, K., Lamy, I., Winterton, P., Bermond, A., Dumat, C.: Interactions between metals and soil organic matter in various particle size fractions of soil contaminated with. Geoderma **149**(3–4), 217–223 (2009)

20. Abdullahi, I. L., Sani, A.: Evaluation of some heavy metals' concentration in body fluids of metal workers in Kano metropolis, Nigeria. Toxicol. Rep. **4**, 72–76 (2017)

21. Olayinka, O.O., Oludare, A.H., Oluwatoyin, D.: Determination of concentrations of heavy metals in municipal dumpsite soil and plants at Oke - Ogi, Iree, Nigeria. Int. Res. J. Pure Appl. Chem. **4**(6), 565–569 (2014)

22. Agbemafle, R., Aggor-Woananu, S.E., Akutey, O., Bentum, J.K.: Heavy metal concentrations in leachates and crops grown around waste dumpsites in Sekondi-Takoradi in the Western Region of Ghana. Res. J. Environ. Toxicol. **14**, 16–25 (2020)

23. Nwaogu, C., Ogbuagu, H.D., Abrakasa, S., Olawoyin, M.A., Pavlů, Y.: Assessment of the impacts of municipal solid waste dumps on soils and plants. Chem. Ecol. **33**(7), 589–606 (2017)

Ten Years After the Deepwater Horizon Disaster - Lessons Learned for a Better Cementing Job

Ghada Bassioni$^{(\boxtimes)}$ (iD)

Chemistry Division, Faculty of Engineering, Ain Shams University, P.O. Box 11517, Cairo, Egypt
Ghada_bassioni@eng.asu.edu.eg

Abstract. The impacts on the Gulf of Mexico's environment and population are enormous after the Deepwater Horizon accident in 2010. Ten years later investigations on the real causes of that accident with systematic simple lab tests started to use all data available at that time and mimic what happened to overcome similar accidents. The approach in this study shows that risk assessment by experiment cannot be replaced by the mathematical models, which many companies use prior oil production. The models are simply too vague to rely on and are not putting into consideration the many factors that play a crucial role for proper oil well cementing in reality. The compatibility between chemical additives is here demonstrated. The cement additives are characterized by different methods. The additives showed slight changes in the dispersant's molecular weight and particle charge that had in turn significant impact on the mechanical properties of the slurry. Static gel and compressive strengths of the different mixtures are tested. The dosage that shows optimum mechanical characteristics is identified for all individual systems as well as for the mixtures. The results show how important experimentation is and that mathematical models would not be able to differentiate between the two implemented chemicals if we rely on chemical composition only. The study is particularly important for future Africa with increasing potential for oil production.

Keywords: Gelation · Chemical additives · Oil well cement

1 Introduction

In 2010 a large trans-ocean drilling rig was operational in the Gulf of Mexico for the Macondo well. The job at the so-called Deepwater Horizon was behind schedule and over budgeted by $58 million facing a lot of challenges: the well was at high pressure, below the seabed by about 4 km. Sixteen hours after the cementing engineering had confirmed that the cementing job went well, hydrocarbons were escaped into the well bore upon which the drilling rig experienced a disastrous blowout. The high pressure oil and gas leaked from the rig and into the ocean causing a huge oil spill [1]. Eleven people died when the rig caught fire. A lot more people were seriously injured [2]. The fire lasted for 36 h until the rig sank. Hydrocarbons continued to leak from the reservoir

A. D. Mambo et al. (Eds.): InterSol 2022, LNICST 449, pp. 175–186, 2022.
https://doi.org/10.1007/978-3-031-23116-2_14

through the wellbore for almost 90 days [3]. The expenditures from this accident are not yet fully captured, but it is clear that the impacts on the region's environment and population are enormous, and that financial losses exceed tens of billions of dollars. As part of the US governmental response, a well integrity crew assessed the geological hazards and determined the factors under which shutting in the well could securely be undertaken. The estimated high shut-in pressure made leakage of oil below the seafloor very likely. This leak could probably result in new geological routes for discharge into the Gulf of Mexico [4].

Shortly after the accident, a project team was established to learn from it and to recognize parallels and variances with other severe incidents. The goal was to identify best practices for improving the authority's supervision and to implement actions which can improve HSE in the oil and gas sector [2].

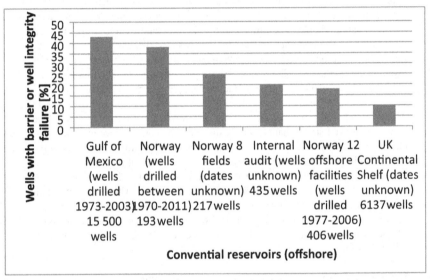

Fig. 1. Percentage of wells with well or barrier integrity failure in different conventional offshore reservoirs.

For enhanced HSE security, wells are planned with multiple fences. The number of these fences or barriers depends on the hazard severity. Figure 1 shows the fraction of wells that have barrier or well integrity failure in different conventional offshore reservoirs. Well documented is the Gulf of Mexico with 15,500 failures resembling 43% of the wells drilled from 1973 to 2003. The documented failures show that about 5% are due to a bad cementing job [5, 6]. The wells that have been affected by sustained casing pressure have been reported in correlation to the well age in years [7]. In the vast majority of cases, wells develop leaks with aging as can be seen in the Fig. 2.

According to the National Commission investigations the oil spill of the Deepwater Horizon was caused by a failure to encompass hydrocarbon pressures in the well. The chief council's report of the National Commission stated that there are several issues that may have contributed to the cement failure. These events incorporate that cement in

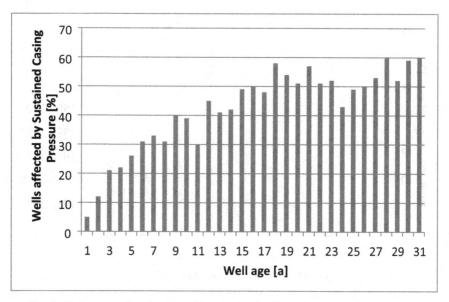

Fig. 2. Percentage of wells affected by sustained casing pressure in aging wells [7].

the annulus may have flown back due to U-tube pressure and drilling mud might have contaminated the cement, cement displacement wasn't properly done leaving channels of mud behind, characteristics of the cement slurry like base slurry stability and rheology, retarder concentration. Sealing properties of the cement might have been compromised due to foam instability and allowed nitrogen gas to escape the slurry. According to a previous statement, large portions of the reservoir strata were not cemented allowing oil and gas to flow at high pressure (900 bar) into the borehole. Another factor proposed that over-retardation of cement slurry exhibited a thickening time more than 10 h and developed no compressive strength even after 24 h. This allowed the gas to migrate through the still plastic cement and ascend to the surface where the blow-out preventer failed.

The percentage of reported wells developing leaks after a certain lifetime in years are represented in Fig. 3 [8]. Surprisingly, the wells between 1970 and 1979 develop the highest number of leaks in comparison to other well-documented data between 1958 to 1970.

A sharp focus on risk assessment is already implemented, compliance, simplification and improvement of the available R&D methodologies and the technical reliability of the lab facilities. Certainly, there will be increasing focus on the team's actions and how to regulate systems and procedures. That means that the importance of precision, quality and excellent HSE performance will increase. A sharp reminder is this accident in the Gulf of Mexico that one can never reduce the efforts to continuously improve HSE [3]. According to the latest statistics, Africa accounts for about 8% of the global oil output in 2020. Nearly 330 million tons (metric) of oil were generated in Africa the same year. The continent produced around 7 million barrels per day, the lowest production level since 2000. Nevertheless, oil remains a crucial driver for the producing countries

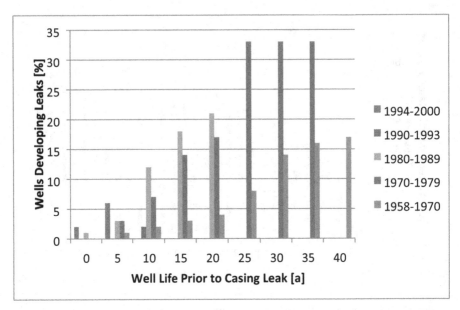

Fig. 3. Percentage of wells developing leaks in correlation to the well life prior casing [8].

economically, and its huge reserves may unveil other African countries as new producers (Fig. 4) [9].

Oil-well cementing is essential for all oil-producing countries. Appropriate design of the used slurry is crucial to a successful cementing job. The best way to get the anticipated compressive strength is by lab experiments which involve testing different recipes and choosing the optimum chemical mixture for a certain cementing job.

Compressive strength is particularly useful to test trustworthiness of the cementing operation since it is the capability of a material to resist distortion with increasing load. It depends on the type and number of raw materials and additives used, method and time of curing of the cement slurry as well as exposure conditions [8]. Good compressive strength means withstanding extremely high temperature, corrosive formations and gas intrusion. Challenges accompanying cementing jobs have led to a lot of investigation in this field using different approaches. Labibzadeh et al. concluded that, in connection to temperature and pressure variations, rapid early-age compressive strength could result in decrease in thickening time in oil well cement class G [10]. It was also reported that the strength of the cement could decrease in case of crystalline silica addition. Despite the ability to withstand pressure, temperature, and sulfate, additives are required to improve the properties of the cement [11]. It was concluded that compressive strength increased by the addition of 0.2% of lignosulfonate [12]. Beyond this value a reduction in compressive strength was observed. Enhancement of cement compressive strength depends on the correct quantity of each of the additives. The optimum dosages of these additives need to be identified by time consuming experimental runs, a process that is tedious and costly [13].

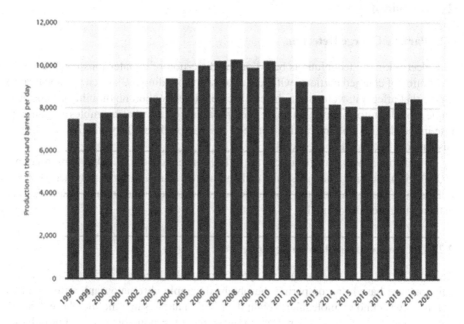

Fig. 4. Oil production in Africa from 1998–2020 [9].

The cement is required to have a minimum strength of about 500 psi before restarting the drilling operations [14]. The time necessary to attain that stage is the so-called wait-on-cement (WOC) which relates to the hydration time and consequently to the drilling cost per hour. That means that a longer waiting time will cause extra cost while a shorter waiting time could cause cement failure due to inadequate setting time of cement. Therefore, correct assessment of required cement strength is significant to reduce cost, in particular at those stages when mechanical and physical characteristics of oil well cement considerably change with time.

The main challenges that face drilling of an oil well include inhibiting gas migration after cementing. This phenomenon bears high risk since the gas can travel to the surface producing annular pressurization leading to a blowout with tragic results and eventually complete loss of the well.

This study presents a methodology to assess gas migration probability after cementing operations by means of the critical static gel strength concept. This study examines one retarder with two dispersants that seem chemically identical but come from two different service companies, namely sodium lignosulfonate (A) as a retarder and naphthalene sulfonate formaldehyde (B1 and B2) as a dispersant, respectively, with the focus on competitive adsorption [15, 16], steric position of anchor groups along with the main chain as well as adsorbed conformation of macromolecules on the cement grain [17, 18]. This work shows that models would fail if they would depend on theoretical structures only.

2 Methodology

2.1 Particle Charge Detection

The electro-kinetic technique is based on the distortion of counter ions resulting from the motion of charged particles with regard to its surrounding [19]. Each particle bears a dipole that affects its velocity in the electric field (electrophoretic mobility). This technique provides information about the effective particle charge that resembles a significant role in the electrostatic interaction between charged particles. The stability of colloidal suspensions is echoed consequently [19].

The chemical admixture solutions are of 100 ppm concentration. The solution sample (10 mL) is placed into the measuring cell and titrated with a cationic polymer (0.001 N polydadmac) solution until the isoelectric point is reached. The anionic charge density is then calculated accordingly.

2.2 Gel Permeation Chromatography

This method is used to determine polymers molecular weight distributions. The calculations are based on comparing the obtained sample chromatograph with standard polymers with known molecular weight distribution at the same mobile phase. Choosing the suitable standards is important in order to get reproducible results. For polydisperse polymers a weight average molecular weight M_w and a number average molecular weight M_n can be calculated using Agilent.

HPLC 1200, Agilent Technologies, USA. $NaNO_3$ aqueous solution of concentration 0.2 mol/L is used as an eluent. By adding 10 drops of 0.01 mol/L NaOH the solution is adjusted to pH = 8. The sample is injected with volume of 50 μL at a flow rate of 1 mL/min. Calibration of the column is carried out using polyethylene oxide/polyethylene glycol (PEO/PEG) standards (separation range = 100 to 1000k Da (Dalton)). Calculations of the molecular weight are carried out using the GPC software and a sixth order polynomial fit.

2.3 Cement Slurry Preparation

The cement paste is prepared at ambient temperature and at a water to cement ratio (w/c) of 0.4.

Preparation and mixing of the cement slurries followed ASTM C-305 using a cement blender,

ToniMIX, Toni Technik Baustoffprüfsysteme GmbH, Germany [20].

2.4 Static Gel and Compressive Strength Development

The compressive strength of oil well cement is important in acquiring long-term integrity of the wellbore. Its development is experimentally not easy to achieve once the cement is placed into the wellbore. During early cement hydration monitoring cement strength development is crucial and failure to do so may necessitate secondary cementing job. The static gel and compressive strengths are measured using a non-destructive method based on an ultrasonic technique as a function of time using Static Gel Strength Analyzer model 5265, Chandler Engineering, USA. After the sample is prepared as in 2.1, the slurry is poured into the autoclave cell and cured for 24 h at 25 °C and atmospheric pressure. The minimum accepted compressive strength for oil well cement is expected to be 500 psi in order to resist the shocks caused by the drilling operation and provides sufficient support to the casing in the wellbore [10]. According to API specifications [21], the static gel strength elapsed time is recorded and compared for different cement/additives slurry systems.

2.5 Compressive Strength by Crush Test

The compressive strength by crush test for different cement/additive systems is measured using an Automated Compressive Load Frame model 250, OFI testing equipment, USA and compared with the results gained by using the ultrasonic method described in Sect. 2.3. A cubical mold with dimensions of $5 \times 5 \times 5$ cm^3 is used. The mold interior surfaces are coated with mold sealing grease and the bottom cover plate is tied enough to prevent any cement leakages. After that, the cement slurry for different studied systems is poured into the prepared mold to approximately one-half of the mold depth [22]. Then, the sample is puddled for 30 times by using a puddling rod. The remaining sample is stirred and poured into the mold until it is overflowing with the slurry, the second layer of the slurry is puddled and any slurry excess is stroked off using a straight edge. The top cover is placed on the mold structure and tied in order to prevent any penetration of water into the sample. The mold is transferred to a water bath (Clifton NE4-14D, Nickel-Electro, England) and the sample is cured at 25 °C and atmospheric pressure for 24 h. The compressive strength is calculated based on the ratio of load applied per unit area of cement sample.

3 Results and Discussion

3.1 Chemical Characterization

The range of molecular weights of the different cement additives in any cementing job is considered as one of the main factors that affect the adsorption behavior of these additives on cement. The results for A, B1 and B2 are demonstrated in Fig. 5.

In case of B1 and B2, the molecular weights distribution results show minor differences and the values are almost identical as can be seen in Fig. 5. Nevertheless, other previous chemical characterization results didn't show any remarkable differences between B1 and B2. As a result, it is expected that both of them behave in the same way on the cement system.

The particle charge densities are evaluated as displayed in Fig. 5. The results show that the dispersants' systems have higher anionic charge density (ACD) by 22% to 26% compared to the retarder's system. Furthermore, B2 shows 4.3% higher anionic charge density than B1. These differences can be attributed to the variation in the degree of sulfonation. In more details, different polar groups are found in lignosulfonate such as phenylic hydroxyl and alcoholic hydroxyl groups as well as sulfonic groups [23] so that the value of charge density for the retarder represents the summation of the charge densities of all those groups Fig. 5. Quyang et al. altered lignosulfonate performance by increasing the sulfonation degree (sulfonic groups) and associated this with zeta potential measurements. It was reported that the modified components possess higher charge densities and thus a higher zeta potential was achieved [24]. These results were in consistence with other work on dispersants in presence of fluid loss additive.

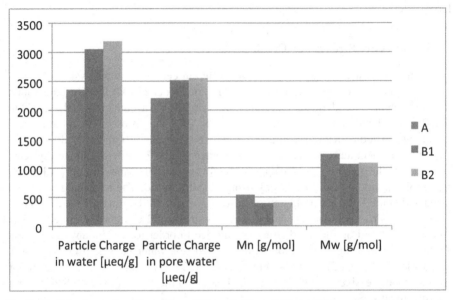

Fig. 5. Particle charge densities of the additives A, B1 and B2 at 0.2% in water and in pore water as well as number average (Mn) and weight average (Mw) molecular weights.

While free A and B1 and B2 show a certain particle charge as can be seen in Fig. 5, only about 8090% of that amount is found in the pore water of the cement under investigation attributed to complexation to free Ca ions in the pore water.

3.2 Mechanical Properties of Oil Well Cement Slurries

Development of high compressive strength and rapid static gel strength are considered as important and critical functions in oil well cementing jobs. That is attributed to the fact that both are directly involved in preventing unpleasant incidences in case the cement fails to achieve zonal isolation. Gas migration through cement matrix can badly compromise the cement job as well as the well production. Gas migration can occur in different ways in addition to bubble flow in a viscoelastic fluid. It can be found in the form of a lengthened slug as channels along cement-formation and cement-casing boundaries, or as a growing plume, where an almost spherical chamber is connected to the formation by a narrow umbilical conduit.

The cement slurry needs to develop rapid and sufficient compressive strength in order to ensure both structural support and hydraulic/mechanical isolation of borehole intervals [10]. Therefore, measuring both early compressive and static gel strengths are conducted for proposed cement/additives systems and compared to the neat cement system in order to evaluate their workability as well as their capability to deliver zonal isolation. Furthermore, the effect of compatibility between the additives on the mechanical properties is studied. As can been seen in Fig. 6 the static gel strength development is measured at 25 °C and atmospheric pressure for different systems at 0.2% bwoc. Unlike the neat cement system, the time to reach certain gel strength for all the cement/additives system is prolonged due to the retardation effect at constant water to cement ratio.

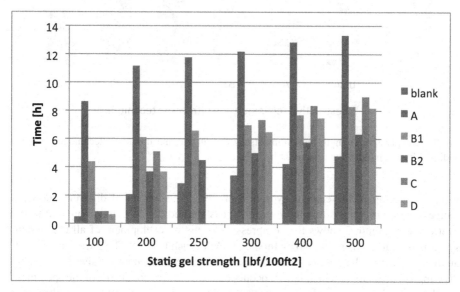

Fig. 6. Static gel strength as a function of time at 0.2% bwoc for the different admixtures.

As illustrated in Fig. 6, for the blank cement system the gel strength at 250 Ibf/100ft2 is reached at 2.85 h while at 0.2% A bwoc and 0.2% B1 bwoc the same gel strength is observed after 11.77 and 6.57 h, respectively. That means that the gel strength is retarded due to the addition of both additives on the cement slurry. For 0.2% B2 bwoc the gel strength at 250 Ibf/100ft2 is obtained approximately after 4.5 h as displayed in Fig. 6. The difference between both dispersants can be attributed to the variation in adsorption amounts as shown in previous results [15].

The systems C (a mixture of A and B1) at 0.2% bwoc and D (a mixture of A and B2) at 0.2% bwoc are negatively affected by the cement hydration time as well as the gel strength development due to competitive adsorption.

During the hydration process the consumption rate for NSF is higher than the rate for lignosulfonate due to variation in anionic charge and adsorption conformation. After a certain time, free NSF concentration in the solution will drop to zero allowing free lignosulfonate to adsorb with higher amounts. Because the compatibility is minimized drastically, the lignosulfonate will adsorb in higher amounts and effectively retard the system. However, the retardation will not be as effective as when lignosulfonate is added

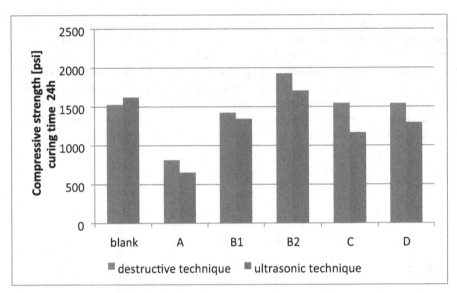

Fig. 7. Compressive strength measurements by destructive and ultrasonic techniques at 0.2% additives bwoc and a curing time of 24 h.

in the beginning of the cement hydration process. The impact of different additives recipes on compressive strength development is studied for 24 h and compared to the neat cement. Figure 7 shows the compressive strength development of all the cement systems is characterized by two methods: (1) API crush test, (2) The ultrasonic cement analyzer (UCA). The former method describes the cement compressive strength by dividing the pressure at which failure occurs by the cross sectional area of the specimen. The latter method is depending on measurement of the sonic travel time of ultrasonic energy through the cement sample while it is curing. As can be seen, there are differences between the results due to the measuring principle. The results obtain by API crush test are higher in compressive strength than the ones by using UCA except for the blank sample. It can be seen that all additives have reduced the compressive strength and prolonged its development for a certain time at constant water to cement ratio.

According to Fig. 7 the blank cement reached 500 psi compressive strength after 13.46 h and its maximum compressive strength value within 24 h is observed to be 1620 psi. Furthermore, the mixtures C and D exhibit the lowest compressive strengths and the minimum value for strength is not reached within the first 24 h. Therefore, those systems have failed to meet the minimum specifications and it's not recommended to be applied in the field at those conditions. The delay in strength development can be attributed to synergistic retardation when higher dosages of additives are used. For B1 and B2 systems the minimum value is reached after 17.93 and 15 h, respectively. This behavior can be attributed to the adsorption amount of B1 in comparison to B2, since by increasing the adsorption amount the compatibility question will arise. Although, all the proposed dosages have good workability, the additive systems can be enhanced by reducing the water to cement ratio with maintaining approximately similar obtained viscosities.

4 Conclusion

The Macondo blowout in 2010 was a wake-up call for seeking better risk assessment tools by experimentation rather than relying on old or imprecise mathematical models. It is crucial for the African countries as oil producers to get improved knowledge on the compatibility of chemical additives and their interactions on class G cement while undertaking oil well cementing. The chemical characterization results show that a retarder in presence of two dispersants of the same chemical structure but from different vendors can lead to misleading expectations and consequently models. The study shows that molecular weights can be considered as one of the factors that play an important role on adsorption behavior. While free A, B1 and B2 show a certain particle charge, only about 80–90% of that amount is found in the pore water of the cement under investigation attributed to complexation to free Ca ions in the pore water. The adsorption capacity and further the understanding of the compatibility between different cement additives is significant. In summary, particle size and microstructure play an essential role in assessing optimum recipes for a successful cementing job. The recommended optimum dosages are 0.2% bwoc for the individual systems under investigation and 0.1% for the combined mixtures due to evaluated synergistic effects. For the blank cement system the gel strength at 250 Ibf/100ft2 is reached at 2.85 h while at 0.2% A bwoc and 0.2% B1 bwoc the same gel strength is observed after 11.77 and 6.57 h, respectively. For 0.2% B2 bwoc the gel strength at 250 Ibf/100ft2 is obtained after 4.5 h. Competitive adsorption is observed in the mixture solutions. The retardation effects for the different systems emphasize that experiment is key, even if theoreticians believe they have reliable models.

Acknowledgement. The author would like to thank Mohammed M. Ali for providing some experimental data. The team at the microanalytical lab of the Technische Universität München is also greatly appreciated for their assistance with the experimental measurements.

References

1. Rhona, F.: Non-technical skills: enhancing safety in operating theatres (and drilling rigs). J Perioperat. Pract. **24**(3), 59–60 (2015)
2. Anda, I., Ebbesen, A.: Deepwater horizon: taking the lessons to heart. Saf. Stat. Signals **2012,** 42–45 (2012)
3. Learning from the Macondo accident. Statoil Annual Report (2010)
4. Hickman, S.H., Hsieh, P.A., Mooney, W.D., Enomoto, C.B., Nelson, P.H., Mayer, L.A., et al.: Scientific basis for safely shutting in the Macondo Well after the April 20, 2010 Deepwater Horizon blowout. Proc. Natl. Acad. Sci. U.S.A. **109**(50), 20268–20273 (2012)
5. King, G.E., King, D.E.: Environmental risk arising from well-construction failure— differences between barrier and well failure, and estimates of failure frequency across common well types, locations, and well age. J. Soc. Pet. Eng. **2013**; SPE-166142-MS

6. Nyap, D.W.V., Shoushtari, M.A., Rashidovich, R.M.: Synergistic assessment of sustained casing pressure on oil well. Res. J. App. Sci. Eng. Tech. **5**(17), 4246–4256 (2013)
7. Ingraffea, A.R., Wells, M.T., Santoro, R.L., Shonkoff, S.B.C.: Assessment and risk analysis of casing and cement impairment in oil and gas wells in Pennsylvania, 2000–2012. PNAS **111**(30), 10955–10960 (2012)
8. Herianto, M., Fathaddin, T.: Effects of additives and conditioning time on compressive and shear bond strengths of geothermal well cement. In: Proceedings World Geothermal Congress 2005, Antalya, Turkey (2005)
9. N. Sönnichsen, 26 August 2021. https://www.statista.com/statistics/265197/oil-production-inafrica-in-barrels-per-day/. Accessed 17 Dec 2021
10. Bassioni, G., Farid, R., Mohamed, M., Hammouda, R.M., Kühn, F.E.: Effect of different parameters on caustic magnesia hydration and magnesium hydroxide rheology: a review. Mat. Adv. **2**(20), 6519–6531 (2021)
11. Bassioni, G., Ali, M.M.: The effect of counterion in lignosulfonates as oil-well cement retarders. Adv. Cem. Res. **25**(5), 245–253 (2013)
12. Bayu, S., Muhammed, T.F., Roby, T.: Effect of lignosulfonate and temperature on compressive strength of cement. In: Proceedings of World Geothermal Congress 2010, Bali, Indonesia, pp. 1–3 (2010)
13. Isehunwa, O.S., Orji, H.I.: Analysis of mud filtration properties using factorial design. In: SPENC 9515, Paper Presented at the SPE Nigerian Council Annual Conference, Lagos, Nigeria (1995)
14. Backe, K.R., Lile. O.B., Lyomov, S.K.: Characterizing curing cement slurries by electrical conductivity. J. Soc. Pet. Eng. **16**(4), 207–207 (2001); SPE 74694
15. Bassioni, G.: Mechanistic aspects on the influence of inorganic anion adsorption on oilfield scale inhibition by citrate. J. Pet. Sci. Eng. **70**, 298–330 (2010)
16. Reader, T.W., O'Connor, P.: The Deepwater Horizon explosion: non-technical skills, safety culture, and system complexity. J. Risk Res. **17**(3), 405–424 (2014)
17. Abbas, G., Irawan, S., Kumar, S., Elrayah, A.A.I.: Improving oil well cement slurry performance using hydroxypropylmethylcellulose polymer. Adv. Mat. Res. **787**, 222–227 (2013)
18. Ghobasgy, M.M., Bassioni, G.: pH stimuli-responsive poly(acrylamide-co-sodium alginate) hydrogels prepared by γ-radiation for improved compressive strength of concrete. Adv. Poly. Tech. **37**(6), 2123–2133 (2018)
19. Al Wahedi, Y., Awayes, J., Bassioni, G.: Influence of classical & modern superplasticizers on the chemical and rheological behavior of oil well cement- A comparative study. Adv. Cem. Res. **23**(4), 175–184 (2011)
20. Böckenhoff, K., Fischer, W.: Determination of electrokinetic charge with a particle-charge detector, and its relationship to the total charge. Fresenius J. Anal. Chem. **371**(5), 670–674 (2001). https://doi.org/10.1007/s002160100897
21. ASTMC305-99. Standard Practice for Mechanical Mixing of Hydraulic Cement Pastes and Mortars of Plastic Consistency, 1st edn. ASTM, West Conshohocken (1999)
22. API RP 10B-6. Recommended Practice on Determining the Static Gel Strength of Cement Formulations, 1st edn. API, Washington, DC (2010)
23. API RP 10B-2. Recommended Practice for Testing Well Cements, 1st edn. API, Washington, DC (2005)
24. Ouyang, X., Qiu, X., Chen, P.: Physicochemical characterization of calcium lignosulfonate - a potentially useful water reducer. Coll. Surf. A Physicochem. Eng. Aspects **282–283**, 489497 (2006)
25. Bassioni, G., Ali, M.M., Almansoori, A., Raudaschl-Sieber, G., Kühn, F.E.: Rapid Determination of complex oil well cement chemistry using mathematical models. RSC Adv. **7**, 51485157 (2017)

Generating Bioelectricity from Traditional Food Processing Wastewater Using an Inoculum of Return Activated Sewage Sludge

S. I. Ocheni, C. C. Ogbaga$^{(\boxtimes)}$ (iD), S. S. D. Mohammed, and G. Mangse

Department of Microbiology and Biotechnology, Nile University of Nigeria, Abuja, Nigeria
chukwuma.ogbaga@nileuniversity.edu.ng

Abstract. Mediatorless, two-chambered microbial fuel cells were developed using activated sewage sludge as the source of exoelectrogenic microorganisms with wastewater from two Nigerian traditional food processing activities (locust Bean Processing and Sorghum processing) as the energy source. The fuel cells were operated in batch mode, with aerobic, instead of anaerobic anode chamber. Carbon felt rolled into cylindrical shapes were used for both electrodes and a Nafion® 117 (Dupont Co., USA) proton exchange membrane was used. The highest voltage (172.3 mV) was reached using Locust bean wastewater as the anolyte. A directly proportional relationship was observed between current density and power generation. These initial results demonstrate that wastewater from traditional food processing activities can be used for power generation in a mediatorless microbial fuel cell with an aerobic anode chamber.

Keywords: Microbial fuel cell · Aerobic anode chamber · Locust beans · Sorghum · Wastewater

1 Introduction

Nigeria is a country known for its diverse cultures and cuisines [1, 2]. The west African country, with a population of over 210 million (2021 est.) [3], has over 250 ethnic groups (2018 est.) [3]. These ethnic groups each have their own distinct cultures, traditions and cuisines.

Iru (Yoruba), also referred to as Ukpehe in Igala land and dadawa in the northern part of the country, is a condiment often used in the preparation of traditional dishes by many ethnic groups in Nigeria. The condiment is made from the fermentation of whole locust beans. However, iru is not the only condiment gotten from this process. Other oil seeds such as soybean, melon seed, castor oil seed and mesquite bean are fermented to yield other condiments [4].

Ogi or akamu also known as pap is a fermented cereal pudding, enjoyed by many Nigerians, which has a custard-like consistency. It can be made from the wet milling of various cereals like maize, millet or sorghum. After milling, it is allowed to settle and the water is decanted off and disposed of.

A. D. Mambo et al. (Eds.): InterSol 2022, LNICST 449, pp. 187–194, 2022.
https://doi.org/10.1007/978-3-031-23116-2_15

The making of these two products generates wastewater. This water is either poured on the ground, in gutters, or water bodies.

This wastewater, however, can be kept out of the environment by using it to produce energy in a process that could also produce electricity [5].

In 2016, Nigeria emitted 120.37 megatons of CO_2 [3]. This figure can be drastically reduced if the country looks towards renewable sources of energy instead of relying on less sustainable sources.

A Microbial Fuel Cell (MFC) is a device that produces electrical current from the microbial degradation of a chosen substrate [6]. If practicalized, MFCs will be a beneficial source of renewable energy as not only can they produce electricity sustainably, they are also invaluable in the treatment of wastewater [5, 7, 8].

MFCs are commonly dual chambered. They have an anodic chamber that contains an anolyte as well as an anode and a cathodic chamber that contains a catholyte and the cathode [9]. These chambers are kept separate by a Proton Exchange Membrane (PEM) which is selectively permeable and prevents the anolyte and catholyte from mixing but serves as a route for protons to migrate from the anodic chamber to the cathodic chamber [9, 10]. The two chambers are also connected by a wire running from the anodic chamber to the cathodic chamber.

The anolyte refers to organic substrates which serve as fuel to the MFC by providing microorganisms present in the anodic chamber with nutrients for their growth [11]. These microorganisms can be referred to as electroactive microorganisms (EAMs), exoelectrogens, electrogens, electro-active bacteria, or anode respiring bacteria. They degrade the feedstock, producing electrons and protons as a by-product. The electrons pass from the anodic chamber to the cathodic chamber through the external wire, creating a current in the process while the protons move from the anodic chamber to the cathodic chamber through the proton exchange membrane where they react with oxygen to produce water.

Typically, the anodic chamber is kept anaerobic because many MFCs use microorganisms that are obligate anaerobes and are unable to survive in the presence of oxygen [12].

In this study, we used both wastewater from the production of iru (Locust Bean Wastewater, LBWW) and wastewater from the production of pap (Sorghum Wastewater, SWW) as the anolytes in an MFC, and return activated sewage sludge (RAS) as the inoculum. A number of studies have already been carried out on the use of different fuels, configurations, consortia of microorganisms, aerobic and anaerobic anode chambers as well as the effects of pH., temperature, magnetic fields, etc., on electricity generation using MFCs. However, no research has been done in relation to what is obtainable in rural communities in Africa. To this effect, this study was carried out using materials from a village in Nigeria (Abocho, Dekina, Kogi state) to determine the possibility of using MFCs in rural settings.

2 Materials and Methods

2.1 Inoculum

Return Activated Sludge was obtained from Wupa Wastewater Treatment Plant (WWTP), Abuja Nigeria. The sludge was collected in sterile sample collection containers and transported on ice to the laboratory. In the Laboratory, it was stored at 4 °C for use as the inoculum in subsequent experiments.

2.2 Physicochemical Analysis

The COD, BOD, Total Suspended Solids, Total Dissolved Solids and pH were analyzed by standard methods (Table 1).

Table 1. Physicochemical analysis of waste water samples

Heading level	LBWW	SWW
COD (mg O_2/L)	1, 950	1, 500
BOD (mg O_2/L)	580	580
TDS (mg of solids/L)	10, 258	176
TSS (mg of solids/L)	2, 480	650
pH	3.84	5.04

COD, Chemical Oxygen Demand; BOD, Biological Oxygen Demand; TDS, Total Dissolved Solids; TSS, Total Suspended Solids

2.3 Microbial Fuel Cell Coupling and Operation

The H-type MFC reactor used in the study was purchased from Huirong E-commerce Co., Ltd., (Hebei, China). Each reactor was assembled by placing a pre-treated Nafion® 117 (Dupont Co., USA) proton exchange membrane between each chamber and holding them together with a clamp. Each chamber contained carbon felt folded cylindrically attached to the external system with copper wires.

The anode chambers were filled with either LBWW, SWW or Distilled Water (DW), as a control.

The cathode chambers were always filled with a sodium percarbonate catholyte (5 g/L) prepared according to Forrestal et al. [13]. The initial pH of all solutions was adjusted to 7.0 and all MFCs were operated at room temperature.

Microorganisms of interest were first immobilized on the anode by filling the anode chamber with 97 mL of the individual anolytes and 3 mL of the RAS inoculum. The system was then run until maximum Open Current Voltage (OCV) was achieved and then the voltage dropped (17 days).

After the immobilization step, the anode chambers were filled with 100 mL of either LBWW, SWW or DW.

2.4 Data Acquisition and Calculations

A multimeter (PeakTech® 2010DMM) was used to measure the voltage across a 1 KΩ resistor and the Open Current Voltage (OCV) of each cell.

The current (I) in amperes (A) was calculated using Ohm's law:

$$I = V / R \tag{1}$$

where V is the potential drop in volts (V) across the external load resistor (R) in Ohms (Ω).

The power output (P) in watts (W), was calculated using the formula:

$$P = I \times V \tag{2}$$

and the power density (PD) in (W m^{-2}) using the formula:

$$PD = I \times V/A \tag{3}$$

where A (m^2) is the area of the anode.

3 Results and Discussion

3.1 Open Current Voltage

Following the immobilization period, which lasted approximately 17 days, the anode chambers of all MFCs were filled with either LBWW, SWW or DW. No electricity was generated in the MFC with DW as the anolyte (control).

However, the LBWW MFC achieved a maximum voltage of 172.3 mV and the SWW achieved a maximum voltage of 112.4 mV.

From Fig. 1, two peaks can be observed in the graph for both nutrient sources. This is believed to be due to the presence of different types of microorganisms in the inoculum. The initial rise in the open current voltage indicates that the exoelectrogens and other microorganisms are using up glucose as their primary energy source. The number of exoelectrogens, as well as other microorganisms, increase and so, there is a further increase in open current voltage. At the peak, these exoelectrogens have utilized all the glucose present. Due to this, they begin to compete for available nutrients. Their number begins to drop, and consequently, the open current voltage does as well. At this point, the other microorganisms in the anolyte begin to use more complex sugars as their energy source. This results in the production of glucose, which the exoelectrogens then use as their energy source, producing electrons in the process. The open current voltage rises again, only for it to permanently fall after all nutrients have been utilized (Fig. 1).

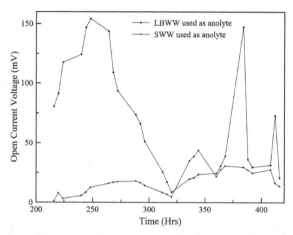

Fig. 1. Open current voltage (OCV) during the first cycle of the operation of the Microbial Fuel Cells (MFCs) with the function of time. (External resistance: 0 Ω; pH of anolyte: 7). (LBWW: Locust bean wastewater; SWW: Sorghum wastewater).

3.2 Extended Performance of the Microbial Fuel Cells Under an External Resistance

Once it was established that a microbial fuel cell using a mixed inoculum obtained from activated sewage sludge could indeed generate an electrical current, the performance of the MFC was monitored during prolonged operation using Locust Bean Wastewater and Sorghum Wastewater as nutrient sources and carbon felt as both the anode and cathode. The cell was operated over an external resistance of 1 kΩ. The potential difference across the external resistance (Fig. 2) reached a maximum of approximately 28 h after the start of the experiment in the case of LBWW and after approximately 44 h for SWW. The potential difference fell to 0 mV after 72 h of running the LBWW MFC and 76 h of running the SWW MFC. Removal of the wastewater, in both cases, and replacement with fresh wastewater restored the potential difference to the maximum. This indicates that the drop in potential difference was due to the exhaustion of nutrients available in the media.

3.3 Effect of Anolyte on Electricity Generation

From Figs. 1, 2 and 3, it is clear that an MFC using LBWW as the anolyte, with all things being equal, will produce higher power than an MFC which uses SWW as the anolyte. This can be due to the fact that LBWW contains higher amounts of nutrients which exoelectrogens can use as an energy source in the process of the current generation. These nutrients may be found in the higher number of dissolved and suspended solids.

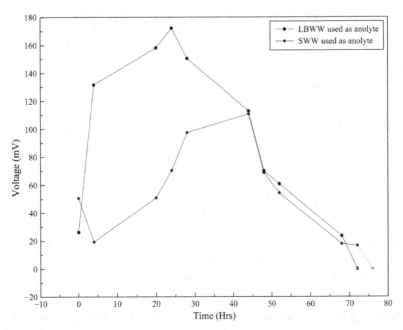

Fig. 2. Voltage during operation of the Microbial Fuel Cells (MFCs) with the function of time. (External resistance: 1,000 Ω; pH of anolyte: 7). (LBWW: Locust bean wastewater; SWW: Sorghum wastewater).

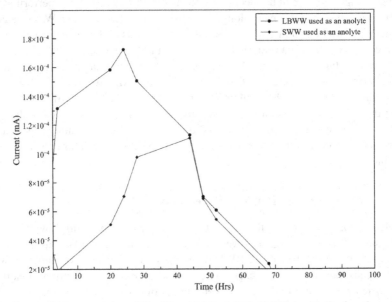

Fig. 3. Current during operation of the Microbial Fuel Cells (MFCs) with the function of time. (External resistance: 1,000 Ω; pH of anolyte: 7). (LBWW: Locust bean wastewater; SWW: Sorghum processing wastewater).

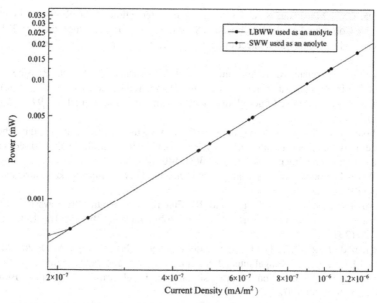

Fig. 4. Logarithmic graph showing the relationship between current density and power during operation of the Microbial Fuel Cells (MFCs). (External resistance: 1,000 Ω; pH of anolyte: 7). (LBWW: Locust bean wastewater; SWW: Sorghum wastewater).

3.4   Relationship Between Current Density and Power Generation

From Fig. 4, we can see that regardless of the feedstock used as the anolyte, current density and power generation are directly proportional. This means that as the current density increase, so also does the power generated by the MFC and to generate greater power, the current density must be increased.

4   Conclusion

This study shows that LBWW is a more feasible anolyte for MFCs which may be operated in rural areas in Nigeria. With an LBWW powered MFC, higher voltages are achieved, more power is produced, and a higher current density can be observed.

Since the process of making the anode chamber anaerobic may not be cost-effective, in rural areas, this study was carried out with an anode chamber that began as aerobic. No oxygen was sparged into the chamber, and there was no shaking of the anode chamber to introduce oxygen. This means that during the course of the experiment, the oxygen concentration changed, therefore altering the active microbial communities.

References

1. Babani, S.I., Ogbaga, C.C., Okolo, D., Mangse, G.: Bioactive compound and rubisco analyses of leaf and seed extracts of Sesamum indicum. In: 2019 15th International Conference on Electronics Computer and Computation (ICECCO), pp. 1–6. IEEE, USA (2019)

2. Ogbaga, C.C., Maishanu, R.A., Okolo, D.: Characterisation of the Rubisco Content and Bioactive Compound Analysis of Leaf and Seed Extracts of Tamarindus indica. In: 2019 15th International Conference on Electronics Computer and Computation (ICECCO), pp. 1–6. IEEE, USA (2019)

3. Mohan, S., Saravanan, R., Raghavulu, S.V., Mohanakrishna, G., Sarma, P.: Bioelectricity production from wastewater treatment in dual chambered microbial fuel cell (MFC) using selectively enriched mixed microflora: effect of catholyte. Biores. Technol. **99**(3), 596–603 (2008)

4. Omafuvbe, B.O., Falade, O.S., Osuntogun, B.A., Adewusi, S.R.: Chemical and biochemical changes in African locust bean (Parkia biglobosa) and melon (Citrullus vulgaris) seeds during fermentation to condiments. Pak. J. Nutr. **3**(3), 140–145 (2004)

5. The World Factbook – Nigeria. https://www.cia.gov/the-world-factbook/countries/nigeria/. Accessed 1 Nov 2022

6. Herrero-Hernandez, E., Smith, T., Akid, R.: Electricity generation from wastewaters with starch as carbon source using a mediatorless microbial fuel cell. Biosens. Bioelectron. **39**(1), 194–198 (2013)

7. Fernández de Dios, M.Á., Del Campo, A.G., Fernández, F.J., Rodrigo, M., Pazos, M., Sanromán, M.Á.: Bacterial–fungal interactions enhance power generation in microbial fuel cells and drive dye decolourisation by an ex situ and in situ electro-Fenton process. Bioresour. Technol. **148**, 39–46 (2013)

8. Lu, N., Zhou, S., Zhuang, L., Zhang, J., Ni, J.: Electricity generation from starch processing wastewater using microbial fuel cell technology. Biochem. Eng. J. **43**(3), 246–251 (2009)

9. Oh, S., Logan, B.E.: Hydrogen and electricity production from a food processing wastewater using fermentation and microbial fuel cell technologies. Water Res. **39**(19), 4673–4682 (2005)

10. Min, B., Cheng, S., Logan, B.E.: Electricity generation using membrane and salt bridge microbial fuel cells. Water Res. **39**, 1675–1686 (2005)

11. Slate, A.J., Whitehead, K.A., Brownson, D.A., Banks, C.E.: Microbial fuel cells: an overview of current technology. Renew. Sustain. Energy Rev. **101**, 60–81 (2019)

12. Zhang, Y., Min, B., Huang, L., Angelidaki, I.: Generation of electricity and analysis of microbial communities in wheat straw biomass-powered microbial fuel cells. Appl. Environ. Microbiol. **75**(11), 3389–3395 (2009)

13. Forrestal, C., Huang, Z., Ren, Z.J.: Percarbonate as a naturally buffering catholyte for microbial fuel cells. Biores. Technol. **172**, 429–432 (2014)

Community Engagements
and Collaboration

The Levels of Crop Raiding by Rodents and Primates in a Subsistence Farming Community, in South Africa

Tlou D. Raphela[1]([⊠]) [iD] and Neville Pillay[2] [iD]

[1] Disaster Management Training and Education Centre for Africa, University of the Free State, Bloemfontein, South Africa
RaphelaTD@UFS.ac.za

[2] School of Animal, Plant and Environmental Sciences, Faculty of Science, University of the Witwatersrand, Johannesburg, South Africa

Abstract. Globally, human-wildlife conflict often arises from crop raiding. Therefore, there is a need to quantify crop damage by the suspected animals around protected areas. We assessed and quantified crop damage by wildlife on subsistence farms on the edge of the Hluhluwe Game Reserve, northern KwaZulu-Natal, South Africa. Twenty farms were assessed monthly from April 2016 to March 2017, using direct observations of wildlife, detectable evidence of their consuming crops and remote camera trap footage of their presence. We recorded the animals involved in raiding, crops affected, and differences in the level of crop damage by season and farm proximity to the reserve boundary. Rodents, arthropods (mainly insects) and birds were found to feed on crops on the 20 farms, with rodents causing the highest levels of crop damage as compared to the other animals. Contrary to expectations, primates (vervet monkey *Chlorocebus pygerythrus* and chacma baboons *Papio ursinus*) identified by our camera traps were not identified as raiders during our study, since these species never left the reserve to raid farms. However, camera trap footage showed that both primate species engaged in feeding behaviour on the inside boundary edge of the reserve (close to farms) during the dry season. Maize (*Zea mays*) was the main affected crop throughout the study. The highest level of crop damage was during the dry season compared to the wet season. The distance of farms from the reserve was not a significant predictor of the level of crop damage in the farms sampled, contrary to the findings of other studies, which mentioned that crop raiding decreases further from protected area boundary. Using trapping, crop assessment and observation, our study showed that small rather than larger animals from the neighbouring conservation area were the main crop raiders and that maize was the most affected crop, especially during the dry season.

Our study showed that small rather than larger animals from the neighbouring conservation area were the main crop raiders and that maize was the most affected crop, especially during the dry season. This study concludes that mitigation measures by our studied farmers should target small mammals, concentrate on maize and should be strengthened during the dry season.

A. D. Mambo et al. (Eds.): InterSol 2022, LNICST 449, pp. 197–209, 2022.
https://doi.org/10.1007/978-3-031-23116-2_17

Keywords: Camera trap survey · Crop raiding · Human-wildlife conflict · Primates · Rodents · Subsistence homesteads

1 Introduction

Crop raiding by wildlife is amongst the most critical problems experienced by farmers, particularly those farming adjacent to protected areas (Siljander et al. 2020). However, the extent of the problem has not been addressed in subsistence farmers (Seoraj-Pillai 2016). Thus, case-specific studies are needed from farmland bordering protected areas, with different potential crop types and crop pests, to enable us to generate a global understanding of crop-raiding patterns. Crop raiding by wildlife has been extensively studied in Africa (Montgomery et al. 2021; Gloriose 2019), with focus being placed on flagship species such as elephant (*Loxodonta africana*). However, raiding by rodents and primates together has received little attention in the scientific literature.

Systematic surveys of rodent damage are scarce in Africa (Dossou et al. 2020). Moreover, the impact of these animals on subsistence homesteads is not well documented. Unsurprisingly, crop raiding by primates is common, yet studies of primate feeding ecology do not adequately consider their impact on subsistence homesteads, as well as seasonal changes in their raiding behaviour for agricultural and non-agricultural food (Naughton-Treves et al. 1998). Most crop raiding by wildlife is reported to occur on farms that are in close proximity to protected areas (Siljander et al. 2020). Naughton-Treves (1997) hypothesized that crop raiding, in general, is limited to a few hundred meters from the protected area boundaries. However, we are not aware of any studies that have tested the distance-related hypothesis for rodents and primates in rural subsistence farmers of South Africa.

We investigated the levels of crop raiding by rodents and primates in a subsistence farming community, abutting the Hluhluwe Game Reserve, KwaZulu-Natal Province, South Africa. The literature maintains that crop-raiding levels vary seasonally (Raphela and Pillay 2021; Mukeka et al. 2019). In particular, it is reported that crop-raiding incidences decrease during the wet season. Therefore, we predicted that the level of crop damage by both rodents and primates would increase during the dry season. We also tested the hypothesis proposed by Naughton-Treves (1997) that crop raiding decreases away from the game reserve boundary. We predicted that the level of crop damage by both rodents and primates would be greater on farms that are closer to the game reserve. We also predicted that maize (*Zea mays*) would experience the highest level of damage as compared to all the other crop types. Previous research has reported that maize is the most depredated crop because of its nutritional value (Ghimirey et al. 2018; Raphela and Pillay 2021).

2 Materials and Methods

2.1 Study Site

The study was conducted at Phindisweni village (28°26' S; 31°43 'E), bordering the Hluhluwe Game Reserve. Subsistence farming is the main source of income in this community (StatsSA 2011). Phindisweni village is vulnerable to crop raiding according to previously undocumented farmer reports. We sampled wildlife in 20 subsistence farms adjacent to the Hluhluwe Game Reserve in the dry (April to August) and wet (September to March) seasons from April 2016 to March 2017.

2.2 Farm Attributes

A Garmin GPSMap62 handheld device was used to record several farm attributes. We recorded the geographical location (GPS coordinates of the farms) and elevation of the central position of each of the 20 farms sampled. The area of each farm and the area cultivated were established by walking the perimeter of each sampled farm and cultivated land separately and calculating the area of each in m^2. The distance between each farm and the reserve boundary was determined by a straight-line shortest distance from the center of the farms to the reserve boundary fence using ArcMap (ArcGIS, V10.3, software package, ESRI). The measurements were grouped into intervals of <1 km, 1–2 km and 2–3 km.

2.3 Farm Sampling

We sampled food crops at Phindisweni farms, during the dry season and the wet seasons. 1 m^2 quadrats were placed to cover at least 20% of the cultivated area for each farm. Quadrats were randomly placed flat on the ground in the farmed areas and left lying there for 10 consecutive days each month per farm throughout the study. The joint ends of the quadrats were covered in bright insulation tape to locate the quadrats later. Most farmers planted their crops in rows (personal observation). Therefore, the quadrats were placed to cover all crop types planted per farm. To cover at least 20% of the cultivated land, we set 6 to 16 quadrants, depending on the surface area of the cultivated land in each farm.

2.4 Crop Damage Assessment

We visited the farms for 10 consecutive days, twice a day every month for the duration of the study to assess the amount of damage caused by animals on food crops. We counted the number of individual food crops damaged daily in each quadrat, irrespective of where the damage occurred (i.e. mostly on the leaves of crops or seeds for maize). The damaged part/s of the plants were pricked with a pin around the destruction sites to identify damage and to avoid later resampling. Crop types were also recorded. Animals that were directly observed causing damage were arthropods (mainly insects) and birds (species unknown).

Even though rodents were trapped inside the farms (see Results), they were never witnessed directly feeding on crops. Therefore, we used impressions and indentations on food crops to identify damage. We used the following evidence to categorise crop raiders: rodents, from tooth marks and ragged breaks with shredded edges and holes; insects from round holes on the leaves; and birds from tears off the food crops.

Crop damage was quantified by counting the total number of damaged crop parts, mostly leaves (sampling unit), of each individual food crop inside each quadrat, and was recorded as the level of crop damage by rodents, insects, and birds in a farm. Since we used impressions and indentations on food crops to identify damage, in cases where more than one crop raider damaged a crop part, we recorded the damage by each crop raider suspected to have caused the damage. The total number of counts per quadrat for a particular crop and pest species was recorded. Because the focus of the study was on rodents, the damage that was caused by other pests (insects and free-living birds) was compared to the damage caused by rodents.

2.5   Rodent Trapping

The capture, mark, identify and release protocol technique was used to sample rodents (Mills et al. 1995). Trapping was done monthly from April 2016 to March 2017. Each trapping session lasted 10 consecutive days each month per farm. PVC live-traps (290 × 60 × 80 mm) were set randomly on each farm, resulting in 1200 (smallest farm) to 1680 (largest farm) trap nights. Traps were baited with a mixture of peanut butter, oats, coarse salt, sunflower oil, and raisins (De Bondi et al. 2011). Cotton wool was inserted into traps to provide insulation for trapped animals during the colder periods. Also, we covered traps with surrounding vegetation for insulation against lethal temperatures. Traps were set in areas preferred by small mammals, such as next to fallen trees/shrubs, next to holes in the ground and areas with small mammal runways.

Traps were checked twice a day, once in the morning (9 am to 10 am) and in the afternoon (3 pm and 5 pm). We identified trapped individuals to species level. The trapped animals were transferred from the traps to a clear plastic bag and weighed (to the nearest gram) using a DKD handheld spring balance. Individuals were sexed based on the ano-genital distance and obvious genital differences. To recognise previously captured individuals, we marked each captured individual by trimming the hair on the back of the neck with a pair of scissors to reveal the different colour undercoat (Mills et al. 1995). Gentian violet was sprayed on the clipped area as a semi-permanent marking to also assist in identifying recaptures. The individuals were released at the point of capture and the traps were re-baited when necessary. Trapping was conducted with the approval of the local government conservation authority, Ezemvelo KZN Wildlife (permit number: OP 711/2016), and the University of the Witwatersrand Animal Ethics Screening Committee (AESC protocol number: 2015/011/48/B). This study followed the guideline for capturing and handling rodents (Mill et al. 1995).

2.6   Monitoring Primates

Direct observation and camera trap methods were used to sample primates for this study. The 20 farms were sampled for four hours a day randomly from 6 am to 8 am and, again, from 4 pm to 6 pm for 10 days a month from April 2016 to March 2017. To assess primate behaviour in the mornings and in the afternoons before they disappeared into the surrounding bush, we walked along the sampled farms to identify whether they raided crops. During these walks, we aimed to record the presence and demographic parameters (number of groups, juveniles, and adult males and adult females) of primates raiding crops and the type of crops they raided. We carried a digital camera during the walks to capture any evidence of crop raiding, as well as other evidence, such as droppings, bite marks on crops, and tracks. However, throughout the study, primates never transgressed the reserve boundary to raid crops. Therefore, their potential to raid crops was analysed from the camera trap footage (see below), to assess their behaviour on the edge of the reserve.

2.7 Camera Trap Surveillance

At 10 sites determined to be frequently visited by primates, according to farmer reports, we set up 10×8-megapixel infrared camera traps (Bushnell®, trophy camera, China), with 32 GB memory cards. The cameras were positioned at appropriate angles at approximately 0.7 m above the ground. All the cameras faced onto the farms and were secured using multiple lengths of coated flexible wire and a padlock to prevent theft. Also, for five farms that were adjacent to the Hluhluwe Game Reserve, the cameras were set up strategically facing the reserve to record the occurrence and behaviour of primates and other mammals, particularly if they transgressed the reserve/farm boundary. The five farms were separated from the reserve by a gravel road that was created by reserve management as a safety measure for fence workers. The five farms shared a fence with the reserve and with each other and were separated by distance of 100 m from each other.

The cameras were housed within an aluminum camera housing to reduce damage from moisture and for protection from rain and tied to tree trunks/logs. The camera started recording when a motion was sensed at a distance up to 18 m and recorded high-definition videos (1280×720 pixels) for 30 s. A delay period of 15 s between recordings was programmed into cameras to avoid too many records of a single motion trigger. The videos were automatically dated, and time stamped. Cameras were operational 24 h a day for 10 days per month in each of the sites throughout the study and checked every three days to replace data storage card and batteries, if necessary. Video footage was downloaded onto a laptop computer from each memory card every three days and organized into folders labelled with the location and date.

All visible animals on the video footage were identified according to primates or in other broad animal categories. The frequency of occurrence of primates and other animal groups on the edge of Hluhluwe Game Reserve were noted. To avoid pseudo-replication of primates and other animals on one video, we scored each animal species as one occurrence per day from the video footage, regardless of the number of times per day they appeared in the footage. We also recorded each primate's behaviour (feeding and traveling) by season separately.

To investigate the potential of primates to raid crops, we scored two behaviours, feeding (i.e., manipulation and ingestion of food), considered to have priority over other activities and traveling (i.e., walking, running) which was found to have a positive relationship with feeding in Japanese macaque (*Macaca fuscata*; Agetsuma et al. 2015). The travelling and feeding behaviours are fundamentally important when addressing the crop-raiding behaviour of primates because these two behaviours are indicative of current or future raiding. Agetsuma et al. (2015) found that Japanese macaques decreased feeding time when fruits are available and increase traveling time when the density of fruit-food trees is low during the dry season, requiring greater travelling and searching for trees.

3 Statistical Analyses of Data

Rodent trapping data were analysed using descriptive statistics first. All other statistical analyses were done using R statistical software (version 4.1.0; 2020). Statistical tests were two-tailed, and significance levels were set at $P \leq 0.05$. Data were mostly categorical and did not meet the assumptions of normality (Shapiro-Wilk test). Accordingly, nonparametric analyses were used.

The Spearman's rank order correlation coefficient (Spearman's rho) was performed to analyse the relationship between farm proximity to the reserve boundary and the level of crop raiding by animal groups separately (rodents, insects, birds) and collectively. For each species, the level of crop damage was set as the response variable and distance from the game reserve was the explanatory variable.

To assess seasonal variations in the level of damage by 1) crop type and 2) crop raiding animals, we applied two separate Generalised linear mixed models (GLMM) with a *glmer* function and a Poisson distribution (lme4 package, Bates *et al.* 2015). For both models, we included farm size as a random factor (intercepts only) to account for the potential sizes effect. We checked the model fit for the variables described below, and used the most appropriate model, based on the plot of the residuals against the fitted values from each model (Crawley 2007). For model 1: we used season, crop raiding animals, and two-way interactions of season*crop raiding animals as independent variables with the level of damage as a dependent variable and for model 2: we used season, crop type and the interaction between season*crop type as independent variables with the level of damage as the dependent variable. We generated P values using likelihood ratio tests (Bates *et al.* 2015).

Primates did not transgress the reserve boundary to raid crops throughout the study. Therefore, we investigated their potential to raid crops by assessing their behaviour on the edge of the reserve. We analysed the numerical frequencies of occurrences (1 occurrence per day; see above) of two behaviours (travelling and feeding) along the reserve boundary for chacma baboon (*Papio ursinus*) and vervet monkey (*Chlorocebus pygerythrus*) separately with Generalised linear models (GLMs), with a *glm* function and Poisson distribution. We included season, species, and the two-way interactions season* species as independent variables. Significance was determined using Wald (χ^2) statistics. Data for this study are presented as boxplots and scatterplots, produced using a Ggplot2 package from R software.

4 Results

4.1 Rodent Trapping

A total of 96 individual rodents were captured in 20 sampled farms from April 2016 to March 2017, in 30600 trap nights (0.3% trap success), comprising of two species: red bush rat (*Aethomys spp.*) and pouched mouse (*Saccostomus campestris*). *Aethomys spp.* (67.7%; 51 males and 28 females) was most trapped and is a common murid rodent in savanna habitats in KwaZulu-Natal Province. The pouched mouse (*Saccostomus campestris*) represented the remaining 32.3% (14 females and three males). Both the *Aethomys spp* and the *Saccostomus campestris* were mostly captured during the dry season.

4.2 Crop Raiding and Farm Proximity to the Game Reserve

The Spearman's rho did not reveal a statistically significant relationship between the level of damage and distance of farms from the reserve boundary ($r_s = -0.07$, P $= 0.438$), although the highest level of damage was in farms further away from the reserve (Fig. 1).

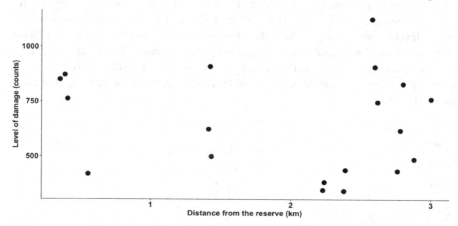

Fig. 1. Scatterplot of the distribution of the overall level of crop damage (counts per farm) across different farm distances for 20 sampled farms abutting the Hluhluwe Game Reserve, South Africa.

We then ran three separate Spearman rank analysis for the different crop raiding animal type (rodents, insects, and birds) to ascertain the relationship between the distance of farms from the reserve boundary and the level of crop damage. There was again no significant correlation between farm distance from the reserve boundary and the level of crop damage by rodents ($r_s = -0.18$, P $= 0.262$), insects ($r_s = -0.06$, P $= 0.700$) and birds ($r_s = -0.09$, P $= 0.601$; Fig. 2).

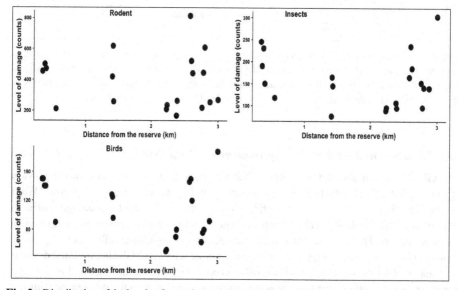

Fig. 2. Distribution of the levels of crop damage (counts per farm) by crop raiding rodents (top left), insects (top right) and birds (bottom left) across 20 sampled farms situated at different distances from Hluhluwe Game Reserve, South Africa.

4.3 Variation in the Level of Crop Damage by Crop Raiding Animals

The results of a GLMM showed that season (Wald $\chi_1^2 = 17.02$; P < 0.001), crop raiding animal type (Wald $\chi_1^2 = 302.76$; P < 0.001) and the interaction between season and crop raiding animal type (Wald $\chi_2^2 = 165.57$; P < 0.001) were significant predictors of the level of damage. Farmers experienced the highest level of crop damage during the dry season as compared to the wet season. Rodents followed by insects and birds caused the highest level of crop damage. The highest level of crop damage was caused by rodents during the dry and wet season as compared to insects and birds, but the highest level of rodent crop damage was during the wet season as compared to the dry season in contrast to the highest level of crop damage caused by insects and birds, which was in the dry season (Fig. 3).

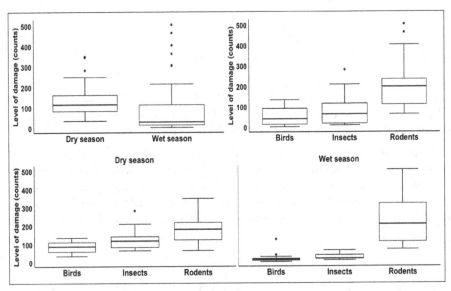

Fig. 3. Levels of damage (counts per farm) by season (top left), crop raiders (top right) and season*crop raiders (bottom) in farms on the edge of Hluhluwe Game Reserve, South Africa. Boxes show medians (solid black line across the box) and 1st (top box) and 3rd (bottom box) quartiles. Whiskers show total range and dots outside of boxes indicate outliers.

4.4 Variation in the Level of Crop Damage by Crop Type

The GLMM results showed that season (Wald $\chi_1^2 = 962.23$; P < 0.001), crop type (Wald $\chi_4^2 = 7725.42$; P < 0.001) and the interaction between season and crop type (Wald $\chi_3^2 = 118.25$; P < 0.001) were significant predictors of the level of damage. Farmers experienced the highest level of crop damage during the dry season as compared to the wet season. The highest level of crop damage was for maize followed by spinach, common bean, and beetroot. Crop damage for maize was higher during both the dry and wet season than the damage for all the other crop types, but the highest level of damage for maize and the other crop types was during the dry season than the wet season (Fig. 4).

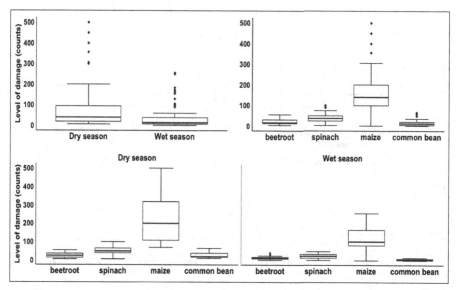

Fig. 4. Levels of damage (counts per farm) by season (top left), crop type (top right) and season*crop type (bottom) in farms on the edge of Hluhluwe Game Reserve, South Africa. Boxes show medians (solid black line across the box) and 1st (top box) and 3rd (bottom box) quartiles. Whiskers show total range and dots outside of boxes indicate outliers.

4.5 Seasonal Variations in Primate Behaviour

Overall, primate occurrence along the reserve boundary was significantly influenced by season (Wald $\chi^2_2 = 1358.33$; P < 0.001) and species (Wald $\chi^2_1 = 12.43$; P = 0.000), with the highest occurrence recorded during the dry season as compared to the wet season and the highest occurrence recorded for vervet monkey compared to chacma baboon. Primate occurrence along the reserve boundary was not significantly influenced by the interaction between season and species (Wald $\chi^2_1 = 2.36$; P = 0.124).

4.6 Feeding Behaviour

Species (Wald $\chi^2_1 = 3.19$; P = 0.073) and the interaction between species and season (Wald $\chi^2_1 = 0.11$; P = 0.736) were not significant predictors of the feeding behaviour of chacma baboons and vervet monkeys along the reserve boundary. Feeding behaviour was significantly influenced by season (Wald $\chi^2_2 = 16.41$; P = 0.000), with the highest feeding behaviour occurring in the wet season as compared to the dry season (Fig. 5).

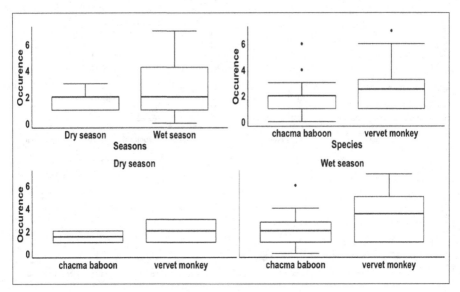

Fig. 5. Frequency of occurrence of primate feeding behaviour by season (top left), species (top right) and by season*species (bottom) along the Hluhluwe Game Reserve boundary in South Africa. Boxes show medians (solid black line across the box) and 1st (top box) and 3rd (bottom box) quartiles. Whiskers show total range and the dot outside of boxes indicate outliers.

4.7 Travelling Behaviour

Season (Wald $\chi^2_2 = 18.70$; P < 0.001), species (Wald $\chi^2_1 = 10.86$; P $= 0.000$), season*species (Wald $\chi^2_1 = 5.28$; P $= 0.021$) had a significant effect on the frequency of the travelling behaviour of primates along the Hluhluwe Game Reserve boundary. The most frequent occurrence of travelling behaviour was recorded during the dry season as compared to the wet season. Vervet monkeys travelled along the reserve borders more frequently than chacma baboons. The highest frequency of occurrence of the travelling behaviour by vervet monkey was during the dry season as compared to the wet season.

5 Discussion

We trapped 96 individual rodents of two species (79 *Aethomys spp* and 17 *Saccostomus campestris*). These two murids are common in the savanna biome (Skinner and Chimimba 2005; De Graaff 1981) and were also reported by other studies in the Hluhluwe-iMfolozi Game Reserve complex (Hagenah et al. 2009; Taylor 1998). However, these two species are not the most common species in the study area (Hagenah et al. 2009). Thus, the diverse assemblage of rodents present at Hluhluwe Game Reserve was not reflected in my study. The reduced rodent species richness and diversity in our study was an indication of a disturbed ecosystem, probably also due to the drought disaster that was experienced during the study in the study area. In summary, the absence of some rodents species which also occurs in the study area, the open habitat and drought conditions might have favored the occurrence of *Aethomys spp*. And *Saccostomus campestris*.

We found differences in the level of crop damage between rodents, insects, and birds, as well as differences in their level of crop damage between the dry and the wet season. Worldwide, rodents are considered as the second most important pest of farms (after insects), but farmers claim to have the least control of rodent pests (Tomass et al. 2020). In Uganda, Hill (1997) found that rodents, insects, and birds caused widespread damage to crops. The higher levels of crop damage caused by rodents in both seasons fond by our study may be due to their not being "controlled", as were insects and birds in the studied farms.

We did not find any indication of raiding by primates. Instead, primates were observed feeding only on the edge of the reserve, so our expectation that crop raiding by primates will occur in farms that are closer to the reserve was not supported. However, we found some evidence to suggest the potential of primates to raid crops based on their behaviour on the reserve edge. Feeding on the edge of the reserve was the most common behaviour for primates during the wet season as compared to the dry season.

Consistent with our prediction, we found that the highest level of crop damage occurred during the dry season as compared to the wet season. Mekonnen et al. (2018) suggested that lower quality and reduced availability of natural food between the wet and dry season encourages and can exacerbate crop raiding.

Crop type is known to influence the level of crop damage (Emberson et al. 2018), as occurred in our study. Maize experienced the highest level of crop damage compared to other crops, especially during the dry season. This was not surprising considering the high nutritional value of this crop (Kontsiotis et al. 2020).

Contrary to the hypothesis by Naughton-Treves (1997), we found that the level of crop damage by rodents, insects and birds was not correlated with distance from the reserve boundary. Consistent with our study, Pittiglio et al. (2014) also found that the impact of crop raiding in three villages in Tanzania did not appear to be consistently related to distance. In contrast, Saj *et al.* (2001) reported that the proximity of farms to protected areas is a significant positive predictor of crop raiding in Uganda, and farms closer to forests were reported to receive more raids than those farther away from the forest.

In conclusion, rodents appeared to be the most important damage-causing agents in the farms considered in our study, although the low diversity of rodents captured in our study might have been due to the drought that was experienced during the study. Nonetheless, some important patterns were highlighted. Even though many studies on crop raiding indicated that farms that are near protected areas are more vulnerable to crop raiding (Branco et al. 2020; Gontse et al. 2018), our study showed no distance relationship. Although no primate raiding was recorded during our study, the potential for increasing human–primate conflict throughout Africa is increasing and the attractiveness of farm crops to primates (from camera trap footage) indicates a high probability of future raids. It is crucial to gain a better understanding of the ecological determinants of primate crop-raiding. Investigations should incorporate more detailed nutritional analyses of cultivated foods consumed at different times of the year, and patterns and changes over longer periods of time. Future studies during periods with greater rainfall should be done to holistically capture the crop raiding behaviour of a range of wildlife and provide an important comparison for the data obtained in our study, conducted during a drought.

Acknowledgements. We are very greatful to the Phindisweni farmers for allowing access into their farms and we would also like to thank the research assistants Sgcino Mdletshe and Sphelele Mdletshe for assisting with data collection for this study.

Nomenclature Acts. This work and the nomenclatural act it contains have been registered in ZooBank.

Conflicts of Interest. The authors declare that there is no conflict of interest that may have influenced either the conduct or the presentation of this research.

Funding. This work was supported by National Research Foundation under Grant number [111309] and the University of the Witwatersrand.

References

Agetsuma, N., Koda, R., Tsujino, R., Agetsuma-Yanagihara, Y.: Effective spatial scales for evaluating environmental determinants of population density in Yakushima macaques. Am. J. Primatol. **77**(2), 152–161 (2015)

Bates, D., Kliegl, R., Vasishth, S., Baayen, H.: Parsimonious mixed models. Statistics. University of Wisconsin-Madison, USA. arXiv preprint arXiv:1506.04967 (2015)

Branco, P.S., et al.: An experimental test of community-based strategies for mitigating human–wildlife conflict around protected areas. Conserv. Lett. **13**(1), e12679 (2020)

Crawley, M.J.: The R book. Imperial College London at Silwood Park, UK (2007)

De Bondi, N., White, J.G., Stevens, M., Cooke, R.: A comparison of the effectiveness of camera trapping and live trapping for sampling terrestrial small-mammal communities. Wildl. Res. **37**(6), 456–465 (2010)

De Graaff, G.: The Rodents of Southern Africa: Notes on Their Identification, Distribution, Ecology, and Taxonomy. Butterworth-Heinemann (1981)

Dossou, H.J., Adjovi, N., Houéménou, G., Bagan, T., Mensah, G.A., Dobigny, G.: Invasive rodents and damages to food stocks: a study in the Autonomous Harbor of Cotonou, Benin. Biotechnologie, Agronomie, Société et Environn./Biotechnol. Agron. Soc. Environ. **24**(1), 28–36 (2020)

Emberson, L.D., et al.: Ozone effects on crops and consideration in crop models. Eur. J. Agron. **100**, 19–34 (2018)

Ghimirey, Y., Acharya, R., Pokhrel, B.M.: Human-assamese macaque conflict in Makalu-Barun National Park Buffer Zone, Nepal. Himalayan Nat. **1**, 3–7 (2018)

Gloriose, U.: Community perceptions of human-wildlife conflicts and the compensation scheme around Nyungwe National Park (Rwanda). Int. J. Nat. Resour. Ecol. Manag. **4**(6), 188–197 (2019)

Gontse, K., Mbaiwa, J.E., Thakadu, O.T.: Effects of wildlife crop raiding on the livelihoods of arable farmers in Khumaga, Boteti sub-district, Botswana. Dev. South. Afr. **35**(6), 791–802 (2018)

Hagenah, N., Prins, H.H., Olff, H.: Effects of large herbivores on murid rodents in a South African savanna. J. Trop. Ecol. **25**(5), 483–492 (2009)

Hill, C.M.: Crop-raiding by wild vertebrates: the farmer's perspective in an agricultural community in western Uganda. Int. J. Pest Manag. **43**(1), 77–84 (1997)

Kontsiotis, V.J., Vadikolios, G., Liordos, V.: Acceptability and consensus for the management of game and non-game crop raiders. Wildl. Res. **47**(4), 296–308 (2020)

Mekonnen, A., Fashing, P.J., Bekele, A., Hernandez-Aguilar, R.A., Rueness, E.K., Stenseth, N.C.: Dietary flexibility of Bale monkeys (Chlorocebus djamdjamensis) in southern Ethiopia: effects of habitat degradation and life in fragments. BMC Ecol. **18**(1), 1–20 (2018). https://doi.org/10.1186/s12898-018-0161-4

Mills, J.N., et al.: Guidelines for working with rodents potentially infected with hantavirus. J. Mammal. **76**(3), 716–722 (1995)

Montgomery, R.A., Raupp, J., Mukhwana, M., Greenleaf, A., Mudumba, T., Muruthi, P.: The efficacy of interventions to protect crops from raiding elephants. Ambio **51**(3), 716–727 (2021). https://doi.org/10.1007/s13280-021-01587-x

Mukeka, J.M., Ogutu, J.O., Kanga, E., Røskaft, E.: Human-wildlife conflicts and their correlates in Narok County, Kenya. Glob. Ecol. Conserv. **18**, e00620 (2019)

Naughton-Treves, L.: Farming the forest edge: vulnerable places and people around Kibale National Park, Uganda. Geogr. Rev. **87**, 27–46 (1997)

Naughton-Treves, L., et al.: Temporal patterns of crop-raiding by primates: linking food availability in croplands and adjacent forest. J. Appl. Ecol. **35**(4), 596–606 (1998)

Pittiglio, C., Skidmore, A.K., van Gils, H.A., McCall, M.K., Prins, H.H.: Small-holder farms as stepping stone corridors for crop-raiding elephant in northern Tanzania: integration of Bayesian expert system and network simulator. Ambio **43**(2), 149–161 (2014). https://doi.org/10.1007/s13280-013-0437-z

Raphela, T.D., Pillay, N.: Quantifying the nutritional and income loss caused by crop raiding in a rural African subsistence farming community in South Africa. Jàmbá J. Disaster Risk Stud. **13**(1), 1040 (2021)

Saj, T.L., Sicotte, P., Paterson, J.D.: The conflict between vervet monkeys and farmers at the forest edge in Entebbe, Uganda. Afr. J. Ecol. **39**(2), 195–199 (2001)

Seoraj-Pillai, N.: Human-wildlife conflict in subsistence and commercial farmers in north-eastern South Africa. Ph.D. thesis, University of the Witwatersrand, Johannesburg, South Africa (2016)

Siljander, M., Kuronen, T., Johansson, T., Munyao, M.N., Pellikka, P.K.: Primates on the farm–spatial patterns of human–wildlife conflict in forest-agricultural landscape mosaic in Taita Hills, Kenya. Appl. Geogr. **117**, 102185 (2020)

Skinner, J.D., Chimimba, C.T.: The Mammals of the Southern African Sub-Region. Cambridge University Press, Cambridge (2005)

Taylor, P.: The Smaller Mammals of KwaZulu−Natal. University of KwaZulu Natal Press (1998)

Tomass, Z., Shibru, S., Yonas, M., Leirs, H.: Farmers' perspectives of rodent damage and rodent management in smallholder maize cropping systems of Southern Ethiopia. Crop Prot. **136**, 105232 (2020)

Survey on Crop Disease Detection and Identification Based on Deep Learning

Demba Faye[✉] and Idy Diop

Ecole Supérieure Polytechnique (ESP) UCAD, Dakar, Sénégal
{demba.faye,idy.diop}@esp.sn

Abstract. Plant diseases lead to a reduction in both quality and quantity of agricultural production. 50% of agricultural losses are due to these diseases. Due to poverty and lack of infrastructures in some countries, their identification remains difficult. Plant pathologists use several techniques to identify these diseases. But these techniques are time-consuming and relatively expensive for farmers. Nowadays, several models based on image processing (IP) techniques, machine learning (ML) algorithms and deep learning (DL) algorithms have been proposed for automatic detection and identification of plant diseases. In this study, we divided these models into two groups: models based on IP and classical ML algorithms, and those based on DL. DL coupled with the transfer learning (TL) technique has become the most widely used method because of its impressive performance. The critical analysis of these models has allowed us to identify potential challenges in the field of automatic plant disease diagnosis.

Keywords: Crop diseases · Automatic detection · Artificial intelligence · Image processing · Machine learning · Deep learning · Transfer learning

1 Introduction

Plant diseases have long been one of the problems leading to a considerable reduction in both quality and quantity of agricultural production [1]. Such diseases are closely related to the long-standing global climate change [2, 3] or caused by pathogens like bacteria, virus, fungi, parasites, etc. [4]. 50% of yield losses are due to these diseases or pests [5]. Its therefore constitute a major threat to global food security and also have disastrous consequences for the economy of small farmers who represent 85% of the world's farmers [6, 7].

Rapid identification of crop diseases remains difficult in many parts of the world (e.g. developing countries) due to the lack of necessary infrastructures [6] and poverty. In practice, a naked eye observation of experts is the main approach adopted for diagnosing such diseases [8, 9]. The techniques used by Plant pathologists include methods related to chemical analysis of the infected area of the plant, and indirect methods such as the use of physical techniques (spectroscopy). These techniques are relatively expensive for farmers [1] and often take a long time to find out exactly what the disease is and to propose the right remedy to treat the pathology.

A. D. Mambo et al. (Eds.): InterSol 2022, LNICST 449, pp. 210–222, 2022.
https://doi.org/10.1007/978-3-031-23116-2_18

However, the search for a fast, automatic, cheaper and accurate method to detect plant diseases before its spread in the field is of great importance [1, 10]. It will prevent agricultural yields losses while at the same time ensuring crop quality and quantity. Today, precision technology based on IP, ML and DL is driving the modern agricultural revolution known as "Agriculture 4.0" which aims to revolutionize agricultural productivity and farm profitability [11]. Currently, AI technology, which crowns ML, which in turn crowns DL, is already considered a reality in the context of precision agriculture [1]. In recent years, several ML models have been proposed for the automatic diagnosis of plant diseases from their leaves, which are usually the first area where the symptoms of most plant diseases appear [12, 13]. These models offer a possibility to easily deploy this technology on mobile devices. In addition, with the important internet penetration[1] all around the world, smartphones and drones offer new tools for real-time detection of plant diseases [7].

This study consists of a critical analysis of recently proposed models based on IP, ML and DL techniques for the automatic diagnosis of plant diseases. It concludes by identifying the limitations and potential challenges that could help researchers in this field.

The paper is organized as follows: Sect. 2 shows the automatic learning algorithms used to identify plant diseases, Sects. 3 and 4 provide a critical analysis of the proposed models based on the classical ML and DL algorithms respectively, Sect. 5 defines and gives the advantages of TL, Sect. 6 shows the potential challenges in the field of automatic plant disease diagnosis and the last section concludes the paper.

2 Algorithms Used for Plant Disease Diagnosis

Several AI-based algorithms are used today to diagnose crop leaf diseases. The most commonly used are K-Nearest Neighbors (K-NN), Logistic Regression, Decision Tree, Random Forest (RF), Support Vector Machines (SVM) and Artificial Neural Networks (ANN) [9, 14, 15]. Such algorithms are combined with different IP methods for better feature extraction. In recent years, ANNs, especially Convolutional Neural Networks (CNNs), are the most widely used in the field of plant leaf disease identification [1, 3, 7, 16, 17]. From an architectural point of view, there are mainly two categories of ANNS: feed-forward ANNs, in which the output of one layer is output from any layer and is not likely to influence that same layer, and feedback ANNs, in which signals flow in both directions, involving loops in the network [18].

3 Detection and Identification of Plant Diseases Based on Classical ML Algorithms

In the field of plant disease detection and classification, classical ML algorithms, combined with IP techniques, have achieved excellent results. Image segmentation and classification are key steps in many proposed systems for plant disease detection. The objective of segmentation is to divide an image into a set of disjoint regions with uniform and

---

[1] The portion of the population that has access to the Internet.

homogeneous attributes such as intensity, color, tone, or texture [19]. Image segmentation approaches can be divided into four categories: thresholding, clustering, edge detection and region extraction [5]. The K-means clustering algorithm and the SVM are the most widely used algorithms in the last decade for image segmentation and classification, respectively [13, 19–21].

For example, Al Bashish et al. [10] used a model based on K-Means and a neural network to detect and classify five plant diseases namely, early scorch, cottony mold, ashen mold, late scorch and tiny whiteness, from their RGB images. K-Means technique provided excellent results in the segmentation of RGB images. The proposed model achieved an accuracy of 93%. [8] is an improvement of [10] by completely removing pixels with zero red, green and blue values and pixels at the boundaries of the infected group (object) from the images. The accuracies obtained range from 83 to 94% and the processing time has been reduced by 20% compared to the approach proposed in [10]. To detect and classify two tomato diseases caused respectively by tomato spotted wilt virus and tomato yellow leaf curl virus, Mokhtar et al. [13] proposed an approach based on four main phases, namely pre-processing, segmentation (k-means clustering algorithm) of the image, feature extraction and classification (SVM). They obtained an overall accuracy of 90% in the classification of images of diseased tomato leaves but system performance can be improved by increasing the number of images used (200 images). Chouhan et al. [19] introduced a method called Bacterial foraging optimization based Radial Basis Function Neural Network (BRBFNN) for the automatic identification and classification of plant leaf diseases using Genetic Algorithm (GA) and K-Means Clustering algorithms and SVM classifier. The accuracies obtained vary between 75.1 and 88.97%. BRBFNN is used to speed up a network and improve classification accuracy. Tian et al. [21] combined a GA to the SVM classifier and performed feature selection based on kernel principal component analysis (KPCA) to identify the best features in the images. The proposed KPCA/GA-SVM recognition model achieved the following results: 98.14%, 94.05% and 97.96% accuracy for apple mosaic virus, apple rust and apple leaf spot, respectively. Kaur et al. [22] proposed a system for detecting, classifying and calculating the severity of three soybean diseases (downy mildew, frog eye, and septoria leaf blight). Authors used color features, texture features and their combinations separately to train three models based on k-means clustering and SVM. The accuracy is ranged from 80.5 to 85%. However, the texture features selected in this study identify frog eye very efficiently but do not work for septoria leaf blight and downy mildew. Camargo et al. [23] use an algorithm for identifying visible symptoms of plant diseases based on color image analysis. The algorithm consists of the following four main phases: pre-processing, enhancement, segmentation and post-processing of images to remove unwanted background regions. To test the accuracy of their algorithm, manually segmented images were compared to automatically segmented ones. The results showed that the developed algorithm was able to identify diseased regions of plant leaves even when that region was represented by a wide range of intensities. Sutrodhor et al. [24] proposed a Mango Leaf Ailment Detection (MLAD) system based on Neural Network and SVM classifier. The MLAD can automatically detect and classify four diseases named Scab, Anthracnose, Red Rust and Sooty Mold with a mean accuracy of 80%. However, the main problem encountered is that there is not enough data on mango diseases.

Studies have shown that ML and IP algorithms have been used to determine disease severity on plant fruits. For example, Kuo et al. [25] presents an application of neural networks and IP techniques to detect and classify the quality of areca nuts, using the Detection Line method for image segmentation and a back-propagation neural network for classification. The proposed algorithm can detect spots and classify the quality of areca nuts with a CCD camera accurately (90.9%) and efficiently, but is unable to inspect for the covered blades (or other face). Table 1 is a summary of classical ML-based approaches. It compares these approaches based on the training and test data used, the ML algorithms used and the results obtained.

Table 1. Comparison of methods based on classical ML algorithms.

Topic	Year	Crop	Diseases	Method	Accuracy
[19]	2018	Orange, apple, tomato, apple	Common rust, cedar apple rust, late blight, leaf curl, leaf spot, and early blight	BRBFNN, GA et K-Means + SVM	75.17 – 88.97%
[22]	2018	Soybean	Downy mildew, frog eye, and Septoria leaf blight	k-means + SVM	80.5 – 85%
[24]	2018	Mango	Scab, Anthracnose, Red Rust and Sooty Mold	Neural Network + SVM	80%
[21]	2012	Apple	Mosaic virus, rust and alternaria leaf spot	KPCA/GA + SVM	98.14%, 4.05% and 97.96%
[25]	2012	Areca nuts	Quality of areca	Detection Line + Back-propagation neural network	90.90%
[8]	2011	Undefined	Early scorch, Cottony mold, Ashen mold, late scorch and tiny whiteness	k-Means + Neural Network	83 – 94%
[10]	2011	Undefined	Early scorch, Cottony mold, Ashen mold, late scorch and tiny whiteness	k-Means + Neural Network	93%
[23]	2009	Banana	Black sigatoka	Histogram of intensity + proposed classifier	93.7%

4 Detection and Identification Based on DL

Today, several DL models (or architectures) are used to identify plant diseases: Finetuned CNN architecture [2], Faster R-CNN [3], Region-based Fully Convolutional Network (R-FCN) [3], GoogleNet CNN [6], Inception V3 based on GoogleNet [7], Shallow CNN Model [9], Nine-layer deep CNN [14], AlexNet CNN [26], AlexNetOWTBn [16], Single-shot multibox (SSD) [28], INC VGGN [29], Deep Residual Neural Network (DRNN) [30], etc. Since AlexNet's success in the ImageNet Large Scale Visual Recognition Challenge (ILSVRC) competition in 2012, increasingly deeper networks [26, 31, 32] have been proposed and have achieved state-of-the-art performance on ImageNet and other benchmark datasets [3].

The latest generation of CNNs has achieved impressive results in image classification and is considered as the leading method for object detection in computer vision. [3, 18, 33]. For example, Ait Elkadi K. et al. [1] built a CNN-based ML model to identify tomato diseases from RGB (Red, Green, Blue) leaves images. The images used were taken from PlantVillage, a public dataset. They compared their model with three CNNs architectures, namely Alexnet, LeNet, Tairu (which provided the best performance). With the Tairu architecture, they were able to predict 8 tomato diseases with 94.35% accuracy. According to the authors, CNNs require special attention, especially in the availability of training data, the adequate choice of network structures and their hyper parameters to be adopted, and the material means available to carry out the training in the best conditions. Fuentes et al. [3] proposed a DL-based approach to detect and recognize nine different types of diseases and pests on plants in real time, using images taken by cameras (smartphones and other digital cameras). The authors used three DL architectures (Faster R-CNN (83% of accuracy), R-FCN (85.98%) and SSD (82.53%)) to find out which one is the most suitable for real-time detection and recognition of plant diseases and pests. The proposed system is able to recognize diseases but also to localize them on plant leaves and shows remarkable performance on the cases evaluated. However, the system is crop specific and, due to the insufficient number of samples, some classes with high pattern variation tend to be confounded with others, resulting in lower average precision. Mohanty et al. [6] used CNNs based on GoogleNet and AlexNet architectures to identify 14 species and 26 different plant diseases with an accuracy of 99.35%. However, for model training, when images taken under different conditions than PlantVillage are used, the accuracy drops to 31.4%. The performance of the model decreases when images taken in real time are used for testing and more training data would be sufficient to increase the accuracy of the model. Ramcharan et al. [7] applied Transfer Learning (TL) to a deep CNN (Inception V3 CNN) to identify three diseases (brown leaf spot (BLS), cassava brown streak disease (CBSD) and cassava mosaic disease (CMD)) and two types of pest damage (red mite damage (RMD) and green mite damage (GMD)). They analyzed the performance of the model with three different architectures: the original inception softmax layer, SVM, and k-nearest neighbor (knn). The model obtained the following accuracies: 98% for BLS and CBSD, 96% for CMD and RMD and 95% for GMD. The overall accuracy is 93%. Their study showed that TL applied to the CNN Inception V3 model offers very promising results in real-time plant disease detection with a relatively small image dataset. Using images or videos taken in real time by the mobile app as training data would increase the overall accuracy of the system. To identify plant diseases from their leaves, Ferentinos et al. [16] developed five CNNs based on the following architectures: AlexNet, AlexNetOWTBn, GoogLeNet, Overfeat and VGG. They used both images from a public dataset and images taken in real field conditions (37.3%) to train and test the models. When the models were trained and tested with images taken under laboratory conditions, the best performing models, VGG and AlexNetOWTBn, achieved 99.53% and 99.49% of accuracy, respectively. On the other hand, when trained and tested with images taken under laboratory conditions and those taken in the field, the accuracies decrease to 33.27% and 32.23% respectively for VGG and AlexNetOWTBn. Sladojevic et al. [18] propose a deep CNN to identify 13 different types of plant diseases with the ability to distinguish leaves of diseased plants from healthy leaves and their environment, with an average accuracy of 96.3%. However, the dataset used by the authors consists of images from Internet, so they are not taken in real conditions. Subetha et al. [27] compared the performance of two DL algorithms, such as ResNet50 and VGG19, in classifying and predicting the apple leaf diseases using images from Kaggle dataset and others real-time images captured in an apple orchard under different environmental conditions such as illumination, varying backgrounds, view-invariant, and various noises. The results show VGG19 can work better in real-time compared to ResNet50 but these architectures can predict the leaf disease with an overall accuracy of 87.7%. Pham et al. [34] proposed a Feed-Forward Neural Network (FFNN) with Hybrid Metaheuristic Feature Selection (HMFS) to classifier 3 mango diseases named Anthracnose, Gall Midge, and Powdery Mildew. The proposed model achieved an accuracy of 89,41% more than comparative CNN named AlexNet (78.64%), VGG1 (79.92%) and ResNet (84.88%). Singh et al. [35] used a multilayer convolutional neural network (MCNN) model for the classification of the mango leaves infected with the fungal disease named as anthracnose. They pre-trained their images using histogram of equalization (for contrast enhancement) and central square crop method (for image resizing) and achieved an accuracy of 97.13%. But images taken in real condition majorly suffers from the problem of Variation in Temperature, Shadowing, Overlapping of leaves, and Presence of multiple objects. Such problems reduce the performance of the model. Gulavnai et al. [36] proposed a ResNet-CNN (ResNet18, ResNet34 and ResNet50) combined with TL for automatic detection and identification of four mango leaf diseases named, anthracnose, powdery mildew, red rust and golmich. Results show that ResNet50 gives better performance with an accuracy of 91.50%. Piyush Singh et al. [37] developed a Deep 2D-Convolutional Neural Network (CNN) to detect stem bleeding disease, leaf blight disease, and pest infection by Red palm weevil in coconut trees by applying IP and DL technology. They used TL technique and compared their model to VGG16, VGG19, InceptionV3, DenseNet201, MobileNet, Xception, InceptionResNetV2 and ASNetMobile. InceptionResNetV2 and MobileNet obtained a classification accuracy of 81.48% and 82.10%, respectively while the hand-designed CNN model achieved 96.94% validation accuracy. Rabia Saleem et al. [38] proposed a model based CNN and named FrCNnet to segment and identify the diseases (Anthracnose and apical nacrosis) on the mango leaves using TL. The proposed model's segmentation accuracy is 99.2%. But a large number of mango images are required to improve the segmentation performance of each class.

Over the years, researchers have continued to develop deeper and more powerful CNN models. Geetharamani et al. [14] developped a deep CNN model with nine layers to solve plant leaf disease identification problems using PlantVillage dataset. To achieve better performance and accuracy (96.46%), they had to improve the model training images using the following methods: image flipping, gamma correction, noise injection, color enhancement by principal component analysis (PCA), rotation and scaling. The authors believe that extending their database with new images of different plant species and from different sources would increase the performance and accuracy of their model.

However, studies have shown that it is not necessary to use deep CNNs just to identify plant diseases. Shallow CNNs have a powerful IP capability which, when combined with classical ML algorithms (e.g. KNN, SVM, Random Forest (RF),…) can provide excellent results exceeding those of the proposed deep CNNs [9]. Shallow CNNs use few parameters, which means that its require little learning time.

Today, researchers are increasingly applying transfer learning (TL) [7, 14, 28, 29, 32] (see Sect. 4) to train their models for better performance. Chen et al. [29] investigated TL of deep CNNs to identify plant leaf diseases with minute lesion symptoms with the objective of reducing computational complexity. The proposed model achieves 91.83% accuracy on the PlantVillage dataset and 92% accuracy for class prediction of rice diseased images collected under real field conditions with fairly complex backgrounds.

Thanks to the benefits of TL (see Sect. 4), these models are increasingly being integrated into applications for use in mobile devices such as smartphones, drones and other autonomous agricultural vehicles. For example, Ramcharan et al. [28] deployed a CNN model in a mobile application to identify leaf symptoms (pronounced and mild) of three diseases (Manihot, esculenta, Crantz), two types of damage (RMD and GMD) caused by pests and the lack of nutrients in cassava. The authors used the SSD model and the MobileNet detector and classifier and tested the system with images and videos taken in real time and real field conditions. They obtained an accuracy of 80.6% for images and 70.4% for videos for named symptoms. But for mild symptoms, they obtained 4.10% for images and 29.4% for videos. The detection of mild symptoms seems to be difficult. One solution would be to use images with mild symptoms as training data.

Studies have shown that using a balanced set of images as the dataset increases the classification accuracy for a given model. For example, Oyewola et al. [30] developed a deep residual neural network (DRNN) and a Plain Convolutional Neural Network (PCNN) for the recognition of cassava leaf diseases. They used the distinct block processing technique and a balanced dataset of cassava leaf images, which was biased towards the CMD and CBSD classes. The proposed DRNN model outperformed PCNN by a significant margin of 9.25% on the Kaggle cassava disease dataset. Therefore, using the imbalanced dataset of cassava leaf images, both PCNN and DRNN fail identify well cassava diseases (PCNN: 50–65%; DRNN: 50% of accuracy).

Information on disease severity is crucial for plant pathologists when proposing remedies (e.g. pesticides) to eradicate a disease. This will allow pesticides to be used more economically while preserving the environment. For example, Ozguven et al. [39] used a faster R-CNN model to automatically detect and estimate disease severity in sugar beet leaves. The model was trained and tested with 155 images and the overall correct classification rate was found to be 95.48%. The authors believe that using more data and improving the quality of the images will also increase the performance of the model. Gensheng Hu et al. [17] developed a DL method based on Faster R-CNN architecture to both detect and estimate the severity of tea leaf blight (TLB). They used Retinex algorithm to enhance quality of original images used. The proposed method reduces the impact of the imbalance in the number of images and improves the accuracy of gravity classification by increasing the image size and separating the detection and classification tasks. Results show that the detection average precision and the severity grading accuracy of the method are improved by more than 6% and 9%, respectively, compared with the classical ML methods.

Table 2 is a summary of the DL-based approaches in terms of the architecture used, the training and test data used and the accuracy of the proposed model.

Table 2. Comparison of deep learning approaches

Topic	Year	Data used	Architecture	Accuracy
[1]	2021	PlantVillage	Alexnet, LeNet, Tairu and proposed model	94%
[17]	2021	Images captured in tea garden	Faster R-CNN	i) Disease detection: 6% more than classical ML methods ii) Disease severity analysis: 9% more than classical ML methods
[24]	2021	Dataset of hand-collected images of coconut	2D-CNN, VGG16, VGG19, InceptionV3, Dense-Net201, MobileNet, Xception, InceptionResNetV2 and SNetMobile	i) 2D-CNN: 96.94% ii) Inception-ResNetV2: 81.48% iii) MobileNet: 82.10%
[27]	2021	Kaggle dataset + 3,651 real-time apple images	ResNet50 and VGG19	87.7%
[30]	2021	Kaggle dataset	DRNN	96.75%
[37]	2021	Hand-collected dataset of 1564 images	Deep 2D-CNN	96.94%
[38]	2021	2286 real-time self-collected mango images	FrCNnet	99.2%
[6]	2020	PlantVillage	GoogleNet et AlexNet	99.35%
[29]	2020	PlantVillage and real time images	INC-VGGN	i) Images from PlantVillage: 91.83% ii) Real time images:92%

(continued)

Table 2. (*continued*)

Topic	Year	Data used	Architecture	Accuracy
[34]	2020	Dataset of 450 images of mango leaves	FFNN with HMFS	89.41%
[14]	2019	PlantVillage	Proposed	96.46%
[28]	2019	COCO dataset and digital camera images	SD-MobileNet	i) images: 80.6%; videos: 70.4% for pre-named symptoms ii)For mild symptoms, images: 4.10%; videos: 29.4%
[35]	2019	1070 mango leaves images captured on real-time and 1130 images from PlantVillage	MCNN	97.13%
[36]	2019	Mango dataset of 8853 images	ResNet-CNN	91.50%
[39]	2019	Dataset of 155 sugar beet images	Faster R-CNN	95.48%
[16]	2018	Public Dataset	AlexNet, lexNetOWTBn, GoogLeNet, Overfeat and VGG	i) VGG: 99.53%; ii) Overfeat: 99.49%
[3]	2017	Images taken by different cameras	Faster R-CNN, R-FCN and SSD	i) Faster R-CNN: 83%; ii) R-FCN: 85.98%; iii) SSD: 82.53%
[7]	2017	Images captured in a field	Inception V3 CNN	93%
[18]	2016	Images downloaded from the Internet	CaffeNet	96.30%

5 Transfer Learning

TL is a ML approach in which a trained CNN for one task is reused as a starting point for a model for a second task [40]. This knowledge sharing method reduces the training data size, time and computational costs when building a DL model [14]. With TL, instead of training a model from scratch, the model can be initialized using a pre-trained network on large labeled datasets, such as public image datasets, etc. [29] (see Fig. 1).

TL has been used in various applications, such as plant classification, software defect prediction, activity recognition and sentiment classification. In recent years, in the field of plant disease detection and identification, this technique has been widely used in DL approaches since the models often used in this field require high computational time and resources. TL has shown excellent results with deep network models. In general, there are three types of TL: from prior knowledge to learning, from learning to new learning and from learning to application [41].

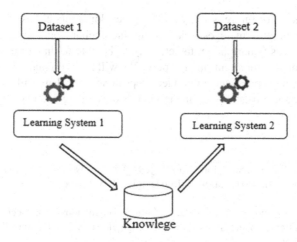

Fig. 1. Transfer learning technique

6   Potential Challenges

Classical ML algorithms and DL algorithms have achieved excellent results in the field of automatic plant disease diagnosis. However, the following challenges remain:

- For DL approaches, training data should be taken in the field and in geographically different locations (or sources). This will allow very good results to be obtained when testing with images taken in real time, in the field.
- For test images, it is important to consider images that are noisy, poorly illuminated or have complex backgrounds.
- One of the limitations of the proposed models is the difficulty of detecting diseases with mild symptoms. Detection of these mild symptoms would allow early detection of plant diseases.
- The symptoms of crop diseases can also appear on roots, stems, flowers or fruits. But until now, researchers are focused on foliar diseases.
- With the advantages of TL, these models should be deployed in mobile devices to help farmers diagnose crop diseases quickly, but also plant pathologists in their decision making. However, it should be taken into consideration that in developing countries (e.g. Sahelian countries), there is no internet in many areas, especially in the most remote areas.

7   Conclusion

This paper presents a review of approaches used for automatic detection and identification of plant diseases. These approaches are divided into two categories: classical ML based approaches and DL-based approaches. In recent years, DL-based approaches are the most widely used and for this purpose, the best performances are obtained with CNNs. In this study, we have critically analyzed these approaches to identify both limitations and potential challenges for future researches in the field of automatic crop diseases diagnosis. For future work, we plan to develop a model based on DL and the TL technique to allow farmers, especially those in Sahelian countries such as Senegal, from mobile devices (smartphone, tablet, etc.), to be able to diagnose the diseases of their crops without the intervention of experts. We will focus on mango diseases, as this fruit is one of the most produced and traded crops in Senegal. This will lead to a smarter and more sustainable production of mango in this developing country.

References

1. Ait Elkadi, K., Bakouri, S., Belbrik, M., Hajji, H., Chtaina, N.: Experimentation of model for early detection of tomato diseases by deep learning. Rev. Marocain. Protect. Plant. **14**, 19–30 (2020)
2. Sladojevic, S., Arsenovic, M., Anderla, A., Culibrk, D., Stefanovic, D.: Deep neural networks based recognition of plant diseases by leaf image classification. Comput. Intell. Neurosci. **2016**, 1–11 (2016)
3. Fuentes, A., Yoon, S., Kim, S., Park, D.: A robust deep-learning-based detector for real-time tomato plant diseases and pests recognition. Sensors **17**(9), 2022 (2017)
4. Arivazhagan, S., Vineth Ligi, S.: Mango leaf diseases identification using convolutional neural network. Int. J. Pure Appl. Math. **120**(6), 11067–11079 (2018)
5. Harvey, C.A., et al.: Extreme vulnerability of smallholder farmers to agricultural risks and climate change in Madagascar. Philos. Trans. Roy. Soc. Lond. B: Biol. Sci. **369**, 1639 (2014)
6. Mohanty, S.P., Hughes, D., Salathé, M.: Using deep learning for image-based plant disease detection. Comput. Electron. Agricult. **173**, 105393 (2020)
7. Ramcharan, A., Baranowski, K., McCloskey, P., Ahmed, B., Legg, J., Hughes, D.P.: Deep learning for image-based cassava disease detection. Front. Plant Sci. (2017). https://doi.org/10.3389/fpls.2017.01852
8. Al-Hiary, H., Bani-Ahmad, S., Reyalat, M., Braik, M., AlRahamneh, Z.: Fast and accurate detection and classification of plant diseases. Int. J. Comput. Appl. **17**(1), 31–38 (2011). https://doi.org/10.5120/2183-2754
9. Li, Y., Nie, J., Chao, X.: Do we really need deep CNN for plant diseases identification? Comput. Electron. Agric. **178**, 105803 (2020)
10. Bashish, D.A., Braik, M., Bani-Ahmad, S.: Detection and classification of leaf diseases using K-means-based segmentation and neural-networks-based classification. Inf. Technol. J. **10**, 267–275 (2011)
11. Raj, M., Atiquzzaman, M., Gupta, S., Chamola, V., Elhence, A., Garg, T., Niyato, D.: A survey on the role of Internet of Things for adopting and promoting Agriculture 4.0 (2021)
12. MahmudulHassan, S.K., Maji, Arnab Kumar, Jasinski, Michał, Leonowicz, Zbigniew, Jasinska, Elzbieta: Identification of plant-leaf diseases using cnn and transfer-learning approach. Electronics **10**(12), 1388 (2021)
13. Mokhtar, U., Ali, M.A.S., Hassanien, A.E., Hefny, H.: Identifying two of tomatoes leaf viruses using support vector machine. In: Mandal, J.K., Satapathy, S.C., Sanyal, M.K., Sarkar, P.P., Mukhopadhyay, A. (eds.) Information Systems Design and Intelligent Applications. AISC, vol. 339, pp. 771–782. Springer, New Delhi (2015). https://doi.org/10.1007/978-81-322-2250-7_77
14. Geetharamani, G., Arun, P.J.: Identification of plant leaf diseases using a nine- layer deep convolutional neural network. Comput. Electr. Eng. **76**, 323–338 (2019)
15. H. Cartwright, Ed (2015). Artificial Neural Networks, Humana Press.
16. Ferentinos, K.P.: Deep learning models for plant disease detection and diagnosis. Comput. Electron. Agric. **145**, 311–318 (2018)

17. Gensheng, H.G., Wang, H., Zhang, Y., Wan, M.: Detection and severity analysis of tea leaf blight based on deep learning. Comput. Electric. Eng. **90**, 107023 (2021)
18. Sladojevic, S., Arsenovic, M., Anderla, A., Culibrk, D., Stefanovic, D.: Deep neural networks based recognition of plant diseases by leaf image classification. Comput. Intell. Neurosci. 1–11 (2016)
19. Chouhan, S.S., Kaul, A., Singh, U.P., Jain, S.: Bacterial foraging optimization based radial basis function neural network (BRBFNN) for identification and classification of plant leaf diseases: An automatic approach towards plant pathology. IEEE Access **6**, 8852–8863 (2018)
20. Steinwart, I., Christmann, A.: Support Vector Machines. Springer Science & Business Media, New York (2008)
21. Tian, J., Hu, Q., Ma, X.X., Han, M.: An improved kpca/ga-svm classication model for plant leaf disease recognition. J. Comput. Inf. Syst. **8**(18), 7737–7745 (2012)
22. Kaur, S., Pandey, S., Goel, S.: Semi- automatic leaf disease detection and classification system for soybean cultivation. IET Image Proc. **12**(6), 1038–1048 (2018)
23. Camargo, A., Smith, J.S.: An image-processing based algorithm to automatically identify plant disease visual symptoms. Biosys. Eng. **102**(1), 9–21 (2009)
24. Sutrodhor, N., Molla Rashied, Md., Firoz, P.K., Nur, T.: Mango leaf ailment detection using neural network ensemble and support vector machine. Int. J. Comput. Appl. **181**(13), 31–36 (2018)
25. Kuo, Y.H.: Detection and classification of areca nuts with machine vision. Comput. Math. Appl. **64**, 739–746 (2012)
26. Saleem, M.H., Potgieter, J., Arif, K.M. Plant Disease Detection and Classification by Deep Learning (2019)
27. Khilar, T.S.R., Subaja Christo, M.: A comparative analysis on plant pathology classification using deep learning architecture – Resnet and VGG19. Mater. Today: Proc. (2021)
28. Ramcharan, A., et al. A mobile-based deep learning model for cassava disease diagnosis. Front. Plant Sci. 10 (2019)
29. Chen, J., Chen, J., Zhang, D., Sun, Y., Nanehkaran, Y.A.: Using deep transfer learning for image-based plant disease identification. Comput. Electron. Agric. **173**, 105393 (2020)
30. Oyewola, D.O., Dada, E.G., Misra, S., Damaševicius, R.: Detecting cassava mosaic disease using a deep residual convolutional neural network with distinct block processing. PeerJ Comput. Sci. **7**, e352 (2021)
31. Arnal Barbedo, J.G.: Digital image processing techniques for detecting, quantifying and classifying plant diseases. Springerplus **2**(1), 1–12 (2013)
32. Wang, G., Sun, Y., Wang, J.: Automatic image-based plant disease severity estimation using deep learning. Comput. Intell. Neurosci. **2017**, 2917536 (2017)
33. Szegedy, C., Vanhoucke, V., Ioffe, S., Shlens, J., Wojna, Z.: Rethinking the inception architecture for computer vision. In: Proceedings of the IEEE Conference on Computer Vision and Pattern Recognition (Las Vegas), pp. 2818–2826 (2016)
34. Pham, T.N., Tran, L.V., Dao, S.V.T.: Early disease classification of mango leaves using feed-forward neural network and hybrid metaheuristic feature selection. IEEE Access **8**, 189960–189973 (2020)
35. Singh, U.P., Chouhan, S.S., Jain, S., Jain, S.: Multilayer convolution neural network for the classification of mango leaves infected by anthracnose disease. IEEE Access **7**, 43721–43729 (2019)
36. Gulavnai, S., Patil, R.: Deep learning for image based mango leaf disease detection. Int. J. Recent Technol. Eng. **8**(3S3), 54–56 (2019)
37. Singh, P., Verma, A., Alex, J.S.R.: Disease and pest infection detection in coconut tree through deep learning techniques. Comput. Electron. Agric. **182**, 105986 (2021)
38. Saleem, R., Shah, J.H., Sharif, M., Ansari, G.J.: Mango leaf disease identification using fully resolution convolutional network. Comput. Mater. Continua **69**(3), 3581–3601 (2021)

39. Ozguven, M.M., Adem, K.: Automatic detection and classification of leaf spot disease in sugar beet using deep learning algorithms. Phys. A Stat. Mech. Appl. **535**, 122537 (2019)
40. Lumini, A., Nanni, L.: Deep learning and transfer learning features for plankton classification. Ecol. Inf. (2019)
41. Kumar, P., Kumar, R., Gupta, M.: Deep learning based analysis of ophthalmology: a systematic review. EAI Endors. Trans. Pervas. Health Technol. **7**(29), e4 (2021)

Pest Birds Detection Approach in Rice Crops Using Pre-trained YOLOv4 Model

Ismael Diakhaby, Mouhamadou Lamine Ba, and Amadou Dahirou Gueye$^{(\boxtimes)}$

Université Alioune Diop de Bambey, Bambey, Senegal
{Ismael.diakhaby,mouhamadoulamine.ba,dahirou.gueye}@uadb.edu.sn

Abstract. In Senegal, farmers in general and rice growers particularly are still facing many issues such as climatic hazards and water-scare environments in their daily life. A very acute and challenging problem for rice crops remains, however, their destruction by pest birds. These latter attack the rice crops when they are mature, leaving the farmers in disarray and without solution. Indeed, such an attack results in a drastic reduction in yields during harvest. Over time, many repellent techniques like scarecrow have been used, but show their limitations. In this paper, we tackle this problem and propose a pest birds detection approach in rice crops using pre-trained YOLOv4 detector and transfer learning. To show the efficiency of our model we conduct experiments on a real bird dataset, exhibiting a mean average precision of 96%.

Keywords: Object detection · Bird · Deep learning · YOLOv4 · Rice crops · Performance evaluation

1 Introduction

Senegalese Agriculture plays an important role in the country's economic development. It contributes about 14% to the Gross Domestic Product (17% for the primary Agricultural sector), employs 60% of the active population and concerns a surface area of more than $2,5$ million out of a potential of $3,8$ million of available arable lands. The irrigable area is estimated to $275,000$ hectares, of which $105,000$ hectares are developed and more than $75,000$ hectares are actually cultivated.

Cereals represent the most predominant crops in Senegal with 2,541,470 tons in 2018: in details we have corn, millet, paddy rices and sorghum with yields of 417,259 tons, 891,069 tons, 1,007,277 tons, and 225,865 tons respectively. Rice yield has increased by a factor of 2,3 between 2010 and 2019. One has to observe that rice is the most used cereals in Senegal. The growth of the production in rice and groundnut noted between 2012 and 2019 is due to the prioritization of these crops given their strategic role in the country's economy and food security Unfortunately, despite all the efforts made by the Senegal government, natural disasters are still hindering the development of the agricultural sector. Some of

A. D. Mambo et al. (Eds.): InterSol 2022, LNICST 449, pp. 223–234, 2022.
https://doi.org/10.1007/978-3-031-23116-2_19

these disasters have a relationship with climate change. For instance, climate change has resulted in a specific scourge that is not negligible, that is *invasion of rice crops by pest birds*. These hamfull birds arrive at a time when the rice is reaching maturity and eat the seeds on a one hand and drop lot of them on another hand. This heavily reduces expected yields during the harvest of the crops. Indeed the amount of lost yields is estimated to one thousands hectares out of fifty thousands hectares planted in 2020.

To fight against the pest birds, local residents have no effective monitoring system so far. Indeed, they are using traditional repellent methods which have quickly shown their limits. For instance, *scarecrows, clap empty bottles or waves of cassette wires* are highly harnessed to scare away birds. For a more productive and efficient Agriculture it is necessary to provide innovations based on new technological advances in particular artificial intelligence, sensors and IoT as sketched in [1,10,15]. Indeed, over the past years, general purpose or domain specific object detection models built on deep learning have received much attention both in the research community and people from industry [5,17–19]. For instance, the one-stage YOLOv4 [2] detector has proven its efficiency for real-time object detection applications.

In this paper, we propose a pest birds detection approach using a pre-trained YOLOv4 detection model for rice crops in the North Valley in Senegal We build our approach by using YOLOv4 as the basis because this latter is suitable for real-time detection and provides a lightweight version which can be deployed on computers with low resources. We rely on transfer learning in order to fine-turne a pre-trained YOLOv4 on two large datasets (ImageNet and MS-COCO) to improve the accuracy of our final model within our setting. To show the efficiency of our model we conduct experiments on a real bird dataset, exhibiting an mean average precision (mAP) (of 96%. The main contributions of this work are as follows.

- Building a real dataset of images about pest and non-pest birds in rice crops in Senegal.
- Designing and evaluating a promising pest birds detection model based on a pre-trained YOLOv4 model.

The remaining of the paper is organized as follows. In Sect. 2, we first review the state-of-the-art. Then, we detail the building block of our proposed detector in Sect. 3 and evaluate its performance over a real dataset in Sect. 4. Finally, we conclude in Sect. 5 by giving some research perspectives.

2   Related Work

We briefly review in this section several research directions pertaining to the problem of object detection using deep learning in general, and in particular for the task of monitoring pest birds in the field of Agriculture.

2.1   Deep Leaning Based Object Detection Models

Over the past years, deep learning based object detection models have received much attention both in the research community and people from industry. A thorough presentation of the state-of-the-art of such types of object detectors is available in [5,17–19]. For instance in [19], Zhengxia et al. have proposed a up-to-date survey of the object detection field in the last 20 years. They made a review of more than 400 papers about object detection in the light of its technical evolution, spanning over a quarter-century's time (from the 1990 s to 2019). They covered a number of topics in the paper, including the milestone detectors in history, detection datasets, metrics, fundamental building blocks of the detection system, speed up techniques, etc. The paper has also reviewed some important detection applications, such as pedestrian detection, face detection, text detection, etc. It made an in-deep analysis of their challenges as well as technical improvements in recent years.

As highlighted in [5], state-of-the-art general purpose and domain-specific object detection models can be categorized into two families: the *one-stage detectors* and *the two-stage detectors*. As examples of popular one-stage detectors we can cite YOLO variants [2,12,13], SDD [9], and RetinaNet [6]. Faster R-CNN [14] is an example of existing two-stage detection models. While methods in both families tackle the same problem, they differ regarding the performance criteria they put in forward. Indeed, two-stage detectors are better in localization and object recognition accuracy, whereas the one-stage detectors are faster. In recent years, proposed object detectors such as YOLOv4 [2] often add some additional layers, seen as the neck of the detector, between backbone and head in order to collect feature maps from different stages. The neck has been introduced in order to improve the accuracy of the prediction, in particular for one-stage detectors. Within the same family, detectors can be also distinguished in terms of performances and application scenarios. For instance, YOLOv4 model proposes a lightweight version that can be used and deployed in computers with low resources such as sensors and micro controllers.

2.2   Pest Birds Monitoring Approaches

Monitoring pest birds is still an acute activity in the field of Agriculture because till now currently used traditional methods remain inefficient in particular for rice crops in Sub-Saharan countries like Senegal. Recently, automatic monitoring and repellent systems for pest birds are starting to be investigated and proposed in the research field [1,10,15]. The most promising works are based on Artificial Intelligence and sensors.

In [15] the authors review the literature of systems and methods employed for autonomous bird pest control in Agriculture. The study points out the fact that using natural bird predator is one of the effective methods used for bird deterring. However, since the predators cannot be controlled, designing artificial predators or systems that act like predators is the focus of most systems reviewed in that paper. A conceptual system was proposed with emphases on the use of offensive strategy when designing an effective bird deterrent system More specifically, [10] presents a CNN based system to detect flocks of birds and to trigger an actuator that will scare the objects only when a flock passes through the monitored space. Before teaching the network, video cameras and a differential algorithm are used to detect all items moving in the vineyard. In terms of function, the algorithm is implemented in a module consisting of a microcomputer and a connected video camera. When a flock is detected, the micro controller will generate a signal to be wirelessly transmitted to the module, whose task is to trigger the scaring actuator. Despite the interesting studies to automate detection and repellent of pest birds in Agriculture, the main observation we can made on the existing proposals is a very few attention made on the use of existing object detection models in the proposed systems or approaches, in particular to fight against the pest birds in rice crops.

To the best of our knowledge this study is the first attempt to use inherent object detection models to automate the monitoring of pest birds in rice crops in Sub-Saharan countries like Senegal.

3   Pest Birds Detection Model

We build and propose our approach to automatically localize and classify pest birds on images (e.g. from a real time image acquisition system) by using YOLOv4 model and transfer learning. The YOLOv4 represents our basis detector model and the transfer learning procedure has been used to mitigate the impact of the limited size of our birds dataset in the learning process of the optimal parameter values of the detection model. The transfer learning helps us to use and fit YOLOv4 in our setting by considering the same hyper-parameter values as those obtained with the basic YOLOV4 model trained and validated on two large and reference datasets in the domain of object detection based on deep learning methods. We start the description of the setting up of our detection model for pest birds in rice crops in Senegal by presenting the architecture of YOLOv4 model.

3.1   YOLOv4 Model Architecture

YOLOv4 [2] belongs to the class of one stage object detectors, also known as dense detectors, which prioritize the inference speeds while ensuring a high detection accuracy. Recall that in one-stage detector models ROI (Region of Interest) is not selected, the classes and the bounding boxes for the complete image are simultaneously predicted. Thus, this makes them faster than two-stage detectors. YOLOv4, corresponding to the fourth version of the YOLO detection model, introduces great improvements of the speed and the accuracy over its predecessors (e.g. [12,13]). Similarly to the other one-stage detectors, YOLOv4 model architecture [2], as shown in Fig. 1, consists of three main components which play each a crucial role in the object detection process: *the backbone, the neck* and *the head* representing the dense prediction layer. In YOLOv4, the following choice has been made for each component of its architecture after intensive performance evaluation on large image datasets (MS COCO and ImagineNet).

- CSPDarknet53 [16], a Convolutional Neural Network based on the DenseNet design, as the backbone. Thanks to its two blocks (Convolutional Base Layer and Cross Stage Partial Block), it concatenates the previous inputs with the current input before proceeding into the dense layers - this is referred to as the dense connectivity pattern.
- SPP [4] additional module and PANet path-aggregation [8] as the neck where feature maps are collected from the different stages of the backbone. Then, it mixes and combines the collected feature maps to prepare them for the next step. To this end, an additional block called SPP (Spatial Pyramid Pooling) is added in between the CSPDarkNet53 backbone and the feature aggregator network (PANet) which latter improves the process of instance segmentation. This helps to increase the receptive field and separates out the most significant context features and has almost no effect on network operation speed. It is connected to the final layers of the densely connected convolutional layers of CSPDarkNet.
- YOLOv3 [13] as the head. The main function here is locating bounding boxes and performing classification. We defer the reader to [2] for the details about this function.

In practical, YOLOv4 models an object-detection task as a regression task followed by a classification task. Regression predicts classes and bounding boxes for the whole input image in single run and helps to identify the object position while classification determines the object's class. More specifically, the model receives an input consisting of the training images which will be fed to the network - they are processed in batches in parallel by the GPU. Then, the Backbone and the Neck components perform the feature extraction and aggregation. The detection Neck and detection Head together can be called as the Object Detector. At last, the head (or dense prediction layer), responsible for the detection (both localization and classification) ends the process. For further improvements of the accuracy without extra running time, YOLOv4 introduces and uses Bag of Freebies (BoF) and Bag of Specials (BoS) strategies which usually represent data augmentation techniques.

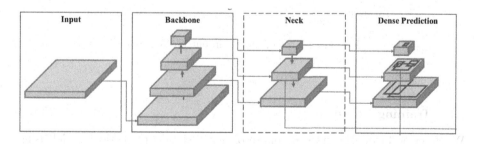

Fig. 1. YOLOv4 main components

3.2   Building Pest Bird Real Data

Our collection of real world data consists of a set of pest bird images and non pest bird images that are frequently present in rice crops in the North Valley in Senegal. As a collection methodology, we first established the list of the names of all such birds. Then, we relied on Web search engines and related tools (Google Search or Bing) and Web scrapping tools to collect images corresponding to the list of bird names of interest. The used tools include *Bing Bulk Image Downloader* script and *Google Chrome extension* for bulk images downloading named *image downloader*. After the collection of the images from the Web, we did a pre-processing stage in order to first delete irrelevant images regarding our application domain, altered images and duplicated images. Then, we proceeded to putting all the images in the same size, i.e. resizing step with 416×416 size. Finally, we proceeded to the labelling of our images needed when fitting our supervised detection model. For the labelling step, we have used *labelImg* which is an open source GUI image annotation tool written in Python[1]. We used bounding-box techniques to draw the ROI of each image and associated the corresponding class name to each box. Using this process, we have generated the labels of our entire set of images according to YOLO format.

We ended up the data collection phase with an annotated dataset of 2443 images with 1338 images belonging to the class of pest birds and 1105 images corresponding to non pest birds. An excerpt of our dataset is given in Fig. 2.

(a) Quelea   (b) Amarante

Fig. 2. Excerpt of images in our bird dataset

3.3   Training Phase

We describe below the training phase of our pest bird prediction model using Yolo v4. We start by detailing the pre-trained YOLOv4 object detection model proposed by Bochkovskiy et al. in [2].

---

[1] https://github.com/tzutalin/labelImg

Pre-training of YOLOv4. YOLOv4 in its basis has been trained and evaluated on two different large datasets: ImageNet (ILSVRC 2012) [3] with $1,000$ distinct classes and MS COCO (test-dev 2017) [7] which latter consists of 80 different object classes. For the purpose of this study, we rely on the same values of YOLOv4 hyper-parameters fitted and tested using those two images datasets. In ImageNet, for the classification of images, the default hyper-parameters of Yolov4 for the various conducted experiments have been set as follows: (i) the training iteration set to $8,000,000$; (ii) the batch size and the mini-batch size are 128 and 32, respectively; (iii) the polynomial decay learning rate scheduling strategy is adopted with initial learning rate of 0.1; (iv) the warm-up steps is 1000; and (v) the momentum and weight decay are respectively set as 0.9 and 0.005. All the BoS (Bag of Specials) experiments use default hyper-parameters while BoF (Bag of Freebies) experiments consider additional 50% training iterations. The training has been done with a 1080Ti or 2080Ti GPU. In MS-COCO object detecton experiments, the authors of YOLOv4 set the default hyper-parameters as follows: (i) the training iterations is $500,500$; (ii) the step decay learning rate scheduling strategy is adopted with initial learning rate 0.01 and multiply with a factor 0.1 at the 400,000 steps and the 450,000 steps, respectively; and (iii) the momentum and weight decay are respectively set as 0.9 and 0.0005 All architectures use a single GPU to execute multi-scale training in the batch size of 64 while mini-batch size is 8 or 4 depend on the architectures and GPU memory limitation. Except for using genetic algorithm for hyper-parameter search experiments, all other experiments use default setting. Genetic algorithm used YOLOv3-SPP to train with IoU loss and search 300 epochs for min-val $5k$ sets. We adopt a search learning rate of 0.00261, momentum of 0.949, IoU threshold forassigning ground truth 0.213, and loss normalizer 0.07 for genetic algorithm experiments. We have verified on a large number of BoF, including grid sensitivity elimination, mosaic data augmentation, IoU threshold, genetic algorithm, class label smoothing, cross mini-batch normalization, self-adversarial training, cosine annealing scheduler, dynamic mini-batch size, Drop Block, Optimized Anchors, different kind of IoU losses. We also conduct experiments on various BoS, including Mish, SPP, SAM, RFB, BiFPN, and Gaussian YOLO. For all experiments in the pre-training phase, we only use one GPU for training, e.g. techniques such as syncBN that optimizes multiple GPUs are not used.

Fine-Tuning Phase. To adapt the pre-trained YOLOv4 model in our application case, we implemented additional layers trained and evaluated on our pest birds dataset. To obtain the final detection model, we used YOLOv4 pre-trained weights by harnessing transfer learning. The fine-tuning phase has been done with the following parameter settings: (i) linebatch = 64; (ii) subdivisions = 16; (iii) width = 416 height = 416 as network input size; (iv) maxbatches = 6000. (v) filters = 21 on each convolutional layer before each YOLOv4 layer; and (vi) number of classes = 2.

4   Experiments and Validation

We detail in the section the experiments we conducted on a real dataset to evaluate the performance of our proposed model. For the details of the description of the used real bird dataset we refer the reader to Sect. 3.2. We start by present our experiment setting.

4.1   Setting Up Experiments

We present here the implementation of our approach and the experimental environment.

Implementation Details. For the purposes of fitting and evaluating our proposed approach, we did the implementation of our detection model using DarketNet library available in C and CUDA. For the labelling of the images in our dataset, we did it using labellImg a graphical user interface written in Python. For the fine-turning of YOLOv4 model it comes out to configure the file *YOLOv4-custom.cfg* by specifying the values of the hyper-parameters that will be considered for the training of the model in our pest bird training set.

Testing Environment. The model has been trained and tested using the Google Colaboratory environment to benefit from the free avalaible GPU and computation power. Colab provides several types of NVIDIA based GPU: GPU NVIDIA K80, P100, P4, T4, V100 and A100 that offer a variety of computation options which suit our workload.

Splitting of the Dataset. With respect to the recommendation of the authors of YOLOv4, we split our dataset considering the following proportions : 90% for the training set and 10% for the testing.

4.2   Performance Measures

We present below the metrics used to evaluate performance of our detection model. Some of them are based on the confusion matrix that sums up the number of true positive (TP), false positive (FP), false negative (FN), and true negative (TN) after the testing of our detection and comparison with the ground truth.

Intersection over Union. Intersection over Union (IoU) measures the difference between the ground truth mask (gt), the predicted objects and the predicted mask (pd) as follows.

$$IoU = \frac{area(gt) \cap area(pd)}{area(gt) \cup (area(pd)}$$

(1)

The value of the IoU metric varies from 0 to 1 where 0 means no overlapping and 1 implies a perfect prediction rate. .

Precision. Precision (P) evaluates the ability of the detector to identify exactly the correct classes of objects.

$$P = \frac{TP}{TP + FP} \tag{2}$$

Recall. Recall (R) measures the ability of the model to find correct classes of the given objects, i.e. the proportion of true positives detected among all object classes to be predicted.

$$R = \frac{TP}{TP + FN} \tag{3}$$

A good model is one that can detect correctly the classes of most of the objects.

F1-Score. It represents the weighted average of the precision and the sensitivity (recall). Therefore, this score takes into account both false positives and false negatives. Intuitively, it is not as easy to understand as precision, but F1-score is generally more useful than precision, especially if you have an unequal class distribution values:

$$F1 - score = 2 \times \frac{P \times R}{P + R} \tag{4}$$

Mean Average Precision. The mean average precision (mAP) is a metric used to measure the accuracy of object detectors over all classes in a specific database. The mAP is simply the average precision over all classes [11] and is given by the following formula:

$$mAP = \frac{1}{n} \sum_{i=0}^{n} AP_i \tag{5}$$

where AP_i being the average precision in the ith class and n is the total number of classes.

Loss Function. We consider the sum-squared error between the predictions and the ground truth to calculate loss. The loss function encompasses the classification loss and the localization loss (errors between the predicted boundary box and the ground truth).

ROC Curve. A receiver operating characteristic curve, or ROC curve, is a graphical plot that illustrates the diagnostic ability of a binary classifier system as its discrimination threshold is varied. The ROC curve is created by plotting the true positive rate (TPR) against the false positive rate (FPR) at various threshold settings.

4.3   Results and Analysis

Figure 3 shows the results of testing our final model on the two images given in Fig. 2; the model successfully detects both birds and classifies them as pest (image in left) and non pest (image in right).

(a) Quelea class detection   (b) Amarante detection

Fig. 3. Examples of detection outputs of our model

The performance of our YOLOv4 pest birds detection model are summarized in Table 1 and Fig. 4. Table 1 contains the precision, recall, F1-score, the mAP, and the IoU measures of the model. The mAP is equal to 96.5% meaning that the average precision of our detection model is very high. This trend is also verify by the recall of our model which is equal to 94%.

Table 1. Performance measures of our detection model

mAP	F1-Score	Precision	Recall	IoU
0.965	0.89	0.84	0.94	63.31

Figure 4 shows the curve representing the evolution of the mAP (red curve) and the loss function (blue curve) as a function of the number of iterations. We note that the loss function exponentially decreases from 1 up to about 200 iterations and then from there, continues to linearly decrease. The loss at the last iteration is 0.1398 showing a very low error rate of our detection model. On the other hand, after the first 1000 iterations, the average accuracy (mAP) is 74%. This percentage grows exponentially until 92%. Then from this point, the average accuracy follows a monotonic trend up to 96% until convergence. The average of the mAP at the end of the training is 96.5%. In sum, we can deduce that our model present promising performance in its ability to correctly detect pest birds and non pest birds. This may be due to the transfer learning process and the high quality of the set of bird images used to fine-turne the pre-trained model in our application case.

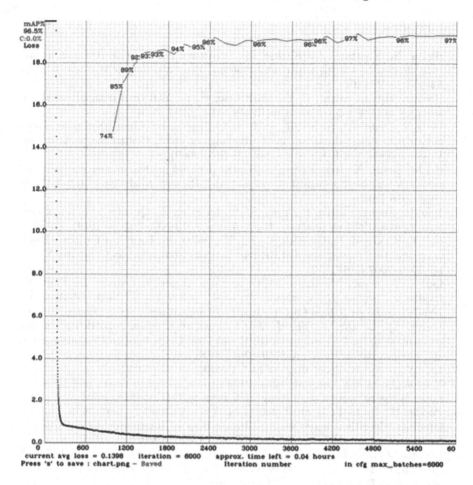

Fig. 4. ROC curve of the training accuracy and lost of our detection model

5   Conclusion and Perspectives

This paper has tackled the problem of pest birds monitoring in rice crops in Senegal and proposed a detection approach built on top of a pre-trained YOLOv4 detector and transfer learning. To show the efficiency of our model we conducted experiments on a real bird dataset, exhibiting a mean average precision of 96%. We use transfer learning to solve the problem of limitations in terms of domain specific data size and resources. As perspectives, we plan to evaluate other one-stage detectors such as SDD and RetinaNet in our setting and compare their performance to those of YOLOv4 in order to see if they can outperform this latter. We also plan to deploy and evaluate our approach in the rice yards in the North Valley in Senegal to see how the model reacts in real environment. At last, we envision to evaluate the running time of our model in order to assess its applicability in real life applications.

References

1. Bhusal, S., Bhattarai, U., Karkee, M.: Improving pest bird detection in a vineyard environment using super-resolution and deep learning. IFAC-PapersOnLine **52**(30), 18–23 (2019)
2. Bochkovskiy, A., Wang, C.-Y., Mark Liao, H.-Y.: YOLOv4: optimal speed and accuracy of object detection. CoRR, abs/2004.10934, 2020
3. Deng, J., Dong, W., Socher, R., Li, L.-J., Li, K., Fei, L.F.: ImageNet: a large-scale hierarchical image database. In: Proceedings of IEEE Conference on Computer Vision and Pattern Recognition, pp. 248–255 (2009)
4. He, K., Zhang, X., Ren, S., Sun, J.: Spatial pyramid pooling in deep convolutional networks for visual recognition. IEEE Trans. Pattern Anal. Mach. Intell. **37**(9), 1904–1916 (2015)
5. Jiao, L., Zhang, F., Liu, F., Yang, S., Li, L., Feng, Z., Qu, R.: A survey of deep learning-based object detection. IEEE Access **7**, 128837–128868 (2019)
6. Lin, T.-Y., Goyal, P., Girshick, R., He, K., Dollár, P.: Focal loss for dense object detection. In: Proceedings of IEEE International Conference on Computer Vision, pp. 2999–3007 (2017)
7. Lin, T.-Y., et al.: Microsoft COCO: common objects in context. In: Fleet, D., Pajdla, T., Schiele, B., Tuytelaars, T. (eds.) ECCV 2014. LNCS, vol. 8693, pp. 740–755. Springer, Cham (2014). https://doi.org/10.1007/978-3-319-10602-1_48
8. Liu, S., Qi, L., Qin, H., Shi, J., Jia, J.: Path aggregation network for instance segmentation. In: Proceedings of IEEE and CVF Conference on Computer Vision and Pattern Recognition, pp. 8759–8768 (2018)
9. Liu, W., et al.: In: Proceedings of ECCV **9905**, 21–37 (2016)
10. Marcon. P., et al.: A system using artificial intelligence to detect and scare bird flocks in the protection of ripening fruit. Sensors **21**(12), 4244 (2021)
11. Padilla, R., Netto, S.L., SilvaEduardo da, A.B.: A survey on performance metrics for object-detection algorithms. In: Proceedings of International Conference on Systems, Signals and Image Processing, pp. 237–242 (2020)
12. Redmon, J., Divvala, S., Girshick, R., Farhadi, A.: You only look once: unified, real-time object detection. In: Proceedings of IEEE Conference on Computer Vision and Pattern Recognition, pp. 779–788 (2016)
13. Redmon, J., Farhadi, A.: YOLOv3: an incremental improvement. arXiv preprint arXiv:1804.02767 (2018)
14. Ren, S., He, K., Girshick, R., Sun, J.: Faster R-CNN: towards real-time object detection with region proposal networks (2016)
15. Suleiman, I., Babawuya, A., Oyewole, A., Salihu, B., Adeoti O., Alhaji, S.Y.: A review of bird pest repellent systems in farms (2021)
16. Wang, C.-Y., Mark Liao, H.-Y., Wu, Y.-H., Chen, P.-Y., Hsieh, J.-W., Yeh, I.-H.: CSPNet: a new backbone that can enhance learning capability of CNN. In: Proceedinds of Conference on Computer Vision and Pattern Recognition, Workshops, pp. 1571–1580. Computer Vision Foundation and IEEE (2020)
17. Abbas Zaidi, S.S., Ansari, M.S., Aslam, A., Kanwal, N., Asghar, M., Lee, B.: A survey of modern deep learning based object detection models. Digit. Sig. Process. **126**, 103514 (2022)
18. Zhao, Z.-Q., Zheng, P., Shou-Tao, X., Xindong, W.: Object detection with deep learning: a review. IEEE Trans. Neural Netw. Learn. Syst. **30**(11), 3212–3232 (2019)
19. Zou, Z., Shi, Z., Guo, Y., Ye, J.: Object detection in 20 years: a survey. CoRR, http://arxiv.org/abs/1905.05055arXiv:1905.05055 (2019)

Energy Conversion and Conservation for Underserved Areas

Truncation Effect of a Three-Dimensional Compound Parabolic Concentrator on the Solar Flux at the Input of the Receiver of a 30 kWe Solar Tower Power Plant

Kory Faye[1]($\boxtimes$), Mactar Faye[1,2], El Hadji Ibrahima Cissé[2], Ababacar Thiam[1,2], and Vincent Sambou[2]

[1] Research Group Energetic System and Efficiency, Department of Physic, Alioune Diop University of Bambey, B.P. 30, Bambey, Senegal
kory.faye@uadb.edu.sn

[2] Laboratory of Water, Energy Environment and Industrial Processes, Polytechnic School, Cheikh Anta Diop University, S-10700 Dakar-Fan, Senegal

Abstract. The length of compound parabolic concentrator affects the performance of solar tower power plant. This study investigates the truncation effect of a three-dimensional compound parabolic concentrator (3D-CPC) on the solar flux at the input of the solar receiver of a 30 kWe solar tower power plant. Firstly, the three-dimensional compound parabolic concentrator (3D-CPC) is firstly sized and designed in SolidWorks software. Then, the 3D-CPC is meshed in Ansys Meshing into 2516 elements before being designed in Soltrace software. Finally, Monte Carlo ray racing (MCRT) method is used to simulate the operation of the solar tower power plant with the 3D-CPC truncated at 0°, 35°, 40° and 55°. The optical simulation results showed that the 3D-CPC increases the concentration ratio by a factor of 4.91 with an optical efficiency of 80.12%. The 3D-CPC truncated at 35° collected a higher solar flux than the others 3D-CPC. This shows that the truncation of 3D-CPC has effect on the solar flux at the input of the receiver.

Keywords: Truncation effect · Tree-dimensional compound parabolic concentrator · Solar flux · Solar receiver

1 Introduction

Solar energy source is considered one of the most renewable energy sources because of its cleanliness, abundance and positive impact on the environment [1]. It can be used for electricity production by two technologies such as Photovoltaic solar panels and Concentrated Solar Power (CSP) [2]. The CSP is the most promising technology due to its high efficiency and its advantage in storing thermal energy [3, 4]. Among the CSP technologies, Solar Tower Power Plant (STPP) is more advantageous for electricity production

© ICST Institute for Computer Sciences, Social Informatics and Telecommunications Engineering 2022
Published by Springer Nature Switzerland AG 2022. All Rights Reserved
A. D. Mambo et al. (Eds.): InterSol 2022, LNICST 449, pp. 237–250, 2022.
https://doi.org/10.1007/978-3-031-23116-2_20

because of its high efficiency and low capital cost [2]. However, the density of solar energy is generally affected by factors related to its intermittent nature such as weather conditions, seasons [5, 6]. This is why, concentrating solar systems are usually equipped with uniaxial or biaxial solar tracking devices to improve their performance. However, solar tracking devices require high control accuracy and considerable investment [5, 7].

Non-imaging concentrator such as three-dimensional compound parabolic concentrator (3D-CPC) can be used in solar tower power plants to eliminate solar tracking systems and thus reduce investment costs [8, 9]. In addition, the use of 3D-CPC can increase the concentration of the solar rays at the input of the receiver [10]. Thus, 3D-CPCs are attracting increasingly attention from researchers because of its importance in collecting solar flux with high efficiency in STPPs [11]. However, the major disadvantage of a 3D-CPC is that it is very long compared to its inlet aperture diameter. This disadvantage should be taken into account when designing a 3D-CPC using STPPs to achieve efficiency, economy, and lightness [12].

Many researchers have studied the 3D-CPC used in STPP. Some of them have focused on truncation to improve the geometric dimensions of 3D-CPC. Winston R. [13] show a relationship between the truncation ratio and the length/aperture ratio with different half acceptance angles. Ari Rabl [14] studied the truncation of a 3D-CPC based on the average number of reflections. He showed that the truncation ratio could be selected based on the average number of reflections and the geometric concentration ratio.

Others researchers have studied the performance of 3D-CPCs by in STPPs. G. Dai et al. [15] studied the solar concentrating performance of a dish concentrator (DC) using a truncated 3D-CPC by the MCRT method. For a DC with a tilt angle of $45°$, the numerical results show that the interception efficiency (η_{int}) is about 4.0% higher than that of the CPC-DC, but the concentration ratio of the CPC-DC is twice that of the DC. Lipinski and Steinfeld [16] proposed an annular 3D-CPC to capture and concentrate the spilled solar radiation, the transmission efficiency (τ) varying with the angle (θ) of incidence was numerically simulated using the MCRT method. Recently, L. Li et al. [10] designed a 3D-CPC for high-temperature solar thermochemical applications, irradiated by a high-flux multisource solar simulator. Optical simulations showed that 3D-CPC increases the concentration ratio by a factor of 4.1 at 85.4% optical efficiency (η_{opt}), reduces the spilling losses (η_{spil}) from 78.9% to 32.1%, and reduces the no-uniformity of the solar flux on the target surface. L. Li et al. [17] studied the thermal and economic performances of a solar central receiver system equipped with 3D-CPC. Using an MCRT model, a heat transfer model, and a cost model based on System Advisor Model (SAM), they showed that a 3D-CPC can improve the thermal (η_{th}) and economic (LCOX) performances of the system only at temperatures between 900 K and 1200 K. However, the truncation effects of these 3D-CPCs have not been studied.

The above-mentioned research work has investigated the truncation effects of 3D-CPCs on the geometrical dimensions and studied the thermal and economic performances of the 3D-CPCs by using central receiver. As far as 1 know, no study has yet been performed on the truncation effects of a 3D-CPC on the solar flux at the input of the receiver. The objective of this study is to investigate the truncation effect of a 3D-CPC on the solar flux at the input of the receiver of a 30 kWe solar tower power plant.

To achieve this objective, a two-dimensional CPC (2D-CPC) is sized firstly and designed in a three-dimensional paraboloid form in SolidWorks software. Then, the 3D-CPC is meshed using Ansys Meshing to calculate the different parameters needed for its design in Soltrace software [18]. Finally, the optical simulations of the STPP with a 3D-CPC truncated at 0°, 35°, 40° and 55° are achieved by the MCRT method. The average solar flux at the input of the receiver is collected for each 3D-CPC truncated during different periods of the year to visualize the truncation effect.

2   Materials and Methods

2.1   3D-CPC description

The 3D-CPC described in Fig. 1 is a no-imaging solar concentrator formed by rotating the cross-section of a 2D-CPC around the optical axis (z) [14]. The half acceptance angle (θ_a) is the angle formed by the optical axis and the line (AC). The half acceptance angle is defined as the maximum angle of incidence that allows incident rays at the inlet aperture of the 3D-CPC to be reflected to the receiver [8]. However, the rays with incidence angles larger than half acceptance angle fail to reach the receiver.

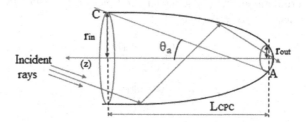

Fig. 1. Schematic diagram of a 3D-CP below the illustration.

2.2   3D-CPC Sizing

The two parameters determining the geometry of a 3D-CPC are the half acceptance angle (θ_a) and the inlet aperture radius (r_{in}). The outlet aperture radius (r_{out}) of the 3D-CPC can be determined by [19, 20]:

$$r_{out} = r_{in} \sin(\theta_a) \tag{1}$$

The length (L_{CPC}) of the 3D-CPC is calculated by the following relationship:

$$L_{CPC} = \frac{f \cos(\theta_a)}{\sin^2(\theta_a)} \tag{2}$$

where f is the focal distance of the 3D-CPC given by the following expression:

$$f = r_{out}(1 + \sin(\theta_a)) \tag{3}$$

In a full 3D-CPC, the upper part is almost parallel to the optical axis (described in red in Fig. 2), thus contributing very low in concentrating solar rays to the receiver. Therefore, the full 3D-CPC can be truncated to a certain length [21]. The 3D-CPC truncated is now defined by three parameters which are the half acceptance angle, the outlet aperture radius and the vertex angle (ϕ_T) which is called the truncation angle (see Fig. 2).

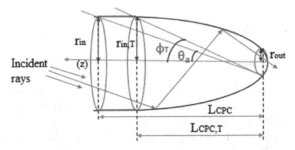

Fig. 2. Schematic diagram of a 3D-CPC showing the upper part parallel to the optical axis

The inlet aperture radius ($r_{in,T}$) and the length ($L_{CPC,T}$) of the 3D-CPC truncated are given by Equations. 4 and 5 respectively [22]:

$$r_{in,T} = \frac{f\sin(\phi_T - \theta_a)}{\sin^2(\phi_T/2)} - r_{out} \tag{4}$$

$$L_{CPC,T} = \frac{f\cos(\phi_T - \theta_a)}{\sin^2(\phi_T/2)} \tag{5}$$

The truncation ratio (r_T) of the 3D-CPC is defined as the ratio of the truncated length to the real length. It is given by:

$$r_T = \frac{L_{CPC,T}}{L_{CPC}} \tag{6}$$

2.3 3D-CPC Design

The method developed by Craig K. et al. in [23] to design a complex solar receiver in Soltrace, is used in this study to design the 3D-CPC. The sizes of the 2D-CPC are used to design the 3D-CPC in SolidWorks software. The 3D-CPC is then meshed using Ansys Meshing with a triangular mesh as described in Fig. 3 [24]. Afterwards, two files containing mesh information are generated by the Ansys Meshing. One contains the elements (triangles) and their nodes (N_1), (N_2), and (N_3) and the other contains the nodes and their coordinates (x, y, z) (see Fig. 3).

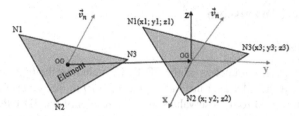

Fig. 3. Mesh element with the nodes of each corner and their coordinates

Thus, the means parameters to define a triangular element in Soltrace are the coordinates of the centroids (OG) and the aim points of each element. The centroid of an element is chosen as the reference point. This reference point is obtained by averaging the coordinates of the three nodes of each element. The coordinates of the reference point are used as input values for the x, y and z coordinates in the stage section of Soltrace. The element is then translated back to the origin by subtracting the reference point coordinates of each node. The relationship that calculates the coordinates of the element after the translation is given by [24]:

$$\begin{pmatrix} x \\ y \\ z \end{pmatrix}_{NiG} = \begin{pmatrix} x \\ y \\ z \end{pmatrix}_{G} - \begin{pmatrix} x \\ y \\ z \end{pmatrix}_{Ni} \tag{7}$$

The normal vector ($\vec{V}_n$) of the element can be calculated by the cross product of the vectors of two nodes. Equation 8 is used to calculate the normal vector of an element.

$$\vec{V}_n = (y_1 z_2 - z_1 y_2)\vec{i} + (z_1 x_2 - x_1 z_2)\vec{j} + (x_1 y_2 - y_1 x_2)\vec{k} \tag{8}$$

The norm of the normal vector ($\|\vec{v_n}\|$) can be calculated by the following expression:

$$\|\vec{v_n}\| = \begin{cases} \left(\dfrac{v_{nx}}{\sqrt{v_{nx}^2 + v_{ny}^2 + v_{nz}^2}} \right) \\ \left(\dfrac{v_{ny}}{\sqrt{v_{nx}^2 + v_{ny}^2 + v_{nz}^2}} \right) \\ \left(\dfrac{v_{nz}}{\sqrt{v_{nx}^2 + v_{ny}^2 + v_{nz}^2}} \right) \end{cases} \tag{9}$$

The coordinates of the aim point of each element can be calculated by the sum of the coordinates of the reference point and the normal vector:

$$\begin{pmatrix} x \\ y \\ z \end{pmatrix}_{Ap} = \begin{pmatrix} x \\ y \\ z \end{pmatrix}_{G} + \begin{pmatrix} x \\ y \\ z \end{pmatrix}_{Vn} \tag{10}$$

3   Results and Discussion

3.1   Results of sizing

The basic geometrical parameters of the 3D-CPC, including the half acceptance (θ_a) angle of 12.5° and the inlet aperture radius (r_{in}) of 0.70 m, are determined by means of optical simulations. From these values, the size results of the 3D-CPC are given in Table 1.

Table 1. Sizes of the three-dimensional compound parabolic concentrator

Parameters	Values (m)
Outlet aperture radius (r_{out})	0.15
Focal distance (f)	0.18
Length (L_{CPC})	3.84

3.2   Results of design

A code is developed in Matlab software to calculate the size of the 3D-CPC and to plot its parabolic profile as shown in Fig. 4. The 2D-CPC consists of two parabolic reflectors symmetrical to the optical axis (z). Thus, the shape of the 3D-CPC is obtained by the rotation of the 2D-CPC cross section around the optical axis of the 2D-CPC. Figure 5 shows the shape of the 3D-CPC designed by SolidWorks software.

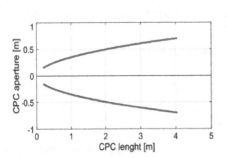

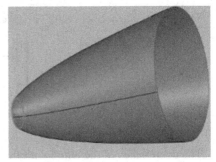

Fig. 4. 2D-CPC parabola profile   **Fig. 5.** 3D-CPC design in SolidWorks

The shape of the 3D-CPC is complex and its design in Soltrace is very problematic. Indeed, Soltrace offers only the users the possibility to design standard geometrical shapes such as circles, triangles, and flat rectangles or curved shapes such as cylinders, cones… [25]. For this reason, the 3D-CPC is meshed in Ansys Meshing by a fine triangular mesh. Figure 6 shows the 3D-CPC meshed into 2516 elements (i.e., small triangles in Fig. 6). Then, the mechanical APDL tool of Ansys Workbench is used to edit the two mesh files. One of the files contains the elements and the nodes of the different corners of the element (N_1, N_2, and N_3) and the other file contains the nodes and their coordinates (x, y, and z) in disorder. Therefore, a script is developed under RStudio software to associate and tidy the elements and nodes with their respective coordinates. After, the coordinates of the centroids (x_G, y_G, z_G) and the aim points ($x_{Aimpoint}$, $y_{Aimpont}$, $z_{Aimpoint}$) of each element are calcuted. These coordinates are used to design the 3D-CPC in Soltrace (see Fig. 7).

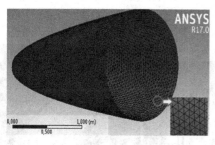 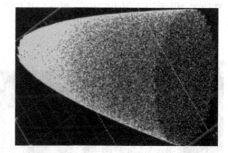

Fig. 6. 3D-CPC mesh in Ansys Meshing   **Fig. 7.** 3D-CPC design in Soltrace

The dimensions of the different subsystems of 30 kWe solar tower power plant are all interdependent parameters that also make the design and positioning of the 3D-CPC complex in Soltrace software. The sizes of the different parameters of the solar field of the 30 kWe STPP found in our previous work [26], are used in this study. The characteristics of the different subsystems of STPP are shown in Table 2.

Table 2. Characteristics of the STPP subsystems 3D-CPC Orientation South.

Subsystems	Parameters	Values
Heliostat	Form	square
	Number	175
	Area (Single-facet)	2 m^2
	Height	1.5 m
3D-CPC	Orientation	South
	Height	26 m
	Inlet aperture radius	0.7 m
	Outlet aperture radius	0.15 m
	Focal distance	0.18 m
	Length	3.84 m
	Tilt angle	55°
Receiver	Form	Circular
	Aperture radius	0.15 m

Figures 8 and 9 show the design of the solar tower power plant without 3D-CPC and with 3D-CPC, respectively, in Soltrace. The parameters listed in Table 2 are taken into account in the optical simulations. For the heliostats and the 3D-CPC, a reflectivity (ρ) of 0.95, a transmitivity (τ) of 0, a slope error (σ_{slop}) of 1 mrad and a specularity error (σ_{spec}) of 0.9 are also taken into account in the optical simulations. In addition, an absorptivity (α) of 0.95, a slope error of 0.90 mrad, and a specularity error of 0.90 are assigned to the solar receiver. For the sun shape, a Pillbox distribution (θ_{sun}=4.65 mrad) is selected. 100,000 solar rays are launched for the optical simulation to determine the average solar flux at the inlet and exit of the 3D-CPC. Figure 10 shows the multiple reflections of solar rays inside the 3D-CPC.

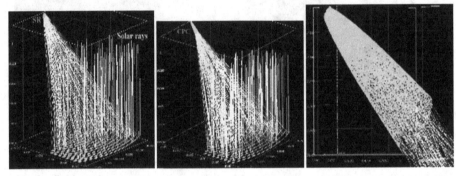

Fig. 8. STPP without 3D-CPC   **Fig. 9.** STPP with 3D-CPC   **Fig. 10.** Solar rays in the 3D-CPC

Figure 11 shows the average solar flux collected at the receiver as a function of time for the STPP with 3D-CPC and without 3D-CPC. The average solar fluxes at 12 h: 00 are 98.79 kW/m^2 without 3D-CPC and 496.89 kW/m^2 with 3D-CPC, i.e., a difference of about 80.12%. This difference is due to the non-uniformity of the solar flux distribution on the receiver without 3D-CPC. This non-uniformity solar flux distribution leads to hot spots on the surface of the receiver and reduces the amount of solar flux. To increase the solar flux and reduce the hot spots, a 3D-CPC is used. Figure 12 shows the average solar flux collected at the input and output of the 3D-CPC as a function of time. The average solar flux collected at the input of the 3D-CPC is 100.99 kW/m^2. Thus, the optical simulations show that the 3D-CPC increases the concentration ratio by a factor of 4.91.

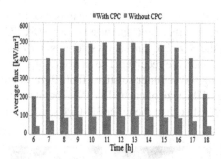

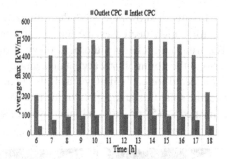

Fig. 11. Average solar flux collected as a function of time (summer solstice)

Fig. 12. Average solar flux as a function of time (summer solstice)

3.3 Results of Truncation Effect

The length of the full 3D-CPC is 3.84 m, which is much longer than its inlet aperture diameter of 1.4 m. For this reason, the 3D-CPC is truncated at 0° (untruncated), 35°, 40° and 55°. The truncation ratio (r_T) of the 3D-CPC is shown in Fig. 13. It can be seen that the truncation ratio decreases when the truncation angle increases. This means that as the truncation angle increases, the length of the 3D-CPC truncated decreases. Figure 14 shows the 3D-CPC truncated at 0°, 35°, 40° and 55°. In this figure, it is clear that if the truncation angle increases from 35° to 55°, the length decreases from 2.62 m to 1.40 m. The truncation also widens the inlet aperture and increases its capacity to collect solar rays that were outside of the nominal half acceptance angle.

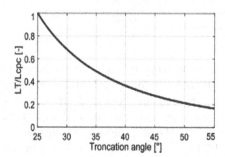

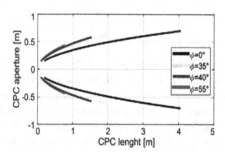

Fig. 13. Truncation ratio via truncation angle of 3D-CPC

Fig. 14. Parabolic profiles of 2D-CPC at 0°, 35°, 40° and 55°

Figure 15 shows the 3D-CPC truncated at 0°, 35°, 40° and 55°. It can be seen that the truncation decreases the length and increases the inlet aperture of the 3D-CPC. The truncation changes the field of view of the 3D-CPC and allows some solar rays, beyond the nominal half acceptance angle, to reach the receiver. The average solar flux is collected for each 3D-CPC at 12 h: 00 during the summer solstice. Table 3 gives the average solar flux at the input of the receiver and the size of each 3D-CPC. The 3D-CPC truncated at 35° provides a higher average solar flux than the other 3D-CPCs.

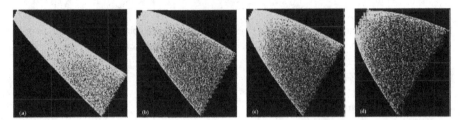

Fig. 15. Three-dimensional compound parabolic concentrator truncated at 0° (a), 35° (b), 40° (c), and 55° (d)

Table 3. Performances of each 3D-CPC

Truncation angle (°)	Length (m)	Inlet aperture radius (m)	Average solar flux (kW/m^2)
0	3.84	0.70	495.82
35	2.62	0.68	514.02
40	1.88	0.63	479.00
55	1.40	0.58	466.76

The results shown in Table 3 are not sufficient to properly assess the effects of the truncation of a 3D-CPC on the solar flux. For this reason, the optical simulations were performed during four periods of the year (spring equinox, autumn equinox, winter solstice, and summer solstice). Figure 16 shows the average solar flux collected at the input of the receiver as a function of time for each 3D-CPC during the four periods. The optical simulation results show that the 3D-CPC truncated at 35° collects a higher average solar flux than the other 3D-CPC for each period. The solar rays that enter the 3D-CPC with incidence angles smaller than the acceptance angle, reach the receiver either directly or after several reflections from the 3D-CPC walls. On the one hand, when the length of the 3D-CPC is long (i.e., the untruncated 3D-CPC), the reflections of the solar rays inside the 3D-CPC are more numerous and therefore the intensity of some solar rays decreases. On the other hand, when the length of 3D-CPC is small (i.e., for 3D-CPCs truncated at 40° and 55°), spilling losses appear. In addition, most of the incident solar rays on the input of the receiver are rejected to the outside after reflection. This shows that the truncation of a 3D-CPC has effects on the solar flux at the input of the receiver.

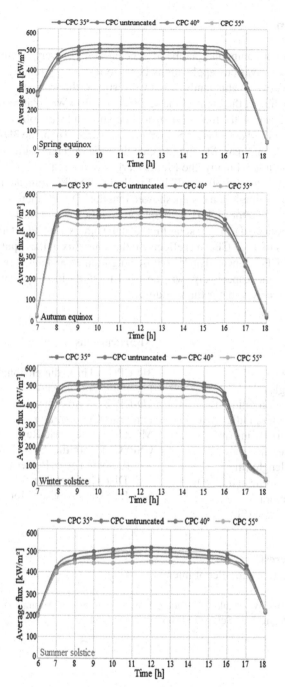

Fig. 16. Average solar flux collected at the input of the receiver via time for each 3D-CPC during four periods

4 Conclusion

A three-dimensional compound parabolic concentrator is a very interesting solar collector technology for various applications because it does not require a solar tracking system. The objective of this study was to investigate the truncation effect of a 3D-CPC on the solar flux at the input of the receiver of a 30 kWe solar tower power plant. To achieve this objective, the three-dimensional compound parabolic concentrator (3D-CPC) is firstly sized and designed in SolidWorks software. Then, the 3D-CPC is meshed into 2516 elements in Ansys Meshing to calculate the different parameters needed for in its design in Soltrace. Finally, the Monte Carlo ray-tracing (MCRT) method is used to simulate the operation of 30 kWe STPP with the 3D-CPC truncated at 0°, 35°, 40° and 55°. The optical simulation results showed that the 3D-CPC increases the solar concentration ratio by a factor of 4.91 with an optical efficiency of 80.12%. The 3D-CPC truncated at 35° collected a higher solar flux than the others 3D-CPC. This shows clearly that the truncation of a 3D-CPC has effects on the solar flux at the input of the receiver.

Thus, the 3D-CPC truncated at 35° whose length, inlet, and outlet radius are 2.62 m, 0.68 m, and 0.15 m, respectively, will be used to study the heat transfer inside the volumetric solar receiver in our future study.

Nomenclature.

θ_a : Acceptance angle (°)
θ: Incidence angle (°)
C_{CPC}: Concentration ratio (-)
r_{out} : Outlet aperture radius (m)
r_{in} : Inlet aperture radius (m)
f: Focal distance (m)
L_{CPC}: 3D-CPC lenght (m)
$L_{CPC,T}$: 3D-CPC truncated length (m)
v_n : Normal vector (-)
ϕ_T : Truncated angle (°)

Abbreviations.

3D-CPC: Three-dimensional Compound Parabolic Concentrator
2D-CPC: Two-dimensional Compound Parabolic Concentrator
MCRT: Monte Carlo Ray Tracing
CSP: Concentrating Solar Power
STPP: Solar Tower Power Plant
DC: Dish Concentrator
SAM: System Advisor Model

Conflicts of Interest
The authors declare no conflict of interest.

Acknowledgements. We thank the academic authorities of the Alioune Diop University of Bambey and the Polytechnic School of Dakar for their support.

References

1. Kalogirou, S.A.: Solar thermal collectors and applications. Progr. Energy Combus. Sci. **30**, 231–295 (2004)
2. Huang, Y., Ma, X., Rao, C., Liu, X., He, R.: An annular compound parabolic concentrator used in tower solar thermal power generation system. Sol. Energy **188**, 1256–1263 (2019)

3. Shahabuddin, M., Alim, M.A., Alam, T., Mofijur, M., Ahmed, S.F., Perkins, G.: A critical review on the development and challenges of concentrated solar power technologies. Sustain. Energy Technol. Assess. **47**, 101434 (2021)
4. Malan, A., Kumar, K.R.: A comprehensive review on optical analysis of parabolic trough solar collector. Sustain. Energy Technol. Assess. **46**, 101305 (2021)
5. Tsegaye, S., Shewarega, F., Bekele, G.: A review on security constrained economic dispatch of integrated renewable energy systems. In: EAI Endorsed Transactions Conference 2020 on Energy Web, vol. 8, no. 32 (2021)
6. Xu, R., Ma, Y., Yan, M., Zhang, C., Xu, S., Wang, R.: Effects of deformation of cylindrical compound parabolic concentrator (CPC) on concentration characteristics. Sol. Energy **176**, 73–86 (2018)
7. Tian, M., Su, Y., Zheng, H., Pei, G., Li, G., Riffat, S.: A review on the recent research progress in the compound parabolic concentrator (CPC) for solar energy applications. Renew. Sustain. Energy Rev. **82**, 1272–1296 (2018)
8. Chandan, S.D., Kumar, P.S., Reddy, K.S., Pesala, B.: Optical and electrical performance investigation of truncated 3X nonimaging low concentrating photovoltaic-thermal systems. Energy Conv. Manag. **220**, 113056 (2020)
9. A. Ustaoglu, J. Okajima, X. Zhang and S. Maruyama.: Truncation effects in an evacuated compound parabolic and involute concentrator with experimental and analytical investigations, Applied Thermal Engineering, 17, 1359–4311 (2018)
10. Li, L., Wang, B., Pottas, J., Lipiński, W.: Design of a compound parabolic concentrator for a multi-source high-flux solar simulator. Sol. Energy **183**, 805–811 (2019)
11. Pozivil, P., Ettlin, N., Stucker, F., Steinfeld, A.: Design and experimental testing of a 50 kWth pressurized-air solar receiver for gas turbines. J. Solar Energy Eng. **137**, 0310021 (2015)
12. Jadhav, A.S., Gudekar, A.S., Patil, R.G., Kale, D.M., Panse, S.V., Joshi, J.B.: Performance analysis of a novel and cost effective CPC system. Energy Conv. Manag. **66**, 56–65 (2013)
13. Ustaoglu, A., Alptekin, M., Okajima, J., Maruyama, S.: Evaluation of uniformity of solar illumination on the receiver of compound parabolic concentrator (CPC). Sol. Energy **132**, 150–164 (2016)
14. Winston, R.: Principles of solar concentrators of a novel design. Sol. Energy **16**, 89–95 (1974)
15. Rabl, A.: Comparison of solar concentrators. Sol. Energy **18**, 93–111 (1976)
16. Dai, G., Xia, X., Sun, C., Zhang, H.: Numerical investigation of the solar concentrating characteristics of 3D CPC and CPC-DC. Sol. Energy **85**, 2833–2842 (2011)
17. Lipinski, W., Steinfeld, A.: Annular compound parabolic concentrator. J. Solar Energy Eng. **128**, 121–124 (2006)
18. Li, L., Wang, B., Pye, J., Lipinski, W.: Temperature-based optical design, optimization and economics of solar polar-field central receiver systems with an optional compound parabolic concentrator. Sol. Energy **206**, 1018–1032 (2020)
19. Wendelin, T.: SolTrace: a new optical modeling tool for concentrating solar optics. In: ASME 2003 Solar Energy Conference, Kohala Coast, HI (2003)
20. Winston, R., Miñano, J.C., Benítez, P.: Non-imaging Optics. Elsevier Academic Press, Cambridge (2005)
21. BarrónDíaz, J.E., et al.: FEM-CFD simulation and experimental study of compound parabolic concentrator (CPC) solar collectors with and without fins for residential applications. Appl. Sci. **11**, 3704 (2021)
22. Indira, S.S., Vaithilingam, C.A., Sivasubramanian, R., Chong, K., Saidur, R., Narasingamurthi, K.: Optical performance of a hybrid compound parabolic concentrator and parabolic trough concentrator system for dual concentration. Sustain. Energy Technol. Assess. **47**, 10538 (2021)

23. Slootweg, M., Craig, K.J., Meyer, J.P.: A computational approach to simulate the optical and thermal performance of a novel complex geometry solar tower molten salt cavity receiver. Sol. Energy **211**, 1137–1158 (2020)
24. Craig, K.J., Slootweg, M., Le Roux, W.G., Wolff, T.M., Meyer, J.P.: Using CFD and ray tracing to estimate the heat losses of a tubular cavity dish receiver for different inclination angles. Sol. Energy **211**, 1137–1158 (2020)
25. Wang, Y., et al.: Verification of optical modelling of sunshape and surface slope error for concentrating solar power systems. Sol. Energy **195**, 461–474 (2020)
26. Faye, K., Thiam, A., Faye, M.: Optimum height and tilt angle of the solar receiver for a 30 KWE solar tower power plant for the electricity production in the Sahelian Zone. Int. J. Photoenergy. 1961134 (2020)

Renewable Energy Transition: A Panacea to the Ravaging Effects of Climate Change in Nigeria

J. O. Mahmud, S. A. Mustapha$^{(\boxtimes)}$, and K. J. Mezue

NASENI Solar Energy Limited, Karshi, Abuja, Nigeria
mustapha.ajibola@naseni.org

Abstract. There have been global concerns about the continuous rise in the surface temperature of the earth. The rise in temperature is due mainly to numerous human activities. Nigeria contributes to this menace due to poor electricity supplies making some of its citizens rely on cutting down woods from forest and others using fossil fuel generators. Another prominent contribution to the release of carbon dioxide and other greenhouse gas emissions is the unrelenting gas flaring during the refining of much relied crude oil. This paper therefore proposes solar photovoltaic (PV) among other recommendations as ways that Nigeria can contribute to limiting global warming to between 1.5 °C and 2 °C which the 2021 report of Intergovernmental Panel on Climate Change (IPCC) alarmed will be exceeded during the 21st century if unchecked. Literatures were reviewed and online survey was carried out to evidently investigate the current state of grid electricity supply in Nigeria. The result from the survey showed that 75% of the respondents who are connected to the grid do not have electricity supply beyond 12 h. The implication of this is that many of these respondents resort to fossil fuel power supply while seeing solar PV as expensive. Therefore, Nigeria can reduce greenhouse gas emissions through political will that ensures that policies that will strictly prohibit gas flaring and encourage the PV industry in the country are enforced in order to make clean energy accessible to all.

Keywords: Renewable energy transition · Solar PV · Climate change

1 Introduction

It is evident from the 2021 Intergovernmental Panel on Climate Change (IPCC) 2021 report that the globe is still warm [1]. The report clearly indicated that the 1.5 °C to 2 °C earth's surface temperature rise limit may be exceeded within the 21st century alone if drastic efforts are not put in place by the nations of the world [1, 2]. It was therefore recommended, based on physical science perspective, that there is the need for firm, sustained and rapid effort at reaching net zero CO_2 emission and minimize other greenhouse gases (GHG) emission. The consequence of continuous neglect of mitigating these GHGs results in rise in temperature, draught, fire, flood and uncertainty in rainfall [3, 4].

A. D. Mambo et al. (Eds.): InterSol 2022, LNICST 449, pp. 251–257, 2022.
https://doi.org/10.1007/978-3-031-23116-2_21

Research works have shown that the major contributing activity to the GHG emission is the use of coal, crude oil and natural gas for electricity generation [3, 5].

In order to solve the negative effects of the climate change and as a result of the fallout of the Paris agreement signed in 2015, the 2021 United Nations Climate Change Conference called COP26 was organized [6]. The participating parties including Nigeria made known their more ambitious commitment towards the mitigation of climate change. This move is pertinent because despite the fact that Africa has 40% of the solar potential of the world, it unfortunately only has 1% of the world's solar panels which contributes to poor electricity access in the continent [7, 8].

Despite efforts by the Nigerian government to improve the poor electricity situation in the country, the rate of access to electricity in Nigeria is still poor [9]. This calls for more drastic policies in order for the nation to effectively transit to the use of renewable energy (RE) for it to significantly contribute to the solution to the ravaging effects of climate change.

This paper therefore presents the respondents' feedback on the status of electricity in Nigeria, effects of climate change on Nigeria, Nigeria's contribution to curbing the effect as well as recommendations on the way towards the transition to RE.

2   Current Status of Electricity in Nigeria via a Survey and Its Effects

There have since been reports of mismatch in the centralized grid electricity demand and supply in Nigeria with demand outweighing supply due to increase in population. This is without a matchup improvement in supply of electricity despite different government interventions [10–12]. In view of this, in this work, an online survey was carried out among 480 respondents across Nigeria as shown in Fig. 1.

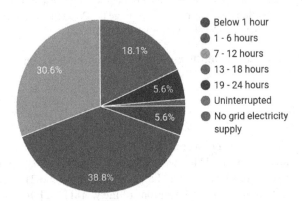

Fig. 1. Status of electricity supply in Nigeria

The results from the survey showed that 5.6% of the respondents reported that they have below 1h daily of electricity supply from the centralized grid. 38.8% of the respondents have between 1 and 6 h electricity supply daily. It was observed that 30.6% of the respondents are supplied electricity between 7 and 12 h daily while 18.1% have power supply for between 13 and 18 h daily and 5.6% have it between 19 and 24 h daily. None of the respondents indicated that they have uninterrupted electricity supply from the grid while 1.2% said they are not connected to the grid at all. Therefore, the result from the survey indicated that 75% of the respondents who are connected to the centralized grid do not have electricity supply beyond 12 h.

This survey has shown that these respondents who are in dire need of energy will resort to any alternative means available to them such as coal and other fossil fuels. With many Nigerians resorting to coal, many trees are continuously fallen especially for cooking and heating. Others resort to fossil fuel powered electric generators all of which contribute to the warming of the earth and affects Nigeria as a country.

3   Climate Change and Its Effects on Nigeria

Energy security has been a long quest for humans. Many industrialized nations such as the USA, China, Germany and Japan have seen energy independence as a key factor to ensure their socio-economic stability as well boosting industrialization thereby utilizing crude oil, gas and coal in large quantity [13]. However, these non-renewable forms of sources of energy are causing more damage to the existence of human race through their emission of GHGs.

Nigeria, among other developing nations have also joined as the use of wood and charcoal as fuel for domestic cooking and heating account for over 80% [14]. Others who can afford or are in the urban centers depend on kerosene and gas. Oil production in Nigeria remains another challenge due to the fact that oil spillage and continuous gas flaring have really contaminated the air, land and crop with about 7.4bn cubic feet of gas being flared in only 2018 and a total of 478.7MT in CO_2 equivalent has been flared between 1970 and 2015 as shown in Fig. 2 [15].

Meanwhile, in commercial utilization as a whole, the major sources of electricity generation in Nigeria are natural gas and hydro. Even though hydro is a form of renewable energy, its commercial utilization is just 10% while other sources such as solar and wind are completely not connected to the national grid as shown in Fig. 3 [15, 16].

With the pervasive epileptic nature of electricity in the country, the use of unclean fuels by many Nigerians is rife. This has made Nigeria to be among the countries of the world with the most deforestation rate with an average annual loss of 525,000 hectares [17]. Evidently, coal has been rated as one of the dirtiest fuel that has added 81% of the carbon dioxide (CO_2) present in the atmosphere of the earth since 1870 and responsible for 40% of the annual CO_2 emission globally [18, 19]. Nigeria is therefore seen as a nation that is contributing to the emission of GHGs and so has not been spared from the ravaging effects of climate change such as flood, inconsistent rainfall and desertification. These have made the Nigerian government to put some effort at adopting REs.

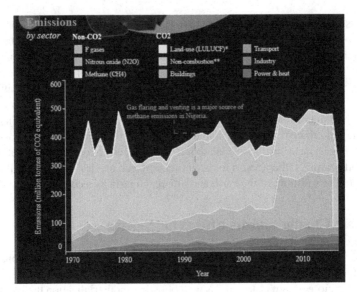

Fig. 2. Gas flaring in Nigeria in CO_2 equivalent [15]

Nigeria electricity production 1985-2018

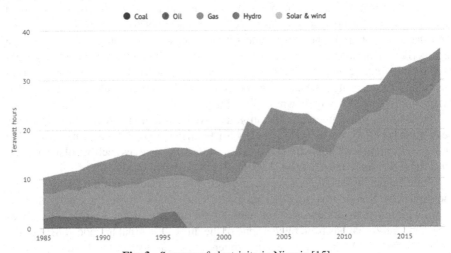

Fig. 3. Sources of electricity in Nigeria [15]

4   Nigeria's Efforts at Mitigating GHGs

Nigeria has been making some frantic efforts at reaching net zero emissions by improving the renewable energy (RE) sector in the country in order to contribute to the mitigation of the ravaging effects of climate change. In 2011, the Federal Government established NASENI Solar Energy Limited for the purpose of doing local manufacturing of solar photovoltaic (PV) modules as well as providing solar energy solutions to the citizens

[20]. The economic recovery and growth plan (ERGP) which ended in 2020, even though has been replaced with National Development Plan (NDP) for 2021–2025, had a good plan of significant inclusion of RE and addition of 1.1GW of solar PV power in particular to the national grid although not achieved [21, 22, 23]. Through one of its agencies, the Rural Electrification Agency (REA), Nigeria has launched solar home systems scheme for 5million home as indicated by Nigerian President during the COP26 conference 2021 in Glasgow [24]. Also, during the conference, Nigeria, having appreciated the level of desertification in the Northern part of the country and its negative socio-economic effects, pledged that it will be net zero by 2060 [24]. Nigeria therein called for investment and partnership as well as financial assistance in the areas of clean technologies especially in solar power [19]. In the area of wind energy, which either in planning stage or abandoned, Nigeria has invested in wind farms including the 10 MW in Katsina state [25, 26]. More efforts are however required especially in the area of effective policy implementation.

5   Conclusion

In this study, it was established through a survey that 75% of respondents among Nigerians who are connected to the centralized grid do not have electricity supply beyond 12 h. It was also evident from this work that poor electricity supply, leading to the use of fossil fuel coupled with gas flaring during oil production, have made Nigeria to be among nations with significant CO_2 and other GHGs emission. Efforts by Nigerian government towards the 2060 net zero were provided. With the provided recommendations, this work will serve as a guide for policy making and implementation towards the realization of energy transition to RE in mitigating the effect of climate change.

6   Recommendations

This study considered the challenges posed by the ravaging effect of climate change in Nigeria in order to provide recommendations that will serve as framework for effective energy transition towards RE. These are as follows:

- Nigeria needs to as a matter of urgency redirect its present resources for capacity development in home grown research, development and commercialization of technologies in the areas of RE and allied solutions such as solar PV manufacturing, storage systems and electric vehicles.
- Emphasis should be more on transfer of RE technologies to developing countries than financial assistance. This is more required because many of the developed countries may deliberately fail or genuinely get affected by the effect of COVID-19 pandemic to redeem their financial pledges as agreed in the COP26 conference.
- Decentralization of the national grid needs to be done urgently with increase in the present limit of 1MW [27] to which mini grid can generate. This will give more degree of freedom for the evolution of privately operated micro and mini grids to supply unserved and underserved communities.

- Since solar PV technology is adjudged to be one of the most economically feasible REs in Nigeria [28], there is the need to give tax holidays for local manufacturers of solar PV modules and balance of system. This will encourage private individuals to establish solar PV manufacturing companies.
- Research works [29, 30] have shown that majority of installed solar power systems in Nigeria are not connected to the grid and are owned by individuals, private and government organizations, there is need for the provision of incentives and subsidies for the adopters of the technology. This will make solar power system components to be cheaper and enticing to adopt.
- Other sources of REs should be embraced. Since hydro is an existing adopted technology for power generation, all available and suitable water sources should be utilized. Wind energy technology also needs to be revived in Nigeria. The technology has high potential with capacity factor ranging between 11% and 45% across the country according to [16].

References

1. IPCC 2021: Summary for policymakers. In: Climate Change 2021: The Physical Science Basis. Cambridge University Press (2021)
2. Kamal, A.S.M., Hossain, F., Shahid, S.: Spatiotemporal changes in rainfall and droughts of Bangladesh for 1.5 and 2C temperature rise scenarios of CMIP6 models. Theoret. Appl. Climatol. 146(1), 527–542 (2021)
3. Eitan, A.: Promoting renewable energy to cope with climate change—policy discourse in Israel. Sustainability 3(3170), 1–17 (2021)
4. Parmesan, C., Yohe, G.: A globally coherent fingerprint of climate change impacts across natural systems. Nature 421, 37–42 (2003)
5. Weisser, D.: A guide to life-cycle greenhouse gas (GHG) emissions from electric supply technologies. Environ. Sci. Technol. 46, 619–627 (2012)
6. United Nations: Climate and Environment. UN News, 29 October 2021. news.un.org/en/story/2021/10/1104142. Accessed 16 Nov 2021
7. Osmundsen, T.: Focus COP26: How can Africa Attract more Solar Investments? PV Magazine, 29 October 2021. https://www.pv-magazine.com/2021/10/29/focus-cop26-how-can-afr ica-attract-more-solar-investments/. Accessed 5 Nov 2021
8. Da Silva, P.P., Cerqueira, P.A., Ogbe, W.: Determinants of renewable energy growth in Sub-Saharan Africa: evidence from panel ARDL. Energy 156, 45–54 (2018)
9. Mahmud, J.O., Mustapha, S.A.: Opportunities for engineers in the solar energy value Chain. In: 1st NSE Minna Branch National Conference, Minna (2021)
10. Sambo, A.S.: Matching Electricity Supply with Demand in Nigeria. International Association for Energy Economics (2008)
11. Sambo, A.S.: Developing local manufacturing capacity for photovoltaic modules and balance-of-system components in Nigeria. In: 2nd Knowledge Sharing Workshop, Sokoto (2021)
12. Ugulu, A.I.: Barriers and motivations for solar photovoltaic (PV) adoption in Urban Nigeria. Int. J. Sustain. Energy Plan. Manag. 21, 19–34 (2019)
13. Dźwigoł, H., Dźwigoł-Barosz, M., Zhyvko, Z., Miśkiewicz, R., Pushak, H.: Evaluation of the energy security as a component of national security of the country. J. Secur. Sustain. Issues 8(3), 307–318 (2019)

14. Olanrewaju, F.O., Andrews, J.I., Li, H., Phylaktou, H.N.: Bioenergy potential in Nigeria. Chem. Eng. Trans. **74**, 61–66 (2019)
15. Dunne, D.: Country Profile. Carbon Brief, 21 August 2020. https://www.carbonbrief.org/the-carbon-brief-profile-nigeria. Accessed 16 Nov 2021
16. Bamisile, O., et al.: An approach for sustainable energy planning towards 100 % electrification of Nigeria by 2030. Energy. **197**, 1–38 (2020)
17. Gobir, A.A., et al.: Climate change awareness and related tree planting practices in a rural community in North-Western Nigeria. J. Commun. Med. Primary Health Care. **33**(1), 41–49 (2021)
18. Burke, A., Fishel, S.: A coal elimination treaty 2030: fast tracking climate change mitigation, global health and security. Earth Syst. Govern. **3**, 100046 (2020)
19. BBC COP26: New global climate deal struck in Glasgow. BBC, 13 Nov 2021. https://www.bbc.com/news/world-59277788.amp. Accessed 13 Nov 2021
20. Giwa, A., Alabi, A., Yusuf, A., Olukan, T.: A Comprehensive Review on Biomas and Solar Energy for Sustainable Energy Generation in Nigeria. Renew. Sustain. Energy Rev. **69**, 620–641 (2017)
21. MBNP: Economic Recovery and Growth Plan 2017–2020," Federal Republic of Nigeria (Ministry of Budget and National Planning), Abuja (2017)
22. Mahmud, J.O., Mustapha, S.A.: Solar photovoltaic technology: a sure pathway to Nigerian economic recovery and growth plan. In: Conference on Engineering Research, Technology Innovation and Practice (CERTIP), Enugu (2020)
23. Ukpe, W.: Federal Executive Council Approves the National Development Plan for 2021 to 2025, Replacing ERGP. Nirametrics, 12 November 2021. https://www.nairmetrics.com/2021/11/11/federal-executive-council-approves-the-national-development-plan-for-2021-to-2025-replacing-ergp/?amp=1. Accessed 13 Nov 2021
24. Channels Television: Full Speech: Nigeria to Reach Net-ZeroEmissions by 2060. Channels Television (2021)
25. Ayodele, T.R., Ogunjuyigbe, A.S.O., Odigie, O.: A multi-criteria GIS based model for wind farm site selection using interval type-2 fuzzy analytic hierarchy process: the case study of Nigeria. Appl. Energy **228**, 1853–1869 (2018)
26. Idris, W.O., Ibrahim, M.Z., Albani, A.: The status of the development of wind energy in Nigeria. Energies **23**(13), 6219 (2020)
27. NERC: Industry Operators. Nigerian Electricity Regulatory Commission (2016). https://www.nerc.gov.ng/index.php/home/operators/mini-grid. Accessed 16 Nov 2021
28. Okoye, C.O., OranekwuOkoye, B.C.: Economic feasibility of solar PV system for rural electrification in Sub-Sahara Africa. Renew. Sustain. Energy Rev. **82**, 2537–2547 (2018)
29. Oji, J.O., Idusuyi, N., Aliu, T.O., Petirin, M.O., Adejobi, O.A., Adetunji, A.R.: Utilization of solar energy for power generation in Nigeria. Int. J. Energy Eng **2**(2), 54–59 (2012)
30. Akinyele, D.O., Rayudu, R.K., Nair, N.K.C.: Development of photovoltaic power plant for remote residential applications: the socio-technical and economic perspectives. Appl. Energy **155**, 131–149 (2015)

Investigation on Concrete with Partial Replacement of Aggregate from Demolition Waste

Abdulhameed Danjuma Mambo, Abdulganiyu Sanusi[✉], Anthony Muoka, Shiloba John Pishikeni, and Abdullahi Isyaka Lawan

Civil Engineering Department, Nile University of Nigeria, Abuja, Nigeria
sanisuabdulganiyu@nileuniversity.edu.ng

Abstract. The world is experiencing rapid infrastructural development. This requires a higher quantity of aggregate resulting in a higher amount of natural resources depletion. Also, waste generated from demolition or collapse of the building ends in landfills unlawfully. The strains and high values on existing lands caused by rapid urbanization are making securing dump sites increasingly difficult. These situations have resulted in an environmental threat that needs urgent attention. This research investigated the potential usage of demolished concrete aggregate (DCA) as a partial replacement of granite to produce structural concrete. Laboratory testing of granite, DCA, and the produced concrete was carried out according to British and ASTM standards. The physical properties of DCA present the material to be a potential construction material for sustainable construction and a greener environment. The strength result of DCA concrete keeps reducing as the percentage replacement increases but yet produced satisfactory structural concrete.

Keywords: Construction waste · Waste management · Concrete strength · Sustainable construction

1 Introduction

Waste creation rises year after year as industries and infrastructure develop rapidly in metropolitan areas. Demolition materials thrown on land are currently classed as garbage, meaning they can't be used for anything (Monish et al. 2013). The first plant for recycling construction trash was built by the Ministry of Urban Development in India but such facilities are not available in Nigeria. This approach is sufficient to address the issue of destroyed garbage generation.

Concrete is responsible for about 4 billion tons of carbon dioxide annually (Ramsden 2021). There is a need to reduce CO_2 emissions in our environment. Currently, the concrete industry requires between 8 and 12 billion tons of natural aggregate per year around the world (Krishna 2015). Another big issue is the continued use of natural resources such as stone and sand, which is causing climate change and depletion

A. D. Mambo et al. (Eds.): InterSol 2022, LNICST 449, pp. 258–266, 2022.
https://doi.org/10.1007/978-3-031-23116-2_22

of natural resources (Ezeudu et al. 2021). Concrete is a composite material made up of a variety of ingredients such as limiting materials (cement), water, aggregates, and admixtures (Sanusi et al. 2020). Aggregate, which makes up 60–75% of the total volume of concrete is the most important material for any construction work (Linch 2010).

Concrete's adaptability as a development material for large-scale development projects stems from its great strength, low maintenance costs, resistance to long-term impact, cost-effectiveness compared to other development materials, and wonderful underlying exhibition (Akadiri et al. 2012). Furthermore, due to the rapid growth of the economy and population, concrete has become the most non-sustainable material, since its production involves the use of the most natural resources which account for 20 billion tons of raw materials (coarse aggregate) annually (Mandloi and Pathak 2015). (Nassar and Soroushian 2016) estimated that aggregate demand for construction could exceed 26 billion tons by 2012.

Aggregate consumption keeps increasing due to global infrastructural development (Sanusi et al. 2021). However, it has been reported that India is among the top ten countries in the world that use the most important natural resource (Somani et al. 2016). Therefore, it can be deduced that the concrete sector burns up a lot of typical assets, resulting in significant environmental, energy, and monetary losses, as half of the raw material is exploited, (Sharma and Singla 2014).

Some of the challenges associated with cement-concrete waste include the risk of contamination with organic substances when disposed of improperly or with the bulk of chemicals (Yang et al. 2008). Also, unlawful disposal could result in contamination of cement-concrete waste with the industrial and hazardous waste which eventually will hamper the desired concrete strength (Evangelista and de Brito 2007). Hence, when using cement-concrete waste to produce new concrete, attention should be paid to the aforementioned and other contaminants.

This research aimed at investigating the replacement of destroyed concrete (demobilization waste) for a coarse aggregate in concrete production to improve environmental sustainability by reducing solid waste generation, energy consumption, and depletion of natural resources.

2 Materials and Methods

In the study, the materials used were tested under laboratory conditions in line with the specification of the British and ASTM Standard.

Materials used for the concrete production include 53 grade of Ordinary Portland Cement (OPC) complying with BS EN 197–1 and BS EN 196–3 (BSI 2003.b, 2003.a), coarse aggregate which was granite and destroyed concrete aggregate, DCA (40%, 50%, and 60% respectively), Fine Aggregate (FA) and water satisfying the requirement of ASTM C-1602 and BS EN 1008 (ASTM 2006; BSI 2002).

The concrete mix proportion adopted for this research was 1:1.1:2.8 and the water-cement ratio of 0.45. However, the batching was carried out in accordance with British Standard. Slump, compressive, and split tensile tests were carried out using concrete moulds of 150mm^3 cubes, and cylinders (150mm diameter and 300mm height) in accordance with (BSI 2019.b, 2019d, 2019.a, 2019.c) respectively. The produced concrete samples were allowed to be set in moulds for 24 h under room temperature and humidity before being demoulded. The curing method used was full immersion of concrete samples in water for 7, 14, and 28 days respectively in accordance with (BSI 2004).

3 Results and Discussion

This section presents the obtained laboratory test result and its discussion.

3.1 Material Test Result

The materials used for this research are cement, coarse aggregate (granite and DCA), fine aggregate, and water.

Cement Test Result. The result of 53 grade Dangote cement used for this study as shown in Table 1 implies that the Portland cement conforms with the specification spelled out by (BSI 2019.c, India Standard 2013) for cement suitable for concrete production. Therefore, the used cement used is adequate for construction purposes and is expected to produce satisfactory concrete.

Table 1. Physical properties of 53 grade Dangote cement used

Test	Result
Specific gravity	3.15
Standard consistency	33.67
Fineness test	1.70
Initial setting time	27 min 8 s
Final setting time	8 h 10 min

Coarse Aggregate Test Result. The coarse aggregate physical properties presented in Table 2 showed that the specific gravity, abrasion, and crushing test results are marginal as compared with the materials. The results are in line with the recommendation of (Neville 2011; Shetty 2010, BSI 2003). The standard states that the impact, abrasion, and crushing strength of aggregate shall not exceed 30% for the wearing surface and 45% for the non-wearing surface. However, the impact, abrasion, and crushing test results fall within the limit of BS aggregate to be used for wearing coarse surfaces. Also, the bulk densities of the two materials are within the acceptable range of (ACI Committee and 318 2011) for normal-weight aggregate. Although, the water absorption capacity of DCA is higher than that of granite. This implies that the pore space between the DCA is much, therefore, more cement will require to produce the same concrete strength of normal granite. In general, DCA appears to possess lesser strength as compared with normal aggregate. However, the test results of DCA are still within the acceptable limit of coarse aggregate for durable concrete (ACI Committee and 318 2011, Sanusi et al. 2020; Neville 2011). Hence, DCA is a suitable and sustainable material for construction.

Table 2. Physical properties of coarse aggregate used

Serial number	Test	DCA	Granite
1	Specific gravity	2.68	2.70
2	Impact value (%)	24.26	13.23
3	Water absorption (%)	3.52	1.00
4	Bulk density (kg/m^3)	1983	1692
5	Crushing test (%)	20.83	17.42
6	Abrasion test (%)	14.6	13.4
7	Size (mm)	20.00	20.00

Fine Test Result. The bulk density and specific gravity test results of the river sand presented in Table 3 revealed that the material falls within the range of 1120 to 1928 kg/m^3 and 2.4 to 2.94 respectively recommended by (ASTM C125, 2000, Sanusi et al. 2020) for concrete aggregate. Also, (BSI 2003) confirms the suitability of the river sand for concrete work.

Table 3. Properties of fine aggregate used

Serial number	Serial number	Description
1	Specific gravity	2.30
2	Bulk density (Kg/m^3)	1678
3	Silt content (%)	4.93

3.2 Laboratory Test on the Produced Concrete

The test conducted on the produced concrete from DCA and normal granite were slump tests on fresh concrete and compressive, and split tensile strength tests on hardened concrete.

Slump Test Result. Figure 1 presents the slump tests. It can be seen from the fig. That as the substitute of DCA for granite increases, the concrete slump reduces. This can be connected to the higher capacity of water absorption for DCA (3.0) as against 1.0 obtained for granite in Table 2. Although, the entire produced concrete slump is within the acceptable range of 10 to 100 mm for satisfactory concrete (Ezeudu et al. 2021).

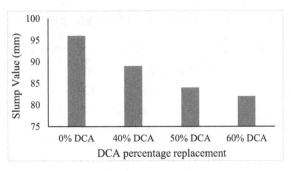

Fig. 1. Slump test

Compressive Test Result from Demolished Concrete Aggregate. The compressive strength test result of each of the produced concrete is presented in Table 4. The results generally show that as the curing age increases, the strength gained of the concrete samples increases irrespective of the materials. However, the result also indicated that an increase in DCA substitutes for granite in the produced concrete leads to a reduction in strength. The strength reduces by 11.86%, 16.27% and 17.73% for 40%, 50% and 60% DCA concrete respectively.

Table 4. Compressive strength of demolished concrete aggregate

Serial number	Mix	7 days	14 days	28 days
1	0% DCA	29.40	35.59	39.70
2	40% DCA	22.06	32.10	34.99
3	50% DCA	21.18	31.42	33.24
4	60% DCA	20.25	30.92	32.66

The strength results also confirm the better strength of conventional granite strength as compared with DCA available in Table 3. Also, the result of 40% DCA concrete agreed with the outcome of (Yehia et al. 2015) which states that the reduction of 7 to 15% compressive strength was recorded for recycled aggregate concrete when the same mix proportion and water-cement ratio were used. Although, 50% and 60% exceeded the range. This is connected to the higher percentage replacement of conventional coarse aggregate with DCA. Figure 2 Presents the graphical representation of the produced concrete compressive strengths.

Split Tensile Test Result from Demolished Concrete Aggregate. Only two levels of headings should be numbered. Lower level headings remain unnumbered; they are formatted as run-in headings.

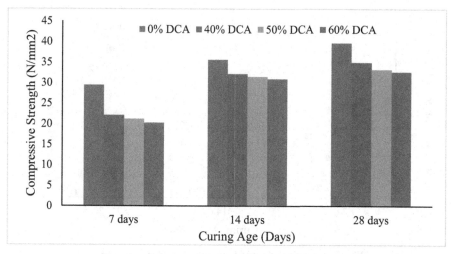

Fig. 2. Produced concrete compressive strength (N/mm^2)

Table 5 shows the split tensile strength of the produced concrete. The result follows the same trend of compressive strength. That is, as the strength of the produced concrete reduces as the percentage of DCA increases in concrete. The percentage reduction to the control (0% DCA) at 28 days curing age are 4.48%, 10.36% and 20.7% for 40%, 50% and 60% DCA replacement with granite in concrete respectively. From the estimation, 50% agreed with the augment of about 10 to 15% reduction in modulus of elasticity discovered in the research of (Yehia et al. 2015). However, 40% and 60% were lesser and higher than the modulus of elasticity reduction limit (10 to 15%).

Table 5. Split tensile strength of demolished concrete aggregate

Serial Number	Mix	7 days	14 days	28 days
1	0%	2.26	2.82	3.57
2	40% DCA	2.15	2.59	3.41
3	50% DCA	2.07	2.53	3.20
4	60% DCA	2.02	2.49	2.83

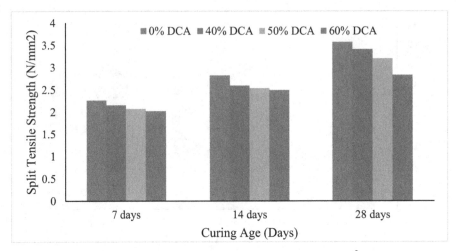

Fig. 3. Produced concrete Split tensile strength (N/mm^2)

4   Conclusion

This paper investigated the mechanical behavior of concrete produced from the partial replacement of conventional coarse aggregate (granite) with demolished concrete aggregate (DCA). 40%, 50%, and 60% DCA replacements were considered in this research. Physical properties of the coarse aggregate were experimental study. Also, laboratory tests conducted on the produced concrete were slump, compressive, and split tensile tests. The entire test conducted was in line with the specification of the British and ASTM standard. The following conclusions are drawn based on the outcome of the laboratory experimental study.

- The bulk density and specific gravity of DCA and conversational granite are within the acceptable limit of 1120 to 1928 kg/m^3 and 2.4 to 2.94 recommended by ASTM standards. Also, abrasion, crushing, and impact value strength test results of the DCA and granite did not exceed 30% and 45% aggregate to be used for wearing surfaces and non-wearing sur-faces recommended by British standards. Although, the granite possesses higher strength than DCA based on the laboratory experiment.
- The slump test of the produced concrete keeps reducing as the partial replacement of DCA increases. Although, the slump of the entire concrete mix was a true slump. The compressive and split tensile strength of the produced concrete also reduces as the percentage of DCA increases. However, the entire produced concrete under laboratory conditions has proven to be structural concrete that can be used for the casting of structural elements. Finally, this research has solved the problem of construction and environment sustainability by keeping the environment clean from construction demolition waste, thereby reducing the depletion of natural resources (granite) and energy efficiency in the construction world.

5 Recommendation

Considering the outcome of the research, the following recommendations are listed.

- The flexural strength of the DCA concrete should be investigated to provide more structural information regarding the material in concrete.
- Reduction of percentage replacement of DCA (such as 5%, 10%, 15%, and so on) with to the conventional aggregate needs further study as the 40% DCA concrete strength shows the close range to the conventional concrete.
- Longer curing ages of DCA concrete require further research to examine its growth in concrete strength after 28 days.

References

ACI Committee 318: Building code requirements for structural concrete (ACI 318-11) and commentary. American Concrete Institute (2011)

Akadiri, P.O., Chinyio, E.A., Olomolaiye, P.O.: Design of a sustainable building: a conceptual framework for implementing sustainability in the building sector. Buildings 2(2), 126–152 (2012). https://doi.org/10.3390/buildings2020126

ASTM: ASTM C 1602: Specification for Mixing Water used in the production of hydraulic cement concrete (2006)

BSI: BS EN 1008. Mixing Water for Concrete – Specification for Sampling, Testing, and Assessing the Suitability of Water, including Water Recovered from Processes in the Concrete Industry, as Mixing Water for Concrete (2002)

BSI (2003a): BS EN 196 Part 3: Methods of testing cement—Determination of Setting Time and Soundness

BSI (2003b): BS EN 197 Part 1: Composition, Specifications, and Conformity Criteria for Common Cements (2002)

BSI: BS 1881 Part 112. Testing Concrete - Methods of Accelerated Curing of Test Cubes (2004)

BSI: BS 1881 Part 102. Testing Concrete: Method for Determination of Concrete Slump (2019a)

BSI: BS EN 12390 Part 2: Testing Hardening Concrete - Making and Curing Specimens for Strength Tests (2019b)

BSI: BS EN 12390 Part 3: Testing Hardened Concrete - Compressive Strength of Test Specimens (2019c)

Evangelista, L., de Brito, J.: Mechanical behaviour of concrete made with fine recycled concrete aggregates. Cement Concr. Comp. 29(5), 397–401 (2007). https://doi.org/10.1016/j.cemcon comp.2006.12.004

Ezeudu, S.N., Mambo, A.D., Sanusi, A., Amuda, A.G., Salihu, A., Muoka, A.: Mechanical behavior of sugar on Palm Kernel Shell Concrete. In: 1st International Conference on Multidisciplinary Engineering and Applied Science (ICMEAS) (2021). https://doi.org/10.1109/ICMEAS 52683.2021.9692394

India Standard: IS 8112: Specification for 43 Grade Ordinary Portland Cement (2013)

Krishna, T.S.: An experimental investigation on flexural behavior of recycled aggregate fiber reinforcement concrete. Int. Res. J. Eng. Technol. (2015). www.irjet.net

Mandloi, A., Pathak, K.K.: Utilization of Waste steel scraps for increase in strength of concrete-waste management. In: IJSRD-International Journal for Scientific Research & Development, vol. 3 (2015). www.ijsrd.com

Monish, M., Srivastava, V., Agarwal, V., Mehta, P., Kumar, R.: Demolished waste as coarse aggregate in concrete. J. Acad. Indus. Res. 1 (2013)

Nassar, R.U.D., Soroushian, P.: Use of recycled aggregate concrete in pavement construction. J. Solid Waste Technol. Manag. 42(2), 137–144 (2016). https://doi.org/10.5276/JSWTM.201 6.137

Neville, A.M.: Properties of Concrete (5th edn.). Pearson Education Limited, London (2011). http://www.pearsoned.co.uk

Sanusi, A., Ndububa, E.E., Amuda, A.G., Mambo, A.D., Mohammed, A., Mohammed, I.: Properties of fine aggregate in Abuja and environs. J. Civil Eng. (NICE) 12(1), 22–35 (2020)

Sanusi, A., Ndububa, E.E., Amuda, A.G., Mohammed, A., Adelake, W.A., Shuaibu, U.A.: Demographic Based Survey on the Use of Abuja River Sand as Fine Aggregate for Concreting. In: 1st International Conference on Multidisciplinary Engineering and Applied Science (ICMEAS) (2021). https://doi.org/10.1109/ICMEAS52683.2021.9692309

Sharma, J., Singla, S.: Study of recycled concrete aggregates. Int. J. Eng. Trends Technol. 13, 123–125 (2014). http://www.ijettjournal.org

Shetty, M.S.: Concrete Technology: Theory and Practice. S Chand and Company Ltd., New Delhi (2010)

Somani, P., Dubey, B., Yadav, L., Kumar, J., Abhishek, Singh, M.: Use of demolished concrete waste in partial replacement of coarse aggregate in concrete. SSRG IJCE. 3, 117–121 (2016). https://doi.org/10.14445/23488352/IJCE-V315P125

Yang, K.-H., Chung, H.-S., Ashour, A.F.: Influence of Type and Replacement Level of Recycled Aggregates on Concrete Properties (2008)

Yehia, S., Helal, K., Abusharkh, A., Zaher, A., Istaitiyeh, H.: Strength and durability evaluation of recycled aggregate concrete. Int. J. Concr. Struct. Mater. 9(2), 219–239 (2015). https://doi. org/10.1007/s40069-015-0100-0

Valorization of the Recovered Lime in Cement-Typha Concretes: Thermal and Mechanical Behavior

Ibrahima Diaw[1]([✉]), Mactar Faye[1], Stéphane Hans[2], Frederic Sallet[2], and Vincent Sambou[3]

[1] Groupe de Recherche Efficacité et Systèmes Énergétiques, Alioune Diop University, BP 30, Bambey, Senegal
ibrahima.diaw@uadb.edu.sn
[2] LTDS UMR CNRS 5513 – École Nationale des Travaux Publics de l'État (ENTPE), Université de Lyon, 3 rue Maurice Audin, 69120 Vaulx en Velin, France
[3] Laboratoire Eau-Energie-Environnement - Procédés Industriels (LE3PI), École Supérieure Polytechnique de Dakar (UCAD-Senegal), BP 5085, Dakar-Fann, Senegal

Abstract. In a context of sustainable development and reduction of energy consumption in the building sector, plant-based concretes are increasingly developed. These materials offer excellent thermal properties, with low mechanical properties, but sufficient for use as a filling material. Moreover, Typha is an invasive plant with harmful consequences on our environment. This work investigates the valorization of recycled lime in Typha-cement thermal insulation materials. The mechanical and thermal properties of these composites are studied according to lime percentage used in substitution of cement. The results show that the compressive strength of the concrete ranges from 1.34 to 2.30 MPa. Thermal results range from 0.078 to 0.192 $W.m^{-1}K^{-1}$ for thermal conductivity and 385.68 to 505.18 $J.m^{-2}.K^{-1}.s^{-\frac{1}{2}}$ for thermal effusivity.

Keywords: Typha · Cement · Recovered lime · Compressive strength · Thermal characterization

1 Introduction

In recent years, the world is confronting an increasing demand for energy. This high demand impacts not only the energy supplies due to the depletion of natural resources but also the environment, in particular global warming and climate change. The contribution of building sector represents 20 to 40% of energy consumption in developed countries [1] against 25 to 30% of total electricity consumption and 49% of carbon dioxide emissions in West Africa [2]. According to the 2019 report of the UEMOA Energy Information System, the Senegalese residential sector accounts for 62% of total final electricity consumption in the UEMOA space [3]. This high energy consumption in the residential sector is due in part to a failure of thermal insulation in buildings.

A. D. Mambo et al. (Eds.): InterSol 2022, LNICST 449, pp. 267–276, 2022.
https://doi.org/10.1007/978-3-031-23116-2_23

Depending on the geographical location and the season, occupants often have to resort to air conditioning or heating to have thermal comfort inside the building. However, a large part of the heating or cooling demand is caused by transmission losses through the building envelope [4]. Energy efficiency of buildings is therefore an important challenge for the reduction of energy consumption in the building sector. In this context, several researchers have developed thermal insulation materials-based plant fibers. Natural fibers are light, renewable, insulating, less expensive than glass fibers and Bio-based materials allow carbon storage during their growing [5]. In addition, bio-based materials respect environmental criteria during their life expectancy, unlike conventional insulation materials like polystyrene, polyurethane and glass wool [6]. However, the development of vegetal concretes is slowed down by their weak mechanical performances resulting from the high compressibility of the vegetal granulate [7]. Moreover, plant fibers contain sugars that can inhibit cement hydration and negatively affect the mechanical performance of composites. Unlike conventional concretes with compressive strengths of about 30 MPa, plant-based concretes have very low compressive strengths that depend on the nature of the particles and the composition of the vegetable concretes [7]. Many studies have been carried out to understand the interactions between plant fibers and the cement matrix. Delannoy et al. [8] studied the impact of hemp extracts on hydration of Portland Cement. Results show that the adsorption of monosaccharide (cellulose and hemicellulose) on anhydrous cement grains delays the setting by physisorption. In the presence of calcium, non-reducing sugars (sucrose) form complexes and bind to hydrates and prevent their growth [8]. Bekir Çomak et al. [9] studied the effect of hemp fibers on the physical and mechanical properties of cement-based mortars. Sedan et al. [10] studied the influence of chemical interactions between cement and hemp fibers on the mechanical behavior of hemp-cement composites. Govin et al. [11] studied the relative effectiveness of polysaccharides and their influence on cement hydration. The retarding effect of polysaccharides depends on the cement composition. To improve the adhesion between the plant fibers and the cement matrix, several methods have been used by researchers, in particular treatment of fibers or addition of additives to the matrix. Weyenberg et al. [12] used an alkaline treatment to improve the mechanical properties of the flax-epoxy composite. Terpáková et al. [13] studied the chemical modification of hemp shives after treatment with sodium hydroxide, calcium hydroxide and ethylene-diamine-tetra acetic acid. Sawpan et al. [14] studied the effect of hemp fiber treatments on the interfacial shear strength of hemp fiber-reinforced unsaturated polylactide and polyester composites. A lot of research has been conducted on the valorization of typha in construction materials. In 2016, Diaw et al. [15] studied the valorization of typha by its incorporation in building materials. In 2017 Dieye et al. [2], studied the thermomechanical properties of a typha-based building material. In 2018, Niang et al. [16] studied the thermal and hygroscopic performance of various typha-clay composites. In 2021, Diaw et al. [5] studied the characterization of cement-reinforced Typha-clay composites. More and more wastes are valorized in building materials. Bal et al. [17] used millet waste in laterite-based building materials to improve their insulation properties. Bouhamou et al. [18] have valorized extracted silt in the development of concrete and construction materials. The objective of this study is to valorize lime recovered in insulation materials cement-typha. The second part of this document deals with the experimental program, the raw materials used, the preparation of the samples as well as the different characterizations are described. The third part is devoted to the results and discussion and finally a conclusion and finally, a conclusion and some perspectives put end this document.

2 Experimental Program

2.1 Raw Materials

The plant particles used in this study are extracted from typha plant. Typha Australis is a monocotyledonous plant belonging to the Typhaceae family [19]. The typha used in this study was harvested from the Senegal River. It was then sun-dried and crushed to obtain typha fibres (tf). Figure 1 and Fig. 2 show the Typha fibers and their particle size analysis, respectively. Fibers are very light with an apparent (or bulk) density of 24 kg/m^3.

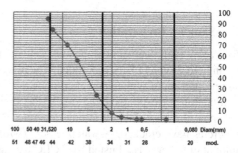

Fig. 1. Typha fiber

Fig. 2. Granulometric analysis of typha particles

The matrix used is composed of cement and recycled lime. The cement (c) is a Portland cement type CEM II/B 32, R with a density of 1.34 g/cm^3. The characteristics of clinker and cement are presented in Table 1. The hydrated lime used in this study comes from the Keur Momar Sarr drinking water treatment plant, 300 km from Dakar, Senegal. The lime was used to improve water quality, especially to soften the water and remove arsenic. After use, the residue was rejected into nature. In this work, the residue was collected and dried in an oven at 50 °C. The product was then crushed and sieved. The powder obtained was conditioned in bags to protect it from humidity and air. The density of lime is 0.58 g/cm^3.

Table 1. Physical and chemical properties of cement

Chemical characteristics of clinker		Physico-chemical characteristics of cement	
C_3A (%)	6.70	Blaine	4330
C_4AF (%)	10.89	beginning of setting time (min)	261
C_3S (%)	60.54	Hot stability (mm)	1.70
C_2S (%)	14.25	S_3O content (%)	2.33
Lime standard	0.982	Loss on ignition (%)	12.0
Silicic modulus	2.48	Insoluble residue (%)	2.00
Aluminum-Ferric Index	1.39	Chlorides content (%)	0.01
		Adding limestone (%)	28.2
		Compressive strength (MPa) 2 days	12.6
		Compressive strength (MPa) – 7 days	24.1
		Compressive strength (MPa) – 28 days	37.8

2.2 Samples Preparation

To prepare typha-cement composites, cement and water were mixed in a pan mixer for 2 min before typha fibers was added. The mixing then continued for another 3 min. The mix proportion of typha-cement composites (TCC) was set at c/tf of 250 kg/1 m^3. This formulation corresponds to the smallest amount of cement that can be mixed with 1 m3 of typha fibres to obtain a strong concrete. Below 250 kg of cement, the formulated concretes have cracked. A water/cement (w/c) ratio of 0.6 was used for TCC and the amount of water was adjusted for TCLC to ensure workability of the concretes. Table 2 presents the mix proportion of TCC and TCLC. The mixture was placed in different cylindrical and parallelepipedic molds for the compressive strength test and thermal test. To improve the mechanical performance of TCC, the cement was substituted by lime recycle at 10, 20 and 30% by weight, respectively. Block specimens with 10, 20 and 30% of lime were named 10TCLC, 20TCLC and 30TCLC, respectively.

Table 2. Mix proportion of TCC and TCLC.

Sample	Typha (g)	Cement (g)	Lime (g)	Water (g)
TCC	700	7291.7	0	4447.9
10TCLC	700	6562.5	729.2	4732.3
20TCLC	700	5833.3	1458.3	5016.7
30TCLC	700	5104.2	2187.5	5301.0

2.3 Mechanical Test Methods

To carry out the mechanical tests, cylindrical specimens of 110 mm diameter and 220 mm height were made. They were then conserved in their mold with one side exposed to the air during 48 h. They were removed from the molds and placed in the open air in the laboratory. Simple compression tests were carried out at 28 days using a hydraulic press with a load of 50 kN. The testing machine can be seen in Fig. 3.

Fig. 3. Compression testing machine

2.4 Thermal Characterization

Thermal characterization of concretes was carried out by hot plate method using parallelepipedic samples of dimensions $10 \times 10 \times 2$ cm^3. This method is used in an asymmetrical configuration because it is almost impossible to find two identical materials in their form and composition in construction [2, 20]. The heating element on which a thermocouple is fixed in its center is placed under the sample to be characterized. A 5 cm thick polystyrene block is placed under the heating element and another on top of the sample. The whole is placed between two 4 cm thick aluminum blocks. Thermal characterization of samples is represented in Fig. 4. The principle of this method consists of to apply a constant thermal flux to the heating element and to record the evolution of the temperature Ts (t) at the center of the heated face of the sample. By overlaying the experimental and theoretical temperature, thermal conductivity and diffusivity of the sample can be determined. The theoretical model of the temperature at the center of the heated face of the sample is presented in [20].

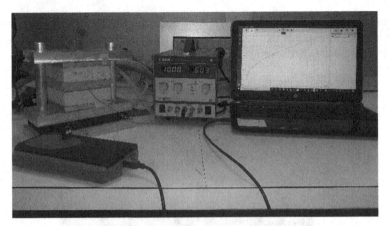

Fig. 4. Thermal characterization of samples.

3   Results

3.1   Bulk Density of Samples

The evolution of samples density as a function of lime percentage is represented in Fig. 5. The results show that increasing lime amount leads to decrease the bulk density. Indeed, cement is denser than lime. The substitution of cement by lime leads to a lightness of the material. Indeed, the density of lime is lower than that of cement. Consequently, a substitution of cement by lime leads to a decrease in the density of concrete.

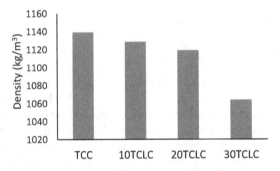

Fig. 5. Bulk density of TCC and TCLC

3.2   Mechanical Results

The results of compressive strength according to lime percentage are shown in Fig. 6. The compressive strength of the composites ranges from 1.342 and 2.297 MPa.

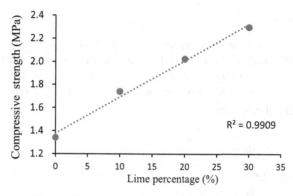

Fig. 6. Compressive strength of TCC and TCLC

The results show that compressive strength increases with increasing lime percentage. These results are slightly higher to compressive strength of Typha-clay concretes which range from 0.279 to 0.796 MPa [2] and cement-reinforced Typha-clay composites which range from 0.14 to 0.71 MPa [5]. Figure 7 shows the evolution of applied load according to lime percentage during the compression test. We can note that applied load increases progressively until it reaches a maximum and then decreases. As can be seen, the increase in the amount of lime leads to an increase in the applied load due to the fact that the material becomes more resistant (but less ductile). Indeed, the loss of performance of typha-based cementitious concretes would be due to the decomposition of the cellulose and hemicellulose of which they are composed in the alkaline environment of the cementitious matrices. In addition, the pectin contained in typha fibres fixes calcium Ca^{2+} and hydroxide OH^- ions on the surface of the fibres. A deficit of calcium and hydroxide ions is then observed in the interstitial phase, leading to an inhibition of calcium silicate hydrates (CSH), the main product of the hydration of a hydraulic binder, and thus a delay in the setting of the cement. The introduction of lime has improved the compressive strength of concrete. The introduction of lime leads to a decrease in the alkalinity and $Ca(OH)_2$ content of the cementitious matrix, responsible for the mineralization and fragility of the fibres.

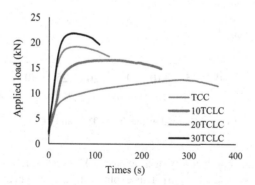

Fig. 7. Applied load according lime percentage

3.3 Thermal Results

The evolution of thermal conductivity and thermal effusivity of the samples are represented in Fig. 8 and Fig. 9, respectively. An increase of thermal conductivity and thermal effusivity is observed as a function of the recovered lime content. These values range from 0.078 to 0.192 $W.m^{-1}.K^{-1}$ for thermal conductivity and 385.68 to 505.18 $J.m^{-2}.K^{-1}.s^{-\frac{1}{2}}$ for thermal effusivity.

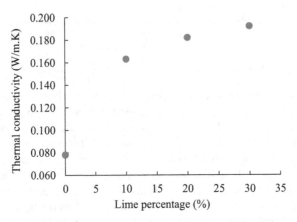

Fig. 8. Thermal conductivity of TCC and TCLC

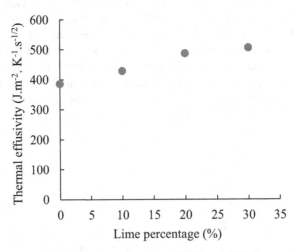

Fig. 9. Thermal effusivity of TCC and TCLC

Indeed, the thermal conductivity of lime paste ($0.7\ W.m^{-1}.K^{-1}$) [21] is higher than that of cement ($0.53\ W.m^{-1}.K^{-1}$) [5]. This explains the increase in thermal conductivity of concrete when the quantity of lime increases. According to Fatim et al. [22] addition of lime deteriorates the thermal inertia of the material.

4   Conclusion

This work consisted in valorizing lime mud recovered in building materials. The mechanical and thermal performances of the materials were evaluated according to the quantity of lime added. The results show an improvement in the compressive strength of the materials and a slight increase in the thermophysical properties of the materials. However. A microstructural study is needed to understand more closely the effect of lime on the interfacial bonding between fiber and cement matrix. This study shows that the valorization of waste materials in construction materials can improve its mechanical performance while maintaining its insulating properties.

References

1. Pérez-Lombard, L., Ortiz, J., Pout, C.: A review on buildings energy consumption information. Energy Build. **40**(3), 394–398 (2008). https://doi.org/10.1016/j.enbuild.2007.03.007
2. Dieye, Y., Sambou, V., Faye, M., Thiam, A., Adj, M., Azilinon, D.: Thermo-mechanical characterization of a building material based on Typha Australis. J. Build. Eng. **9**, 142–146 (2017). https://doi.org/10.1016/j.jobe.2016.12.007
3. Système d'Information énergétique des États membres de l'UEMOA. RAPPORT 2019 Chiffres clés sur l'énergie au Sénégal et dans l'espace UEMOA (2019)
4. Berggren, B., Wall, M.: Calculation of thermal bridges in (Nordic) building envelopes - risk of performance failure due to inconsistent use of methodology. Energy Build. **65**, 331–339 (2013). https://doi.org/10.1016/j.enbuild.2013.06.021
5. Diaw, I., Faye, M., Bodian, S., Sambou, V.: Characterization of cement-reinforced Typha-clay composites. J. Sci. Eng. Res. **8**(12), 123–128 (2021)
6. Osseni, S.O.G., Apovo, B.D., Ahouannou, C.: Caractérisation thermique des mortiers de ciment dopés en fibres de coco par la méthode du plan chaud asymétrique à une mesure de temperature. Afrique Sci. **12**(6), 119–129 (2016)
7. Akkaoui, A.: Bétons de granulats de bois : Étude expérimentale et théorique des propriétés thermo-hydro-mécaniques par des approches multi-échelles. Ph.D. thesis (2014)
8. Delannoy, G., et al.: Impact of hemp shiv extractives on hydration of Portland cement. Constr. Build. Mater. **244**, 118300 (2020). https://doi.org/10.1016/j.conbuildmat.2020.118300
9. Çomak, B., Bideci, A., Bideci, Ö.S.: Effects of hemp fibers on characteristics of cement based mortar. Constr. Build. Mater. **169**, 794–799 (2018). https://doi.org/10.1016/j.conbuildmat.2018.03.029
10. Sedan, D., Pagnoux, C., Smith, A., Chotard, T.: Mechanical properties of hemp fibre reinforced cement: influence of the fibre/matrix interaction. J. Eur. Ceramic Soc. **28**(1), 183–192 (2008). https://doi.org/10.1016/j.jeurceramsoc.2007.05.019
11. Peschard, A., Govin, A., Grosseau, P., Guilhot, B., Guyonnet, R.: Effect of polysaccharides on the hydration of cement paste at early ages. Cement Concr. Res. **34**(11), 2153–2158 (2004). https://doi.org/10.1016/j.cemconres.2004.04.001
12. Van de Weyenberg, I., Truong, T.C., Vangrimde, B., Verpoest, I.: Improving the properties of UD flax fibre reinforced composites by applying an alkaline fibre treatment. Compos. Part A: Appl. Sci. Manuf. **37**(9), 1368–1376 (2006). https://doi.org/10.1016/j.compositesa.2005.08.016
13. Terpáková, E., Kidalová, L., Eštoková, A., Čigášová, J., Števulová, N.: Chemical modification of hemp shives and their characterization. Procedia Eng. **42**, 931–941 (2012). https://doi.org/10.1016/j.proeng.2012.07.486

14. Sawpan, M.A., Pickering, K.L., Fernyhough, A.: Effect of fibre treatments on interfacial shear strength of hemp fibre reinforced polylactide and unsaturated polyester composites. Compos. Part A: Appl. Sci. Manuf. **42**(9), 1189–1196 (2011). https://doi.org/10.1016/j.compositesa.2011.05.003

15. Diaw, A.S., Sow, D., Ndiaye, M.B., Abdelakh, A.O., Wade, M., Gaye, S.: Valorization of Typha Australis by its integration in building construction materials. Int. J. Emerg. Technol. Adv. Eng. **6**(1), 34–37 (2016)

16. Niang, I., et al.: Hygrothermal performance of various Typha–clay composite. J. Build. Phys. **42**(3), 316–335 (2018). https://doi.org/10.1177/1744259118759677

17. Bal, H., Jannot, Y., Quenette, N., Chenu, A., Gaye, S.: Water content dependence of the porosity, density and thermal capacity of laterite based bricks with millet waste additive. Constr. Build. Mater. **31**, 144–150 (2012). https://doi.org/10.1016/j.conbuildmat.2011.12.063

18. Belas, N., Belaribi, O., Mebrouki, A., Bouhamou, N.: Valorisation des sédiments de dragage dans les bétons. Séminaire International, Innovation et Valorisation en génie Civil et Matériaux de construction, Rabat (Maroc), vol. 23, p. 25 (2011)

19. Ba, L., Abbassi, I.E., Kane, C.S.E., Darcherif, A.M., Ndongo, M.: The challenges of local and bio-sourced materials on thermal performance: review, classification and opportunity. Int. J. Eng. Res. Africa **47**, 85–101 (2020). https://doi.org/10.4028/www.scientific.net/JERA.47.85

20. Diaw, A.S., Bal, H.M., Diallo, O., Ndiaye, M.B., Wade, M., Gaye, S.: Thermophysical characterization of Typha's concrete for its integration into construction. J. Build. Constr. Plann. Res. **9**(1), 56–65 (2021). https://doi.org/10.4236/jbcpr.2021.91005

21. Brzyski, P., Lagód, G.: Physical and mechanical properties of composites based on hemp shives and lime. In: E3S Web of Conferences, vol. 49, pp. 1–8 (2018). https://doi.org/10.1051/e3sconf/20184900010

22. Zoma, F., Yonli, F.H., Malbila, E., Toguyeni, D.Y.K., Hassel, I.B.: Adding hydrated lime in a material made of clayey soil and fibres: formulation and effects on thermo-mechanical properties. J. Miner. Mater. Charact. Eng. **8**(3), 149–161 (2020). https://doi.org/10.4236/jmmce.2020.83010

Engineering and Science Education in Underserved Areas

The Need for Nigerian Universities to Collaborate for Quality Research Output

Chukwuma C. Ogbaga[1,2]([✉]) [ID], Terkuma Chia[3], Oluwatosin Imoleayo Oyeniran[4],
Menizibeya Osain Welcome[4], George Mangse[2], Habib-ur-Rehman Athar[5],
and Nugun P. Jellason[6] [ID]

[1] Department of Biological Sciences, Faculty of Natural and Applied Sciences,
Nile University of Nigeria, Abuja, Nigeria
chukwuma.ogbaga@nileuniversity.edu.ng, chukwumaogbaga@gmail.com
[2] Department of Microbiology and Biotechnology, Faculty of Natural and Applied Sciences,
Nile University of Nigeria, Abuja, Nigeria
[3] Department of Anatomy, Faculty of Basic Medical Sciences, College of Health Sciences,
Nile University of Nigeria, Abuja, Nigeria
[4] Department of Physiology, Faculty of Basic Medical Sciences, College of Health Sciences,
Nile University of Nigeria, Abuja, Nigeria
[5] Institute of Pure and Applied Biology, Bahauddin Zakariya University, Multan 60800, Pakistan
[6] School of Agriculture, Policy and Development, University of Reading, Reading, UK

Abstract. The sustainable development of nations globally is highly influenced
by the knowledge economy. Growth in the knowledge economy is driven by higher
education with quality research being a major contributor to an excellent education.
Over the years, universities in high-income countries have put research excellence
at the core of their strategies with collaboration being a major tool utilised in
improving the universities' global recognition and ranking. However, low-income
countries lag behind in global recognition and ranking of universities. This is
worsened by difficulties in securing collaboration. In this perspective, we examine,
the situation in Nigeria- a low-income country. We compare public and private
Nigerian universities in terms of research excellence and argue for collaboration
between local private and public universities, and between the local and foreign
universities to overcome the challenges associated with researchers working alone.
We also highlight the barriers that could limit effective collaboration in Nigerian
universities. These barriers include funding and finding collaborators, personal
or family worries, lack of trust and respect for diversity of disciplines and poor
internet infrastructure and the high cost of international calls. Finally, we conclude
that collaboration is key to knowledge sharing, the attraction of research grants
and meeting sustainability targets. Hence, Nigerian universities should reach out to
researchers with mutual research interests at home and abroad for more successful
and impactful research.

Keywords: Nigerian universities · Research collaborations · Quality research

© ICST Institute for Computer Sciences, Social Informatics and Telecommunications Engineering 2022
Published by Springer Nature Switzerland AG 2022. All Rights Reserved
A. D. Mambo et al. (Eds.): InterSol 2022, LNICST 449, pp. 279–289, 2022.
https://doi.org/10.1007/978-3-031-23116-2_24

1 Introduction

The sustainable development of nations globally is knowledge-driven. Central to the knowledge economy is education and specifically higher education [1]. Research is acclaimed to be one of the core mandates of universities alongside innovation and knowledge dissemination [2]. Research drives innovation, creates and improves already established knowledge that informs teaching and learning and is disseminated to the scientific community. Perhaps this informs the choice of research productivity as a common criterion for ranking universities globally [3, 4]. Owing to its vital place in universities, authorities often strive for research excellence, which is a tool for projecting a positive image of an institution. Research excellence enhances the attraction of institutional funding through research grants [5–7]. Arguably, citations garnered by a research publication reflect the quality of the research [8]. The contribution of research to economic growth is limited by factors such as lack of funding, ineffective higher education policies and recently technology deficiency [1]. High-income countries (HICs) have largely tackled these limitations over time with low-income countries (LICs) still struggling to overcome these challenges [9].

Nigeria is a LIC faced with multifaceted challenges hindering the growth of higher education. The Nigerian university system is plagued with numerous challenges principal among them is poor funding [10, 11]. Generally, public universities in Nigeria are funded by the government with little or no private participation [12]. The paucity of funds may be due to the dwindling government revenues, growing needs of universities as well as an increase in the number of universities. Consequently, university staff unions have often embarked on lengthy industrial actions to press home their demands for improved university funding and working conditions [13, 14]. These industrial actions have caused severe disruptions to academic activities at Nigerian universities. The situation has resulted in the gradual fall of standards and consistent low ranking of Nigerian universities globally and within the African continent [15]. According to Times Higher Education World Ranking of Universities for 2021 based on 1500 institutions cutting across 93 countries and territories, the best Nigerian university was ranked 401–500th position in the world and 27th position out of over 1225 universities in Africa [16].

Inter-university cooperation both locally and internationally holds much promise in enhancing research within the university system. Private and public research funding bodies increasingly require collaboration at disciplinary, institutional and international levels [17]. Through such collaborations, universities are able to interdepend on one another both for expertise and equipment to make up for areas they are lacking. Collaboration is the rule and not the exception and it ranges from an interpersonal, team and corporate partnership [18]. Hence, the notion of 'collaborative capability' which Blomqvist and Levy argue is a pre-requisite for knowledge creation based on communication, commitment, and mutual trust [19]. The existence of different layers of collaboration has led to a mixed understanding of the benefits of collaboration [18]. However, when properly defined, collaboration has been found to lead to several benefits such as better organisational performance with regards to knowledge creation, transfer and ingenuity [20]. Other benefits associated with well-defined collaborations are the ability to utilise resources optimally and the creation of positive competition amongst collaborators [20]. Within Nigeria, universities have differed from one another; whereby the earlier established universities have relatively more experts well versed in research compared to the recently established universities. However, much attention has not been given to inter-university collaboration that may address some of the challenges faced by Nigerian universities.

In this perspective, we discuss the need for enhanced research collaboration in Nigerian universities for quality research output that will considerably raise the ranking and favourably position Nigerian universities among their peers globally. First, we briefly discuss the history of Nigerian universities to highlight potential aspects or peculiarities that may promote research collaboration. Second, we consider the common traits and differences between private and public Nigerian universities. Third, we discuss both local and international aspects of Nigerian university collaboration, focusing on knowledge sharing, collaborative research grant applications and meeting sustainable development targets. Finally, we consider the barriers to effective research collaboration.

2 Historical Perspectives on Nigerian Universities

Four generations of universities exist in Nigeria based on the year of creation. The oldest higher institution in Nigeria was established around the middle of the last century. The university college Ibadan was established in 1947 as an affiliate of the University of London following the recommendation of the Asquith commission of 1943 [21, 22]. This was followed by the establishment of the University of Nigeria, Nsukka (UNN) in 1960 which unlike the university college Ibadan was an autonomous university [23]. In anticipation of the manpower needs that may arise following Nigeria's independence in 1960, the Ashby commission of 1959 recommended the establishment of additional universities to train manpower in each of the regions and Lagos the then country's capital. This birthed the Ahmadu Bello University (ABU) Zaria in the north, the University of Ife (now Obafemi Awolowo University) and the University of Lagos in 1962 both in the west [22, 23].

Additionally, the University College Ibadan gained its autonomy and was now known as the University of Ibadan. With the creation of the mid-west region, another university was established at Benin, the University of Benin [22, 23]. These universities collectively formed what is regarded as first-generation universities in Nigeria. The first generation universities had strong ties with local and international research institutions especially in the UK and USA at the time – which promoted the training of research personnel, scholars, and enhanced research funding, and hence capacity building with great potential for becoming leading global frontiers of the knowledge economy [21–23].

The second-generation universities were established around 1975 in Ilorin, Calabar, Jos, Port Harcourt, Maiduguri, Sokoto, and Kano [22, 24]. They were a consequence of the military government's third national development plan of Nigeria. Third-generation universities were specialized universities focusing on technology and agriculture. These universities were established in the 1980s in Owerri, Akure, Makurdi, Bauchi, and Yola [22]. Also, about the same time, individual state governments began establishing their universities aside from those of the federal government. States such as Imo, Cross River, Lagos, Akwa-Ibom and Ondo state universities were established in the 80s [22, 25].

From the early 1990s, fourth-generation universities came into existence [26]. Several state government-owned universities fall into this category. Nigeria thereafter witnessed the boom of university expansion through private sector participation beginning from early 1999/2000s and upwards [27, 28]. Additional Federal and State universities have also been established during this period. A total of three private universities were established at the onset following the approval by the government in 1999, namely: Igbinedion University, Babcock University and Madonna University [29]. As of the first quarter of 2021, Nigeria had 195 licensed universities, comprising 44 Federal, 52 State, and 99 private universities [30]. Of these universities, only one, the National Open University of Nigeria (NOUN) is an exclusive open and distance learning institution. Recently, a few of the conventional universities now run some limited open and distance learning programmes [31]. The creation of more universities in the country gradually resulted in dwindling international research ties with renowned and leading global institutions due to a reduction in standards of teaching, quality staff and research facilities [32].

3   Common Traits and Differences Between the Universities: Private vs Public

In order to meet the rising demand for higher education by the growing populace, and to improve the quality of education in Nigeria, the Federal Government of Nigeria through the Ministry of Education and Nigerian Universities Commission (NUC) augmented the efforts of public universities and colleges of education by approving the establishment of private universities in 1999 [33]. The increase in the number of universities did not seem to have any significant effect on the number of students gaining admission into the universities. Documented reports reveal that out of over one million candidates seeking admission to Nigerian Universities through the Joint Admission and Matriculation Board (JAMB) exams, only about 450,000 representing approximately 30% were able to gain entrance into 112 universities in the country [34]. It is important to note that both public and private universities are established by acts of parliament and are both regulated by the same regulatory body – the NUC. Entry requirements for fresh students as well as the academic curricula used for teaching is the same for both institutions.

At the same time, both public and private Nigerian universities have their peculiarities. For instance, public universities have access to funding from the government. A certain percentage of the government's annual budget is allocated to the public universities in order to subsidize the running costs of the universities. Over N500billion (approx. $1billion) has been released by the Federal Government of Nigeria to the federally funded universities between 2000 and 2008 [35]. In addition to the government subventions, the Education Tax Fund (ETF), established by law in 1993 was empowered to carry out major projects within the public universities using funds from the profit of private business organisations operating within the country [35]. The private universities on the other hand rely almost solely on the income realised from tuition fees from students running various degree programmes.

Another notable difference between public and private universities is access to research grants from the Nigerian government. While researchers from public universities are able to access research grants from the Tertiary Education Trust (TET) Fund, a government agency, researchers from private universities mostly depend on their salaries or seek alternative sources of research grants e.g., from international sources. However, the quality of teaching facilities and manpower are believed to be much better in the private schools because the students pay relatively higher tuition fees than in the public schools [33], and can therefore place a demand on value for their money. This is not the case in most public universities, where tuition fees are quite low and affordable, consequently leading to a higher number of students depending on very few facilities and manpower to cater for them.

Cognisant of these peculiarities, there is a need for both public and private universities to work together to advance the Nigerian knowledge economy. Furthermore, multi-university collaborative research on economy-oriented innovations may substantially help to gradually close the gap between private and public universities, and address some of the critical threats facing the Nigerian university system.

4 Collaborative Research in Nigerian Universities May Drive the Knowledge Economy: Local and International Perspectives

4.1 Knowledge Sharing

Knowledge sharing entails learning, understanding and sharing information, ideas, views and resources [36]. The majority of the universities in Nigeria just like most of sub-Saharan Africa (SSA) are economically challenged and have had negative experiences with research [37] such as lack of research funds, minimal or no government support and limited research-oriented facilities. Oftentimes, researchers from these regions produce less rigorously researched papers that have little or no impact on society [38–41]. Thus, it is crucial to acknowledge the need for collaborative projects and the expertise that partners bring that are central to knowledge sharing.

Indeed, international collaboration, which promotes knowledge sharing, is not new as it has been ongoing in countries like the UK, USA, Germany, France, Japan, Canada, Brazil, South Africa, Pakistan, China [36, 42, 43]. A wide gap exists in knowledge sharing between the universities in SSA, particularly in Nigeria. In Nigeria, incentives exist for academics to work in silos. For example, universities offer higher rewards when research is done individually. Higher points are rewarded for single-authored research papers during the annual appraisal or promotion of academic staff.

Collaboration between universities results in sharing of ideas, resources and skills. Also, researchers are exposed to cutting-edge technologies which they may not likely have access to in their institutions [36]. More importantly, effective collaboration reduces the time required to complete a given research project, leading to faster research output for maximum societal impact and contribution to the knowledge economy.

4.2 Collaborative Research Grants

Research grants are essential means of funding research that promote quality research output and the knowledge economy. The massive research grants awarded by industrialized nations can be harnessed via cutting-edge collaborative research between local and international institutions. Inter-nation agreements or research funding can also considerably promote research collaboration amongst different institutions.

In addition to helping the career path, productivity and growth of the researcher [44, 45], research grants, indeed, foster a multi-disciplinary collaboration amongst investigators and institutions that results in the acquisition of data or other products that inform decision making for societal benefit. For instance, the National Institutes of Health provides over $32 billion in research grants per year to conquer diseases, promote a healthy life and reduce disability – which has resulted in life-changing discoveries that established new methods of disease treatments, advancing healthier lives and societal as well as economic growth [45, 46]. In contrast, research funding institutes in Africa, especially SSA countries are poorly developed with very little or no grant mechanisms to inform decision-making or drive monumental changes in the lives of the people [47]. As a result, research output from SSA tends to be weak.

4.3 Meeting Sustainability Targets

Universities are increasingly being challenged to respond to sustainability-oriented problems. These problems could be economically, socially or environmentally based. Economic problems include low GDP growth, low regional net profit and low production per employee [48]. Socially-based problems include diminishing demographic trends and a high unemployment rate whilst environmental problems on the other hand are linked to waste management strategies [48]. Universities are expected to develop curricula to address these problems in terms of quality teaching, research and outreach [48] and introduction of sustainability pedagogy in higher education to tackle sustainability issues at the university level [49].

Embedding sustainability in higher education curriculum is likely to lead to the development of future sustainability leaders [6, 7]. Furthermore, it is essential for universities in the country to adjust to recent developments in research collaboration that includes integrated knowledge translation, in which research partnership between the researcher and the knowledge user provides for productive research through co-generation and implementation of knowledge that ultimately lead to greater knowledge use and societally impactful opportunities in practice [50, 51]. Achieving these sustainability targets would pose substantial difficulties when universities do not align with international best practices.

5 Barriers to Effective Research Collaboration

5.1 Funding and Finding Collaborators

Funding is crucial for the successful take-off and execution of any collaboration. It is also an important aspect of fulfilling the internationalization mandate of universities [52]. However, securing funding is challenging for researchers in Nigeria due in part to the highly competitive nature of the grant application processes [53]. In addition, finding collaborators is also considered a major challenge as Nigerian researchers usually have limited knowledge on how to initiate or follow up the process [47, 53]. Hence, Nigerian researchers tend to work alone with minimal motivation.

5.2 Personal or Family Worries

Nigerian researchers find it challenging to travel especially when they have family commitments. This problem affects women more than men [52, 54]. For instance, women who have children or are nursing are less willing to travel for research purposes [54]. Also, Nigerians have a strong attachment to family members and relatives and have a culture of caring for elderly parents [54]. Thus, leaving family responsibilities for research is onerous.

5.3 Lack of Trust and Respect for Diversity of Disciplines

A major challenge to data sharing in science is the lack of trust in terms of data misuse, ethical or legal infringements [55]. There is a need for researchers and collaborators to establish close working relationships based on mutual trust [55]. Also, another daunting challenge is the diversity of disciplines. A situation whereby researchers collaborate on interdisciplinary research and need to work together including in common and rare languages [55]. For effective collaboration, the researchers will require a working guide to ensure that the views of all the collaborators are respected.

5.4 Poor Internet Infrastructure and the High Cost of International Calls

Poor access to good broadband or fluctuations in internet connection can limit engagement in research [56]. For instance, a recent study conducted in rural and small-town schools showed that a lack of home internet affected researchers' digital skills. This limitation could have a lifelong repercussion for affected researchers [56]. Similarly, the high cost of international phone calls limits global linkage preventing communication between researchers in different countries [57].

Both poor internet infrastructure or fluctuations in internet connectivity and the high cost of international calls are major limitations to research progress and output between collaborators in Nigeria and abroad [58]. Digital infrastructure is still grossly underdeveloped in Nigeria with the country ranking 105th out of a total of 137 for access to the internet [59]. Only about 0.05% of people residing in the country have access to fixed broadband subscriptions according to documented reports [59]. Although the Nigeria University's Commission (NUC) in collaboration with the World Bank established the Nigerian Research and Education Network (NgREN), which is meant to support digital communication, and sharing of resources across about 40 universities, there is still, no national repositories that hold research publications or data for the purposes of research and learning.

6 Conclusion

Collaborative research requires careful planning and is key to improving knowledge sharing, the attraction of research grants and the attainment of sustainability goals. However, this is not straightforward, as barriers such as inadequate funding and lack of trust and respect for diversity of disciplines could affect smooth collaboration.

A decrease in inter-university ties and research collaboration results in a considerable reduction in quality research output by the universities in the country [32]. Hence, activating sustainable research collaboration and inter-university ties once enjoyed by first-generation universities may serve as a panacea to some of the current challenges faced by Nigerian universities.

There is a need to create a collaborative space by bringing researchers from different backgrounds together to understand the language of each other, foster respect for each other's approaches to research and provide more training on interdisciplinarity in research. Also, there is a need to advise all university stakeholders on the advantage of collaboration and increased funding. The funding can also be extended to include the private universities to compete for the grants based on merit.

In addition, it is pertinent to call the attention of university stakeholders to encourage collaboration by discouraging single-authored publications (it should be given the least points during promotion exercises) and promoting collaborative work to be published in high-impact journals. Also, to solve contemporary and local problems, there is a need to encourage inter-governmental agencies and industry collaborations in SSA countries, as it used to be in developing countries. Finally, Nigerian universities should reach out to researchers with mutual research interests at home and abroad for more successful and impactful research.

References

1. Saint, W., Hartnett, T.A., Strassner, E.: Higher education in Nigeria: a status report. High Educ. Pol. 16(3), 259–281 (2003)
2. Boulton, G., Lucas, C.: What are universities for? Chin. Sci. Bull. 56(23), 2506–2517 (2011)
3. Liu, N.C., Cheng, Y.: The academic ranking of world universities. High. Educ. Eur. 30(2), 127–136 (2005)
4. Piro, F.N., Sivertsen, G.: How can differences in international university rankings be explained? Scientometrics 109(3), 2263–2278 (2016). https://doi.org/10.1007/s11192-016-2056-5
5. Hicks, D.: Performance-based university research funding systems. Res. Policy 41(2), 251–261 (2012)
6. Lozano, R., Merrill, M.Y., Sammalisto, K., Ceulemans, K., Lozano, F.J.: Connecting competences and pedagogical approaches for sustainable development in higher education: a literature review and framework proposal. Sustainability 9(10), 1889 (2017)
7. Taimur, S.: Pedagogical training for sustainability education. In: Leal Filho, W., Azul, A.M., Brandli, L., Özuyar, P.G., Wall, T. (eds.) Quality Education. Encyclopedia of the UN Sustainable Development Goals, pp. 611–621. Springer, Cham (2020). https://doi.org/10.1007/978-3-319-95870-5_51
8. Leydesdorff, L., Bornmann, L., Comins, J.A., Milojević, S.: Citations: indicators of quality? The impact fallacy. Front. Res. Metrics Analyt. 1, 1 (2016)
9. Schendel, R., McCowan, T.: Expanding higher education systems in low-and middle-income countries: the challenges of equity and quality. High. Educ. 72(4), 407–411 (2016)
10. Afolayan, F.O.: Funding higher education in Nigeria. J. Res. Method Educ. 1, 63–68 (2015)
11. Gambo, O.O., Fasanmi, S.A.: Funding university education in Nigeria: the challenges and way forward. Bulg. J. Sci. Educ. Policy 13(1), 80–91 (2019)
12. Onuka, A.: Funding the Nigerian University Education: Role of Various Stakeholders (2008)

13. Offem, O.O., Anashie, A.I., Aniah, S.A.: Effect of strikes on management and planning of educational activities in Nigerian universities. Glob. J. Educ. Res. **17**(1), 1–8 (2018)
14. Odiagbe, S.A.: Industrial Conflict in Nigerian Universities: A Case Study of the Disputes Between the Academic Staff Union of Universities University of Glasgow ASUU) and the Federal Government of Nigeria (FGN). (2012)
15. Omonijo, D., Uche, C., Okunlola, O., Anyaegbunam, M., Adeleke, V.: Exploring factors responsible for the poor ranking of scholars and tertiary institutions in Nigeria In: Exploring Factors Responsible for the Poor Ranking of Scholars and Tertiary Institutions in Nigeria, p. 4250. Nigeria (2018)
16. https://www.timeshighereducation.com/world-university-rankings/2021/world-ranking#!/page/0/length/-1/sort_by/rank/sort_order/asc/cols/stats
17. Sonnenwald, D.H.: Scientific collaboration. Ann. Rev. Inf. Sci. Technol. **41**(1), 643–6819 (2007)
18. Smith, D.: Collaborative research: policy and the management of knowledge creation in UK universities. High. Educ. Q. **55**(2), 131–157 (2001)
19. Blomqvist, K., Levy, J.: Collaboration capability–a focal concept in knowledge creation and collaborative innovation in networks. Int. J. Manag. Concepts Philos. **2**(1), 31–48 (2006)
20. Sepuru, M., Musonda, I., Okoro, C.S.: An assessment of factors influencing collaboration impacts on organisational performance: a review. In: Collaboration and Integration in Construction, Engineering, Management and Technology, pp. 321–325 (2021)
21. Abrokwaa, C.: Colonialism and the development of higher education. In: Re-thinking Post-colonial Education in Sub-Saharan Africa in the 21st Century, pp. 201–220. Sense Publishers, Rotterdam (2017). https://doi.org/10.1007/978-94-6300-962-1_12
22. Ejoigu, A., Sule, S.: Sixty-Five Years of University Education in Nigeria: Some Key Cross Cutting Issues. Bulgarian Comparative Education Society (2012)
23. Anyebe, A.A.: Nigerian University and its mandate in a changing world. e-Bangi 11(2), 048–062 (2014)
24. Awe, B.A.: Quality and stress in Nigerian Public Universities. Am. J. Educ. Res. **8**(12), 914–925 (2020)
25. Nyewusira, B.: Politics and the establishment of public universities in Nigeria: Implications for University Education. Politics **5**(19) (2014)
26. Otonko, J.: University education in Nigeria: history, successes, failures and the way forward. Int. J. Technol. Incl. Educ. **1**(2), 44–48 (2012)
27. Obasi, I.N.: Analysis of the emergence and development of private universities in Nigeria (1999–2006). J. Higher Educ. Afr./Revue de l'enseignement supérieur en Afrique **5**(2–3), 39–66 (2007)
28. Okoro, N.P., Okoro, E.O.: Time and change: development of private universities in Nigeria. Time Change: Dev. Private Univ. Nigeria **5**(9), 1–7 (2014)
29. Ademola, E., Ogundipe, A., Babatunde, W.: Students'enrolment into tertiary institutions in Nigeria: the influence of the founder's reputation–a case study. Stud. Enrol. Tertiary Inst. Nigeria **5**(3), 1–28 (2014)
30. National Universities Commisssion homepage. http://nuc.edu.ng. Accessed 10 Jan 2022
31. Ofole, N.M.: Social loafing among learner support staff for open and distance education programmes in south-western Nigeria: the imperative for counselling intervention. Open Learn. J. Open, Dist. e-Learn 37, 1–18 (2020)
32. Asiyai, R.I.: Challenges of quality in higher education in Nigeria in the 21st century. Int. J. Educ. Plan. Admin. **3**(2), 159–172 (2013)
33. Ajadi, T.O.: Private universities in Nigeria–the challenges ahead. Am J. Sci. Res. **1**(7), 1–10 (2010)
34. Iruonagbe, C., Imhonopi, D., Egharevba, M.E.: Higher education in Nigeria and the emergence of private universities. Int. J. Educ. Res. **3**(2), 49–64 (2015)

35. Ogbogu, C.: Modes of funding Nigerian universities and the implications on performance. J. Int. Educ. Res. **7**(4), 75–82 (2011)

36. Parekh, R.A.: Knowledge sharing: collaboration between universities and industrial organisations. In: International Conference on Academic Libraries (ICAL-2009), pp. 146–151. University of Delhi, India (2009)

37. Bosma, L.M., Sieving, R.E., Ericson, A., Russ, P., Cavender, L., Bonine, M.: Elements for successful collaboration between K-8 school, community agency, and university partners: the lead peace partnership. J. Sch. Health **80**(10), 501–507 (2010)

38. Rohwer, A., Wager, E., Young, T., Garner, P.: Plagiarism in research: a survey of African medical journals. BMJ Open (11), e024777 (2018)

39. Thomas, A., De Bruin, G.P.: Plagiarism in South African management journals. S. Afr. J. Sci. **111**(1–2), 01–03 (2015)

40. Adeleye, O.A., Adebamowo, C.A.: Factors associated with research wrongdoing in Nigeria. J. Emp. Res. Hum. Res. Ethics **7**(5), 15–24 (2012)

41. Okonta, P., Rossouw, T.: Prevalence of scientific misconduct among a group of researchers in Nigeria. Dev. World Bioeth. **13**(3), 149–157 (2013)

42. Niu, F., Qiu, J.: Network structure, distribution and the growth of Chinese international research collaboration. Scientometrics **98**(2), 1221–1233 (2013). https://doi.org/10.1007/s11192-013-1170-x

43. Sabah, F., Hassan, S.-U., Muazzam, A., Iqbal, S., Soroya, S.H., Sarwar, R.: Scientific Collaboration Networks in Pakistan and Their Impact on Institutional Research Performance: A Case Study Based on Scopus Publications. Library Hi Tech (2019)

44. Bajaj, S.S., et al.: National institutes of health R01 grant funding is associated with enhanced research productivity and career advancement among academic cardiothoracic surgeons', In: National Institutes of Health R01 Grant Funding Is Associated with Enhanced Research Productivity and Career Advancement Among Academic Cardiothoracic Surgeons. Elsevier (2020)

45. Jacob, B.A., Lefgren, L.: The impact of research grant funding on scientific productivity. J. Public Econ. **95**(9–10), 1168–1177 (2011)

46. Schneider, W.H.: The origin of the medical research grant in the United States: the Rockefeller Foundation and the NIH extramural funding program. J. Hist. Med. Allied Sci. **70**(2), 279–311 (2015)

47. Osagie, R.O.: Federal Government Funding of Research in Universities in Nigeria, the University of Benin as a Case Study. Int. Educ. Stud. **5**(6), 73–79 (2012)

48. Lukman, R., Krajnc, D., Glavič, P.: Fostering collaboration between universities regarding regional sustainability initiatives–the University of Maribor'. J. Clean. Prod. **17**(12), 1143–1153 (2009)

49. Sandri, O.: What do we mean by 'pedagogy' in sustainability education?. Teach. High. Educ. **27**(1), 1–16 (2020)

50. Sibbald, S.L., Kang, H., Graham, I.D.: Collaborative health research partnerships: a survey of researcher and knowledge-user attitudes and perceptions. Health Res. Policy Syst. **17**(1), 1–10 (2019)

51. Zych, M.M., Berta, W.B., Gagliardi, A.R.: Conceptualising the initiation of researcher and research user partnerships: a meta-narrative review. Health Res. Policy Syst. **18**(1), 1–18 (2020)

52. Fox, M.F., Realff, M.L., Rueda, D.R., Morn, J.: International research collaboration among women engineers: frequency and perceived barriers, by regions. J. Technol. Transf. **42**(6), 1292–1306 (2016). https://doi.org/10.1007/s10961-016-9512-5

53. Yozwiak, N.L., et al.: Roots, not parachutes: research collaborations combat outbreaks. Cell **166**(1), 5–8 (2016)

54. Karatepe, O.M., Magaji, A.B.: Work-family conflict and facilitation in the hotel industry: a study in Nigeria. Cornell Hosp. Q. **49**(4), 395–412 (2008)
55. Parsons, M.A., et al.: A conceptual framework for managing very diverse data for complex, interdisciplinary science. J. Inf. Sci. **37**(6), 555–569 (2011)
56. Hampton, K., Fernandez, L., Robertson, C., Bauer, J.M.: Broadband and student performance gaps. SSRN 3614074 (2020)
57. Vertovec, S.: Cheap calls: the social glue of migrant transnationalism. Global Netw. **4**(2), 219–224 (2004)
58. Oyelaran-Oyeyinka, B., Adeya, C.N.: Internet access in Africa: empirical evidence from Kenya and Nigeria. Telemat. Inform. **21**(1), 67–81 (2004)
59. Fosci, M., Loffreda, L., Chamberlain, A., Naidoo, N.: Assessing the Needs of the Research System in Nigeria. Report for the SRIA Programme (2019)

SenTekki: Online Platform and Restful Web Service for Translation Between Wolof and French

Alla Lo[1], Elhadji Mamadou Nguer[2(✉)], Sileye O. Ba[3],
Cheikh M. Bamba Dione[4], and Moussa Lo[2]

[1] Université Gaston-Berger, Dakar, Senegal
[2] Université Virtuelle, Diamniadio, Senegal
{elhadjimamadou.nguer,moussa.lo}@uvs.edu.sn
[3] Dailymotion, Paris, France
sileye.ba@dailymotion.com
[4] University of Bergen, Bergen, Norway
dione.bamba@uib.no

Abstract. In this article, we propose a machine translation Web Service and Platform for Wolof, a low-resource Niger-Congolese language. We first developed a Transformer model, and different configurations adapted to these models to translate between Wolof and French. We trained the model on a very limited amount of French-Wolof parallel data of approximately 85,000 parallel sentences. The best model was able to achieve a good performance of around 28 BLUE score. We then developed a web platform that allows text to be translated between French and Wolof, but also a RestFull Web Service that will allow other applications to benefit from the translation service.

Keywords: Neural machine translation platform · Neural machine translation web service · Low resource language · Wolof

1 Problem Statement

These days, web applications are changing individuals' life everywhere. Applications such as Google-Map permit individuals to find themselves. Facebook, Snapchat, Instagram permit people to be associated with their companions. Amazon, Alibaba permit individuals to do easy internet based shopping. Netflix permits individuals to watch video substance. For smooth communication, these applications require an understanding of web predominant dialects like English, Spanish, Chinese, Arabic, French, etc. Others dialects, spoken in Africa, for example, Eastern Ethiopian Amharic, Southern African Swahili, Western African Fulani or Wolof can not be utilized with these applications. The fundamental reason being that contrasted with English, for example, large numbers of these dialects are spoken by little sized populations.

© ICST Institute for Computer Sciences, Social Informatics and Telecommunications Engineering 2022
Published by Springer Nature Switzerland AG 2022. All Rights Reserved
A. D. Mambo et al. (Eds.): InterSol 2022, LNICST 449, pp. 290–298, 2022.
https://doi.org/10.1007/978-3-031-23116-2_25

In machine learning, natural language processing models have been created to extricate pertinent information from electronic documents on the web. These models for the most part address documents written in well-resourced languages like English, Mandarin, Spanish, Arabic, French, and so on. Aside from rare cases, low-resource language, like Eastern Ethiopian Amharic, Southern African Swahili, Western African Fulani or Wolof, are seldom addressed. Having machine learning models such as machine translation frameworks that can change data from high to low resource languages would have incredible effect. This will permit population communicating in low-resource dialects to make full utilization of web substance and applications.

This is the reason why we conducted some researches in building neural system for translation between Wolof and French language. This research led to the construction of a translation model between Wolof and French based on the architecture of the Transformer. This is a model that performed well for a low-resourced language with more than 28 BLUE points.

However, for this model to benefit the public, it must be accessible and usable via the Internet. It is with this in mind that we have started the development of a translation platform accessible online. We have also developed a RESTful web service to allow other applications to consume the services of the model to have text translation between Wolof and French.

The remainder of this paper is organized as follows. Section 2 discusses related work . Section 3 presents the translation platform we developed. Section 4 gives details about the Neural machine translation model we have investigated so far. Section 5 concludes the discussion and outlines future work.

2   Related Work

Because of the importance of language in human interaction, natural language understanding has been widely investigated in computer science. Natural language understanding can be approached either from speech or text inputs. In this paper our focus is on text inputs. Without being exhaustive, natural language understanding can have as object parts-of-speech tagging, named entity recognition, text classification, automatic translation, etc. [1,2].

Many applications in these aforementioned areas are developed for Western languages. However, for poorly resourced languages such as local African languages, few investigations have been conducted so far. To our knowledge, [3–6] are among the very few studies that have so far explored that language using neural network-based methods. These investigations led to the creation of an automatic translation model between French and Wolof [5]. There are other translation platforms between French and Wolof. However, it is not machine translation strictly speaking. They just put a list of French sentences with their Wolof translations. This kind of system will not be able to translate a sentence which is not part of the pre-recorded sentences.

The purpose of this paper is to provide a platform and a service to address the aforementioned model [5]. So far, investigations about Wolof have mostly been about building dictionaries [7], and studying the grammatical structures [8–10] of the language. Other African languages such as Swahili (Southern Africa) and Amharic (Eastern Africa) have been subject of research about automatic statistical based machine translation [11–13]. However, to our knowledge, this work (our Neural Machine Translation model) is the first to address Wolof (Western Africa) using Neural Network based Machine Translation.

3   Machine Translation Platform and RestFull Web Service

In this section we will present the global architecture of our system. It is composed of three main modules. Namely a web and mobile client, a web server, a REST API, and a translation model. Figure 1 presents the overall architecture of the application.

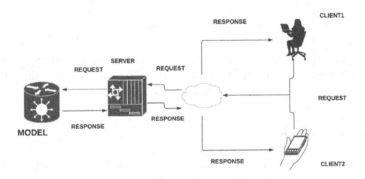

Fig. 1. Overall architecture

In general, the scenario is as follows: a web client sends text to be translated to the web server. The server retrieves this text, performs some processing before sending it to the translation model. The model translates the text and sends it back to the server. The server returns the result to the client. We will detail each module of the system to explain its real operation.

3.1   Client

The client designates the person who will request a translation of a text. It sends the text to be translated via the internet, this text ends up in the server which will do the necessary work. We have two types of client as described below.

3.2   Web and Mobile Client

The web client has a simple interface in which he can choose the languages and the direction of the translation (eg., French to Wolof). He has a text zone where he must type the text to be translated before clicking on the translate button. Once he clicks on the translate button, the result of the translation will be displayed to him in the text area located at the bottom of the said button. It also has a button to download the translation results in .txt format (see Fig. 2).

The same principle is used for the mobile client with a similar interface, but the mobile interface do note allow to download the results of the translation into a file (Fig. 3).

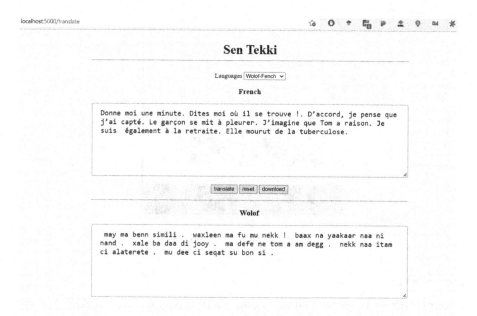

Fig. 2. Web client interface

3.3   Application Client

In the case where the client is an application, it sends the text to be translated into the provided endpoint. The text must be in JSON format where we have key **sent** and the value is the list of sentences to be translated.

Example:

```
texte = {
        "sent" : ["Je veux aller à Dakar demain",
                  "Je dois acheter une voiture"]
        }
```

Fig. 3. Mobile client interface

3.4 Server

In our server we have two main elements. A Web App and a Rest API. We will explain both components in the following.

Web Server. The web server receives a request from the client, extracts the content of the request (the text to be translated) and gives it to the tokenizer. The latter cuts the text into a list of sentences and then send them to the translation model. The model does the translation and sends the results back to the server, which then will send it back to the client. The server will also at the same time keep the client's sentences and their translation in a database (see Fig. 4).

RESTfull Web Service. To access the API, the client application must send a JSON file to an URL given by the web service. The JSON data must have as **key** *sent* and as value the list of sentences to translate.

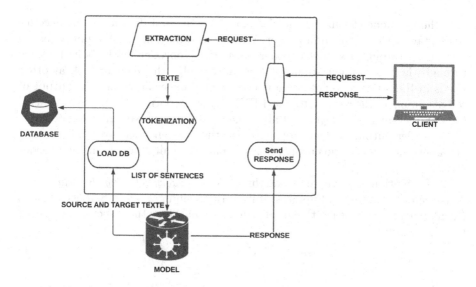

Fig. 4. Web application server side

```
url='http://localhost:5000/tekki'
sentences = str(['Donne-moi une minute.',
    'Dites-moi où il se trouve !',
    "D'accord, je pense que j'ai capté.",
    "Mais les enfants de Coré ne moururent point.",
    "Le garçon se mit à pleurer.",
    "J'imagine que Tom a raison.",
    "Je suis également à la retraite.",
    "Elle mourut de la tuberculose.",
    "Jésus leur répondit: Vous croyez maintenant?",])

res = requests.post(url, data= {"sent":sentences}).json()
```

The API receives the JSON data, extracts the sentences and sends it to the translation model. The latter translates the sentences and returns the result. They will be returned in JSON format before being sent back to the client application.

4   The NMT Model

The Transformer is a new architecture introduced by the article *Attention Is All You Need* [14]. This architecture transforms one sequence into another using a block of encoders and a block of decoders. Encoder block and decoder block are multiple identical encoders and decoders stacked on top of each other.

Encoder and decoder have the same number of units. Each encoder consists of two layers: self-attention and Feed Forward Neural Network. The first (and only the first) encoder in the encoder block and the first decoder in the decoder block start with an embedding layer. Word embeddings from the input sequence are passed through the first encoder layer of the encoder block. It first passes through the layer of self-attention. This layer helps the encoder look at other words in the input sentence while it is encoding a specific word. The output of self-attention is then given to the FFNN layer. A normalization layer is used after the self-attention layer and after the Feed Forward Neural Network layer. The encoder output is then propagated to the next encoder layer. The output of the last encoder in the encoder stack is passed to all decoders in the decoder stack.

Self-attention is calculated using three vectors: *query (Q), key (K), value (V)*. This vector is trained and updated during the training process. Self-attention is calculated for each word of the input sentence using these three vectors according to this formula:

$$Attention(Q, K, V) = softmax(\frac{QK^T}{\sqrt{d_k}}) \tag{1}$$

Like the encoder, each decoder in the decoder block has a self-attention layer and an anticipation neural network layer. But between these layers is an attention layer that helps the decoder focus on the relevant part of the input sentence.

Our transformer follows the architecture proposed by [14]. It has a block of 3 encoders and a block of 3 decoders which process source sequences and target sequences respectively (see Fig. 5).

During encoding, each input word is transformed into a vector using an embedding layer. Next, positional encoding is used to inject positional information into the input embeddings. Each encoder uses two layers to convert the input into a continuous representation with attention information: multi-head attention and a position-dependent feedforward neural network (FFN). Multi-headed attention uses the self-attention mechanism, which allows models to associate each word in the input with other words. Self-attention is achieved by first creating the query ($\mathbf{Q}$), key ($\mathbf{K}$), and value ($\mathbf{V}$) vectors from the input. Next, we calculate a score matrix by multiplying the query with the key vector and dividing by the square root of the dimension of the key vectors (denoted by d_k).

We apply softmax on the scaled score matrix to obtain the attention weights which are used to obtain an output vector. Adding this last vector to the original positional input integration creates a residual connection. The residuals pass through layer normalization and are projected through the point FFN, i.e. a few linear layers with ReLU activation in between. The output of this is then again added to the input of the point lookahead network and further normalized. The point anticipation layer is used to project attention outputs potentially giving it a richer representation.

$$Warning(Q, K, V) = softmax(\frac{Q \times K^T}{\sqrt{d_k}}) \tag{2}$$

The decoder has two multi-head attention blocks in a layer, one for the target sequences and one for the encoder output.

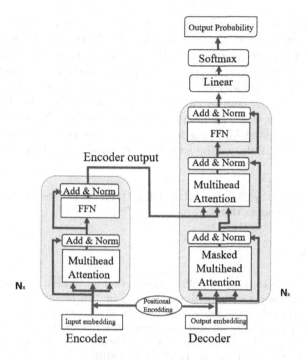

Fig. 5. Our basic transformer model

The old multi-headed attention is hidden to prevent the calculation of attention scores for future words. The decoder also has a point lookahead layer, residual connections, and layer normalization after each sublayer. As with encoding, during decoding the input goes through an integration layer and a positional encoding layer to achieve positional integrations. Then, these integrations are fed into the first multi-head attention layer which computes the attention scores for the decoder input. The second multidirectional attention layer uses the encoder outputs as requests and keys, and the first multidirectional attention layer outputs are the values. This process matches the encoder input to the decoder input, allowing the decoder to decide which encoder input to focus on. The output of the second multidirectional attention passes through a point FFN layer for further processing. The output of the final point lookahead layer goes through a final linear layer, which acts as a classifier.

5   Conclusion

In this article, we presented the investigations we carried out to build a translation platform between Wolof and the French language. The system also provides a RestFull web service that allows other applications to use the translation service. The overall architecture can be described as a client-server application. The application provides a user-friendly interface that allows a user to type text in the source language and simply click a button to get the translation. The interface gives the possibility to the user to download the results of the translation in text format. So this work resulted in the first Wolof translation platform, with a model that achieved encouraging results for a language so poorly endowed with resources. The platform also allows at the same time to increase our corpus because keeping all the translations that it will have to operate in a database.

In the rest of our work, we plan to add a feature that allows users to correct the translation of the machine in order to allow it to make fewer mistakes the next time. This corrected data will be added to our corpus to re-train the translation model.

Acknowledgments. Authors thank the CEA MITIC of Universite Gaston Berger in Senegal for partly funding this work.

References

1. Collobert, R., Weston, J.: A unified architecture for natural language processing: deep neural networks with multitask learning. In: Proceedings of the ICML (2008)
2. Young, T., Hazarika, D., Poria, S., Cambria, E.: Recent trends in deep learning based natural language processing. arXiv:1708.02709 (2018)
3. Alla, L., Sileye, B., El Hadji Mamadou, N., Moussa, L.: 2019 Neural words embedding: Wolof Language Case. In: IREHI 2019 (2019)
4. Alla, L., Bamba, D.C., El Hadji Mamadou, N., Sileye, B., Moussa, L.: 2020 building word representations for Wolof using neural networks. In: CNRIA 2020 (2020)
5. Alla, L., Sileye, B., El Hadji Mamadou, N., Moussa, L.: 2019 Neural words embedding: Wolof Language Case. In: ICLR workshop 2020 (2020)
6. Bamba, D.C.: LSTM based Language models for wolof. human language technologies as a challenge for computer science and linguistic. 190–194 (2019). 978-83-65988-30-0
7. Khoule, M., Thiam, M.N., Nguer, E.M.: Towards the establishment of a LMF-based Wolof language lexicon. Traitement Automatique des Langues Africaines (TALAf) (2014)
8. Dione, C.B.: LFG parse disambiguation for Wolof. J. Lang. Model. **2**, 105 (2014)
9. Dione, C.B.: Valency change and complex predicates in Wolof: an LFG account. In: LFG Conference (2013)
10. Dione, C.B.: An LFG approach to Wolof cleft constructions. In: LFG Conference (2012)
11. Pauw, G.D., Wagacha, P.W., Schryver de, G.-M.: Towards English - Swahili Machine Translation. In: Research Workshop of the Israel Science Foundation (2011)
12. Ombui, E.O., Wagacha, P.W., Ng'ang'a, W.: InterlinguaPlus machine translation approach for under-resourced languages: Ekegusii and Swahili. In: Workshop on the Use of Computational Methods in the Study of Endangered Languages (2014)
13. Gebreegziabher, M., Besacier, L.: English-amharic statistical machine translation. In: Workshop on Spoken Language Technologies for Under-Resourced Languages (2012)
14. Vaswani, A., Shazeer, N., Parmar, N., Uszkoreit, A.: Attention is all you need. arXiv:1706.03762v5 [cs.CL] (2017)

Towards an Optimal Placement of Learning Resources in a Fog Computing Based E-Learning System: The Case of UVS

Serigne Mbacke Gueye[1(✉)], Alassane Diop[2], and Amadou Dahirou Gueye[1]

[1] University Alioune Diop de Bambey (UADB), Diourbel, Senegal
{serignembacke.gueye,dahirou.gueye}@uadb.edu.sn
[2] Université Virtuelle du Senegal (UVS), Diamniadio, Senegal
alassane.diop@uvs.edu.sn

Abstract. With the growing number of its students, Virtual University of Senegal is often faced with a lack of quality of service during synchronous learning activities. Thus, the University has set itself the challenge of reinforcing its technological device to make it even more robust in order to support the increasing number of students with a more powerful infrastructure. In this perspective, we have, in this paper, proposed an online teaching platform based on fog computing. Thus, we have proposed an optimal placement of educational resources at the fog layer nodes in order to relieve the backbone network and, consequently, reduce the response time of students' requests during synchronous activities, which are very sensitive to delay.

Keywords: Distance learning · Fog computing · Optimization · Placement of learning resources in fog nodes

1 Introduction

In recent years, many universities and training institutes have taken advantage of ICT (Information and Communication Technology) to improve their educational strategies in order to attract the maximum number of students [1]. In this perspective, e-learning is widely adopted to offer a quality and more flexible educational service. Accordingly, this form of learning is getting more and more popular worldwide and the number of learners in these online courses increasing exponentially. In this mode of education, all the educational resources are stored in the cloud to allow the various learners to access via the internet.

UVS, with more than 50,000 students in 15 Open Digital Spaces, has adopted this teaching model in order to offer a wide range of training to its students [2]. At this university, two types of learning activities are carried out: Synchronous activities, where learners and the teacher (or tutor) interact live via a dedicated platform (blackboard collaborate, bigbluebutton, Google Meet, etc.) and asynchronous activities i.e. that those students can do at any time. Thus, with

© ICST Institute for Computer Sciences, Social Informatics and Telecommunications Engineering 2022
Published by Springer Nature Switzerland AG 2022. All Rights Reserved
A. D. Mambo et al. (Eds.): InterSol 2022, LNICST 449, pp. 299–308, 2022.
https://doi.org/10.1007/978-3-031-23116-2_26

this large number of students who are supposed to connect at the same time to the university's cloud servers with their respective teacher (or tutor) in a synchronous session, the university is often confronted with problems of computing resources of its cloud servers (I/O, RAM, CPU, etc.). In this respect, the quality of service (QoS) during synchronous activities remains poor.

To address these kinds of QoS issues, particularly response time, fog computing has emerged. It is a recent paradigm that aims to extend cloud computing to the network edge to address the challenges associated with the exponential growth of connected objects at the network edge. In fact, fog computing relies on network resources available at the edge of the network, known as fog nodes, to provide services with reduced response times. These devices, although characterized by limited computing and storage capacity, benefit from a proximity to the end-users which allows the location of learners, saves backbone bandwidth and reduces transmission delays [3].

In this work, we study in the context of the UVS pedagogical model, the implementation of a distance learning platform deployed on geo distributed computing in the form of an optimization problem.

In this context, we propose a heuristic, based on the Greedy algorithm, capable of proposing a better placement of educational resources, at the level of fog nodes, in the form of containerized applications (for requests concerning synchronous learning activities) in order to minimize the response time (transmission delay).

Thus, we will :

- Define a relevant use case, in line with the UVS pedagogical model, for a distance learning platform based on fog computing;
- Give a mathematical formulation of the latency problem of our e-learning platform based on fog computing by an optimization problem whose objective is to maximize the number of containerized learning resources to be deployed to satisfy the requirements of delay of the requests of the learners, under several constraints which we will detail in Sect. 4;
- Proving such a problem is NP-hard;
- Propose a heuristic based on the greedy algorithm.

The rest of the paper will be organized as follows: In Sect. 2, we will review the literature about fog computing based e-learning platforms. Section 3 will be devoted to the study of our proposed platform, in which we describe its components and their functioning. In the last section, we will describe the model system, the mathematical formulation of the problem, and finally propose a heuristic for solving the problem.

2   Related Work

In this section, we will review the literature in order to identify all the existing works with the aim of detecting their limits in relation to our field of study.

In recent years, being aware of the contribution that fog computing can have on e-learning, many researchers have become interested in this new field of research.

In [4], the authors presented a model based on fog computing for accessing educational content in a virtual learning environment. It presents an optimized use of bandwidth that significantly reduces latency, thus improving the quality of teaching/learning. Their results show that fog computing could make virtual learning environments more relevant to the needs of students and teachers.

The authors of [5] proposed an e-learning environment architecture enhanced by fog computing and big data streams. They discussed virtual learning environments and their limitations and then explained the paradigms of big data streams and fog computing to introduce an e-learning architecture integrating both to enhance the ability of virtual learning environments to approximate the needs of all stakeholders.

In [6], the authors have proposed a new secure e-learning scheme based on fog computing. Their solution extends educational content from the cloud to the edge of the network, closer to the learners and teachers. They provided precise access control to learning content by encrypting courses and exams using IBBE and CP-ABE techniques.

In [7], the authors present an IoT-Fog-Cloud framework to provide security factors in sharing E-exam which poses several security challenges, such as fine-grained access control and security preservation of E-exam. Further, there proposed framework supports bringing closer the services to the students. Besides, there paper improves the efficiency of E-exam data analysis, reduces the encryption burden in terms of computation cost on user's devices by offloading part of encryption cost to fog servers, and provides fine-grained access control to E-exam content by encrypting with different cryptographic techniques.

A recommendation system based on fog computing to improve e-learning environments is proposed in [8]. Their system is based on three modules: A class identification module that calculates the desired course category based on the user's query keyword by calculating the correlation between the queries and all domain classes. A subclass identification module that calculates the subclass of the desired subject by applying the association rule technique. A Matching module to retrieve the selected items (classes) and classify them according to their relevance to the user's query.

In [9], a fog-assisted cyber physical system is proposed that deals with the various aspects of the panic well-being of the student, including the virtual reality platform for remote learning. The proposed system utilizes the concepts of physical and cyberspace. The physical space facilitates real-time data acquisition, and cyberspace determines and predicts the panic well-being of the student. The performance assessment of the proposed model acknowledges the efficiency of the virtual learning system and panic well-being determination and prediction. The proposed system also discussed a virtual learning system that provides a virtual classroom environment to the students at remote sites and reduces the panic due to stressful times during the COVID-19 pandemic.

Through all these works, it can be noted that fog computing is widely used in the field of e-learning with a view to improving teaching/learning, even going as far as securing learning objects. However, to our knowledge, no proposal has been made concerning the optimal placement of learning objects in the form of containers at the level of fog nodes for better support of synchronous activities in e-learning systems.

Thus, in the following part, we will, according to the pedagogical model of the UVS, try to propose an online teaching platform based on fog computing (PELBFC - UVS). We will also propose an optimal placement of pedagogical resources in the form of containerized applications according to an optimization problem. Finally, we will propose a heuristic for solving this problem.

3   PELBFC - UVS: Components and Functioning

The proposed system, illustrated in Fig. 1, is based on geo distributed computing (*fog computing*) and works according to the collaboration of three hierarchical layers: the cloud layer, the fog layer and the user layer (Learners, Teachers, Tutors, Administrative staff) according to the following architecture.

The user layer is mainly made up of all the students spread over the 15 Open Digital Spaces of the University across the country. Teachers, tutors and pedagogical administrative staff are also part of the users. In our scenario, we consider learners who wish to access a set of synchronous learning activities via requests sent to the orchestration module of the fog layer. This orchestration module communicates with all the fog controllers in order to determine the most appropriate fog node (the fog node offering the best quality of service) for the execution of the learner's request.

The fog layer, on the other hand, is made up of intelligent devices (routers, switches, gateways, access points, proxy servers, etc.) better known as *fog node*. A fog node may be mobile or static (fixed) and capable of processing, routing or storing data. They are usually grouped into domains which are placed under the authority of a fog controller responsible for assigning Learner's requests to the most appropriate fog nodes according to the required delay of the request, the resources available at the nodes and the position of the learner. However, it should be noted that the computational and storage resources of the fog nodes are limited compared to those of the cloud.

Thus, resource-intensive requests are offloaded to the cloud layer to take advantage of the large computer and storage capacities of its data centers with a higher delay. The orchestration module coordinates services between the fog controllers and the cloud layer data centers.

4   Mathematical Formulation

In this section, we will give a mathematical formulation of our e-learning platform based on fog computing with consideration of delay requirements for learner requests for synchronous learning activities.

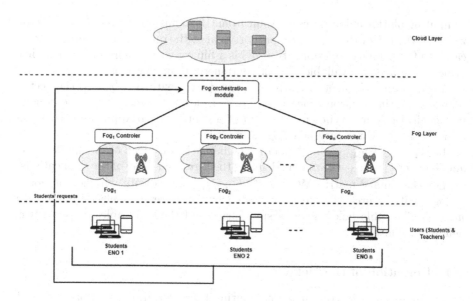

Fig. 1. Architecture PELBFC-UVS

4.1 Problem Description (Use Case)

Consider a set of synchronous learning activity teaching resources to be deployed on the fog nodes in order to allow students access in a reasonable time frame (real time).

A fog controller will be responsible for deploying a resource allocation strategy to maximize the number of learner requests that meet the delay requirements by taking into account the location of the learners, the fog nodes and their available resource capacity.

After setting up this allocation strategy, the learning resources, in the form of containerized applications, are deployed on the *fog nodes* with support for the delay requirements.

For reasons of resource optimization, a container will be able to run multiple compatible learning resources from multiple learners.

4.2 Variables Definition

Let $\mathcal{K}$ be a set of fog domains. Each domain is managed by a fog controller k. $\mathcal{F}_k$ represents a heterogeneous set of fog nodes in a given domain managed by a k controller. It is assumed that each fog node $f \in \mathcal{F}_k$ integrates a containerization platform for better management of the containers assigned to it. Let $\mathcal{F}$ be a set of *fog nodes*. Let us consider the following vectors :

The vector $\mathbf{l} = [l^f]$ expresses the locations of the *fog nodes* and $\mathbf{c} = [c^f]$ denotes their remaining carrying capacity. As the load supported by the dedicated functions varies over time, the amount of resources available on the fog computing platform fluctuates as result from [10]. Thus, we express by the vector $\mathbf{z} = [z^f]$, the use of the *fog nodes*, proportional to the quantity of resources dedicated to the primary functions. $\mathbf{b} = [b^f]$ is a binary vector representing whether or not a *fog node* is available to host containerized applications.

We define by $\mathcal{A}$, a set of learners in the system with $\mathbf{p} = [p^a]_{|\mathcal{A}|}$, the vector representing the location of learners. We consider $\mathcal{Y}$ to be a set of synchronous pedagogical resource types in the form of a containerized application that are available in the University pedagogical model.

Let $\mathbf{Q} = [Q^{a,y}]_{|\mathcal{A}| \times |\mathcal{Y}|}$ be the matrix defining the task load of the applications and $\mathbf{T} = [T^{a,y}]_{|\mathcal{A}| \times |\mathcal{Y}|}$ the matrix defining the threshold delay of the applications.

Let the binary matrix $\mathbf{W} = [w^{a,y,f}]_{|A| \times |\mathcal{Y}| \times |\mathcal{F}|}$ indicate whether or not a pedagogical resource of type y, requested by a learner a, is placed on the *fog node* f. The table below gives a summary of all these variables we have just defined (Table 1).

4.3   Definition of the Delay

In the implementation of our fog computing based e-learning platform, we will consider the delay (response time) as a QoS parameter. In the following lines, we will give its expression that we have considered in the realization of this work.

Table 1. Tables of variables

$\mathcal{K}$	Set of fog domains
$\mathcal{F}$	Set of fog nodes
$\mathcal{F}_k$	Set of *fog nodes* in fog domaine $k \in \mathcal{K}$
$\mathcal{A}$	Set of Learner
$\mathcal{Y}$	All types of learning resources
l	$|\mathcal{F}|$ location vector of the fog nodes
c	$|\mathcal{F}|$ vector representing the remaining load capacity of the fog nodes
z	$|\mathcal{F}|$ Vector representing the use of *fog nodes*
b	$|\mathcal{F}|$ Vector where the element b^f is a binary vector representing if $f \in \mathcal{F}$ is free to host containers or not
p	$|\mathcal{A}|$ Learner location vector
Q	$|\mathcal{A}| \times |\mathcal{Y}|$ matrix representing the load of the containerized applications
T	$|\mathcal{A}| \times |\mathcal{Y}|$ matrix indicating applications threshold latency requirements
W	$|A| \times |\mathcal{Y}| \times |\mathcal{F}|$ binary matrix representing whether a learning resource of type y, requested by learner a, is deployed on *fog node* f or not

The delay $d^{a,y}$ of the tasks of an application y for a learner a is composed of three delays:(1) the communication delay (round trip) between the fog node and the learner, (2) the task processing delay, and (3) the waiting delay, which is included in the processing delay, in this work. Thus, the latency of an application can be written as follows :

$$d^{a,y} = d^{a,y}_{cmp} + d^{a,y}_{com} \quad \forall\, a \in \mathcal{A}, y \in \mathcal{Y} \tag{1}$$

where $d^{a,y}_{cmp}$ and $d^{a,y}_{com}$ represent the processing time and the communication time respectively.

Since a learning resource can be available on several fog nodes, the processing time $d^{a,y}_{cmp}$ of a learner's tasks a for an application y is equal to the minimum of the fog nodes' processing times $d^{f,a,y}_{cmp}$. Furthermore, if a node is not available, we assume that its processing time will take a very large value such that :

$$d^{a,y}_{cmp} = \min_{f \in \mathcal{F}}(d^{f,a,y}_{cmp} \cdot w^{a,y,f}), \quad \forall a \in \mathcal{A}, y \in \mathcal{Y} \quad and \quad w^{a,y,f} = 1. \tag{2}$$

For simplicity purpose, and to make our platform compatible with other threading models, we have derived $d^{a,y}_{cmp}$ using an M/M/1 threading model. Thus, $d^{f,a,y}_{cmp}$ is represented as follows :

$$d^{f,a,y}_{cmp} = \frac{1}{\rho^f - Q^{a,y,f}} \tag{3}$$

where ρ^f is the service rate of a node f.

In the same way as for the processing delay, the communication delay associated with a learner a for an application y is the minimum of the communication delays of the fog nodes which hosted this resource y. The communication delay is given by the following expression :

$$d^{a,y}_{com} = \min_{f \in \mathcal{F}}(d^{f,a,y}_{com} \cdot w^{a,y,f}) \quad \forall f \in \mathcal{F}, a \in \mathcal{A}, y \in \mathcal{Y} \quad and \quad w^{a,y,f} = 1. \tag{4}$$

The communication delay $d^{f,a,y}_{com}$ of a resource y, hosted in the fog node f and requested by the learner a is broken down as follows :

$$d^{f,a,y}_{com} = d^{f,a,y}_{com,a,f} + d^{f,a,y}_{com,f,a} \tag{5}$$

where $d^{f,a,y}_{com,a,f}$ represents the transmission delay of the wireless communication from learner a to node f and $d^{f,a,y}_{com,f,a}$ vice versa. It is expressed as follows :

$$\frac{Q^{a,y,f}}{B \cdot \log_2(1 + SNR)} \tag{6}$$

where B is the bandwidth of the transmission medium, SNR is the signal-to-noise ratio and $Q^{a,y,f}$ is the load on the resource y.

Following the model, our objective is to determine the optimal placement of the containerized learning resources. We seek to maximize the number of satisfied learner's requests within the threshold time required for the learning resource under the constraints of the fog nodes capacity.

4.4   Problem Formulation

In this section, we will give the problem formulation of placing containerized learning resources in a fog computing infrastructure. We will start by describing the constraints that the system must satisfy before completing the objective function of the problem which will be the maximization of the number of containerized learning resources to be deployed that satisfies the required delay.

Constraints Definition: We start by defining the constraint to satisfy a threshold time for learners' requests.

$$T^{a,y} - d^{a,y} \geq G \cdot (S^{a,y} - 1), \quad \forall a \in \mathcal{A}, y \in \mathcal{Y} \tag{7}$$

where G is a large positive number chosen arbitrarily and $\mathbf{S}^{a,y}$ is a binary variable indicating whether the delay $d^{a,y}$ is less than the threshold delay $T^{a,y}$ of the application.

The following constraint will ensure that the total load allocated to each fog node does not exceed its capacity (C^f). It is represented as follows :

$$C^f \geq \sum_{a \in \mathcal{A}} \sum_{y \in \mathcal{Y}} Q^{a,y,f}, \quad \forall f \in \mathcal{F}. \tag{8}$$

Objective Function: As the latency of learners' requests can vary depending on the location of the fog nodes and the learners, the objective of our problem is to maximize the number of deployed applications satisfying the specified delay requirements.

$$\max_{W,Q} \sum_{a \in \mathcal{A}} \sum_{y \in \mathcal{Y}} (S^{a,y}) \tag{P1}$$
$$\text{s.t.} \quad (7) - (8).$$

The problem (P1) presented above is NP-hard. Indeed, it consists in placing containerized applications on fog nodes with the objective of maximizing the number of applications to be deployed that satisfy the required deadline. Thus, the problem can be trivially modelled as the GAP (Generalized Assignment Problem) which is a well known problem in the literature [11].

The objective of the GAP problem is to find a mapping between m agents and n heterogeneous tasks in order to maximize the total profit. Each task is assigned, exactly, to one agent, given that it has sufficient capacity. Moreover, depending on the assigned agent, each task may have a different profit. By analogy to our problem, agents can be likened to fog nodes, containerized applications as tasks and the number of requests answered with latency satisfaction are profit. Given that it is well known that GAP is NP-hard, according to the previous explanation, our problem (P1) is also NP-hard.

4.5 Strategy Greedy First Fit

According to [12], an NP-hard problem is synonymous with the impossibility of finding an optimal solution in reasonable time. Thus, we propose this heuristic based on Greedy First Fit in order to have a solution close to the optimal one in polynomial time.

The Greedy First Fit is an algorithmic strategy which, at each stage of solving a problem, considers the first best choice which satisfies the constraints as being the best optimal choice with the aim of finally leading to an optimal global solution, without taking into account the consequences that this choice may have on the global solution of the problem [13].

Our strategy for solving (P1) is to deploy, as much as possible, the containerized learning resources on fog nodes that satisfy the delay requirements of student requests during synchronous learning activities, taking into account the 7–8 constraints. The details are described in the algorithm below.

Algorithm 1: Strategy Greedy First Fit

Input:

    $\mathbf{F}$: Set of fog nodes,

    $\mathbf{L}_{|\mathcal{F}|}$: Location vector of the fog nodes,

    $\mathbf{C}_{|\mathcal{F}|}$: vector representing the remaining load capacity of the fog nodes,

    $\mathbf{P}_{|\mathcal{A}|}$: Learner location vector,

    $\mathcal{Y}$: All types of learning resources,

    $\mathbf{Q}_{|\mathcal{A}| \times |\mathcal{Y}|}$:Matrix representing the load of the containerized applications,

    $\mathbf{T}_{|\mathcal{A}| \times |\mathcal{Y}|}$, : Matrix indicating applications threshold latency requirements

Output:

    Deployment scheme : $\mathbf{W}_{|\mathcal{A}| \times |\mathcal{Y}| \times |\mathcal{F}|}$

1   *Random initialization of the matrix $\mathbf{W}_{|\mathcal{A}| \times |\mathcal{Y}| \times |\mathcal{F}|}$;*

2   **for** *each learning resource to be deployed :* **do**

3   Randomly select a fog node f_{al} with respect to the constraints 7 and 8;

4   Updating the matrix $\mathbf{W}_{|\mathcal{A}| \times |\mathcal{Y}| \times |\mathcal{F}|}$;

5   **for** *each $f_j \in F \setminus f_{al}$* **do**

6   **if** *f_j is better than f_{al}* **then**

7   Replace f_{al} by f_j in $\mathbf{W}_{|\mathcal{A}| \times |\mathcal{Y}| \times |\mathcal{F}|}$;

8   break ;

9   **end**

10   **end**

11   Update of $\mathbf{C}_{|\mathcal{F}|}$;

12 **end**

13 **return** $\mathbf{W}_{|\mathcal{A}| \times |\mathcal{Y}| \times |\mathcal{F}|}$

---

5   Conclusion

To address the deterioration of the quality of service/quality of experience of teaching/learning during synchronous activities, caused by the increase in the number of students, we proposed an online teaching/learning platform based on fog computing. We have subsequently optimized the placement of educational resources, in the form of containerized applications, at the fog layer nodes in order to relieve the bandwidth of the backbone network and reduce the response time of student requests during synchronous activities, which are very sensitive to the delay.

In perspective, we intend to improve our heuristic by reinforcement learning for the solution of our problem in order to have a better solution in polynomial time.

References

1. Rana Lone, C.P., Ahmad, Z., Ajay.: Architecture du système d'apprentissage en ligne pour le cloud computing - un examen
2. Gueye, S.M., Diop, A., Gueye, A.D.: A machine learning model on virtual university of senegal's educational data based on lambda architecture. In: 2020 7th International Conference on Electrical Engineering, Computer Sciences and Informatics (EECSI), pp. 270–275. IEEE (2020)
3. OpenFog Consortium Architecture Working Group et al.: Openfog reference architecture for fog computing. OPFRA001 **20817** 162 (2017)
4. Pecori, R.: Augmenting quality of experience in distance learning using fog computing. IEEE Internet Comput. **23**(5), 49–58 (2019)
5. Pecori, R.: A virtual learning architecture enhanced by fog computing and big data streams. Future Internet **10**(1), 4 (2018)
6. Amor, A.B., Abid, M., Meddeb, A.: Secure fog-based e-learning scheme. IEEE Access **8**, 31920–31933 (2020)
7. Khairy, D., Amasha, M.A., Abougalala, R.A., Alkhalaf, S., Areed, M.F.: A security system for e-exams using an IoT and fog computing environment. J. Theor. Appl. Inf. Technol. **100**(2), (2022)
8. Ibrahim, T.S., Saleh, A.I., Elgaml, N., Abdelsalam, M.M.: A fog based recommendation system for promoting the performance of e-learning environments. Comput. Electr. Eng. **87**, 106791 (2020)
9. Sood, S.K., Rawat, K.S.: Fog-assisted virtual reality-based learning framework to control panic. Expert Syst. **39**(4), e12700 (2022)
10. Mseddi, A., Jaafar, W., Elbiaze, H., Ajib, W.: Joint container placement and task provisioning in dynamic fog computing. IEEE Internet Things J. **PP**(99), 1 (2019)
11. Ross, S., Terry, G., Richard, M.: A branch and bound algorithm for the generalized assignment problem. Mathe. Program. **8**(1), 91–103 (1975)
12. Hochba, D.S.: Approximation algorithms for NP-hard problems. ACM Sigact News **28**(2), 40–52 (1997)
13. Cormen, T.H, Leiserson, C.E., Rivest, R.L., Stein, C.: Introduction to algorithms. MIT press, Cambridge (2009)

Author Index

Printed in the United States
by Baker & Taylor Publisher Services